Dogs

UNIVERSITY PRESS OF FLORIDA

Florida A&M University, Tallahassee
Florida Atlantic University, Boca Raton
Florida Gulf Coast University, Ft. Myers
Florida International University, Miami
Florida State University, Tallahassee
New College of Florida, Sarasota
University of Central Florida, Orlando
University of Florida, Gainesville
University of North Florida, Jacksonville
University of South Florida, Tampa
University of West Florida, Pensacola

Dogs

ARCHAEOLOGY BEYOND DOMESTICATION

Edited by Brandi Bethke and Amanda Burtt

UNIVERSITY PRESS OF FLORIDA
Gainesville / Tallahassee / Tampa / Boca Raton
Pensacola / Orlando / Miami / Jacksonville / Ft. Myers / Sarasota

Financial support was provided from the Office of the Vice President
for Research and the Office of the Provost, University of Oklahoma.

First cloth printing, 2020
First paperback printing, 2024

29 28 27 26 25 24   6 5 4 3 2 1

Library of Congress Cataloging-in-Publication Data
Names: Bethke, Brandi, editor. | Burtt, Amanda, editor.
Title: Dogs : archaeology beyond domestication / edited by Brandi Bethke, Amanda Burtt.
Description: Gainesville : University Press of Florida, 2020. | Includes bibliographical
    references and index.
Identifiers: LCCN 2019034306 (print) | LCCN 2019034307 (ebook) | ISBN 9780813066363
    (hardback) | ISBN 9780813057460 (pdf) | ISBN 9780813080574 (pbk.)
Subjects: LCSH: Dogs—History. | Dog owners—History. | Human-animal relationships—
    History.
Classification: LCC SF422.5 .D645 2020 (print) | LCC SF422.5 (ebook) | DDC 636.7—dc23
LC record available at https://lccn.loc.gov/2019034306
LC ebook record available at https://lccn.loc.gov/2019034307

The University Press of Florida is the scholarly publishing agency for the State
University System of Florida, comprising Florida A&M University, Florida Atlantic
University, Florida Gulf Coast University, Florida International University, Florida State
University, New College of Florida, University of Central Florida, University of Florida,
University of North Florida, University of South Florida, and University of West Florida.

University Press of Florida
2046 NE Waldo Road
Suite 2100
Gainesville, FL 32609
http://upress.ufl.edu

Contents

Figures

Tables

1

Introduction

BRANDI BETHKE AND AMANDA BURTT

The relationship between humans and dogs has garnered significant attention within archaeological research around the world. To date, no single piece of evidence has convinced scholars the world over of the precise origins of the domestic dog. While considerable debate over the timing, mechanisms, and motivations of dog domestication persist among anthropologists and researchers across disciplines, we know that dogs have been living in close proximity to humans for thousands of years in most habitable parts of the planet. Domestic dogs have accompanied humans in life (and sometimes death), and evidence of this relationship is widely distributed in the archaeological record. The dog's ubiquity makes them an ideal subject for cross-cultural studies of human-animal relationships around the globe and over a broad time scale.

As a result, numerous works have explored the human-dog relationship through time presented from a range of perspectives. Major contributions from archaeologists such as Stanley J. Olsen, Juliet Clutton-Brock, Susan J. Crockford, and Darcy Morey, among many others, have been instrumental in forming our understanding of the origins of domestic dogs, as well as how these origins may further contextualize the bonds humans and dogs have shared beyond initial domestication. Books written for a more popular audience, such as the works of Barbara King and Mark Derr, have aided in forming a greater picture of the universality of the human-dog bond while also drawing attention to the deep time histories of these relationships. Researchers in the fields of cognitive science, ethology, and anthrozoology are also beginning to expand our understanding of the sociobiological aspects of human-dog codevelopment (e.g., Miklósi 2014). Although this body of research explores a diverse set of topics relating to the human-canine connection, many of these works deal primarily with questions involving the domestication process and its immediate consequences. While studying the details and complexities of domestication is instrumental in understanding how past peoples cooperated with and altered their environments, this volume begins later in the dog-human story to investigate the diverse expressions this relationship has taken as result of the dog's inclusion in human groups. Our format follows in the research tradition of previous edited volumes, such as those compiled by James Serpell (1995), Susan Crockford (2000), Lynn Snyder and Elizabeth Moore (2006), and Robert Losey, Robert Wishart, and Jan Peter Luarens Loovers (2018). These investigations into domestic dogs' lived experiences have proven to be intellectually productive avenues for better understanding humanity in the past.

This volume adds to these discussions by exploring the multiplicity of human-canine relationships in a variety of cultures to investigate the many ways dogs have been conceptualized by their human counterparts in terms of both their practical and symbolic value. Contributing authors explore several universal questions about the human-canine past: How do dogs contribute to human communities, and what does this relationship tell us about the practical and ideological organization of different cultures? How and why do human groups maintain personal relationships with individual dogs or with dog communities? How might dogs, as nonhuman social actors, influence or be influenced by cultural change? The goal of this volume is to emphasize the interrelation of these themes across a range of communities worldwide.

Since the varied beginnings of the human-canine connection, dogs have served many functions, from practical, economic purposes (as hunting aids, guards, transport animals, food, or raw materials) to more complex social ones (as pets, spiritual helpers, objects of ritual or religious significance, or symbols of wealth) (Morey 2006, 2010; Russell 2012; Serpell 1995; Snyder and Moore 2006; Stahl 2016). These functions hold significance that speak to the dog's perceived place within human social worlds. The ways dogs are both used and understood within a given community, *their roles,* are conditioned by what that community values, so our relationships with dogs are often expressions of those values (Gilhus 2006). Contributing authors explore the many ways human needs and wants shape a dog's purpose and standing within different cultures.

The dog's ability to hunt with humans, for example, has been argued to be a vital connection that tethered the two species, human and dog, together. In Chapter 2, Angela Perri provides an overview of dogs used for hunting in the past and how the development of this relationship may be understood as the advent of animal biotechnology. Perri also discusses key elements at archaeological sites that can aid in the documentation of hunting dogs within the archaeological record. The ways dogs have been utilized as a hunting adaptation in the past, Perri argues, are manifestations of human needs and thus speak to human behavior, preference, and necessity.

While Perri presents a broad overview of dogs as hunting tools, Victoria Monagle and Emily Lena Jones investigate how nonexclusive categories in which precontact southwestern peoples placed dogs can be understood from an Indigenous framework. In Chapter 3, Monagle and Jones incorporate osteological data with the ethnohistoric record to interpret the life histories of canids found at an Ancestral Puebloan site located in Mancos Canyon, Colorado. Their work illustrates how the dog was not just a caloric or ritual resource for the people living in this place but a multifaceted, integral community member in the Ancestral Puebloan cultural landscape. Similar findings are presented by Edouard Masson-MacLean, Ellen McManus-Fry, and Kate Britton in Chapter 4. Their investigations at the precontact site of Nunalleq in coastal Alaska reveal the varied tasks and perceived meaningfulness of dogs living alongside Arctic peoples. Excellent preservation has given the authors a unique opportunity to analyze not only the physical remains of dogs but also associated organic materials that represent dog-keeping practices. The inclusion of these data with a textured ethnohistoric record allows the authors to better explore the many ways dogs served their community, including their roles in hunting, transport, protection, and meat, fur, and other raw materials, all vital for surviving the Arctic environment.

Several authors seek to further illuminate the human-canine connection as a complex social relationship by exploring the care and maintenance of dogs by humans. In Chapter 5 Amanda Burtt and Larisa R. G. DeSantis employ the latest in dental microwear methodology to study dog teeth and investigate access to food resources. Their work better contextualizes domestic dogs' scavenging behavior by distinguishing between dogs as provisioned consumers and non-provisioned scavengers to explore dog maintenance practiced by precontact people of the North American Midwest and Northwest Plains. Their research shows that dogs are fed in varying ways between and within communities.

Understanding past relationships between humans and dogs helps us not only recognize the dog's economic, social, and symbolic value within their communities but also provides insight into how humans conceptualized their own place within these systems. Chapter 6 explores the changing roles of dogs with the advent of settled farming communities in the Near East. Nerissa Russell's analysis of dog remains from Çatalhöyük suggests that during the Neolithic period dogs no longer played a major role as hunting and herding companions but instead were utilized as sentries and garbage processers to better suit the needs of village life.

Categories in which animals are placed within the human social structure are molded on principles of human interactions, meaning human social categories may be extended to the animal world (Gilhus 2006; Russell 2012; Walker 2008). As such, for some cultures dogs also functioned as important nonhuman social actors beyond just the practical or religious. Building off these themes, several contributors frame human-dog relationships within culturally specific ontologies to consider how the needs of human and dog communities may affect or be affected by cultural change. In Chapter 7 Brandi Bethke explores this theme through a study of the changing relationship between the dog and Blackfoot people in the North American plains following the introduction of the horse into the region. Focusing on the key differences between dogs and horses, her work explores how the use and value of dogs was reimagined within equestrian Blackfoot culture as the horse fostered new ways of thinking about domesticated animals.

Peter W. Stahl explores how the use of dogs as hunting aides helped to create a critical bond between foreign dogs and Indigenous people living in northeastern South America. In Chapter 8, he explains that it was this bond that allowed the dog's incorporation into the community in ways that were markedly different than other exotic domesticates or captives. Chapter 9 authors Loukas Koungoulos and Melanie Fillios also present research on introduced species, focusing on the dingo's long and complex relationship with Indigenous Australians over the past 4,000 years. This chapter critically examines the use of ethnography and early colonial written records to better understand the often variable precontact human-dingo relationship, questioning the recent suggestion that dingoes, acting as hunting companions, may have changed the gendered division of labor in Aboriginal societies.

In addition to serving the practical needs of humans, dogs may also exemplify their caregivers' beliefs and practices. For example, dogs have factored into the spiritual beliefs of many cultures across the world. In Chapter 10, Victoria

Moses focuses on the analysis of animal remains from one of Rome's earliest temples to explore the role of dogs in Roman sacrificial rites. While the majority of animals sacrificed by the Romans were herd animals (sheep, goats, pigs, and cattle), the Romans also sacrificed dogs regularly. This case study highlights the role of dogs in religious rituals and the motivation behind these rites.

In his concluding chapter, Robert J. Losey reflects on many themes explored in these chapters and comments on current trajectories in the study of human-canine relationships. He reminds us that while human relationships with dogs have taken many forms since incipient domestication, dogs are and will always be on a domestication continuum. Researchers may move the conversations about dogs beyond domestication theories, but these processes are still central to tracking the changing roles of dogs within human communities over time.

Assessing the physical ways humans have altered domestic dogs may be relatively straightforward, but it takes several theoretical and methodological avenues to understand how the ever-present dog influenced and was influenced by human communities' needs, belief systems, and relationships with their natural and social environments. Despite their cross-cultural ubiquity and importance in human lifeways, dogs are often silent actors in the retelling of the past. In order to better understand the lived experiences of dogs coexisting with humans, scholars must examine multiple lines of evidence. Archaeologists are especially fit for these topics because they are able to not only trace the physical evidence of these relationships (both the remains of dogs and how they are found contextually) but also incorporate diverse data sets and theoretical frameworks to enhance our understanding of human and nonhuman interactions.

The physical remains of dogs can hold biological histories that exemplify past people's treatment and use of dogs. At the same time, a rich array of techniques for furthering this understanding exists beyond traditional zooarchaeological methods. These include not only the use of scientific techniques to assess physical remains, such as isotope, DNA, and chemical residue analyses, but also the integration of history, ethnography, multispecies scholarship, traditional cultural knowledge, and findings from animal behavioral studies. These multidisciplinary investigative techniques have broadened our ability to ask new archaeological questions about the human-canine relationship. Today, anthropological studies of human-animal relationships are firmly grounded in this multidisciplinary approach, and contributions to this volume attest to this.

Overall, this volume demonstrates that dogs, like humans, fill multiple social functions that create complex and often contradictory relationships. By considering these relationships between humans and dogs through an archaeological lens, this volume adds to our understanding of how the human-canine bond shaped and was shaped by the practical and ontological realities of human caregivers. These chapters contribute a wide-ranging narrative of the human-dog relationship across space and time while also participating in broader anthropological discussions about how the story of the dog is really the story of ourselves.

References Cited

Crockford, Susan J. (editor)
2000 *Dogs through Time: An Archaeological Perspective.* BAR International Series 889. Archaeopress, Oxford.
Gilhus, Ingvild Sælid
2006 *Animals, Gods and Humans: Changing Attitudes to Animals in Greek, Roman and Early Christian Ideas.* Routledge, New York.
Losey, Robert J., Robert P. Wishart, and Jan Peter Laurens Loovers (editors)
2018 *Dogs in the North: Stories of Cooperation and Co-Domestication.* Routledge, London.
Miklósi, Ádám
2014 *Dog Behaviour, Evolution, and Cognition.* 2nd ed. Oxford University Press, Oxford.
Morey, Darcy F.
2006 Burying Key Evidence: the Social Bond between Dogs and People. *Journal of Archaeological Science* 33(2):158–175.
2010 *Dogs: Domestication and the Development of a Social Bond.* Cambridge University Press, Cambridge.
Russell, Nerissa
2012 *Social Zooarchaeology: Humans and Animals in Prehistory.* Cambridge University Press, Cambridge.
Serpell, James (editor)
1995 *The Domestic Dog: Its Evolution, Behaviour and Interactions with People.* Cambridge University Press, Cambridge.
Snyder, Lynn M., and Elizabeth A. Moore (editors)
2006 *Dogs and People in Social, Working, Economic, or Symbolic Interaction.* Proceedings of the 9th ICAZ Conference, Durham. Oxbow Books, Oxford.
Stahl, Peter W.
2016 Old Dogs and New Tricks: Recent Developments in Our Understanding of the Human-Dog Relationship. *Reviews in Anthropology* 45(1):51–68.
Walker, William H.
2008 Practice and Nonhuman Social Actors: The Afterlife Histories of Witches and Dogs in the American Southwest. In *Memory Work: Archaeologies of Material Practices,* edited by Barbara J. Mills and William H. Walker, pp. 137–158. School for Advanced Research, Santa Fe.

2

Prehistoric Dogs as Hunting Tools

The Advent of Animal Biotechnology

ANGELA R. PERRI

The role of hunting dogs in the past and present has always been a topic of great interest in hunter-gatherer studies (e.g., Guagnin et al. 2018; Hayden 1975; Jones 1970; Kent 1993; Koster 2009; Lupo 2011, 2017; Perri 2014, 2016a; Perri et al. 2015; Shipman 2015; White 1972). Although some researchers have argued that the utilization of hunting dogs cannot be documented in the archaeological record (Morey 2010), there are potential paths toward a better understanding of the use of dogs as prehistoric hunting technology. While many records from modern forager groups document the utilization of hunting dogs, similar analyses from the archaeological record are scarce (but see Guagnin et al. 2018; Lupo 2017; Perri 2016a). Karen Lupo (2011, 2017) has noted that the impact of different dog deployment strategies and their effect on human behavior and the zooarchaeo-logical record are still underexplored. To advance our understanding of the use of dogs as hunting weapons in prehistory, we must first identify the ways dogs can be used as hunting biotechnology, including the costs and benefits their use may incur, particularly within different environmental contexts. Next, we must distinguish how hunting dogs can be incorporated into existing subsistence models. Finally, beginning with observations from the ethnographic and ethno-historic record, we must evaluate how we can identify the use of hunting dogs within the archaeological record. Following this, I 1) argue that dogs represent the advent of animal biotechnology, an important cognitive and innovative step in human evolution, 2) explore ways in which hunting dogs have been used in the ethnographic and ethnohistoric record, 3) propose we begin to consider the effects and implications of dogs as hunting technology in the archaeological record, and 4) suggest ways of identifying hunting dogs in the archaeological record.

Animal Biotechnology as Innovation

A hunting partnership between dogs and humans has long been postulated in the archaeological literature. Juliet Clutton-Brock (1995, 1999) suggested that dog domestication was the result of a relationship between wolves and humans, formed due to similar social structures and targeted prey, leading to a natural alliance and collaborative hunting team. Similarly, Brian Hayden (1975) suggested Australian Aborigines first adopted dingoes for their use as hunting aids and Michael Kennedy (1980) suggested hunting dogs as one of the critical components for hunting large game in Mesolithic Europe. Pat Shipman (2015) has even proposed that protodogs assisted human hunters in outcompeting Neanderthals up to 32,000 years ago as part of her "domesticated canid hypothesis."

The use of dogs as hunting weapons represents a first innovative step in human cognition, whereby tasks that were previously performed by humans (or were never performed before) are transferred to animals. This represents not only a novel innovation but the inception of a dynamic relationship between humans and animals whereby humans harness the innate properties of animals as technology (e.g., tools, weaponry, machinery), leading to their ubiquitous use as modes of production (e.g., hunting, transport, draught). This new relationship signifies an important cognitive shift in regarding animals not only for their material products (meat, bones, hides, horns) but for their physiological and behavioral properties. This process likely took place over time, beginning with observations of the innate hunting tendencies of newly domesticated dogs (or wolves, previously) and the later domestication of dogs to look to humans for direction (Udell 2015), thus promoting effective cooperative hunting strategies.

The process of controlled animal biotechnology as first seen in hunting dogs undoubtedly began with observations of the foraging ecology and hunting behaviors of non-domesticated animals in both passive and non-passive forms. These include following vultures to carcasses (Tappen 2001) and scavenging other predators' kills (O'Connell et al. 1988). These relationships, which are often symbiotic, frequently continue today, for example, the tracking of honeyguide birds to beehives (Isack and Reyer 1989; Spottiswoode et al. 2016).

Technological development is seen as a general trend toward less expenditure of human energy (Creswell 1996; Deforge 1989) and an evolutionary force that "propels cultures up the ladder of cultural complexity" (O'Brien and Shennan 2010:4). Discussion of increasing technological complexity and tool use in the archaeological record focuses primarily on stone and bone tool technology. Applications of optimal foraging theory (Smith et al. 1983; Winterhalder 1981) to the behavioral ecology of foragers have not incorporated the use of living, adaptable technology, such as hunting dogs. Their use can incur unexpected costs and benefits, and these should be incorporated as additional constraints when modeling prey choice and dietary breadth. Jeremy Koster (2008a) first outlined how the use of hunting dogs could be modeled within an optimal foraging perspective, but archaeologists have yet to carry over this approach to analyses of past human subsistence practices.

Karen Lupo (2017) reviewed changes in hunting productivity associated with dogs using the diet breadth model, which assumes that resources can be ranked along a single dimension of profitability (usually kcals obtained per unit of handling time or the post-encounter return rate). She noted that resource acquisition is generally divided between two costs—searching and handling. Changes in these costs as a result of technological developments such as the advent of hunting dogs have significant implications for optimal foraging models (Hawkes et al. 1982; Winterhalder 1978, 1981). Citing ethnographic and ethnohistoric sources, Lupo (2017) observed that the use of hunting dogs can affect these costs (both positively and negatively) but that the dogs' effectiveness as hunting technology is also correlated to additional factors, such as other hunting technologies utilized, local prey communities, and environmental contexts.

Dogs as Animal Biotechnology

Current research places domesticated dogs' origin in Eurasia, with domestication likely occurring sometime around 20,000–15,000 years ago (Frantz et al. 2016; Larson et al. 2012). This period saw the end of the Last Glacial Maximum and the beginning of Late Glacial warming. Throughout Eurasia human populations were recolonizing previously glaciated regions, which were increasingly populated by boreal and deciduous forests and their associated prey species (Blackwell and Buck 2003). Although this was a time of overall increased warming, the end of the Pleistocene also saw some dramatic fluctuations in climate, including a sharp decline in temperature and return to glacial conditions across the Northern Hemisphere associated with the Younger Dryas between circa 12,900 and 11,700 BP (Firestone et al. 2007). Fitzhugh (2001:145) proposed that invention and innovation of technology, leading to new tool classes and deployment methods, would be generated by movement into unfamiliar environments and ecosystems, particularly in the case of rapid major environmental change. Though referencing primarily raw materials and lithic tool technology, these predictions can be applied to the use of domesticated dogs as a novel hunting technology beginning in the Late Pleistocene and early Holocene, not long after their domestication. Domesticated dogs have previously been proposed as one of the major technological innovations in the Upper Paleolithic (Hoffecker 2005).

One of the key factors in shaping forager technology is the recognition of risk and the technological strategies employed to reduce risk associated with food acquisition (Bamforth and Bleed 1997; Bleed 1997; Torrence 1989). Though forager technology and risk have been analyzed for decades, the discussion largely focuses on lithic tool technology (Bousman 1993; Collard et al. 2011; Elston and Brantingham 2002; Hiscock 1994; Torrence 2001). In her discussion of forager technologies, Torrence (2001:79) defined a hunting weapon as that which restricts the mobility of prey, allowing the hunter to get closer for a kill. Fitzhugh (2001:127–128) defined technology as "the totality of the means employed to provide objects necessary for . . . sustenance and comfort." Foragers carefully choose their technology to manage their energy and to prevent loss and failure (Torrence 2001). While hunting dogs are commonly listed among the important hunting tools used by groups in the ethnographic record (e.g., Ngima Mawoung 2006), dogs have not been comprehensively discussed as a substantive hunting tool in the archaeological literature, though some recent work has begun to focus on this subject (Guagnin et al. 2018; Lupo 2017; Perri 2014, 2016; Perri et al. 2015; Shipman 2015).

The most productive way to consider dogs as hunting technology and incorporate them into optimal foraging models is to evaluate their costs and benefits in the same way we consider other modes of technology. For example, Peter Bleed (1986) analyzed tool technology using the same design goals

Angela R. Perri

employed by engineers, namely quicker production time, increased use life, increased effectiveness, and increased production volume. Following these goals, we can consider how dogs may be viewed as effective technology in decreasing hunting risk.

Quicker Production Time

Hunting dogs often receive little to no training within forager groups, instead learning by example when they are brought along on hunts (Koster and Tankersley 2012). This often means there is very little, if any, time invested. Yet many dogs are weaned by two months and do not begin effectively hunting until they are between eight months and one year old (Fiorello et al. 2006), leaving between six and ten months of care and feeding investment without immediate return. In some instances this may be managed by killing pups without apparent hunting potential, expecting pups to fend for themselves on wild forage, garbage, or feces or feeding them game scrap or leftovers, incurring little or no cost.

Increased Use Life

Dogs may serve as a useful hunting weapon well into later adulthood (Koster and Tankersley 2012). Hunting dog life expectancies can be variable depending on local conditions and environment. For example, in the neotropical forests of Nicaragua, hunting dogs average short lives due to jaguar attacks, snake bites, and various diseases, which may not be present at other locations (Koster 2008b). Hunting dog "use life" should be evaluated individually given local cultural and environmental contexts.

Increased Effectiveness

The increased effectiveness potential of dogs is based primarily on their providing superhuman skills beyond typical human sensory perception. For example, dogs may be used to initially sniff out prey or track blood trails, effectively overcoming biological shortfalls in human predatory adaptations. They may also act as stand-ins for human hunters, freeing individuals to pursue other activities.

The ethnographic literature on the use of hunting dogs suggests three factors are critically important in their effectiveness: environment, species type, and overall species diversity. While hunting dogs seem to be used in a variety of environments for different purposes, the amount of vegetation and other hunting techniques used in this environment appear to affect their usefulness. For example, hunters in open environments often avoid using dogs because prey can see or smell dogs from long distances (Krober 1941). Furthermore, hunters in these environments often use ambush techniques to hunt prey, which may not be conducive to the assistance of dogs.

Prey species type also appears to be a critical factor in the importance of hunting dogs. There is ethnographic evidence for humans' use of dogs while hunting many different types of prey, but hunting dogs appear to be particularly effective with prey that live individually or in small groups. Large groups of animals that travel in herds are often hunted via ambush to avoid spooking them (Harako 1981), so hunters avoid the use of dogs. However, they are often used in open environments for persistence hunting, chasing prey that are sprinters but tire quickly (Liebenberg 2006). For example, dogs have been used in desert environments for millennia to chase-hunt quick prey, like gazelle, to exhaustion (Guagnin et al. 2018). They are also useful in hunting dangerous prey, such as bears or boar, creating a barrier between the hunter and animal, as well as prey that hide when escaping or injured, such as some deer species.

Finally, overall species diversity appears to be an important factor in hunting dog effectiveness. The relationship between hunting dog effectiveness and species diversity is most apparent in the lower latitudes, where species diversity is often high but desirable prey may make up only a small portion of available species. For example, Jeremy Koster and Andrew Noss (2013) describe the variable outcomes of hunting dog use in the neotropics of Nicaragua, finding that hunting dogs often led human hunters on long chases after undesirable prey. Koster (2008a) applied the optimal foraging model and found that while dogs can be valuable hunting tools in the region, improving both encounter rates and pursuit times of several prey types, they also often lead hunters on extended, fruitless chases. Given this possibility, an environment in which most, if not all, available species present are considered desirable prey would increase the effectiveness of hunting dogs.

The ethnographic and ethnohistoric records exhibit the wide geographic, environmental, and prey species range in which dogs are utilized to increase hunting effectiveness. Dogs are used to hunt everything from rodents (Lupo 2011; Ngima Mawoung 2006) to ratites such as emu (Boyce 2006; Gusinde 1937; Lyons 1926), monkeys (Pannell and O'Connor 2010), and other carnivores

(Laugrand and Oosten 2002; Liebenburg 2006). They are particularly useful in hunting forest ungulates like deer and boar, for which their utilization is widely documented worldwide (e.g., Brown and Emery 2008; Nobayashi 2006; Perri 2014). A review of this literature suggests the effectiveness of hunting dogs, like other tool technology, cannot be evaluated broadly but must be analyzed within individual contexts.

Many foragers and other subsistence hunters have asserted that it would be impossible to track or kill certain types of game without dogs (Brown and Emery 2008; Caldecott 1988; Ikeya 1994; Serpell 1995; Tate 1931; White 1972). The Bakola of Cameroon considered the dog their most valuable domesticated animal and a critical hunting weapon (Ngima Mawoung 2006). Similarly, Dwyer (1983) commented that access to a capable hunting dog was a critical determinant of successful Etolo hunting in Papua New Guinea, and Paige West (2005) stated some highly prized marsupials were impossible to hunt there without dogs. In Malaysia, more than 86% of the wild bearded pigs killed by the Sarawak were taken with the help of a dog (Caldecott 1988), and Louis Liebenberg (2006) has suggested that in the Kalahari Desert (and perhaps as a general rule) the highest hunting success rates and meat yields were achieved by hunting with dogs. A famous example from Richard Lee (1965) stated that one San man with a trained pack of hunting dogs brought in 75% of the meat to a camp, while six other hunters without dogs brought only the remaining 25% combined.

Yet dogs may also be a detriment in some environments. Although dogs can be trained to successfully hunt multiple species (e.g., Newton et al. 2008), training is rarely observed among forager hunting dogs, and dogs can prove problematic when blindly targeting undesirable prey types (Koster 2008a). Everard Thurn (1967) and Kevin Jernigan (2009) both reported that dogs in the neotropics were trained to hunt specific animals, likely a result of the vast array of possible prey and loss of time if dogs chase after low-ranking species (Koster and Noss 2013). A. L. Krober (1941) noted that dogs were not turned on animals like antelope and buffalo in open country because such prey might run or stampede and thus be lost, and subsistence elephant hunters avoid using dogs due to the need for silent stalking and ambush (Harako 1981). Samuel Dira and Barry Hewlett (2018) observed that even in locations where dogs are used regularly for hunting, such as the highland forests of Ethiopia, they may not be used for hunting techniques that require stealth ambushing.

Increased Production Volume

Production volume in dogs is directly related to reproduction and puppies as a renewable resource. Although there may be a trade-off in hunting time loss with a pregnant female, overall female dogs tend to be worth more in subsistence groups, which acknowledge their value as technology producers (Lupo 2011).

Like other tools, quicker production time, increased use life, increased effectiveness, and increased production volume affect the way dogs are evaluated as hunting technology. Limitations in understanding hunting dogs as technology and integrating them into, for example, optimal foraging models has been restrained by the apparent inability to quantify their costs and benefits as for non-living tools. Evaluating hunting dogs through the same design goals as other tool technology, including assessing their strengths and weaknesses and defining the tasks they performed, offers a meaningful way of considering hunting dogs as biotechnology.

Hunting Dog Tasks

The tasks hunting dogs undertake vary based on location, environment, prey species, and human hunting goals. As documented in the ethnographic record, hunting dogs appear to be most useful in performing tasks that are difficult or impossible for human hunters to perform or in replacing human hunters, freeing individuals to perform other activities. For example, Peter Mitchell (2008) stated that hunters in southern Africa used dogs to harry prey, a task previously assigned to one of the men, thus reducing human energy expenditure and allowing individuals to undertake other responsibilities. Dogs are also used as human substitutes to flush out prey, thus requiring fewer people to accompany the hunting party (Bulmer 1968; Ellen 1999). Importantly, this role as a human replacement can also allow hunters to successfully hunt alone (Buxton 1968; Nobayashi 2006), which may be impossible otherwise. Of the tasks undertaken while on hunts, the ethnographic record documents dogs being particularly adept at the following.

Locating and Encountering

Hunting dogs are most commonly employed by humans for locating game, which is often the most difficult skill to learn for human hunters (Walker et al. 2002). Robert Carneiro (1970) documented the Amahuacas' use of hunting dogs in the Amazon Basin, where dogs enable hunters to locate game more easily, particularly by locating animals living in burrows or hollow tree trunks. Similarly, in Malaysia the Sarawak used dogs to seek out and hold prey, for which "they were indispensable . . . and can virtually guarantee a successful day's hunt" (Caldecott 1988:27). John Grant (1980:342) likewise noted that the Saulteaux of Canada used dogs to find beavers in low, swampy ground "where the most experienced hunter very often cannot succeed."

Indicating

In nearly all instances of the use of dogs for hunting, one of the dogs' primary tasks is indicating the location of prey to human hunters through a variety of methods, including chasing, barking, and pointing. Ferdinand Rühe and colleagues (2006) found that 91% of red deer hunts and 100% of wild boar hunts in Germany were successful when hunters managed an unbroken acoustic tie with their hunting hounds. Similarly, Angela Perri (2014) documented that boar hunters in Japan targeted their prey by following their hunting dogs' barking through thick mountain forests.

Restricting Movement

One of hunting dogs' most valuable advantages may be their holding of dangerous animals, reducing the risk encountered by the human hunter. Such dangerous animals include prey such as gemsbok or boar that can bite or attack with sharp horns or tusks, deer and kangaroo with violent kicks, venomous snakes, and carnivores such as hyena and jaguar. For example, when hunting wild pigs, some hunters mitigate risk by using their dogs to chase the animals into water where they can be killed (Caldecott 1988) or until the prey turns and posts, at which point dogs can hold the animal long enough for the hunter to make the final kill (Nobayashi 2006; Saïd et al. 2012).

Pursuing and Recovering

Dogs are commonly used to chase-hunt and tree game, often to the point of exhaustion (e.g., Chitwood et al. 2011; Nobayashi 2006). Deer hunters use them to track blood trails of fleeing, injured animals and cite them as one of the main reasons for high wounded prey recovery rates (Campo and Spencer 1991). Richard Morton and colleagues (1995) reported that it took an average of only 30 minutes for hunting dogs to recover a deer once on the blood trail; the method is so effective that Norwegian law requires hunters to have a hunting dog available to track wounded red deer (Olaussen and Mysterud 2012).

Procuring

There have been some extraordinary instances where dogs have been documented procuring prey almost entirely for their human masters. Ole Grøn and Michail Turov (2007:71) document the case of a disabled Evenk man in Siberia whose exceptional hunting dog led moose to his tent where he could shoot them at close range. William Pferd (1987) recounts a similar story of dogs corralling moose in seventeenth-century North America for a lone hunter to kill.

The Koster Model

Some of the most comprehensive studies on the economy of hunting dogs, which acutely document these hunting dog tasks, have been undertaken by Koster and colleagues in their work with Miskito and Mayangna hunters in Nicaragua (Koster 2006, 2008a, 2008b, 2008c, 2009, 2011; Koster and Noss 2014; Koster and Tankersley 2012). For the first time, Koster (2008a) approached the use of dogs as hunting technology from an optimal foraging perspective, focusing on how their utilization affects prey encounter rates and pursuit times. While his findings are specific to the particular environment (lowland tropical rain forest) and prey species (diverse neotropical species) in which the data was collected, this work provides critical insight into the economy of hunting dog use by subsistence hunters.

Following work by human behavioral ecologists in applying optimal prey choice models and cost-benefit analyses (Alvard 1993; O'Connell and Hawkes 1981; Smith 1983; Winterhalder 1981), Koster (2008a) collected quantitative evidence on the ways in which the use of hunting dogs affected a number of parameters. These include, for each prey type, encounter rate, energetic return per pursuit, dog-commitment time per pursuit, and "handling time" per pursuit, which includes hunting and processing time. These studies provide quantifiable findings associated with, for example, how long hunting dogs take to find prey, which prey types hunting dogs target, how many years hunting dogs are effective, and the return rates of hunting dogs as compared to other technology (Koster 2006, 2008a, 2008b, 2009; Koster and Noss 2014).

Koster (2008a) noted that there can be important costs associated with decision-making when hunting with dogs. For example, while hunters without dogs visually mark their prey before pursuit or attack, hunters with dogs often rely on dogs to locate prey, leading to a chase in which the human hunter pursues the prey and dog(s). In environments such as lowland neotropical Nicaragua with dense vegetation, which may affect prey species identification, encounter rates, and anti-predator strategies, and high rates of undesirable prey, these chases may be lengthy but ultimately fruitless, resulting in long pursuit times with no prey return. Alternatively, in more open environments or those where most or all available species represent desirable prey, this pursuit time may result in higher prey returns, potentially making dogs more effective as hunting technology.

Koster (2008a:939–940) showed that the trade-off for potential high dog-handling costs in certain environments is increased encounter rates with desired prey types. Encounter rates were up to nine times higher for some species, as compared to hunting without dogs, and dogs contributed to 86% of mammalian prey kills in the community studied (Koster 2008b). Koster (2008b) also noted that dogs can be considered particularly useful for only specific prey types. This can be applicable to varied locations, meaning hunting dogs may be entirely inadequate in some settings or specific locations. Thus, in some locations hunting dogs are useful for some local prey but detrimental for others, leading to potentially high costs when chasing unprofitable prey. Therefore, dogs may be most advantageous as hunting technology where most or all prey they encounter and pursue is within hunters' optimal diet set. Alternatively, if the environment is full of species that may distract dogs unprofitably, then they are likely not considered a valuable tool.

While this work documents the extent to which hunting dogs act as significant participants in hunting outcomes within the ethnographic record, there has been little research into how the use of hunting dogs may have affected hunting practices and prey return in the past. Applicable insights from the work of Koster and colleagues and others may help explain why ancient foragers began using dogs as hunting technology, why purported hunting dogs are found in particular environments, and how dog remains and prey profiles at archaeological sites are related. One particularly key finding, which is relevant to archaeological prey choice modeling, is that when using hunting dogs to locate and chase prey, initial pursued prey choice is invariably made by the dog, not the human hunter, though the hunter may choose to kill the quarried prey or abandon the pursuit or kill. Dog-driven prey choice has important implications for how archaeologists interpret prey profiles and optimal foraging decisions made by past populations that may have used dogs as critical hunting technology.

Identifying Hunting Dogs in the Archaeological Record

One of the first challenges in assessing the role of hunting dogs in the past is identifying hunting dogs in the archaeological record. Hunter-gatherer sites with domesticated dog remains are fairly ubiquitous from about 10,000 years ago onward, but identifying which, if any, of these dogs may have been used as hunting aids is less simple. While the ethnographic and ethnohistoric records document that dogs may be useful to hunters, at some level, across a variety of contexts, hunting dogs may be most visible in the archaeological record in locations where they were perceived as critical technology. The documentation of potential hunting dogs may include not only the skeletal remains of these dogs but also potential contextual elements suggesting the use of hunting dogs in a particular location.

Shelters and Pits

Working dog shelters are ubiquitous throughout the ethnographic literature but are particularly prevalent in harsh environments where dogs need to be protected from excessively hot or cold temperatures. When analyzing data from ethnographic work with Native Americans in the western United States, Alfred L. Kroeber (1941) noted various types of dog shelters, from brush shelters and domes to lean-tos made of bark, specifically made for hunting dogs or favored pets. Similarly, James O'Connell (1987) and Paul Memmott (2007) have both described small, domed brush huts built for dogs by Australian Aborigines. In the higher latitudes hunting dogs are often protected with snow shelters or kennels (e.g., Savelle 1984), and Taksami (1961) documented lean-to summer shelters and large structures which served as winter shelters for dogs built by the Nivkh near lower Amur River, Russia.

Small shelters are also sometimes constructed for females that are pregnant or have litters of puppies (Savelle 1984; Seligmann and Seligmann 1911). B. Reynolds (1968), working with the Gwembe Tonga in Zambia, who use dogs for hunting, documented the digging of shallow holes for bitches with litters, either in the open or in the floors of old houses. The shelters were then covered with cowhides weighed down with large stones (Reynolds 1968:21). In prehistory, stillborn pups or those that died shortly after birth may have been left in floor pits like these and later interpreted as intentional burials (e.g., Emslie 1978).

Dog shelters often leave traces that may be archaeologically visible, such as gravel floors, stone-lined borders, and postholes. The ethnographic record suggests some may be difficult to distinguish from human dwellings as they are often in the same location and can be roughly the same size. James Savelle (1984), in discussing remains from a historic Inuit site in Arctic Canada, noted that snow dog shelters were similar to human shelters but were smaller with fewer, more dispersed, gnawed and fragmented faunal remains and fewer artifacts. Holt (1946) observed the Shasta of the western United States kept hunting dogs in kennels built against the back of a house. Hunting dogs were sometimes kept within human dwellings as well. Tom Harrisson (1965) described the close relationship between hunters in Borneo and their hunting dogs; family huts have special raised platform beds for dogs, while humans sleep on the floor. Similar wooden sleeping platforms for hunting dogs have been described among the Yanomami and Carib groups of Brazil (Becher 1960). All of these areas may show increased occurrence of feces, carnivore-gnawed bones, or digging pits.

Other domestic evidence of hunting dogs may include postholes used to tether hunting dogs to keep them from wandering, fighting, or getting un-derfoot. Tethering often results in a concentrated area of digging pits, gnawed bones, and excrement (O'Connell 1987). Variation in bone damage by dogs that were spatial-restricted and destructively chewed bones versus those that were allowed to range freely and only damaged bones as an effect of meat removal is well documented (Hudson 1993; Kent 1981). C. Claassen (2010:96–97), noticing a curious absence of carnivore gnawing from Midsouth US Archaic sites with large numbers of dogs, proposed they may have been tied up or penned, which is in line with the practice of keeping hunting dogs separated to prevent fighting or undesirable mating. Special feeding conditions have also been documented, as among the Chenchu in India, who feed their hunting dogs from homemade bamboo feeders or alternatively from natural depressions on rock surfaces (Reddy 2006).

The intentional burial of food and bones to keep dogs from scavenging is also widely documented in the ethnographic literature (e.g., Lehtisalo 1964; Schapera 1930). In the archaeological record this may be misinterpreted as some other form of storage or preservation. Pits can also be created by dogs as a means of hunting, storage, or bedding. O'Connell (1987) described shallow pits, roughly 1 m wide and 50 cm deep, which Australian Aboriginal hunting dogs dug to keep cool. His example fits well within the range of pits and wallows dug by dogs in experimental work by Robert J. Jeske and Laurence A. Kuznar (2001;

see also Kuznar and Jeske 2006), which showed that canine digging behavior can easily be confused with human-produced features. Susan Kent (1981, 1993) documented similar issues related to the spatial distribution and taphonomy of faunal remains at sites with dogs.

Hunting-Associated Equipment

There are several references to keeping hunting dogs on collars and leashes in the ethnographic record, though many of these are made from material that would not survive well in the archaeological record, such as leather or plant materials (Harrisson 1965; Huntingford 1929). Gusinde (1937) discussed the keeping of hunting dogs on leashes in Tierra del Fuego to keep them from hunting alone, which was thought to reduce their prey drive. The earliest depictions of hunting dogs on leashes date back to pre-neolithic rock art from Saudi Arabia (Guagnin et al. 2018), suggesting their use began in early prehistory.

The use of collars is also common among modern foragers. Bell collars made of wood, large nut shells, and bone are often used to track hunting dogs in Africa due the dense vegetation and the lack of vocalization in local breeds (Huntingford 1929). T. I. Itkonen (1984) also recorded the use of collars and leashes made of wood and antler for hunting dogs by Lapps in Finland. These were similar to the antler-toggled leather halters used with hunting dogs by the Nlaka'pamux in British Columbia (Teit 1900). The shape, material, and perforation of these examples are remarkably similar to prehistoric artifacts often identified as shaft straighteners. Julian Haynes Steward (1941) recorded the stringing of shell collars around the neck of hunting dogs by the Shoshone in the western United States, and Verne F. Ray (1942) suggested deer hooves were used to make hunting dog collars in British Columbia.

Other hunting apparatuses include the tying of fetishes such as animal horn or the claws of predators (Roscoe 1923) around the necks of hunting dogs and whistles. Whistles made of various materials are used by modern foragers to communicate with their hunting dogs (MacGaffey 1991; Söderberg 1966; Torday and Joyce 1905). Antler, bone, stone, and clay whistles are known from prehistoric forager sites worldwide (Hickmann and Hughes 1988; Morley 2013), including regions with large numbers of dog burials (Martin 1976; Tsuge 1988). These are often interpreted as musical instruments or animal calls but may in fact be whistles used for dog-assisted hunting.

Depictions of Hunting Dogs in Art

The depiction of hunting dogs in art is one of the more obvious ways of identifying them in the archaeological record. Hunting dogs, especially in association with bow hunters, are known from rock art in many locations around the world (e.g., Francfort et al. 1990; Ranov 2001). Dog-shaped clay figurines are common from Jōmon (ca. 13,000–2,500 BP) forager sites in Japan, where prehistoric hunters likely used dogs to hunt deer and boar (Perri 2016a). This includes a set of figurines from the site of Fujioka Jinja that appears to show a dog barking at three wild boars (Fujinuma 1997). Another depiction of hunting dogs, this time encircling a wild boar with a human bow hunter, is shown in relief on a ritual bronze bell from the same region of Japan (Perri 2016a). Maria Guagnin and colleagues (2018) documented some of the earliest dog depictions in the world, from Saudi Arabia, where groups of dogs on leashes are shown hunting a variety of prey alongside humans. Similar depictions of dogs within hunting scenes are also evident in the prehistoric rock art of Fennoscandia (Viranta and Mannermaa 2018).

Dog Burials

The prevalence of hunting dog burials in the ethnographic record indicates their importance within some groups. These dogs often acquired the status of valued group members based on their hunting proficiency, frequently extending to the giving of proper names (Ikeya 1994; Ellen 1999). In many groups, dogs that are useful for hunting are considered separate from all other dogs, leading to their burial in a remarkably human-like manner (Perri 2014). Edward Winslow Gifford (1940), writing on the Apache and Pueblo, stated that good dogs were buried, while useless dogs were thrown into the bushes. Deliberate, individual burials of hunting dogs (e.g., Perri 2017) have been well documented globally in forager groups (Elmendorf and Kroeber 1960; Lupo 2011; Perri 2014), as well as more ephemeral methods such as placing the animal in a sacred tree (Koler-Matznick et al. 2007; Whiting 1941), wrapping the remains in bark (Meehan et al. 1999), or placing the remains in an aboveground wooden coffin (Grøn and Turov 2007).

Dog burials seem to be particularly common when the death occurred during a hunting expedition (e.g., Olowo Ojoade 1990; Nobayashi 2006). Though the details of dog burials are rarely recorded, there are some discussions of grave goods, including deer skins (Nobayashi 2006) and loincloths (Blackwood 1935). The burial of some prehistoric dogs under deliberate rock markers (DeJarnette and Wimberly 1942; Kerber 1997; McMillan 1970) parallels the burial of hunting dogs under similar conditions in the ethnographic record (Hambly 1934). Other prehistoric dogs have been buried with grave goods like projectile points and deer antlers (Larsson 1990; Walker et al. 2005), which are closely associated with hunting.

Though Lupo (2011) reported the hunting prowess of male and female dogs was equivalent, Koster and Kenneth Tankersley (2012) suggested male dogs and older dogs (probably due to gained experience) may be better hunters. A preference for male hunting dogs has been noted from many forager groups, including those in Papua New Guinea (Koler-Matznick et al. 2007), Nigeria (Bohannan and Bohannan 1968), and Russia (Ohnuki-Tierney 1974). This may be due to hunting variation between the sexes but may also be influenced by hunting downtime in pregnant or nursing females. In an analysis of Archaic dog burials from the Midsouth United States, Warren (2004:63) noted that as dogs increased in age, the representation of the sexes changed dramatically. The sub-adults had a 1:1 ratio of males and females, mature adults favored male dogs by a 3.41:1 ratio, and in the oldest age category all dogs were identified as male. This apparent preference toward the burial of male dogs may reflect a belief, either real or imagined, that male dogs are better suited to hunting.

Variation in Diets

Though dogs in forager villages are often treated roughly and made to scavenge for refuse and scraps (Jackson 1983; Kracke 1981), there is ample documentation of good hunting dogs receiving better care than other dogs (Koster 2009; McSweeney 2000). This differentiation between types of dogs is apparent in the use of different words for common village dogs and hunting dogs among some foragers (Schulting 1994). Hunting dogs are often fed the spoils of a successful hunt, including meat and bones (Gayton 1948; Lupo 2011), viscera (Kagwa 1934), fetuses (Forline 1997), and blood (Lupo 2011). Dogs of all ages are also sometimes fed human breast milk (Alexiades 1999; Descola 1994; Gifford 1940). Although some analytic work has been done on isotopic variation in modern and ancient dog diets (e.g., Cannon et al. 1999; Clutton-Brock and Noe-Nygaard 1990; Ewersen et al. 2018; Guiry 2012; Guiry and Grimes 2013; Monagle et al. 2018; Tankersley and Koster 2009), additional work should be undertaken to address questions of differential feeding and dietary variation between intentionally buried and "refuse" dogs from the same archaeological site.

In addition to feeding, there is significant documentation of hunting dogs being treated with various hallucinogenic or medicinal plants. These remedies are put in the nose, eyes, anus, or given to the dog to drink or eat (Carneiro 1970; Jernigan 2009). Among the Aguaruna Jivaro of Peru, Jernigan (2009) documented 35 plant species given to dogs. The majority of these are used to improve hunting ability, including plants from the pepper family, which are used to improve the olfactory senses. Other plants are used to cure gastrointestinal illness, including those caused by parasites. Additional uses include cures for snake or insect bites, skin infections, lice, and witchcraft. Hallucinogenic plants are also used to improve hunting success (Bennett et al. 2002; Koster 2009). Bradley Bennett and Rocío Alarcón (2015) documented 21 psychoactive species used by the Shuar and Quichua of Ecuador to improve hunting by enhancing the sensory perception of hunting dogs. They proposed that the prevalence of the practice suggests it garners positive results. The possibility of similar uses of medicinal or hallucinogenic plants with hunting dogs in the prehistoric record could be examined by analyzing the stomach contents and dental calculus of excavated dog remains.

Injuries and Disease

Serious injury or death as a result of interactions with prey, particularly large ungulates, is well documented in interspecies interactions between prey, wolves, and coyotes (MacNulty 2002; Mech and Nelson 1990; Wobeser 1992). Rausch (1967) documented many skull compression fractures among Alaskan wolves, presumably due to interaction with large ungulate prey, some leading to death. In the archaeological record, such skull fractures in dogs are usually assumed to be related to blunt-force trauma at the hands of humans, but the risk of injury or death in hunting dogs increases in relation to environments with large or dangerous prey.

Koster and Tankersley (2012) reported hunting dog deaths as a result of snakebites, which would leave no evidence but are limited to certain environments. Similarly, they and others (e.g., Neto et al. 2011) have documented high rates of hunting dog death by jaguar attack, which is again limited to particular geographic locations. Hunting dogs are also prone to injury or death at the hands of other prey or predators such as wild boar, bears, wolves, or large felids (Hanson and Karstad 1959). The presence of dogs often diverts the attention of predators or dangerous prey away from humans and onto the dogs (Swenson et al. 1999; Koster 2009).

Unfortunately, detailed data on specific injuries or deaths of hunting dogs are rarely documented in ethnographic accounts. Christina Ingendaay and colleagues (2008) documented injuries sustained by non-hunting dogs as a result of wild boar interactions in Germany. They noted the majority of injuries occurred in the torso, resulting in lacerations, bone fractures, and death. In a study of Archaic dogs from the Midsouth United States, Warren (2004) noted high frequencies of skull and rib fractures consistent with large animal encounters that may have occurred while hunting. Canine and premolar fracture frequencies also suggest increased contact with large, struggling animals, likely the white-tailed deer that were the most commonly exploited prey species in the region (Madrigal and Holt 2002). Warren (2004:248–249) concluded that consistent trauma seen on the bones of intentionally buried dogs suggested burial treatment was preferentially applied to dogs that performed an economically important function, such as hunting. This conclusion complements observations by Tuck (1976:78), who found well-developed muscle attachments in buried dogs as compared to non-buried dogs at the Archaic site of Port au Choix, suggesting use in hunting.

Due to documentation of pathogen exposure through ethnoveterinary medicine, we know that forager hunting dogs are exposed to a wide range of disease and parasites (Fiorello et al. 2006). These are often the result of proximity to live game or the consumption of infected raw game flesh, organs, or blood. Infection may be particularly problematic in environments which promote the development and spread of disease, such as warm, humid locations. R. P. Hanson and Lars Karstad (1959) documented the rabies death of a hunting dog as a result of being wounded by a feral boar, and E. Szabová and colleagues (2007) found a higher than average infection rate with the *Toxocara* spp. parasite in Slovak hunting dogs, probably as a result of exposure to wild animal feces. Similarly, Sun Lim and colleagues (2010) found a significantly higher rate of infection for a range of diseases among wild boar– and pheasant-hunting dogs when compared to urban dogs. A. B. Cay and C. Letellier (2009) reported the deaths of two hunting dogs in Belgium due to Aujeszky's disease after consuming the raw viscera of wild boar and Carl Armstrong and colleagues (1987) reported the death of four dogs from blastomycosis after hunting raccoons. Importantly, the transmission of disease and parasites between prey and hunting dogs may increase the probability of infection in their human owners. Future work on diseases and their physical manifestations in archaeological dog remains will contribute to this line of research.

Prey Profiles

The ethnographic record confirms that hunting dogs have been used in nearly every environment with every type of prey species. The identification of hunting dogs in the archaeological record using faunal assemblages at sites may, then, require a comparison of those prey profiles to other contemporary sites or time periods. For example, Bruce Winterhalder (1977, 1981) estimated that technological advances (snowmobiles, in this case) cut Cree hunting search cost times by 75% but also limited the types of species pursued, effectively decreasing their dietary breadth. If the same is true for archaeological sites with hunting dogs, people inhabiting those sites will likely specialize in hunting species where the use of dogs increases hunting returns or decreases hunting costs and risk (such as time or chance of injury), as compared to sites without dogs. If these are prey specifically targeted by dogs (e.g., if individual animals tracked and held or prey decision-making falls to dogs), then prey profiles may mirror the attritional mortality profiles seen in other nonhuman predators—the young, the old, and the sick or injured.

The use of hunting dogs may also be signaled by a shift in the type or number of particular prey species, as evidenced in the ethnographic record. The introduction of dogs as hunting technology revolutionized the hunting practices and success of many groups. L. Cipriani (1966) noted that the introduction of the dog to the Onges of the Andaman Islands transformed their hunting methods. Previously subsisting on primarily fish and shellfish, the group's use of dogs as hunting aids allowed them to prey on the more desirable wild pig. Similarly, the Batak of the Philippines abandoned their traditional hunting technique of using blowguns for smaller prey in favor of spears and hunting dogs in order to hunt the preferred wild boar (Eder 1988). Using his own ethnographic hunting correlations in his discussion of the prehistoric hunting record in Malaysia, Julian O. Caldecott (1988) argued that the high proportion of wild boar identified from archaeological sites would have been impossible to take without the use of hunting dogs.

In Australia and Tasmania the introduction of hunting dogs, specifically those of European origin, changed the way local forager groups interacted with their environment. Dogs brought to Tasmania by British colonists proved more important than guns, allowing Tasmanians to significantly increase their success in hunting kangaroo (Jones 1970). In some parts of Australia, introduced dogs have had similar effects to those in Tasmania. Some hunters relied entirely on dogs for the taking of larger prey, as their skill was so great in hunting kangaroo that I. M. White (1972) reported not one kangaroo was killed without the use of dogs at one camp. As a result of this success, the traditional weapons of a spear and club were no longer used in favor of the easier method of hunting with dogs.

Sex and age variation within prey profiles may also be affected by the use of hunting dogs, suggesting the use of hunting dogs may result in observable prey profiles. Koster (2008b:216) noted similar sex profiles among prey harvested by humans with and without dogs, except in the case of two prey species (iguana and agouti), suggesting dogs may be more proficient at locating females (and their offspring) of some species. Christopher Godwin and colleagues (2013) found that dog-assisted white-tailed deer hunters harvested more fawns than did hunters without dogs. Innate prey selection in dogs may lead them to target more vulnerable individuals—the young, the sick or weak, the old, and mothers defending their young, as is observed in wolves (Evans et al. 2006; Sand et al. 2012). Guagnin and colleagues (2018) documented pre-neolithic rock art from Arabia depicting hunting dogs specifically targeting males in rut, signifying a weak state, and mothers with their young. Teresa E. Steele (2003, 2004) has discussed the use of mortality profiles to infer behavior in the fossil record, suggesting prey deaths as a result of nonhuman predators often result in attritional mortality profiles (high numbers of the young and old with fewer adults) while humans tend to target more prime-aged adults. Importantly, Koster and Noss (2014) note that the effects of hunting dogs on the age-sex classes of harvested prey are influenced by the dog-assisted method used. For example, methods that utilize dogs to independently kill or chase-hunt individuals versus methods that use dogs to unselectively flush prey may result in different mortality profiles.

One factor that may be more difficult to document is the time loss incurred by hunters when using dogs that pursue unprofitable prey. For example, Koster (2008) notes that hunters in the neotropics of Nicaragua are often led on long, fruitless chases by their hunting dogs. While similar situations would incur hunting costs for prehistoric hunters, these unprofitable species may never show up archaeologically. This scenario appears to be contingent on the hunting environment and ratio of profitable to unprofitable species available, so an understanding of the overall species landscape around an archaeological site is important. Using dogs to hunt in an environment where a majority of the species it may pursue are desirable is a less risky strategy compared to using hunting dogs in an environment with a high number of unprofitable prey, any of which a dog may pursue.

Often the use of hunting dogs can be so effective that the surrounding populations of prey species are severely affected. Charles Darwin (1839) noted that the use of the introduced hound to Australia was so effective in killing emus and kangaroos that the species were doomed to be exterminated if the use of hunting dogs continued. In Central and South America, the use of dogs has been blamed for the extinction of several wildlife species in Panama, and the use of hunting dogs has been banned in some parts of Brazil due to their devastation of local fauna (Ventocilla et al. 1995). Ikeya (1994) noted that the San were forced to hunt further and further away from their camps as the increased hunter population with dogs depleted nearby prey resources.

Implications for Hunting Dogs in Prehistory

While dogs are rarely discussed as hunting technology in the prehistoric record, they may have played a pivotal role in the lives of past populations. The use of dogs as hunting technology has proven an invaluable advance to many hunting groups. Dogs may have been an important part of changing hunting strategies—allowing human hunters to hunt alone or in smaller groups or freeing hunters to perform other tasks and reducing human energy expenditure. They likely also allowed hunters to target desirable prey that was previously low ranked due to the danger or difficulty of hunting them (e.g., wild pigs) prior to the use of hunting dogs. The Bambuti said it would be impossible to track or kill certain types of game without dogs (Serpell 1995), as did the San (Ikeya 1994), the Sarawak (Caldecott 1988), and hunters in the Guatemalan highlands (Brown and Emery 2008) and parts of South America (Tate 1931).

Prehistoric hunting dogs may have also played a critical role in the local economy and trade relations, including increasing prestige positions of their owners. The Bakola of Cameroon consider the hunting dog their most valuable domesticated animal and a hunting weapon they cannot do without. Their ability to hunt for meat, which is then used for trade, makes the dog a critical factor in the entire life of their small-scale society (Ngima Mawoung 2006). In many groups, the successful hunting dog's owner, whether a direct participant in the hunt or not, is entitled to a portion of the kill. For Aborigines at the Yalata Aboriginal Reserve (White 1972) and the San (Ikeya 1994), the entire kill belonged to the dog's owner, while the Efe gave roughly 21% of the meat to the dog's owner (Bailey 1991). Bailey (1991) told of one Efe man who was ranked very low when it came to killing prey himself but was one of the highest ranked in total meat procurement because he owned a very good hunting dog that was involved in a large number of successful kills. Takeda (1996) stated that for the Ngandu in Zaire, the man who brought the dog that catches a monkey receives one of the monkey's arms in return. For any other animal caught with dogs, the majority portion of the kill is given to the dog's owner. The ethnographic record documents that the communal use of hunting dogs and the resulting meat share builds social relations of cooperation among groups (Ramírez 2004), which may be reflected in prehistory.

There is also trade in hunting dogs themselves, which Steward (1941), for example, documented among the Shoshone. Here, the price of a hunting dog was a string of shell money, which the dogs often wore as collars. The trade of good hunting dogs, both within and between groups, appears to be a widespread practice in the ethnographic record (e.g., Becher 1960; Turnbull 1965). Similar trade in hunting dogs may be documented in the archaeological record through analysis of stable isotopes, which document variation in diet and localities.

Hunting dogs may have also had a number of other effects on the prehistoric record. Their successful use may have slowed the progression to agriculture in some parts of the ancient world (e.g., in Japan; Perri 2016a), as proposed by James Boyce (2006) of Tasmania. In some locations their effective use may have also had deleterious effects on local prey populations(Ikeya 1994; Ventocilla et al. 1995). This may be documented in the archaeological record in the taking of younger animals, increased carcass utilization (e.g., bone marrow processing), a sudden shift in utilized prey species, or the taking of animals from further afield.

Discussion and Conclusions

The initial use of dogs as hunting technology has usually been associated with the process of domestication. Several authors have argued that domestication may have been the result of a hunting partnership between wolves and humans, eventually leading to the domesticated dog (Clutton-Brock 1981, 1995; Germonpré et al. 2012; Shipman 2012, 2015). Conversely, Lupo (2017) has discussed the circumstances surrounding the emergence and spread of dogs as hunting technology in the Upper Paleolithic. She found no clear evidence that prehistoric hunting dogs would have been beneficial in the hunting of the megafauna associated with these groups, particularly given the debates surrounding whether the remains at so-called mammoth megasites are the result of human targeting or natural deaths (Pitulko et al. 2014, 2016; Svoboda et al. 2005). Perri and colleagues (2015) made similar arguments regarding the use of proposed protodogs in the Upper Paleolithic. Nevertheless, early evidence of hunting dogs in the archaeological record confirms their importance as the first animals utilized as biotechnology by prehistoric groups (Guagnin et al. 2018; Perri 2014, 2016a).

The insights provided by groups using hunting dogs in the ethnographic and ethnohistoric record are critical in considering the use of hunting dogs in the past. Though these records are often biased toward hunting in lower latitudes where dogs arrived long after initial domestication and hunting is influenced by the high species diversity associated with more tropical environments, they provide a foundation for thinking about the ways dogs may have been utilized by past human groups. Specifically, the ethnographic record shows that dogs can be useful for hunting a variety of wild game across different environments. Given the behavioral ecology of dogs and prey species in combination with these environments, dogs appear to be most useful in hunting methods that utilize their natural propensity for tracking, chasing, and holding prey. Conversely, they can prove to be a detriment in the taking of game in open landscapes, where they can be seen easily, or with methods that require stealth and ambush. Groups that successfully use hunting dogs often report that their assistance is vital to minimizing hunting risk among dangerous or difficult prey while maximizing returns. Those that have acquired hunting dogs fairly recently often see a significant increase in their hunting success, often also targeting more desirable game that was previously avoided.

Future ethnographic work on hunting dogs which provides additional detail following the work of Koster (2008a), including cost-benefit analyses, age-sex profiles of dogs and their prey, and treatment and care of hunting dogs, will further benefit archaeological approaches. Applications of this work to the archaeological record should be mindful to the effects that environmental and cultural contexts, local prey species types, and prey species diversity can have on the effectiveness of dogs as hunting technology.

Traditional optimal foraging approaches such as the prey choice model make several assumptions that leave the incorporation of dogs as hunting technology difficult. One such assumption is that the searching and handling of prey are mutually exclusive activities and that foragers have no impact on resource abundance or distribution (Kaplan and Hill 1992). Conversely, there is some evidence that the use of hunting dogs may have long-term effects on the spatial behavior of prey (Scillitani et al. 2010) or can be so effective as to deplete local prey populations (Ikeya 1994). Utilizing the hunting dog optimal foraging model outlined by Koster (2008a), archaeologists can better approach the ways in which hunting dogs may have been employed in prehistoric hunting strategies and their effect on the archaeological record.

One way forward in understanding how the use of hunting dogs may have affected optimal foraging decisions in the past is to consider the effects of dogs on the faunal record. Koster (2008a) showed that both encounter rates and the profitability of prey types can vary dramatically between hunters with and without dogs. Hunters with dogs encountered significantly more of some species, while other species were encountered only by hunters with dogs. Given similar variation in the archaeological record, it may be reasonable to infer that targeted species composition varies between hunters with and without dogs in the archaeological record. Future work may identify variation in faunal remains from sites with the introduction of or increases in the presence of dogs or a change in their treatment. This may include not only the introduction of hunting dogs but their loss or discontinued use, which may be associated with a shift in subsistence faunal remains.

Dogs have played an important role in the innovative and cognitive progression of human prehistory. As the first in a long line of species, dogs served as the model for the domestication of the wild. Their use as hunting weapons represents the advent of animal biotechnology, a significant step in human innovation, beginning with prehistoric forager groups. Their earliest uses may also extend to sledging and hauling not long after their initial domestication (Pitulko and Kasparov 2017). This use of animals as biotechnology later encompassed the use of other species as hunting aids, transport, traction, material production, and part of extensive breeding programs and represents the foundation of our modern use of science and engineering to modify living organisms. Using the ethnographic and ethnohistoric records, archaeologists can better understand the technological costs and benefits incurred through the use of hunting dogs, as well as the specific tasks undertaken by these dogs and the effects of those tasks on local hunting economies. The quantification of these tasks allows hunting dogs to be evaluated within optimal foraging models, similarly to other non-living technology. Finally, the identification of hunting dogs in the archaeological record through skeletal observations, such as hunting-related injuries, or more indirect evidence within the zooarchaeological record or material culture serves as the initial step in pinpointing the use of dogs as the advent of animal biotechnology.

Acknowledgments

I am grateful to Jeremy Koster, Bruce Winterhalder, Dave Meltzer, and Luis Pacheco-Cobos for their helpful comments on this manuscript, as well as the anonymous reviewers and editors.

References Cited

Alexiades, Miguel N.
1999 Ethnobotany of the Ese Eja: Plants, Health, and Change in an Amazonian Society. PhD dissertation, Department of Anthropology, City University of New York.
Alvard, Michael S.
1993 Testing the "Ecologically Noble Savage" Hypothesis: Interspecific Prey Choice by Piro Hunters of Amazonian Peru. *Human Ecology* 21(4):355–387.
Armstrong, Carl W., Suzanne R. Jenkins, Leo Caufman, Thomas M. Kerkering, Betty S. Rouse, and Grayson B. Miller
1987 Common-Source Outbreak of Blastomycosis in Hunters and Their Dogs. *Journal of Infectious Diseases* 155(3):568–570.
Bailey, R. C.
1991 *The Behavioral Ecology of Efe Pygmy Men in the Ituri Forest, Zaire*. University of Michigan, Ann Arbor.
Bamforth, Douglas B., and Peter Bleed
1997 Technology, Flaked Stone Technology, and Risk. *Archeological Papers of the American Anthropological Association* 7(1):109–139.
Becher, Hans
1960 *Die Surára und Pakidái: Zwei Yanonami-Stämme in Nordwestbrasilien*. Mittei-lungen des Museums für Völkerkunde 26.
Bennett, Bradley C., and Rocío Alarcón
2015 Hunting and Hallucinogens: The Use of Psychoactive and Other Plants to Improve the Hunting Ability of Dogs. *Journal of Ethnopharmacology* 171:171–183.
Bennett, Elizabeth L., Eleanor Jane Milner-Gulland, Mohamed Bakarr, Heather E. Eves, John G. Robinson, and David S. Wilkie
2002 Hunting the World's Wildlife to Extinction. *Oryx* 36(4):328–329.
Blackwell, Paul G., and Caitlin E. Buck
2003 The Late Glacial Human Reoccupation of North-Western Europe: New Approaches to Space-Time Modelling. *Antiquity* 77(296):232–240.
Blackwood, Beatrice
1935 *Both Sides of Buka Passage: An Ethnographic Study of Social, Sexual and Economic Questions in the North-Western Solomon Islands*, Vol. 1. Clarendon Press, Oxford.

Bleed, Peter

1997 Content as Variability, Result as Selection: Toward a Behavioral Definition of Technology. *Archeological Papers of the American Anthropological Association* 7(1):95–104.

Bohannan, Paul, and Laura Bohannan

1968 *Tiv Economy*. Longmans Green, London.

Brown, Linda A., and Kitty F. Emery

2008 Negotiations with the Animate Forest: Hunting Shrines in the Guatemalan Highlands. *Journal of Archaeological Method and Theory* 15:300–337.

Bousman, C. Britt

1993 Hunter-Gatherer Adaptations, Economic Risk and Tool Design. *Lithic Technology* 18(1–2):59–86.

Boyce, James

2006 Canine Revolution: The Social and Environmental Impact of the Introduction of the Dog to Tasmania. *Environmental History* 11:102–129.

Bulmer, R.

1968 The Strategies of Hunting in New Guinea. *Oceania* 38:302–318.

Buxton, Jean

1968 Animal Identity and Human Peril: Some Mandari Images. *Man* 3(1):35–49.

Caldecott, Julian O.

1988 *Hunting and Wildlife Management in Sarawak*. International Union for the Conservation of Nature and Natural Resources, Gland, Switzerland.

Campo, J. J., and G. E. Spencer

1991 Regulatory Response to Deer Hunting with Dogs in Eastern Texas. *Proceedings of the Annual Conference of the Southeastern Association of Fish and Wildlife Agencies*, pp. 235–240. Southeastern Association of Fish and Wildlife Agencies, Flora, Mississippi.

Cannon, Aubrey, Henry P. Schwarcz, and Martin Knyf

1999 Marine-Based Subsistence Trends and the Stable Isotope Analysis of Dog Bones from Namu, British Columbia. *Journal of Archaeological Science* 26(4):399–407.

Carneiro, Robert L.

1970 Hunting and Hunting Magic among the Amahuaca of the Peruvian Montaña. *Ethnology* 9(4):331–341.

Cay, A. B., and C. Letellier

2009 Isolation of Aujeszky's Disease Virus from Two Hunting Dogs in Belgium after Hunting Wild Boars. *Vlaams Diergeneeskundig Tijdschrift* 78(3):194–195.

Chitwood, M. C., M. N. Peterson, and C. S. Deperno

2011 Assessing Dog Hunter Identity in Coastal North Carolina. *Human Dimensions of Wildlife* 16:128–141.

Cipriani, L.

1966 *The Andaman Islanders*. Weidenfeld and Nicolson, London.

Claassen, C.

2010 *Feasting with Shellfish in the Southern Ohio Valley: Archaic Sacred Sites and Rituals*. University of Tennessee Press, Knoxville.

Clutton-Brock, Juliet

1995 Origins of the Dog: Domestication and Early History. In *The Domestic Dog: Its Evolution, Behaviour, and Interactions with People*, edited by James Serpell, pp. 7–20. Cambridge University Press, Cambridge.

1999   *A Natural History of Domesticated Mammals.* Cambridge University Press, Cambridge.

Clutton-Brock, Juliet, and Nanna Noe-Nygaard

1990   New Osteological and C-Isotope Evidence on Mesolithic Dogs: Companions to Hunters and Fishers at Star Carr, Seamer Carr and Kongemose. *Journal of Archaeological Science* 17(6):643–653.

Collard, Mark, Briggs Buchanan, Jesse Morin, and Andre Costopoulos

2011   What Drives the Evolution of Hunter-Gatherer Subsistence Technology? A Reanalysis of the Risk Hypothesis with Data from the Pacific Northwest. *Philosophical Transactions of the Royal Society of London B: Biological Sciences* 366(1567):1129–1138.

Creswell, Robert

1996   *Prométhée ou Pandore? Propos de Technologie Culturelle.* Éditions Kimé, Paris.

Darwin, Charles

1839   *Journal of Researches into the Geology and Natural History of the Various Countries Visited by HMS Beagle: Under the Command of Captain Fitzroy, RN, from 1832 to 1836.* Henry Colburn, London.

Deforge, Yves

1989   Simondon et les Questions Vives de l'Actualité. Postface. In *Du Mode d'Existence des Objets Techniques,* edited by Gilbert Simondon, pp. 269–331. Éditions Aubier, Paris.

DeJarnette, David Lloyd, and Steve Boynton Wimberly

1942   *The Bessemer Site: Excavation of Three Mounds and Surrounding Village Areas near Bessemer, Alabama.* Vol. 17. Geological Survey of Alabama, Tuscaloosa.

Descola, Philippe

1994   *In the Society of Nature: A Native Ecology in Amazonia,* Vol. 93. Cambridge University Press, Cambridge.

Dira, Samuel Jilo, and Barry S. Hewlett

2018   Cultural Resilience among the Chabu Foragers in Southwestern Ethiopia. *African Study Monographs* 39(3):97–120.

Dwyer, P. D.

1983   Etolo Hunting Performance and Energetics. *Human Ecology* 11:145–174.

Eder, J. F.

1988   Batak Foraging Camps Today: A Window to the History of a Hunting-Gathering Economy. *Human Ecology* 16(1):35–55.

Ellen, Roy

1999   Categories of Animality and canine Abuse: Exploring Contradictions in Nuaulu Social Relationships with Dogs. *Anthropos* 94(1):57–68.

Elmendorf, W. W., and A. L. Kroeber

1960   The Structure of Twana Culture with Comparative Notes on the Structure of Yurok Culture. Washington State University Research Studies 28(3), Monographic Supplement 2.

Elston, Robert G., and P. Jeffrey Brantingham

2002   Microlithic Technology in Northern Asia: A Risk-Minimizing Strategy of the Late Paleolithic and Early Holocene. *Archeological Papers of the American Anthropological Association* 12(1):103–116.

Emslie, Steven D.

1978   Dog Burials from Mancos Canyon, Colorado. *Kiva* 43(3–4):167–182.

Evans, Shaney B., L. David Mech, P. J. White, and Glen A. Sargeant

2006   Survival of Adult Female Elk in Yellowstone following Wolf Restoration. *Journal of Wildlife Management* 70(5):1372–1378.

Ewersen, Jörg, Stefan Ziegler, Britta Ramminger, and Ulrich Schmölcke

2018   Stable Isotopic Ratios from Mesolithic and Neolithic Canids as an Indicator of Human Economic and Ritual Activity. *Journal of Archaeological Science: Reports* 17:346–357.

Fiorello, Christine V., Andrew J. Noss, and Sharon L. Deem

2006   Demography, Hunting Ecology, and Pathogen Exposure of Domestic Dogs in the Isoso of Bolivia. *Conservation Biology* 20(3):762–771.

Firestone, Richard B., A. West, J. P. Kennett, L. Becker, T. E. Bunch, Z. S. Revay, P. H. Schultz, T. Belgya, D. J. Kennett, J. M. Erlandson, O. J. Dickenson, A. C. Goodyear, R. S. Harris, G. A. Howard, J. B. Kloosterman, P. Lechler, P. A. Mayewski, J. Montgomery, R. Poreda, T. Darrah, S. S. Que Hee, A. R. Smith, A. Stich, W. Topping, J. H. Wittke, and W. S. Wolbach

2007   Evidence for an Extraterrestrial Impact 12,900 years Ago that Contributed to the Megafaunal Extinctions and the Younger Dryas Cooling. *Proceedings of the National Academy of Sciences* 104(41):16016–16021.

Fitzhugh, Ben

2001   Risk and Invention in Human Technological Evolution. *Journal of Anthropological Archaeology* 20(2):125–167.

Forline, Louis Carlos

1997   The Persistence and Cultural Transformation of the Guajá Indians: Foragers of Maranhao State, Brazil. PhD dissertation, Department of Anthropology, University of Florida.

Francfort, Henri-Paul, Daniel Klodzinski, and Georges Mascle

1990   Pétroglyphes archaïques du Ladakh et du Zanskar. *Arts Asiatiques* 45:5–27.

Frantz, Laurent A. F., Victoria E. Mullin, Maud Pionnier-Capitan, Ophélie Lebrasseur, Morgane Ollivier, Angela Perri, Anna Linderholm, Valeria Mattiangeli, Matthew D. Teasdale, Evangelos A. Dimopoulos, Anne Tresset, Marilyne Duffraisse, Finbar McCormick, László Bartosiewicz, Erika Gál, Éva A. Nyerges, Mikhail V. Sablin, Stéphanie Bréhard, Marjan Mashkour, Adrian Bălăşescu, Benjamin Gillet, Sandrine Hughes, Olivier Chassaing, Christophe Hitte, Jean-Denis Vigne, Keith Dobney, Catherine Hänni, Daniel G. Bradley and Greger Larson

2016   Genomic and Archaeological Evidence Suggest a Dual Origin of Domestic Dogs. *Science* 352(6290):1228–1231.

Gayton, A. H.

1948   Yokuts and Western Mono Ethnography, II: Northern Foothill Yokuts and Western Mono. *University of California Anthropological Records* 10:1–138.

Germonpré, Mietje, Martina Lázničková-Galetová, and Mikhail V. Sablin

2012   Palaeolithic Dog Skulls at the Gravettian Předmostí Site, the Czech Republic. *Journal of Archaeological Science* 39(1):184–202.

Gifford, Edward Winslow

1940   *Apache-Pueblo,* Vol. 4(1). University of California Press, Berkeley.

Godwin, Christopher, James A. Schaefer, Brent R. Patterson, and Bruce A. Pond

2013   Contribution of Dogs to White-Tailed Deer Hunting Success. *Journal of Wildlife Management* 77(2):290–296.

Grant, John Webster

1980   Missionaries and Messiahs in the Northwest. *Studies in Religion/Sciences Religieuses* 9(2):125–136.

Grøn, O., and M. G. Turov

2007   Resource "Pooling" in Hunter-Gatherer Resource-Management Strategies: An Ethno-Archaeological Study of the Evenki in Katanga County, Siberia. In *On the Road: Studies in Honour of Lars Larsson*, vol. 26, pp. 67–72. Almqvist and Wiksell International, Stockholm.

Guagnin, Maria, Angela R. Perri, and Michael D. Petraglia

2018   Pre-Neolithic Evidence for Dog-Assisted Hunting Strategies in Arabia. *Journal of Anthropological Archaeology* 49:225–236.

Guiry, Eric J.

2013   A Canine Surrogacy Approach to Human Paleodietary Bone Chemistry: Past Development and Future Directions. *Archaeological and Anthropological Sciences* 5(3):275–286.

Guiry, Eric J., and Vaughan Grimes

2013   Domestic Dog (*Canis familiaris*) Diets among Coastal Late Archaic Groups of Northeastern North America: A Case Study for the Canine Surrogacy Approach. *Journal of Anthropological Archaeology* 32(4):732–745.

Gusinde, M.

1937   *Die Feuerland Indianer: Band I die Selk'nam, Vom Leben und Denken eines Jägervolkes auf der Grossen Feuerlandinsel.* Anthropos-Bibliothek, Vienna.

Hambly, Wilfrid Dyson

1934   Occupational Ritual, Belief, and Custom among the Ovimbundu. *American Anthropologist* 3(2):157–167.

Hanson, R. P., and Lars Karstad

1959   Feral Swine in the Southeastern United States. *Journal of Wildlife Management* 23(1):64–74.

Harako, Reizo

1981   The Cultural Ecology of Hunting Behavior among Mbuti Pygmies in the Ituri Forest, Zaire. In *Omnivorous Primates*, edited by Robert Harding and Geza Teleki, pp. 499–555. Columbia University Press, New York.

Harrisson, Tom

1965   Three "Secret" Communication Systems among Borneo Nomads (and Their Dogs). *Journal of the Malaysian Branch of the Royal Asiatic Society* 38:67–86.

Hawkes, Kristen, Kim Hill, and James F. O'Connell

1982   Why Hunters Gather: Optimal Foraging and the Ache of Eastern Paraguay. *American Ethnologist* 9(2):379–398.

Hayden, Brian

1975   Dingoes: Pets or producers? *Mankind* 10:11–15.

Hickmann, Ellen, and David W. Hughes

1988   *The Archaeology of Early Music Cultures: Third International Meeting of the ICTM Study Group on Music Archaeology*, Vol. 51. Verlag für systematische Musikwissenschaft, Bonn.

Hiscock, Peter

1994   Technological Responses to Risk in Holocene Australia. *Journal of World Prehistory* 8(3):267–292.

Hoffecker, John F.

2005 Innovation and Technological Knowledge in the Upper Paleolithic of Northern Eurasia. *Evolutionary Anthropology: Issues, News, and Reviews* 14(5):186–198.

Holt, C.

1946 *Shasta Ethnography,* Vol. 3(4). University of California Press, Berkeley.

Hudson, Jean

1993 The Impacts of Domestic Dogs on Bone in Forager Camps; or, the Dog-Gone Bones. In *From Bones to Behavior: Ethnoarchaeological and Experimental Contribution to the Interpretation of Fauna Remains,* edited by Jean Hudson, pp. 301–323. Southern Illinois University Press, Carbondale.

Huntingford, G. W. B.

1929 Modern Hunters: Some Account of the Kamelilo-Kapchep-kendi Dorobo (Okiek) of Kenya Colony. *Journal of the Royal Anthropological Institute of Great Britain and Ireland* 59:333–378.

Ikeya, Kazunobu

1994 Hunting with Dogs among the San in the Central Kalahari. *African Study Monographs* 15:119–134.

Ingendaay, Christina, Michael Burger, Helge Linzmann, and Leo Brunnberg

2008 Injuries in the Dog due to Wild Boar. *KLEINTIERPRAXIS* 53(1):13.

Isack, Husein Adrian, and Heinz-Ulrich Reyer

1989 Honeyguides and Honey Gatherers: Interspecific Communication in a Symbiotic Relationship. *Science* 243(4896):1343–1346.

Itkonen, T. I.

1984 *The Lapps in Finland up to 1945,* Vol. 2. Werner Söderström Osakeyhtiö, Porvoo, Helsinki.

Jackson, Jean E.

1983 *The Fish People: Linguistic Exogamy and Tukanoan Identity in Northwest Amazonia,* Vol. 39. Cambridge University Press, Cambridge.

Jernigan, Kevin A.

2009 Barking Up the Same Tree: A Comparison of Ethnomedicine and Canine Ethnoveterinary Medicine among the Aguaruna. *Journal of Ethnobiology and Ethnomedicine* 5(1):33.

Jeske, Robert J., and Lawrence A. Kuznar

2001 Canine Digging Behavior and Archaeological Implications. *Journal of Field Archaeology* 28(3–4):383–394.

Jones, R.

1970 Tasmanian Aborigines and Dogs. *Mankind* 7:256–271.

Kagwa, Apolo

1934 *The Customs of the Baganda,* Vol. 22. Columbia University Press, New York.

Kennedy, Kenneth A. R.

1980 Prehistoric Skeletal Record of Man in South Asia. *Annual Review of Anthropology* 9:391–432.

Kent, Susan

1981 The Dog: An Archaeologist's Best Friend or Worst Enemy, The Spatial Distribution of Faunal Remains. *Journal of Field Archaeology* 8(3):367–372.

1993 Variability in Faunal Assemblages: The Influence of Hunting Skill, Sharing, Dogs, and Mode of Cooking on Faunal Remains at a Sedentary Kalahari Community. *Journal of Anthropological Archaeology* 12:323–385.

Kerber, Jordan E.

1997 Native American Treatment of Dogs in Northeastern North America: Archaeological and Ethnohistorical Perspectives. *Archaeology of Eastern North America* 25:81–95.

Koler-Matznick, J., Bonnie Yates, S. Bulmer, and I. L. Brisbin

2007 The New Guinea Singing Dog: Its Status and Scientific Importance. *Australian Mammalogy* 29(1):47–56.

Koster, Jeremy

2006 Hunting and Subsistence among the Mayangna and Miskito of Nicaragua's Bosawas Biosphere Reserve. PhD dissertation, Department of Anthropology, Pennsylvania State University.

2008a Hunting with Dogs in Nicaragua: An Optimal Foraging Approach. *Current Anthropology* 49(5):935–944.

2008b The Impact of Hunting with Dogs on Wildlife Harvests in the Bosawas Reserve, Nicaragua. *Environmental Conservation* 35(3):211–220.

2008c Giant Anteaters (*Myrmecophaga tridactyla*) Killed by Hunters with Dogs in the Bosawas Biosphere Reserve, Nicaragua. *Southwestern Naturalist* 53(3):414–416.

2009 Hunting Dogs in the Lowland Neotropics. *Journal of Anthropological Research* 65(4):575–610.

2011 Interhousehold Meat Sharing among Mayangna and Miskito Horticulturalists in Nicaragua. *Human Nature* 2(4):394–415.

Koster, Jeremy M., and Andrew Noss

2013 Hunting Dogs and the Extraction of Wildlife as a Resource. In *Free-Ranging Dogs and Wildlife Conservation*, edited by Matthew E. Gompper, pp. 265–285. Oxford University Press, Oxford.

Koster, Jeremy M., and Kenneth B. Tankersley

2012 Heterogeneity of Hunting Ability and Nutritional Status among Domestic Dogs in Lowland Nicaragua. *Proceedings of the National Academy of Sciences* 109(8):E463–E470.

Kracke, Waud H.

1981 Kagwahiv Mourning: Dreams of a Bereaved Father. *Ethos* 9(4):258–275.

Kroeber, Alfred L.

1941 Culture Element Distributions: XV Salt, Dogs, Tobacco. *Anthropological Records* 6(1):1–20.

Kuznar, Lawrence A., and Robert Jeske

2006 Analogic Reasoning, Ethnoarchaeology, and the Impact of Canines on the Archaeological Record. *Archeological Papers of the American Anthropological Association* 16(1):37–46.

Larson, Greger, Elinor K. Karlsson, Angela Perri, Matthew T. Webster, Simon Y. W. Ho, Joris Peters, Peter W. Stahl, Philip J. Piper, Frode Lingaas, Merete Fredholm, Kenine E. Comstock, Jaime F. Modiano, Claude Schelling, Alexander I. Agoulnik, Peter A. Leegwater, Keith Dobney, Jean-Denis Vigne, Carles Vilà, Leif Andersson, and Kerstin Lindblad-Toh

2012 Rethinking Dog Domestication by Integrating Genetics, Archeology, and Biogeography. *Proceedings of the National Academy of Sciences* 109(23):8878–8883.

Larsson, Lars

1990   Dogs in Fraction—Symbols in Action. In *Contributions to the Mesolithic in Europe*, edited by P. M. Vermeersch and P. van Peer, pp. 153–160. Leuven University Press, Leuven.

Laugrand, Frédéric, and Jarich Oosten

2002   Canicide and Healing: The Position of the Dog in the Inuit Cultures of the Canadian Arctic. *Anthropos* 97(1):89–105.

Lee, Richard B.

1965   Subsistence Ecology of !Kung bushmen. PhD dissertation, Department of Anthropology, University of California, Berkeley.

Lehtisalo, Toivo V.

1964   *Sketch of a Mythology of the Yurak Samoyed*. Human Relations Area Files, Vol. 17, New Haven.

Liebenberg, Louis

2006   Persistence Hunting by Modern Hunter-Gatherers. *Current Anthropology* 47:1017–1026.

Lim, Sun, Peter J. Irwin, SeungRyong Lee, MyungHwan Oh, KyuSung Ahn, BoYoung Myung, and SungShik Shin

2010   Comparison of Selected Canine Vector-Borne Diseases between Urban Animal Shelter and Rural Hunting Dogs in Korea. *Parasites & Vectors* 3(1):32.

Lupo, Karen

2011   A Dog Is for hunting. In *Ethnozooarchaeology*, edited by Umberto Albarella, pp. 4–12. Oxbow Books, Oxford.

2017   When and Where do Dogs Improve Hunting Productivity? The Empirical Record and Some Implications for Early Upper Paleolithic Prey Acquisition. *Journal of Anthropological Archaeology* 47:139–151.

Lyons, A.

1926   Notes on the Gogodara Tribe of Western Papua. *Journal of the Anthropological Institute of Great Britain and Ireland* 56:329–359.

MacGaffey, Wyatt

1991   *Art and Healing of the Bakongo, Commented by Themselves*. Indiana University Press, Bloomington.

MacNulty, Daniel Robert

2002   The Predatory Sequence and the Influence of Injury Risk on Hunting Behavior in the Wolf. PhD dissertation, University of Minnesota, Minneapolis.

Madrigal, T. C., and J. Z. Holt

2002   White-Tailed Deer Meat and Marrow Return Rates and Their Application to Eastern Woodlands Archaeology. *American Antiquity* 67(4):745–759.

Martin, Katherine Lee Hall

1976   Bone Flutes and Whistles from Archaeological Sites in Eastern North America. Master's thesis, Department of Anthropology, University of Tennessee, Knoxville.

McMillan, R. Bruce

1970   Early Canid Burial from the Western Ozark Highland. *Science* 167:1246–1247.

McSweeney, Kendra

2000   In the Forest Is Our Money: The Changing Role of Commercial Extraction in Tawahka Livelihoods, Eastern Honduras. PhD dissertation, Department of Anthropology, McGill University, Montreal.

Mech, L. David, and Michael E. Nelson

1990   Evidence of Prey-Caused Mortality in Three Wolves. *American Midland Naturalist* 123(1):207–208.

Meehan, B., R. Jones, and A. Vincent

1999   Gulu-Kula: Dogs in Anbarra Society, Arnhem Land. *Aboriginal History* 23:83.

Memmott, Paul

2007   *Gunyah, Goondie and Wurley: The Aboriginal Architecture of Australia.* University of Queensland Press, Brisbane.

Mitchell, Peter

2008   The Canine Connection: Dogs and Southern African Hunter-Gatherers. In *Animals and People: Archaeozoological Papers in Honour of Ina Plug*, edited by Shaw Badenhorst, Peter Mitchell and Jonathan C. Driver, pp. 104–116. BAR Publishing, Oxford.

Monagle, Victoria, Cyler Conrad, and Emily Lena Jones

2018   What Makes a Dog? Stable Isotope Analysis and Human-Canid Relationships at Arroyo Hondo Pueblo. *Open Quaternary* 4(1):6.

Morey, Darcy

2010   *Dogs: Domestication and the Development of a Social Bond.* Cambridge University Press, Cambridge.

Morley, Iain

2013   *The Prehistory of Music: Human Evolution, Archaeology, and the Origins of Musicality.* Oxford University Press, Oxford.

Morton, R. T., D. C. Guynn Jr., R. Horton, and J. G. Williams

1995   Efficiency of Archery Hunting for White-Tailed Deer on Medway Plantation. *Proceedings of the Southeastern Association of Fish and Wildlife Agencies*, pp. 432–438. Southeastern Association of Fish and Wildlife Agencies, Flora, Mississippi.

Neto, Manoel Francisco Campos, Domingos Garrone Neto, and Vidal Haddad Jr.

2011   Attacks by Jaguars (*Panthera onca*) on Humans in Central Brazil: Report of Three Cases, with Observation of a Death. *Wilderness & Environmental Medicine* 22(2):130–135.

Newton, Peter, Nguyen Van Thai, Scott Roberton, and Diana Bell

2008   Pangolins in Peril: Using Local Hunters' Knowledge to Conserve Elusive Species in Vietnam. *Endangered Species Research* 6(1):41–53.

Ngima Mawoung, Godefroy

2006   Perception of Hunting, Gathering and Fishing Techniques of the Bakola of the Coastal Region, Southern Cameroon. *African Study Monographs* 33:49–70.

Nobayashi, Atsushi

2006   An Ethnoarchaeological Study of Chase Hunting with Gundogs by the Aboriginal Peoples of Taiwan. In *Dogs and People in Social, Working, Economic or Symbolic Interaction*, edited by Lynn Snyder, pp. 77–84. Oxbow Books, Oxford.

O'Brien, Michael J. and Stephen J. Shennan

2010   *Innovation in Cultural Systems: Contributions from Evolutionary Anthropology.* MIT Press, Cambridge.

2010   Issues in Anthropological Studies of Innovation. In *Innovation in Cultural Systems: Contributions from Evolutionary Anthropology*, edited by Michael J. O'Brien and Stephen J. Shennan, pp. 3–17. MIT Press, Cambridge.

O'Connell, James F.

1987   Alyawara Site Structure and Its Archaeological Implications. *American Antiquity* 52(1):74–108.

O'Connell, James F., and Kristen Hawkes

1981   Alyawara Plant Use and Optimal Foraging Theory. *Hunter-Gatherer Foraging Strategies: Ethnographic and Archaeological Analyses*:99–125.

O'Connell, James F., Kristen Hawkes, and Nicholas Blurton Jones

1988   Hadza Scavenging: Implications for Plio/Pleistocene Hominid Subsistence. *Current Anthropology* 29(2):356–363.

Ohnuki-Tierney, Emiko

1974   *The Ainu of the Northwest Coast of Southern Sakhalin.* Holt, Rinehart and Winston, New York.

Olaussen, J. O., and A. Mysterud

2012   Red Deer Hunting—Commercializing versus Availability. *European Journal of Wildlife Research* 58(3):1–11.

Olowo Ojoade, J.

1990   Nigerian Cultural Attitudes to the Dog. In *Signifying Animals: Human Meaning in the Natural World*, edited by R. G. Willis, pp. 215–221. Unwin Hyman, London.

Pannell, S., and S. O'Connor

2010   Strategy Blurring: Flexible Approaches to Subsistence in East Timor. In *Archaeological Invisibility and Forgotten Knowledge*, edited by Karen Hardy, pp. 115–130. British Archaeological Reports, Oxford.

Perri, Angela R.

2014   Global Hunting Adaptations to Early Holocene Temperate Forests: Intentional Dog Burials as Evidence of Hunting Strategies. PhD dissertation, Department of Archaeology, Durham University, Durham, England.

2016a Hunting dogs as Environmental Adaptations in Jōmon Japan. *Antiquity* 90 (353):1166–1180.

2016b A Wolf in Dog's Clothing: Initial Dog Domestication and Pleistocene Wolf Variation. *Journal of Archaeological Science* 68:1–4.

2017   A Typology of Dog Deposition in Archaeological Contexts. In *Economic Zooarchaeology: Studies in Hunting, Herding and Early Agriculture*, edited by Peter Rowley-Conwy, Dale Serjeantson, and Paul Halstead, pp. 89–99. Oxbow Books, Oxford.

Perri, Angela R., Geoff M. Smith, and Marjolein D. Bosch

2015   Comment on "How Do You Kill 86 Mammoths? Taphonomic Investigations of Mammoth Megasites" by Pat Shipman. *Quaternary International* 368(11):112–115.

Pferd, W.

1987   *Dogs of the American Indians.* Denlinger's, Fairfax.

Pitulko, Vladimir V., Aleksandr E. Basilyan, and Elena Y. Pavlova

2014   The Berelekh Mammoth "Graveyard": New Chronological and Stratigraphical Data from the 2009 Field Season. *Geoarchaeology* 29(4):277–299.

Pitulko, Vladimir V., Alexei N. Tikhonov, Elena Y. Pavlova, Pavel A. Nikolskiy, Konstantin E. Kuper, and Roman N. Polozov

2016   Early Human Presence in the Arctic: Evidence from 45,000-Year-Old Mammoth Remains. *Science* 351(6270):260–263.

Pitulko, Vladimir V., and Aleksey K. Kasparov

2017   Archaeological Dogs from the Early Holocene Zhokhov Site in the Eastern Siberian Arctic. *Journal of Archaeological Science: Reports* 13:491–515.

Ramírez, Cristina Rosero

2004   Women Hunters and Men Gatherers: Gender Role Changes among the Shuar. PhD dissertation, Department of Anthropology, University of Florida.

Ranov, Vadim

2001   Petroglyphs of Tadjikistan, In *Petroglyphs*, edited by Tashbayeva, pp. 122–150. International Institute of Central Asian Studies, Bishkek.

Rausch, R. A.

1967   Some Aspects of the Population Ecology of Wolves, Alaska. *American Zoologist* 7(2):253–265.

Ray, Verne F.

1942   Culture Element Distributions: XXII, Plateau. *Anthropological Records* 8(2):98–262.

Reddy, Anjana

2006   From "Banda" to "Bailu"(The Hills to the Plains): An Ethnographic Model of Chenchu Settlement Systems in Nallamala Hills, Andhra Pradesh, for the Reconstruction of Prehistoric Settlement Patterns. *Man and Environment* 30(1):1–18.

Reynolds, B.

1968   The Material from Gwembe Valley: National Museum of Zambia. *Kariba Studies*, Vol. III. Manchester University Press, Manchester.

Roscoe, John

1923   *The Bakitara*. Cambridge University Press, Cambridge.

Rühe, F., Andreas Baumgart, and Thomas Riemer

2006   Tracking Down Wounded Game with the Aid of Hannoverian Bloodhounds: The Effect of the Acoustic Tie of the Dog Handler to His Chasing Hound on the Lengths of the Chases and on the Tracking Success. *Allgemeine Forst-und Jagdzeitung* 177(5):91–96.

Saïd, S., V. Tolon, S. Brandt, and E. Baubet

2012   Sex Effect on Habitat Selection in Response to Hunting Disturbance: The Study of Wild Boar. *European Journal of Wildlife Research* 58:107–115.

Sand, Håkan, John A. Vucetich, Barbara Zimmermann, Petter Wabakken, Camilla Wikenros, Hans C. Pedersen, Rolf O. Peterson, and Olof Liberg

2012   Assessing the Influence of Prey-Predator Ratio, Prey Age Structure and Pack Size on Wolf Kill Rates. *Oikos* 121(9):1454–1463.

Savelle, James M.

1984   Cultural and Natural Formation Processes of a Historic Inuit Snow Dwelling Site, Somerset Island, Arctic Canada. *American Antiquity* 49(3):508–524.

Schapera, I.

1930   *The Khoisan Peoples of South Africa: Bushmen and Hottentots*. Routledge, London.

Schulting, Rick

1994   The Hair of the Dog: The Identification of a Coast Salish Dog-Hair Blanket from Yale, British Columbia. *Canadian Journal of Archaeology/Journal Canadien d'Archéologie* 18:57–76.

Scillitani, L., A. Monaco, and S. Toso

2010   Do Intensive Drive Hunts Affect Wild Boar (*Sus Scrofa*) Spatial Behaviour in Italy?

Some Evidences and Management Implications. *European Journal of Wildlife Research* 56(3):307–318.

Seligmann, C. G., and B. Z. Seligmann

1911   *The Veddas.* Cambridge University Press, Cambridge.

Serpell, James

1995   *The Domestic Dog: Its Evolution, Behaviour, and Interactions with People.* Cambridge University Press, Cambridge.

Shipman, Pat

2012   "Those Puppy-Dog Eyes" Response. *American Scientist* 100(5):356–357.

2015   How Do You Kill 86 Mammoths? Taphonomic Investigations of Mammoth Megasites. *Quaternary International* 368(11):38–46.

Smith, Eric Alden, Robert L. Bettinger, Charles A. Bishop, Valda Blundell, Elizabeth Cashdan, Michael J. Casimir, Andrew L. Christenson, Bruce Cox, Rada Dyson-Hudson, Brian Hayden, Peter J. Richerson, Eric Abella Roth, Steven R. Simms, and W. A. Stini

1983   Anthropological Applications of Optimal Foraging Theory: A Critical Review. *Current Anthropology* 24(5):625–651.

Söderberg, Bertil

1966   Antelope Horn Whistles with Sculptures from the Lower Congo. *Ethnos* 31(1–4):5–33.

Spottiswoode, Claire N., Keith S. Begg, and Colleen M. Begg

2016   Reciprocal Signaling in Honeyguide-Human Mutualism. *Science* 353(6297):387–389.

Steele, Teresa E.

2003   Using Mortality Profiles to Infer Behavior in the Fossil Record. *Journal of Mammalogy* 84(2):418–430.

2004   Variation in Mortality Profiles of Red Deer (*Cervus elaphus*) in Middle Palaeolithic Assemblages from Western Europe. *International Journal of Osteoarchaeology* 14(3–4):307–320.

Steward, Julian Haynes

1941   *Nevada Shoshone.* University of California Press, Berkeley.

Svoboda, Jiří, Stéphane Péan, and Piotr Wojtal

2005   Mammoth Bone Deposits and Subsistence Practices during Mid-Upper Palaeolithic in Central Europe: Three Cases from Moravia and Poland. *Quaternary International* 126:209–221.

Swenson, Jon E., Finn Sandegren, Arne Soderberg, Morten Heim, Ole Jakob Sφrensen, Anders Bjarvall, Robert Franzen, Steinar Wikan, and Petter Wabakken

1999   Interactions between Brown Bears and Humans in Scandinavia. *Biosphere Conservation: For Nature, Wildlife, and Humans* 2(1):1–9.

Szabová, E., P. Juriš, M. Miterpáková, D. Antolová, I. Papajová, and H. Šefčíková

2007   Prevalence of Important Zoonotic Parasites in Dog Populations from the Slovak Republic. *Helminthologia* 44(4):170–176.

Takeda, J.

1996   The Ngandu as Hunters in the Zaïre River Basin. *African Study Monographs* 23:1–61.

Taksami, Ch. M.

1961   Issledovatel', Drug i Uchitel' Nivkhov. In *Issledovateli Sakhalina i Kuril*, edited by Ivan A. Senclienko, pp. 108–131. Sakhalinskoe Knizhnoe Izdatel'stvo, Iuzhno-Sakhalinsk.

Tappen, Martha

2001   Deconstructing the Serengeti. In *Meat-Eating and Human Evolution*, edited by Craig B. Stanford and Henry T. Bunn, pp. 13–32. Oxford University Press, Oxford.

Tate, G. H. H.

1931 Random Observations on Habits of South American Mammals. *Journal of Mammalogy* 12(3):248–256.

Teit, James Alexander

1900 *The Thompson Indians of British Columbia,* Vol. 1. Nicola Valley Museum Archives Association, Merritt, British Columbia.

Thurn, Everard Ferdinand Im

1967 *Among the Indians of Guiana.* Dover, New York.

Torday, Emil, and Thomas Athol Joyce

1905 Notes on the Ethnography of the Ba-Mbala. *The Journal of the Anthropological Institute of Great Britain and Ireland* 35:398–426.

Torrence, Robin

1989 Tools as Optimal Solutions. In *Time, Energy and Stone Tools*, edited by Robin Torrence, pp. 1–6. Cambridge University Press, Cambridge.

2001 Hunter-Gatherer Technology: Macro-and Microscale Approaches. In *Hunter-Gatherers: An Interdisciplinary Perspective*, edited by Catherine Panter-Brick, Robert H. Layton and Peter Rowley-Conwy, pp. 73–98. Cambridge University Press, Cambridge.

Tsuge, Gen'ichi

1988 Stone and Clay Aerophones in Early Japan. In *The Archaeology of early music cultures: Third International Meeting of the ICTM Study Group on Music Archaeology*, Vol. 51, edited by Ellen Hickmann and David W. Hughes, p. 89. Verlag für systematische Musikwissenschaft, Bonn.

Tuck, J. A.

1976 Ancient People of Port Au Choix: The Excavation of an Archaic Indian Cemetery in Newfoundland. Institute of Social and Economic Research, Memorial University of Newfoundland, St. John's.

Turnbull, Colin

1965 The Mbuti Pygmies: An Ethnographic Survey. *Anthropological Papers of the American Museum of Natural History* 50(3):139–282.

Udell, Monique A. R.

2015 When Dogs Look Back: Inhibition of Independent Problem-Solving Behaviour in Domestic Dogs (*Canis lupus familiaris*) Compared with Wolves (*Canis lupus*). *Biology Letters* 11(9). DOI:20150489.

Ventocilla, Jorge, Heraclio Herrera, Valerio Núñez, and Hans Roeder

1995 *Plants and Animals in the Life of the Kuna.* Austin: University of Texas Press.

Viranta, Suvi, and Kristiina Mannermaa

2018 Prehistory of Dogs in Fennoscandia: A Review. In *Dogs in the North: Stories of Cooperation and Co-Domestication*, edited by Robert J. Losey, Robert P. Wishart, and Jan Peter Laurens Loovers, pp. 233–250. Routledge, London.

Walker, Renee B., Darcy F. Morey, and John H. Relethford

2005 Early and Mid-Holocene Dogs in Southeastern North America: Examples from Dust Cave. *Southeastern Archaeology* 24(1):83–92.

Walker, Robert, Kim Hill, Hillard Kaplan, and Garnett McMillan

2002 Age-Dependency in Hunting Ability among the Ache of Eastern Paraguay. *Journal of Human Evolution* 42(6):639–657.

Warren, Diane M.

2004 Skeletal Biology and Paleopathology of Domestic Dogs from Prehistoric Alabama,

Illinois, Kentucky and Tennessee. PhD dissertation, Department of Anthropology, Indiana University.

West, P.

2005   Translation, Value, and Space: Theorizing an Ethnographic and Engaged Environmental Anthropology. *American Anthropologist* 107:632–642.

White, I. M.

1972   Hunting Dogs at Yalata. *Mankind* 8:201–205.

Whiting, John Wesley Mayhew

1941   *Becoming a Kwoma: Teaching and Learning in a New Guinea Tribe*. Yale University Press, New Haven.

Winterhalder, Bruce

1978   Foraging Strategy Adaptations of the Boreal Forest Cree: An Evaluation of Theory and Models from Evolutionary Ecology. PhD dissertation, Department of Anthropology, Cornell University, Ithaca, New York.

1981   Optimal Foraging Strategies and Hunter-Gatherer Research in Anthropology: Theory and Models. In *Hunter-Gatherer Foraging Strategies: Ethnographic and Archaeological Analyses*, edited by Bruce Winterhalder and Eric Alden Smith, pp. 13–35. University of Chicago Press, Chicago.

Wobeser, G.

1992   Traumatic, Degenerative, and Developmental Lesions in Wolves and Coyotes from Saskatchewan. *Journal of Wildlife Diseases* 28(2):268–275.

3

Dog Life and Death in an Ancestral Pueblo Landscape

VICTORIA MONAGLE AND EMILY LENA JONES

Dogs were the first animals to engage with humans in the process of domestication, resulting in a relationship that crosses cultural and geographical boundaries. Archaeologists have used genetics, morphological data, stable isotope analysis, and other ways of analyzing faunal remains to better understand this relationship, and through it the nature of domestication in general. These data have resulted in many different interpretations of canid-human connections across the globe (e.g., Guagnin et al. 2017; Janssens et al. 2018; Kemp et al. 2017; Lupo 2017; Morey 2010; Perri 2016).

Regional analyses of human-dog relationships can contribute to this broader research program while simultaneously promoting cultural heritage for descendant communities. The archaeological record of dog remains may be viewed through a landscape paradigm (*sensu* Sauer 1925) to explore the roles of past dogs in human societies in a manner that transcends the cultural/natural dichotomy. Such analyses can be used to strengthen repatriation claims (see examples in Darling et al. 2015; Dongoske et al. 1997; Foster and James 2002; Kakaliouras 2012) as well as to provide guidelines for the management of present-day dog populations within Indigenous and other communities. The study of dog remains in the Americas may thus be relevant to tribal heritage and cultural resource ownership as well as to archaeological study.

The archaeological record from the prehispanic American Southwest contains a large number of canid specimens. At the same time, dogs are important agents in the Southwestern Indigenous world today; dog dances, dog kachinas, and stories, traditions, and myths about dogs are a part of life in many Southwestern Indigenous communities (Malotki 2001; Malotki and Gary 2001; Parsons 1939, 1994; Simmons 1980; Smith and Hayes 1992). In this chapter, we discuss Southwestern dogs' roles within an Ancestral Pueblo community—5MTUMR 2347, a prehispanic Southwestern archaeological site in southern Colorado—in light of the historic and ethnographic record from Pueblo communities to explore the role of canids in the Ancestral Pueblo landscape.

The Puebloan Southwest

As an archaeological region, the American Southwest and Mexican Northwest includes both the Southwestern United States (Arizona, New Mexico, and parts of Utah, Colorado, and Nevada) and parts of Northern Mexico (Chihuahua and Sonora). Differences in archaeological material culture in the last 2,000 years within this region have led to the identification of subregions, including Hohokam (south-central Arizona), Mogollon (southwestern New Mexico and southeastern Arizona), and Ancestral Puebloan (sometimes termed Anasazi; northern Arizona and New Mexico and southern Utah and Colorado). Here, we focus on the Ancestral Puebloan subregion. Ancestral Pueblo peoples have been extensively studied by archaeologists, and much information is available about their history, subsistence, and architecture (Kantner 2004).

Present-day Indigenous Pueblo communities maintain strong connections to the Ancestral Pueblo—including maintenance of linguistic, religious, and subsistence traditions—despite changes to traditional lifeways in the wake of colonization (Debenport 2015; Levin 2017; Sando 1992; Swentzell and Perea 2016; Wenger 2009). The robust connection between present-day Pueblo people and their ancestors makes the Puebloan Southwest an ideal context in which to study the human-dog relationship.

The Archaeology of Dogs in the Southwest

Dogs have a long history within the American Southwest. Damage on mammoth bones at Blackwater Draw, a Clovis site in New Mexico dating to about 13,000 cal BP, represents the oldest archaeological evidence suggesting "tame" canids (Bartelle et al. 2010; Fiedel 2005; Saunders and Daeschler 1994). Dog remains dated to 800 BCE–150 CE from the Santa Cruz Bend Site in Arizona are the earliest known dog burials in the Southwest (Hill 2000; Thiel 1998). Later in time, dogs become more common: dog interments at Ancestral Puebloan sites occur in New Mexico and Colorado between 450 CE and 1,200 CE (see Hill 2000 and citations therein). These interments are more variable than other prehispanic animal interments in the Southwest, which suggests a broad range of human-dog relationships. Some dog remains exhibit butchering patterns similar to animals used as food or supplies (Foster and James 2002; Kelley 1975); other dogs were likely sacrificed as dedicatory offerings (Foster and James 2002; Hill 2000).

Archaeological material culture also provides insight into human-dog relationships in the prehispanic Southwest. Dogs were sometimes a source of raw materials: woven sashes made from human and dog hair were found in Obelisk Cave in northeast Arizona (Freer and Jacobs 2008), and pendants, tools, beads, effigies, and at least one arrow point carved from canid skeletal elements have been found across the Southwest (Allen 1954). They also appear to have been companions: 2,500-year-old side-by-side human and dog footprints occur at the Sunset Road site in Arizona (Davidson 2016). There is evidence of dogs serving other roles as well. The Los Guanacos dog effigies of the Hohokam, found crushed in caches on pithouse floors, suggest dogs that served as guardians in the afterlife (Foster and James 2002; James and Foster 2008), and depictions on Mimbres bowls from the Mogollon region show dogs participating in everyday activities such as hunting and firewood collecting (Brody 2008). Dog-shaped ceramic vessels and effigies from Ancestral Pueblo sites also exist. While their meaning is not well-understood by anthropologists, they do indicate the presence of dogs within those communities (Ferg 2008a, 2008b).

There is, in short, an abundance of evidence that dogs filled a multiplicity of roles within the human societies of the prehispanic Southwest. This places dogs as an intrinsic part of the prehispanic Southwestern landscape.

Dogs in the Ancestral Pueblo Landscape

Dogs, like people, continue to occupy both urban and rural spaces in the Southwest. In cities dogs are commonly fenced-in pets and companions, service animals, and guards for homes, car lots, and commercial properties. Leashed dogs accompany people to dog-friendly restaurants, dog parks, and nature trails and on walks around the neighborhood. Dogs in rural areas, including reservations, are often free roaming and less supervised (e.g., *Indian Country Today*, 13 January 2011; Lohmann 2012); they have roles that overlap with but are not always the same as their urban counterparts. While some rural dogs are companions, others guard homes, ranches, farms, and livestock against theft, vandalism, and wild predators (Black 1981; Black and Green 1985). Dogs in rural areas in the Southwest in some cases pose challenges for management by humans (e.g., Clausing 2011; Diniz et al. 2010; Kane 2016).

Present-day human-dog relationships are represented in material culture (leashes, collars, tags, toys) and specialized spaces (dog beds, enclosed runs, dog houses). Dogs are commonly represented in quotidian contexts (mascots, stuffed animals, toys, cartoon characters) and are also the focus of large-scale events (dog races, dog shows). At death dogs may be buried, cremated, or even stuffed.

These present-day human-dog relationships are visible in the Southwestern archaeological literature. Many interpretations of archaeological dogs are rooted in binaries that make sense given the roles of dogs in Western societies today: domestic/non-domestic, natural/cultural, functional/ritual. Such binaries are common in archaeological research as a whole (Harrison 2013), but they are particularly marked in research on dogs, perhaps because dog domestication and what constitutes the strongest evidence for it remains a matter of debate (e.g., Drake et al. 2015; Germonpré et al. 2009; Larson et al. 2012; Morey 2006). In the Southwest, archaeological research on dogs typically consists of metric analyses to determine breed type and size (for example Clark et al. 1987; Colton 1970; Douglas and Leslie 1981; Olsen 1968) and/or studies of interment context to determine if dogs served as food or a source of raw materials (functional role) or played a role in ritual (Ambler 1994; Dove 2012; Emslie 1978; Ezzo and Stiner 2000; Hill 2000). Studies of interment context typically assign canids to only one category; a dog can be "functional" or "ritual" but not both.

Research suggests, however, that a dichotomous approach to analysis of Ancestral Pueblo dog remains is at best problematic. The line between domestic and non-domestic canids, for example, so fundamental to archaeological interpretations, does not seem to have been important to Ancestral Puebloans, with wild canids (particularly coyotes) occasionally taking roles (such as companions) typically ascribed only to domestic dogs (for example, Monagle et al. 2018; Stephen 1929). And ethnographic work documents that dogs in historic and present-day Pueblo communities hold multiple roles, many of which transcend the natural/cultural and functional/ritual binaries. The potential of dogs to be witches is one example of this. Archaeologists (e.g., Walker 2008) do occasionally note the ethnographic evidence that dogs may be considered witches in Pueblo societies (Beals 1934; Dumarest 1920; Espinosa 1936; Malotki and Gary 2001; Parsons 1927, 1940; Stephen 1929; White 1932, 1962). But, as William H. Walker (2008) discusses, witch or potential witch is only one of the many documented roles a dog may hold. Ethnographies and historical accounts also describe dogs as protectors (Ortiz 1969; Roberts and Schneider 1965; Talayesva 2013), hunting assistants (Henderson and Harrington 1914; Hill 1982; Talayesva 2013; Titiev 1971; Tyler 1975), spirits (Cushing 1979; White 1932), messengers (Stephen 1969), warriors (Akins et al. 2012), ceremonial agents and/or participants (Fewkes 1990; Hill 1982; Parsons 1929, 1939; Reagan 1906; Stephen 1969), sickness-absorbers (Cushing 1920; Snow 2008), pests (Beaglehole and Beaglehole 1937; Cushing 1998; Roberts and Schneider 1965; Whitman and Whitman 1969), substitutes for humans (Cushing 1979; Henderson and Harrington 1914), witch deterrents (Espinosa 1936), trash-eaters (Roberts and Schneider 1965), eagle food (Beaglehole 1936; Olsen 1982), friends and companions (Cushing 1998; Espinosa 1936; Henderson and Harrington 1914; Roberts and Schneider 1965; Talayesva 2013; Whitman 1940)—and, on occasion, food for humans (Henderson and Harrington 1914; Simoons 1967; Stephen 1969) and a source of raw materials for tools (Stephen 1969). One indicator of the centrality of canids to village life is the numerous accounts of culling dogs that were a nuisance (Cushing 1920, 1979; Stephen 1969; Whitman and Whitman 1969). Another indicator, which also attests to the complexity of canid roles within the Puebloan world, is their role in oral tradition: while coyote talks are well known, there are also many stories that feature domestic dogs (e.g., Courlander 1982; Cushing 1992; Malotki and Gary 1984; Stephen 1929).

The role of dogs in Pueblo societies can thus perhaps best be described as members of the Pueblo—agents in their own right rather than animals with limited roles. This poses a problem if one is relying on an interpretive approach rooted in binaries. Socially oriented interpretations of Ancestral Pueblo dogs thus far largely focus on the end point—the interment context—and assign the dog a role based on those data. When a dog shows evidence of multiple roles (e.g., Emslie 1978; Lang and Harris 1984), a researcher using a binary approach can only conclude that the evidence is ambiguous.

To avoid this problem, we frame our interpretation of Ancestral Pueblo dogs in a landscape paradigm, which allows contrasting theories and perspectives to coexist (Anschuetz et al. 2001). Landscape, as we use the term here, is the dynamic space generated by the interactions between humans and their environments. Dogs both before and after their deaths were a part of this landscape in the prehispanic Southwest, both through their relationship with humans and through their capacity to fill roles that transcend binaries. With this in mind, we use osteological and contextual analysis in tandem with these ethnographic and historical accounts of dogs' roles in Pueblo communities to interpret the dog remains from the Ancestral Pueblo site 5MTUMR 2347.

The 5MTUMR 2347 Dogs

The dogs from 5MTUMR 2347 were initially recovered in the course of a larger salvage project in Mancos Canyon, Colorado, which was conducted by the University of Colorado for the Ute Mountain Indian Park (Gillespie 1975). The faunal remains from the Mancos Canyon sites were initially analyzed with the goal of environmental reconstruction (Emslie 1977); the dog remains were further studied to determine breed and age (Emslie 1978). These analyses identified dogs ranging in age from puppy to mature and found that they were associated with kivas, kiva vent shafts, and Pueblo room floors. Of the six dogs recovered from a kiva, four were found within a kiva vent shaft and two were 10 cm above the floor. Two other dogs came from room contexts, one within the fill and one placed on the floor. Human remains were not found in association with the dog burials; however, other animal remains (including unidentified mammal bones, *Lepus* [hare] tibiae, an *Ovis canadensis* [mountain sheep] skull, a *Sylvilagus* [cottontail] mandible, and a *Canis lupus* [wolf] skull) and objects (bone tools and awls, shell pendants, ceramics, cores, hammerstones, anvils, manos and metates, and flakes) were interred nearby (Gillespie 1975). In addition, some dogs were buried with or near other dogs. The contextual information from the Mancos Canyon dog burials is summarized in Table 3.1.

In the original analyses, dogs associated with kivas were interpreted as having been buried as part of ritual practice. At the same time, however, the presence of "twist breaks" (spiral fractures) on long bones and breakage patterns on scapulae suggested butchering (Emslie 1977:147). In addition, the changing abundance of dog remains through time at these sites also suggested that many of the Mancos dogs were used as food for humans, that is, that they had a functional role within this community (Emslie 1977, 1978). Despite the ambiguous conclusions, these studies have been widely cited as examples of the role of dogs in the Ancestral Pueblo world (e.g., Ambler 1994; Dove 2012; Ezzo and Stiner 2000; Hill 2000; Lupo and Janetski 1994; Petersen et al. 1987).

The Reanalysis Project

The impetus for our reanalysis stemmed from the interpretation of the Mancos dogs as food. Given changes in how zooarchaeologists identify butchering since the original analysis (i.e., Binford 1981), a reexamination of the evidence seemed in order. We also wanted to add paleopathological and age-at-death data to the analysis, which could further support or negate the original interpretations. The most important goal of our reanalysis, however, was to model the use of an alternative, multi-role framework for interpretation of dog remains.

Accordingly, we test two questions: 1) Were these dogs used as food by Ancestral Puebloans? 2) Do the dogs associated with an architectural feature share a predetermined cause of death suggesting a pattern of ritual culling? We present data on butchering patterns, paleopathology, and interment context to establish individual life and death histories as a means of answering these questions. Given our landscape approach to these data, we investigate roles these dogs played while considering the multiple dog roles documented in ethnographic and historical accounts of Pueblo societies.

Sampling and Data Recording

Curation Challenges

The zooarchaeological assemblage from the Mancos Canyon project presents many challenges, including disassociation between different components of the assemblage, a lack of associated provenience information, and varying states of curation and preservation of the osteological remains. Of the assemblages originally analyzed by Steven D. Emslie, only the 5MTUMR 2347 dogs were available for reanalysis. With some effort, we were able to match these remains with provenience data from the original reports. Dealing with previous conservation efforts presented a larger challenge: many specimens were glued together, limiting our ability to observe bone surface modifications, and some bones were too glued to examine for pathologies or surface modifications. Visibility of surface modifications was also affected by bone preservation: in some cases, fragmentation, carnivore damage or severe weathering made it impossible to see cutmarks or other alterations.

Table 3.1. Descriptive results of reanalysis

ID	Interment Date/ Phase	Context	Age	Pathology/Taphonomy
FS 204	Pueblo I— 770–900	PS 2, Kiva Vent Shaft	Adult	Mature individual (consisting of skull and mandibles) as indicated by teeth health/eruptions. Tooth wear and condition indicate an older individual. Right P4 and P2 have periodontal disease. Loss of right P1 and left P2. Fractured and healed nasal bone. Skull had been glued together along a fracture line connecting two inner orbital incomplete fractures indicating trauma this dog would not have survived.
F. 18, F.A. 21	Pueblo II— 950–1025	PS 8, Kiva Vent Shaft	Juvenile	Juvenile individual around 8–9 months old. Remains have 10 cutmark like traces occurring on skull and two scapulae. Unknown perforations on dorsal border of left scapula. Antemortem trauma on both scapulae spinous processes; right scapula resembles documented projectile point traumas on larger game animals. Left inner orbital has a perimortem/antemortem puncture.
F. 18, F.A. 19	Pueblo II— 950–1025	PS 8, Kiva Vent Shaft	Juvenile	Juvenile individual around 6 months old and buried with F. 18 F.A. 20 in a Kiva vent shaft. Two distinct antemortem wounds and infections on left scapula and a large antemortem healed trauma on frontal bone. Majority of dog skeleton had carnivore gnawing marks. Perimortem trauma on left inner orbital that dog would not have survived.
FS 160	Pueblo I and Pueblo II—900–975	Pueblo A, Room 6 Floor	Juvenile	Juvenile individual around 8–9 months old. Lower portion of skeletal elements are missing. Antemortem puncture marks on bregma, creating two punctures with flaking in skull and consequential osteophytic growth. Left parietal has circular bumpy and grey area indicative of healed infection or trauma. Skull is hollow, and the trauma on left side of face with a distinct circular, incomplete fracture and missing zygomatic arch might indicate a perimortem injury dog did not survive or possibly postmortem damage (as indicated by glue). Upper portion of skeleton has gnawing patterns including channeling, pitting, and punctures most likely from postmortem carnivore activity.

FS	Period	Location	Age	Description
FS 156	Pueblo I and Pueblo II—900–975	Pueblo A, Room 5 Fill	Adult	Mature male dog without a skull. Periodontal disease around both mandibular P4s. Bent and healed baculum and vertebrae. Perimortem trauma to both scapula, left humeral head, and left carpals and tarsals (resulting in fusion). Based on deformation of tarsals, carpals, vertebrae and baculum, dog might have suffering from a genetic condition that limited healing from human or canid aggression. There isn't an obvious reason for death, but dog was able to survive painful conditions that might have limited movement or ability to hunt or defend itself against other animals.
FS 159	Pueblo I and Pueblo II— 925–1000	PS 3, Kiva, 10 cm above floor	Adult	Mature individual with multiple healed fractures most likely from other dogs or from human aggression. Based upon teeth health, this dog would have had trouble eating hard food. Some genetic and developmental disorders responsible for malformations of vertebrate are also associated with poor tooth health. This dog most likely suffered from a developmental disorder affecting spine morphology and health. Spina bifida is possible, as indicated by bifurcated spinous process of T1 and weaker vertebrae susceptible to injury. Majority of the vertebral spinous processes are bent to one side (sometimes immediately switching directions), with T7 showing signs of a healed fracture on the spinous process and tail trauma indicated by two fused caudal bones. A break on the humerus shaft and femoral neck do not show signs of healing and might be perimortem/postmortem injuries. Healed head lesion, healed ischium lesion, and a healed mandible fracture.
FS 120	Pueblo I and Pueblo II—875–950	PS 5, Kiva, 10 cm above ante- chamber floor	Juvenile	Juvenile individual around 9–10 months. Potential for perimortem wound on inner left orbital (might be taphonomy). Healed wound on right parietal, antemortem trauma on right scapula, bent vertebrae, fractured and healed baculum. Taphonomy has limited the interpretation of this individual.
FS 95	Pueblo I and Pueblo II— 875–1000	PS 7, Kiva Vent Shaft	Adult	Mature individual without a skull. Both scapula have healed fractures on dorsal borders. Both scapulae are incomplete, most likely due to a combination of carnivore gnawing and taphonomy (the structure was open to the elements). T7 and T9 have a fracture and infection on spinous processes and most all other skeletal elements were too incomplete or weathered to analyze.

To deal with these issues, we excluded specimens that had been severely affected by weathering or carnivore damage as well as those specimens that had been glued. While this limited the total number of dog burials we could analyze, our analytical interest in surface modifications and paleopathologies made this exclusion necessary. Our final sample consists of eight discrete dog burials from site 5MTUMR 2347.

Analytical Methods

Analysis was conducted by Monagle at the Smithsonian Institution in October 2016. Each specimen was aged and assessed for pathologies, butchery marks, and other surface modifications. To assess age, we used a combination of tooth wear (Horard-Herbin 2000), tooth eruption (Evans and De Lahunta 2013) and epiphyseal fusion (Silver 1969) to group specimens into 5 age classes: less than 6 months old, between 6 months and 8 months, between 8 and 10 months, 10 months to 1.5 years, and 1.5 years or older. Osteological anomalies identified include antemortem traumas (identified by the presence of healing), postmortem traumas (identified in cases with no evidence of healing) and signs of potential human aggression (e.g., blunt-force trauma to the head and around the inner orbitals; Bartosiewicz and Gál 2013:74). Additionally, specimens were analyzed for evidence of modification. We used Binford (1981) and Fernandez-Jalvo and Andrews (2016) to interpret surface modifications.

We also analyzed interment context, using the descriptive categories established by Erica Hill (2000): ceremonial trash, dedicatory offering, and simple interment. Ceremonial trash consists of burial outside of habitation areas, usually in a sacred space or shrine. One example of this are the "eagle cemeteries" from Homol'ovi, in which eagles and their feathers (ritually important objects requiring ceremonial disposal) were buried (Strand 1998; Walker 1995). Dedicatory offerings typically consist of partial to whole objects or animals (with evidence of traumatic injury) placed in a specific spot for a specific function, such as the crushed Los Guanacos recovered from a pithouse floor at Pueblo Grande (Foster and James 2002). Finally, simple interments are usually found in a midden and suggest expedient disposal of remains. While these categories are descriptive rather than definitive, interment categories do suggest the role a dog filled during death. For example, a witch would likely be buried as ceremonial trash, a companion animal might be found in a simple interment in a floor or midden, and a guardian or ritual sacrifice would likely be a dedicatory offering for the ceremonial closure of a kiva (Hill 2000).

Results

The results of our analysis of age at death are consistent with the initial analysis (Table 3.1). The four dogs originally identified as adults were classed as older than 1.5 years in this analysis, while three specimens initially classified as juveniles were reclassified as 8–10 months old and one as 6–8 months old.

We identified consistent antemortem traumas on the skulls, scapulae, and vertebral columns of the 5MTUMR 2347 dogs. Three of the four dogs with complete crania had fractured and healed nasal bones (Figure 3.1), and five of the six dogs with intact skulls had trauma located on their inner left orbitals (Figure 3.2). Of the 7 dogs with postcranial remains, 4 had bent and malformed cervical, thoracic, and lumbar vertebrae (Figure 3.3), and 9 of 16 total scapulae had healed blunt traumas and healed puncture holes (Figure 3.4). The individual with the most severe vertebral and scapular malformations (FS 159) also had a healed

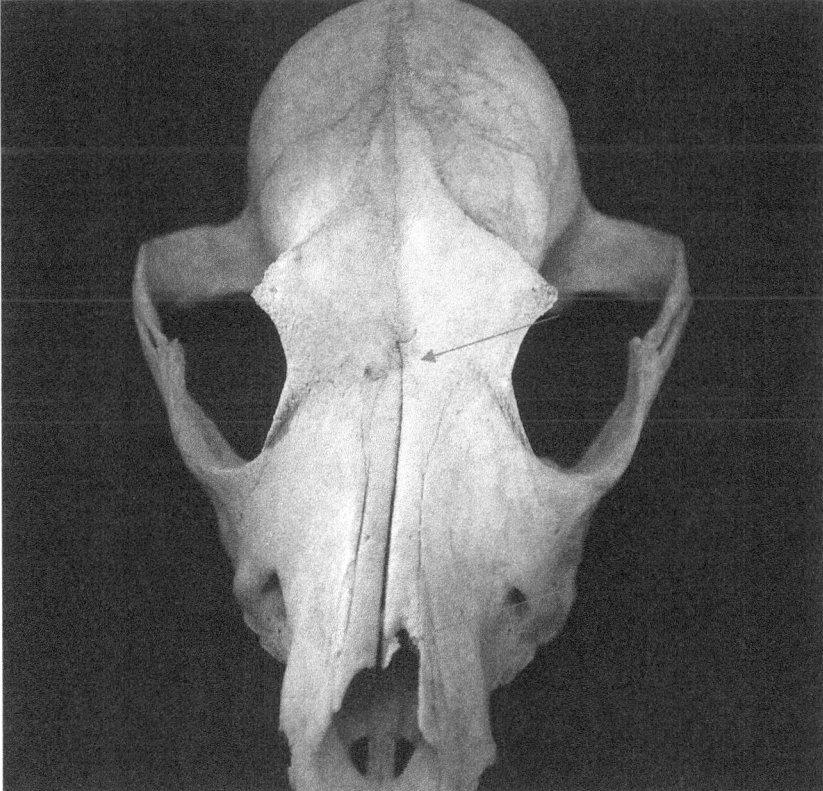

Figure 3.1. Antemortem skull trauma and nasal fractures on FS 204.

ischium lesion and fused caudal bones. Another adult dog (FS 156) had bone fusion from healed traumas as well. In addition, two dogs had fractured and healed baculae (FS 156, FS 120) and five dogs had healed broken long bones. One juvenile dog (F. 18 F.A. 21) exhibited parallel striations on the skull and on both scapulae (Figure 3.5). Finally, all the individual dogs we studied showed evidence

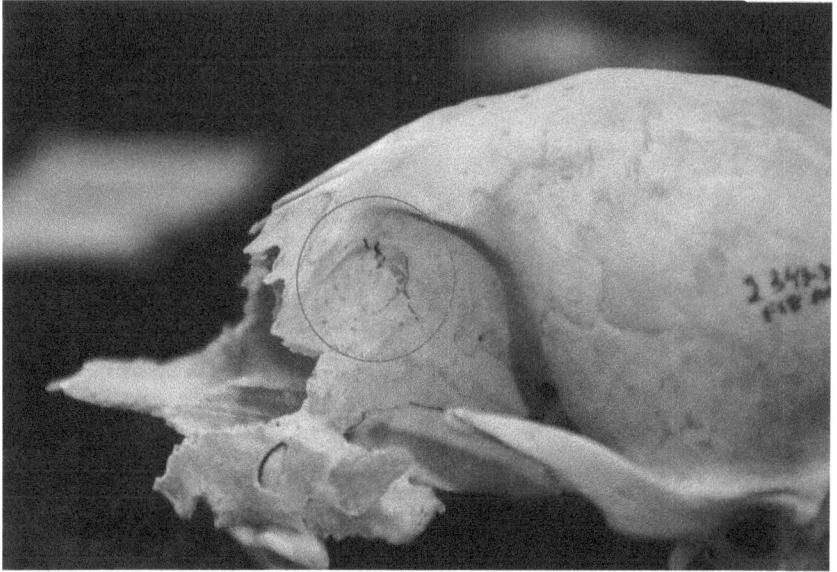

Figure 3.2. Trauma on inner orbital of F.18 F.A. 19.

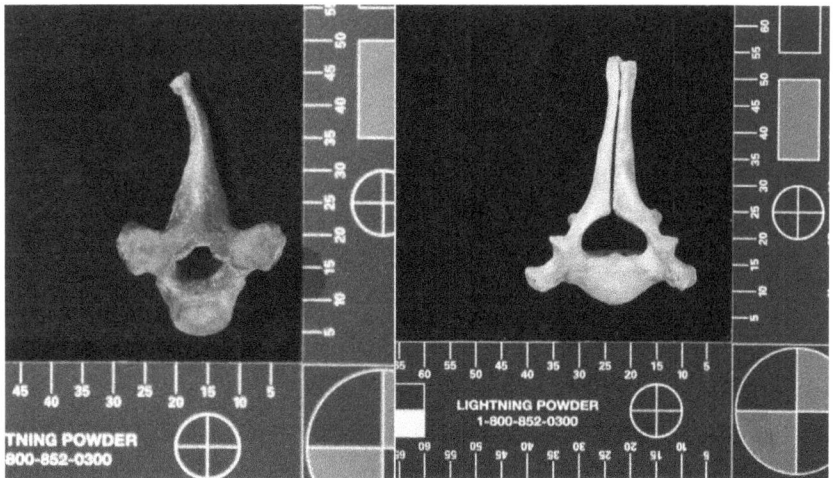

Figure 3.3. Examples of malformed vertebrae from FS 156 (T8, *right*) and FS 159 (T1, *left*).

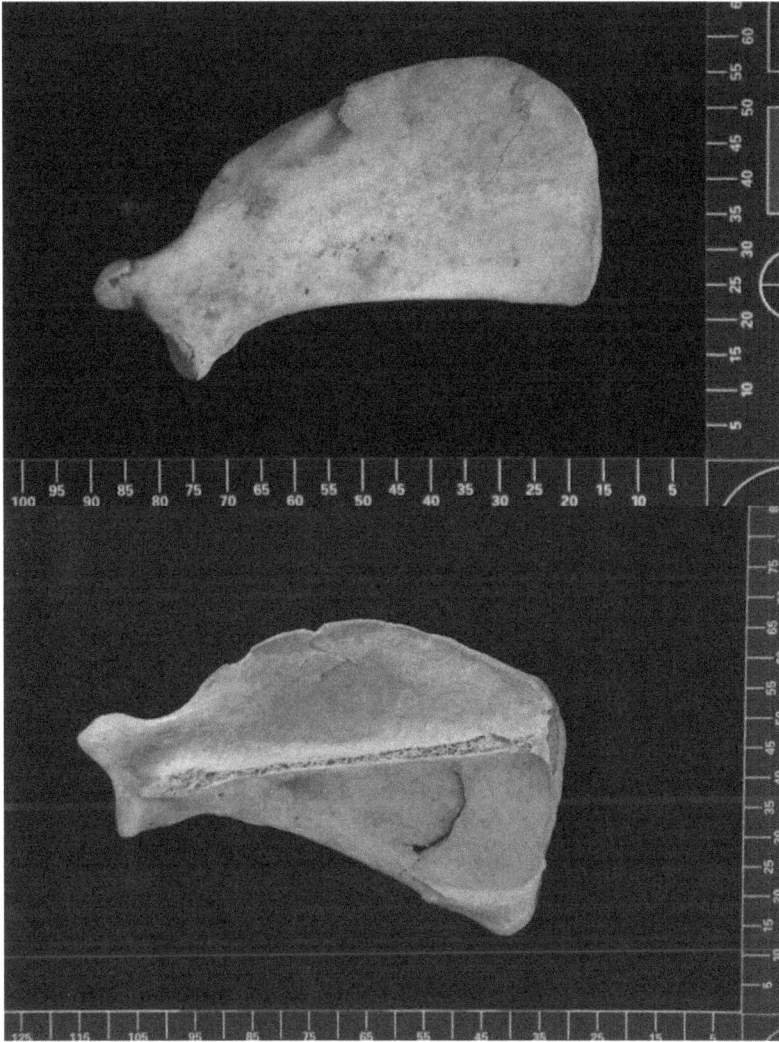

Figure 3.4. Examples of scapula traumas on FS 120 (*top*) and FS 159 (*bottom*).

of non-anthropogenic surface modifications on the bone, including varying degrees of weathering and, in some cases, carnivore gnawing.

Our analysis of interment context found that most of the 5MTUMR 2347 dogs were buried associated with architecture, as might be expected in the case of dedicatory offerings, but there was significant variation in specimen age, in specific burial location, in the presence and type of associated objects, and in other details of the burial (Table 3.2).

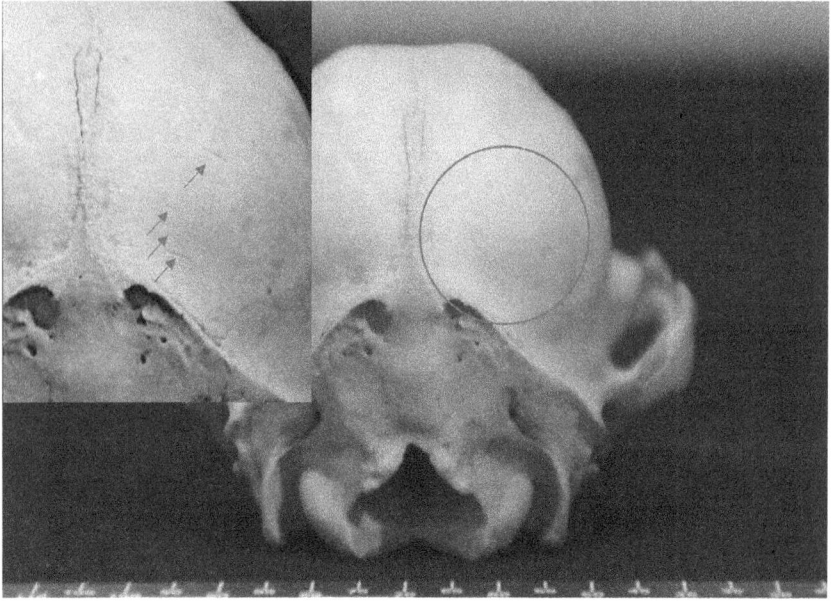

Figure 3.5. Cut marks on F.18 F.A. 21.

Table 3.2. Patterns of interment

ID	Single	Group	Headless	Cranial Trauma	Pit Context	Floor of Room or Kiva	Ventilator Shaft	With Artifacts in Proximity	Juvenile
FS 204	X			X			X	X	
F. 18 F.A. 21		X		X			X	X	X
F. 18 F.A. 19		X		X			X	X	X
FS 160	X			X		X			X
FS156	X		X						
FS 159		X		X		X		X	
FS 120	X			X		X		X	X
FS 95	X		X				X	X	

Discussion

Our results suggest the dogs from 5MTUMR 2347 filled a number of roles both before and after death. All eight dog burials had evidence of trauma associated with human behavior (Table 3.3). Antemortem trauma of the kind we observed on the dog skulls is usually associated with beatings from humans aimed at the

Victoria Monagle and Emily Lena Jones

facial area, typically in an effort to control the animal but not to kill it (Baker and Brothwell 1980; Bartosiewicz and Gál 2013:76; Park 1987:6). Lesions around the rim of the orbit and zygomatic processes of the frontal bone are particularly associated with such beatings (Baker and Brothwell 1980:93). In addition, the adult dogs in our sample had multiple instances of osteophytic growth around joints, deformed vertebrae, and healed traumatic wounds on postcranial remains. Such pathologies might be expected among dogs that survived by scavenging around a village and received negative attention when they crossed boundaries into "human only" space. This kind of interaction between humans and canids has been observed among the Teenek Indians, who beat dogs with a stick or throw a stone at them for peeking inside a house for scraps or approaching their master without invitation (de Vidas 2002).

The traumas on the scapulae and vertebrae are consistent with fracture and healing patterns found on dogs used as pack animals in the North American Plains groups (Latham and Losey 2019; Morey 2010:96; Snyder 1995:222–239). The frequency of skeletal anomalies consisting of flattened and damaged scapulae and vertebral spinous processes on the dogs in our sample indicate that these dogs could have been used to carry packs during their lifetimes. However, there is no historic or ethnographic evidence of this type of dog use in Pueblo communities, and more recent research has indicated that spondylosis deformans are not necessarily reliable indicators of dog transport in the past (Latham and Losey 2019). Given this, what other factors may have caused these traumas? One possible explanation is intraspecies aggression. The scapula traumas we

Table 3.3. Traumas by age at death

Age at death	n	With Skulls	With Healed Head Traumas	With Inner Orbital Trauma	With Long Bone Post Mortem Breaks	With Healed Postcranial Trauma	With Antemortem Vertebral Deformations	With Antemortem Scapular Trauma	With Baculum
1.5 years or older	4	2	2	1	3	3	3	2	1
8–10 months	3	3	2	3	3	3	1	3	1
6 months +	1	1	1	1	1	1	0	1	0
Less than 6 months	0	0	0	0	0	0	0	0	0
Total	8	6	5	5	7	7	4	6	2

identified are similar to those found in archaeological dogs from San Nicolas Island, which were interpreted as blunt-force traumas from collisions with an uneven surface (Bartelle et al. 2010:8). The scapula traumas in the 5MTUMR 2347 dogs, in this light, may reflect injuries from hunting, from assault by a human or other animal, or from rough play with other dogs.

This last possibility is further supported by some of the other antemortem traumas we identified, which are also consistent with interspecies aggression. We observed two baculum fractures, which are often caused by fighting during the mating season (Bartosiewicz and Gál 2013:69); we also observed puncture wounds and fractured frontal bones, which may result from dogs fighting with each other (Bartosiewicz and Gál 2013; Park 1987).

There is solid evidence for both genetic anomalies and nutritional stress in the 5MTUMR 2347 dogs analyzed. In addition to the pathologies on the vertebrae mentioned earlier, two juvenile dogs interred together (F.18 F.A. 21 and F. 18 F.A. 19) showed signs of abnormally formed teeth (the tips of the upper fourth premolars are growing into each other instead of down), indicative of a genetic condition (Carol Breslin, DVM, personal communication, 2017). Signs of nutritional stress identified among the 5MTUMR 2347 dogs include heavily worn teeth (abrasion), broken and dead teeth, and advanced cases of periodontal disease (see Table 3.1). This type of periodontal disease can lead to holes in teeth, tooth sensitivity, and inability to eat and may also impact vision (Frost 1985; Lawler et al. 2016).

The combination of genetic conditions and nutritional stress among the 5MTUMR 2347 dogs suggests a small, resource-limited dog population. If there were not enough resources to support a large dog population, both nutritional stress and a small breeding population of dogs would be expected, which might then result in genetic conditions due to interbreeding. Perhaps more significantly in terms of human-dog interactions, the presence of dogs with advanced periodontal disease indicates that these dogs were being cared for, presumably by humans since they would have required specially prepared foods (MacKinnon 2010).

Our analysis shows that the 5MTUMR 2347 dogs were living alongside (and potentially fighting with) other dogs and humans, and that they were being cared for by humans, possibly at some cost to the humans providing this care. Given this, it is perhaps not surprising that we found no evidence that the 5MTUMR 2347 dogs were used as food. The completeness and lack of burning of the analyzed specimens suggests they were not butchered, cooked, or consumed by humans. Spiral fractures and breakage patterns were found on some individual dog elements; in our view, however, these were most likely caused by channeling from carnivore gnawing rather than butchering, as they were accompanied by pitting and punctures and did not have evidence of burning (see Binford 1981:51) The snapped ends of long bones and lack of proximal ends, previously thought to result from human chewing, may instead be the result of gnawing by carnivores (Binford 1981:69).

It is possible, however, that the 5MTUMR 2347 dogs were ritually killed. A consistent pattern of inner orbital trauma was observed for five of the six skulls we studied. Despite differences between fracture type, shape, and size of these injuries, this evidence is certainly suggestive of intentional and patterned culling. As discussed earlier in this chapter, dog roles that might have resulted in death include the animal's being a witch, a nuisance, a companion animal to a deceased human, or a sacrifice. Witch killing is not a likely fit for any of the 5MTUMR 2347 dogs examined here, as such burials would likely be away from habitation areas (Hill 2000). The culling of dogs that behaved unusually (excessive barking and whining, digging the ground around the house, etc.) is also an unlikely explanation in this case; the burials for such dogs would most likely be expedient disposals since the dogs would not be expected to fulfill afterlife roles (Malotki and Gary 2001). While killing of a companion animal is a possibility for some of these specimens (FS 120 and FS 159; see Ambler 1994), a more likely suggestion, given that none of the 5MTUMR 2347 dogs were found in association with human remains, is that these and the other five dogs were dedicatory offerings. In Pueblo societies, dedicatory offerings are typically part of ceremonial closures of pit structures and kivas (Hill 2000:386)—events that would certainly qualify as ritual killings.

Additional evidence suggesting ritual sacrifice comes from specimen F. 18 F.A. 21 (Table 3.1). As mentioned earlier, this juvenile dog exhibited ten parallel striations on its cranium and scapulae. It is likely that these marks result from carnivore activity, as they resemble claw and beak markings found on the bones of animals that have been preyed upon by raptors (Hockett 1991; Reeves 2009). Specimen F. 18 F.A. 21 also had perforations on the dorsal border of the left scapula and antemortem trauma on the right scapula, which resemble beak punctures from eagles (Sanders et al. 2003). These findings point to a potential role for this dog—and possibly the other sacrificed dogs as well—as eagle food. At Hopi, eagles and hawks were kept in villages for religious use and were fed rabbits and sometimes puppies and older dogs (Beaglehole 1936:22). Any such dogs would have served both functional (food for important animals) and ritual (activities involving religion) roles in their death. We cannot say for certain that any of the 5MTUMR 2347 dogs were used in this way, though the presence of eagle remains in the larger 5MTUMR 2347 faunal assemblage does provide some additional support. Additional research is necessary to fully assess this hypothesis. While to our knowledge the use of dogs as eagle food in Ancestral Pueblo societies has not been studied, it is testable: if dogs served as food for raptors, marks similar to the ones we observed on specimen F. 18 F.A. 21 should be present on canids recovered from kivas at other sites across the Southwest.

It is thus too soon to reach a conclusion on the role of eagles in the deaths of the 5MTUMR 2347 dogs, but we do believe our results indicate that at least some of these canids were ritually killed as sacrifices. However, although these dogs shared similar roles in death, they had different life experiences. The variation in antemortem traumas, ranging from intraspecies trauma (nasal punctures, scapula puncture marks, fractured bacula) to human-caused injuries (trauma on frontal bones and around orbital region, fused caudal bones, and blunt-force trauma to scapulae, vertebrae, and pelvis), and the presence of advanced diseases that would have necessitated human care, suggests differences in these dogs' relationships with humans (MacKinnon 2010).

Conclusion

Rather than serving in strict and mutually exclusive functional or ritual roles, the 5MTUMR 2347 dogs filled multiple roles within their Ancestral Pueblo community. Dogs analyzed were neither butchered nor consumed, and a majority of skulls had patterns of trauma within the same area of their inner orbitals, indicating a patterned killing. All appear to have been dedicatory offerings rather than ceremonial trash or expedient disposals; they were not objects whose function had ended. Instead, they were associated with (and possibly necessary for) the closing of kivas at this Ancestral Pueblo site. This interpretation has implications for the management of these remains today. Just as the Los Guanacos dog figurines from Tempe, Arizona, were identified as sacred objects to the Gila River Indian Community and repatriated to the tribe (Foster and James 2002), dog remains associated with ceremonial activity could be acknowledged as religiously significant and justified for repatriation.

However, despite the consistency in their deaths, the 5MTUMR 2347 dogs had different life experiences. When alive, they likely filled a variety of roles within the community. Given the pathologies and surface modifications we identified, these dogs were probably companions to humans. However, the variation in antemortem trauma and health are indicative of differences in care and diet for these animals, which in turn suggests differences in the degree to which they were companions. This finding also has implications for present-day Pueblo communities. Dog populations living on tribal lands today are threatened by regulations that impose a different set of cultural standards on Indigenous human-dog relationships (see Clausing 2011; Kane 2016; Lohmann 2012; *Indian Country Today*, 13 January 2011; Vaughn 2016). Understanding how dogs functioned within past Indigenous communities may support more cooperative and culturally respectful approaches to the management of dog populations on tribal lands today, while simultaneously promoting dog welfare.

Acknowledgments

We thank Bruce Huckell, Loa Traxler, Hannah Mattson, Melinda Zeder, and Teresa Hsu for support and feedback, as well as Brandi Bethke, Amanda Burtt, and two anonymous reviewers for extremely helpful editorial comments. V. M. would also like to thank Dody Fugate and Dr. Steven Emslie for their research on Southwest dogs and taking the time to discuss it; Dr. Carol Breslin of Advanced Veterinary Dentistry in Albuquerque, New Mexico, for sharing her knowledge and time; and Cyler Conrad, Jacque Kocer, Milena Carvalho, Caitlin Ainsworth, Lexi O'Donnell, and Will Taylor. This project was funded by the following grants to V. M.: the Archaeological Society of New Mexico, the Patrick Orion Mullen Fund of the George C. Frison Institute of Archaeology and Anthropology, University of New Mexico's El Centro de la Raza, and the National Science Foundation (Graduate Research Fellowship ID 2016227866).

References Cited

Akins, Nancy J., Susan Moga, Pamela McBride, Mollie Toll, Jessica A. Badner, and Richard Holloway
2012 *Excavations along NM 22*, Vol. 5, *Analytical Studies: Fauna and Flora*. Museum of New Mexico, Office of Archaeological Studies, Santa Fe.

Allen, Grover M.
1954 Canid Remains from Pueblo Bonito and Pueblo del Arroyo. In *The Material Culture of Pueblo Bonito*, edited by N. M. Judd, pp. 385–389. Smithsonian Miscellaneous Collections, Washington, DC.

Ambler, J. Richard

1994 The Shonto Junction Doghouse: A Weaver's Field House in the Klethla Valley. *Kiva* 59(4):455–473.

Anschuetz, Kurt F., Richard H. Wilshusen, and Cherie L. Scheick

2001 An Archaeology of Landscapes: Perspectives and Directions. *Journal of Archaeological Research* 9(2):157–211.

Baker, John R., and Don R. Brothwell

1980 *Animal Diseases in Archaeology*. Academic Press, New York.

Bartelle, Barney G., René L. Vellanoweth, Elizabeth S. Netherton, Nicholas W. Poister, William E. Kendig, Amira F. Ainis, Ryan J. Glenn, Johanna V. Marty, Lisa Thomas-Barnett, and Steven J. Schwartz

2010 Trauma and Pathology of a Buried Dog from San Nicolas Island, California, U.S.A. *Journal of Archaeological Science* 37(11):2721–2734.

Bartosiewicz, László, and Erika Gál

2013 *Shuffling Nags, Lame Ducks: The Archaeology of Animal Disease*. Oxbow, Oxford.

Beaglehole, Ernest

1936 *Hopi Hunting and Hunting Ritual*. Yale University, New Haven.

Beaglehole, Ernest, and Pearl Beaglehole

1937 *Notes on Hopi Economic Life*. Yale University Press, New Haven.

Beals, Ralph L.

1935 *Preliminary Report on the Ethnography of the Southwest*. National Park Service, Berkeley.

Binford, Lewis R.

1981 *Bones: Ancient Men and Modern Myths*. Academic Press, New York.

Black, Hal L.

1981 Navajo Sheep and Goat Guarding Dogs: A New World Solution to the Coyote Problem. *Rangelands* 3(6):235–237.

Black, Hal L., and Jeffrey S. Green

1985 Navajo Use of Mixed-Breed Dogs for Management of Predators. *Journal of Range Management* 38(1):11–15.

Brody, J. J.

2008 When Is a Dog in Mimbres Art? *Archaeology Southwest* 22(3):10.

Clark, Cherie, Timothy W. Canaday, and Kenneth Lee Petersen

1987 Domestic Dog in the Dolores Archaeological Program Faunal Assemblage. In *Dolores Archaeological Program: Supporting Studies: Settlement and Environment*, pp. 275–288. USDI, Bureau of Reclamation, Engineering and Research Center, Denver.

Clausing, Jeri

2011 Stray Reservation Dogs Blamed for Attacks. *NBC News*, August 16: 1–2. http://www.nbcnews.com/id/44165591/ns/us_news-life/t/reservation-dogs-roam-unchecked-attacks-common/#.W2cZg9hKjOQ.

Colton, Harold S.

1970 The Aboriginal Southwestern Indian Dog. *American Antiquity* 35(2):153–159.

Courlander, Harold

1982 *Hopi Voices: Recollections, Traditions, and Narratives of the Hopi Indians*. University of New Mexico Press, Albuquerque.

Cushing, Frank Hamilton

1920 *Zuñi Breadstuff*. Museum of the American Indian, New York.

1979   *Zuñi: Selected Writings of Frank Hamilton Cushing.* University of Nebraska Press, Lincoln.

1992   *Zuni Folk Tales.* University of Arizona Press, Tucson.

1998   *My Adventures in Zuñi.* Filter Press, Palmer Lake, Colorado.

Darling, J. Andrew, Barnaby V. Lewis, Robert Valencia, and B. Sunday Eiselt

2015   Archaeology in the Service of the Tribe: Three Episodes in Twenty-First-Century Tribal Archaeology in the US–Mexico Borderlands. *Kiva* 81(1–2):62–79.

Davidson, Osha G.

2016   Ancient Footprints Discovered in Arizona. *Scientific American*, 11 February: 1–9.

Debenport, Erin

2015   *Fixing the Books: Secrecy, Literacy, and Perfectibility in Indigenous New Mexico.* School for Advanced Research Press, Santa Fe.

de Vidas, Anath Ariel

2002   A Dog's Life among the Teenek Indians (Mexico): Animals' Participation in the Classification of Self and Other. *Journal of the Royal Anthropological Institute* 8(3):531–550.

Diniz, P. P., M. J. Beall, K. Omark, R. Chandrashekar, D. A. Daniluk, K. E. Cyr, J. F. Koterski, R. G. Robbins, P. G. Lalo, B. C. Hegarty, and E. B. Breitschwerdt

2010   High Prevalence of Tick-Borne Pathogens in Dogs from an Indian Reservation in Northeastern Arizona. *Vector Borne and Zoonotic Diseases* 10(2):117–123.

Dongoske, Kurt E., Michael Yeatts, Roger Anyon, and T. J. Ferguson

1997   Archaeological Cultures and Cultural Affiliation: Hopi and Zuni Perspectives in the American Southwest. *American Antiquity* 62(4):1–9.

Douglas, Charles L., and David M. Leslie

1981   Two Kinds of Small Indian Dogs from Black Mesa, Arizona. *Journal of the Arizona-Nevada Academy of Science* 16(3):88–90.

Dove, David M.

2012   Multiple Animal Offerings in an Early Kiva: Champagne Spring (Greenlee) Ruins, 5DL2333. *Southwestern Lore* 78(2):1–17.

Drake, Abby Grace, Michael Coquerelle, and Guillaume Colombeau

2015   3D Morphometric Analysis of Fossil Canid Skulls Contradicts the Suggested Domestication of Dogs during the Late Paleolithic. *Scientific Reports* 5:8299.

Dumarest, Noël

1920   *Notes on Cochiti, New Mexico.* Translated by E. C. Parsons. Memoirs of the American Anthropological Association, Vol. 6(3). American Anthropological Association, Lancaster, Pennsylvania.

Emslie, Steven D.

1977   Interpretation of Faunal Remains from Archaeological Sites in Mancos Canyon, Southwestern Colorado. Master's thesis, Department of Anthropology, University of Colorado, Boulder.

1978   Dog Burials from Mancos Canyon, Colorado. *Kiva* 43(3–4):167–182.

Espinosa, Aurelio M.

1936   Pueblo Indian Folk Tales. *Journal of American Folklore* 49(191/192):69–133.

Evans, Howard E., and Alexander De Lahunta

2013   *Miller's Anatomy of the Dog.* Elsevier Health Sciences, St. Louis.

Ezzo, Joseph A., and Mary C. Stiner

2000   A Late Archaic Period Dog Burial from the Tucson Basin, Arizona. *Kiva* 66(2):291–305.

Ferg, Alan

2008a Dogs in the Desert: Repatriation. *Archaeology Southwest* 22(3):14–15.

2008b A Rare Breed. *Archaeology Southwest* 22(3):7.

Fernandez-Jalvo, Yolanda, and Peter Andrews

2016 *Atlas of Taphonomic Identifications: 1001+ Images of Fossil and Recent Mammal Bone Modification.* Springer, Dordrecht.

Fewkes, Jesse Walter

1990 *Tusayan Katcinas and Hopi Altars.* Avanyu, Albuquerque.

Fiedel, Stuart J.

2005 Man's Best Friend—Mammoth's Worst Enemy? A Speculative Essay on the Role of Dogs in Paleoindian Colonization and Megafaunal Extinction. *World Archaeology* 37(1):11–25.

Foster, Michael S., and Steven R. James

2002 Dogs, Deer, or Guanacos: Zoomorphic Figurines from Pueblo Grande, Central Arizona. *Journal of Field Archaeology* 29(1/2):165–176.

Freer, Rachel, and Mike Jacobs

2008 Basketmaker Dog-Hair Sashes from Obelisk Cave. *Archaeology Southwest* 22(3):6.

Frost, Patricia

1985 Canine Dentistry: A Compendium. Nabisco Brands, East Hanover, New Jersey.

Germonpré, Mietje, Mikhail V. Sablin, Rhiannon E. Stevens, Robert E. M. Hedges, Michael Hofreiter, Mathias Stiller, and Viviane R. Després

2009 Fossil Dogs and Wolves from Palaeolithic Sites in Belgium, the Ukraine and Russia: Osteometry, Ancient DNA and Stable Isotopes. *Journal of Archaeological Science* 36(2):473–490.

Gillespie, William B.

1975 Preliminary Report of Excavations at the Ute Canyon Site, 5MTUMR 2347, Ute Mountain Ute Homelands, Colorado. Submitted to the Bureau of Indian Affairs, Albuquerque.

Guagnin, Maria, Angela R. Perri, and Michael D. Petraglia

2018 Pre-Neolithic Evidence for Dog-Assisted Hunting Strategies in Arabia. *Journal of Anthropological Archaeology* 49:225–236.

Harrison, Rodney

2013 *Heritage: Critical Approaches.* Routledge, New York.

Henderson, Junius, and John Peabody Harrington

1914 *Ethnozoology of the Tewa Indians.* Smithsonian Institution Bureau of American Ethnology Bulletin 56. US Government Printing Office, Washington, DC.

Hill, Erica

2000 The Contextual Analysis of Animal Interments and Ritual Practice in Southwestern North America. *Kiva* 65(4):361–398.

Hill, W. W.

1982 *An Ethnography of Santa Clara Pueblo, New Mexico.* University of New Mexico Press, Albuquerque.

Hockett, Bryan Scott

1991 Toward Distinguishing Human and Raptor Patterning on Leporid Bones. *American Antiquity* 56(4):667–679.

Horard-Herbin, Marie-Pierre

2000 Dog Management and Use in the Late Iron Age: the Evidence from the Gallic Site of Levroux, France. In *Dogs through Time: An Archaeological* Perspective, edited by S. J. Crockford, 115–122. BAR International Series, Vol. 889. Archaeopress, Oxford.

Indian Country Today

2011 Putting a Leash on the "Rez Dog" Problem. *Indian Country Today*, 13 January. https://newsmaven.io/indiancountrytoday/archive/putting-a-leash-on-the-rez-dog-problem-RIDHL7X-IEKor5O2M9wXtA/, retrieved April 2, 2019.

James, Steven R., and Michael S. Foster

2008 Hohokam Dogs and Iconography at Pueblo Grande. *Archaeology Southwest* 22(3):12–13.

Janssens, Luc, Liane Giemsch, Ralf Schmitz, Martin Street, Stefan Van Dongen, and Philippe Crombé

2018 A New Look at an Old Dog: Bonn-Oberkassel Reconsidered. *Journal of Archaeological Science* 92:126–138.

Kakaliouras, Ann M.

2012 An Anthropology of Repatriation: Contemporary Physical Anthropological and Native American Ontologies of Practice. *Current Anthropology* 53(S5):S210–S221.

Kane, Rich

2016 Dog Daze: Life for Stray Canines on Navajo Nation can lead to Lingering Hunger or Sudden Death (with video). *Salt Lake Tribune*, 3 October:1–3.

Kantner, John

2004 *Ancient Puebloan Southwest.* Cambridge University Press, New York.

Kelley, James E.

1975 Zooarchaeological Analysis at Antelope House: Behavioral Inferences from Distribution Data. *Kiva* 41(1):81–85.

Kemp, Brian M., Kathleen Judd, Cara Monroe, Jelmer W. Eerkens, Lindsay Hilldorfer, Connor Cordray, Rebecca Schad, Erin Reams, Scott G. Ortman, and Timothy A. Kohler

2017 Prehistoric Mitochondrial DNA of Domesticate Animals Supports a 13th Century Exodus from the Northern US Southwest. *PLoS ONE* 12(7):e0178882.

Lang, Richard W., and Arthur H. Harris

1984 The Faunal Remains from Arroyo Hondo Pueblo, New Mexico: A Study in Short-Term Subsistence Change. Arroyo Hondo Archaeological Series. School of American Research Press, Santa Fe.

Larson, G., E. K. Karlsson, A. Perri, M. T. Webster, S.Y.W. Ho, J. Peters, P. W. Stahl, P. J. Piper, F. Lingaas, M. Fredholm, K. E. Comstock, J. F. Modiano, C. Schelling, A. I. Agoulnik, P. A. Leegwater, K. Dobney, J. D. Vigne, C. Vila, L. Andersson, and K. Lindblad-Toh

2012 Rethinking Dog Domestication by Integrating Genetics, Archeology, and Biogeography. *Proceedings of the National Academy of Sciences* 109(23):8878–8883.

Latham, Katherine J., and Robert J. Losey

2019 Spondylosis Deformans as an Indicator of Transport Activities in Archaeological Dogs: A Systematic Evaluation of Current Methods for Assessing Archaeological Specimens. *PLoS ONE* 14(4):e0214575.

Lawler, Dennis F., Chris Widga, David A. Rubin, Jennifer A. Reetz, Richard H. Evans, Basil P. Tangredi, Richard M. Thomas, Terrence J. Martin, Charles Hildebolt, Kirk Smith, Daniel Leib, Jill E. Sackman, James G. Avery, and Gail K. Smith

2016 Differential Diagnosis of Vertebral Spinous Process Deviations in Archaeological and Modern Domestic Dogs. *Journal of Archaeological Science: Reports* 9:54–63.

Levin, Jennifer

2017   Someone Else's Manifest Destiny: Theresa Pasqual on Protecting Sacred Places. *Santa Fe New Mexican*, 28 April. http://www.santafenewmexican.com/pasatiempo/art/someone-else-s-manifest-destiny-theresa-pasqual-on-protecting-sacred/article_4bcf474a-4a6e-5ecd-a817-c799139e53ec.html, retrieved April 2, 2019.

Lohmann, Patrick

2012   Serious "Rez" Dog Problem. *Albuquerque Journal*, 31 December:1–4.

Lupo, Karen D.

2017   When and Where Do Dogs Improve Hunting Productivity? The empirical Record and Some Implications for Early Upper Paleolithic Prey Acquisition. *Journal of Anthropological Archaeology* 47:139–151.

Lupo, Karen D., and Joel C. Janetski

1994   Evidence of Domesticated Dogs and Some Related Canids in the Eastern Great Basin. *Journal of California and Great Basin Anthropology* 16(2):199–220.

MacKinnon, Michael

2010   "Sick as a Dog": Zooarchaeological Evidence for Pet Dog Health and Welfare in the Roman World. *World Archaeology* 42(2):290–309.

Malotki, Ekkehart

2001   *Hopi Animal Stories.* University of Nebraska Press, Lincoln.

Malotki, Ekkehart, and Ken Gary

2001   *Hopi Stories of Witchcraft, Shamanism, and Magic.* University of Nebraska Press, Lincoln.

Monagle, Victoria, Cyler Conrad, and Emily L. Jones

2018   What Makes a Dog? Stable Isotope Analysis and Human-Canid Relationships at Arroyo Hondo Pueblo. *Open Quaternary* 4(1):6. http://doi.org/10.5334/oq.43.

Morey, Darcy F.

2006   Burying Key Evidence: The Social Bond between Dogs and People. *Journal of Archaeological Science* 33(2):158–175.

2010   *Dogs: Domestication and the Development of a Social Bond.* Cambridge University Press, New York.

Olsen, Stanley J.

1968   Canid Remains from Grasshopper Ruin. *Kiva* 34(1):33–40.

Olsen, Sandra L.

1982   Faunal Analysis. In *Archaeological investigations at Zuni Pueblo, New Mexico, 1977–1980*, edited by T. J. Ferguson and B. J. Mills, pp. 390–428. Zuni Archaeology Program, Zuni, New Mexico.

Ortiz, Alfonso

1969   *The Tewa World: Space, Time, Being and Becoming in a Pueblo Society.* University of Chicago Press, Chicago.

Park, Robert W.

1987   Dog Remains from Devon Island, N.W.T.: Archaeological and Osteological Evidence for Domestic Dog Use in the Thule Culture. *Arctic* 40(3):184–190.

Parsons, Elsie C.

1927   Witchcraft among the Pueblos: Indian or Spanish? *Man* 27:106–112.

1929   *The Social Organization of the Tewa of New Mexico.* Memoirs of the American Anthropological Association. American Anthropological Association, Menasha, Wisconsin.

1939   *Pueblo Indian Religion.* University of Chicago Press, Chicago.

1940   *Taos Tales.* American Folk-Lore Society, New York.

1994   *Tewa Tales.* University of Arizona Press, Tucson.

Perri, Angela R.

2016   Hunting Dogs as Environmental Adaptations in Jōmon Japan. *Antiquity* 90(353): 1166–1180.

Petersen, K. L., J. D. Orcutt, Dolores Archaeological Program, Engineering and Research Center

1987   *Dolores Archaeological Program: Supporting Studies, Settlement and Environment.* US Department of the Interior, Bureau of Reclamation, Engineering and Research Center.

Post, Stephen S., Lynne Drake, and Timothy D. Maxwell

2002   *Archaeological Investigation of Two Multicomponent Sites along Interstate 40, near the State Road 6 Exit, Cibola County, New Mexico.* Museum of New Mexico, Office of Archaeological Studies, Santa Fe.

Reagan, Albert B.

1906   Dances of the Jemez Pueblo Indians. *Transactions of the Kansas Academy of Science* 20:241.

Reeves, Nicole M.

2009   Taphonomic Effects of Vulture Scavenging. *Journal of Forensic Sciences* 54(3):523– 528.

Roberts, John M., and David M. Schneider

1965   *Zuni Daily Life.* Behavior Science Reprints. Human Relations Area Files, New Haven.

Sanders, William J., Josh Trapani, and John C. Mitani

2003   Taphonomic Aspects of Crowned Hawk-Eagle Predation on Monkeys. *Journal of Human Evolution* 44(1):87–105.

Sando, Joe S.

1992   *Pueblo Nations: Eight Centuries of Pueblo Indian History.* Clear Light, Santa Fe.

Sauer, Carl Ortwin

1925   The Morphology of Landscape. *University of California Publications in Geography* 2:19–54.

Saunders, Jeffrey J., and Edward B. Daeschler

1994   Descriptive Analyses and Taphonomical Observations of Culturally-Modified Mammoths Excavated at "The Gravel Pit," near Clovis, New Mexico in 1936. *Proceedings of the Academy of Natural Sciences of Philadelphia* 145:1–28.

Silver, I. A.

1969   The Ageing of Domestic Animals. In *Science in Archaeology: A Survey of Progress and Research*, edited by D. R. Brothwell, E. S. Higgs and G. Clark, pp. 283–302. Revised and enlarged ed. Thames and Hudson, London.

Simoons, Frederick J.

1967   *Eat Not This Flesh: Food Avoidances in the Old World.* University of Wisconsin Press, Madison.

Simmons, Marc

1980   *Witchcraft in the Southwest: Spanish and Indian Supernaturalism on the Rio Grande.* University of Nebraska Press, Lincoln.

Smith, Anne M., and Alden C. Hayes

1992   *Ute Tales.* University of Utah Press, Salt Lake City.

Snow, David H.

2008   Pueblo Dog Tales. *Archaeology Southwest* 22(3):5.

Snyder, Lynn M.

1995   Assessing the Role of the Domestic Dog as a Native American Food Resource in the Middle Missouri Subarea A.D. 1000–1840. PhD dissertation, Department of Anthropology, University of Tennessee, Knoxville. UMI International, Ann Arbor.

Stephen, Alexander MacGregor

1929   Hopi tales. *Journal of American Folk-Lore* 42:2–72.

1969   *Hopi Journal of Alexander M. Stephen.* Columbia University contributions to anthropology 23. AMS Press, New York.

Strand, Jennifer G.

1998   An Analysis of the Homol'ovi Fauna with Emphasis of Ritual Behavior. PhD dissertation, Department of Anthropology, University of Arizona, Tucson. University Microfilms, Ann Arbor.

Swentzell, R., and P. M. Perea (editors)

2016   *The Pueblo Food Experience Cookbook: Whole Food of Our Ancestors.* Museum of New Mexico Press, Santa Fe.

Talayesva, Don C.

2013   *Sun Chief: The Autobiography of a Hopi Indian.* 2nd ed. Yale University Press, New Haven.

Thiel, Homer J.

1998   Faunal Remains. In *Archaeological Investigations of Early Village Sites in the Middle Santa Cruz Valley: Analysis and Synthesis, Part I,* edited by J. B. Mabry, pp. 165–208. Anthropological Papers, Vol. 19. Center for Desert Archaeology, Tucson.

Titiev, Mischa

1992   *Old Oraibi: A Study of the Hopi Indians of Third Mesa.* University of New Mexico Press, Albuquerque.

Tyler, Hamilton A.

1975   *Pueblo Animals and Myths.* University of Oklahoma Press, Norman.

Vaughn, Jacqueline

2016   Rez Dog Problem Remains Unresolved. *Flagstaff-Sedona Dog Magazine*, February/March. http://tubacityhumanesociety.org/wp-content/uploads/2016/08/Rez_Dog_article_in_Flagstaff-Sedona_Dog_magazine03-0416.pdf, retrieved April 2, 2019.

Walker, William H.

1995   Ceremonial Trash. In *Expanding Archaeology*, edited by J. M. Skibo, W. H. Walker, and A. E. Nielsen, pp. 67–79. University of Utah Press, Salt Lake City.

2008   Practice and Nonhuman Social Actors: The Afterlife Histories of Witches and Dogs in the American Southwest. In *Memory Work: Archaeologies of Material Practices,* edited by B. J. Mills and W. H. Walker, pp. 137–157. School for Advanced Research Press, Santa Fe.

Wenger, Tisa J.

2009   *We Have a Religion: The 1920s Pueblo Indian Dance Controversy and American Religious Freedom.* University of North Carolina Press, Chapel Hill.

White, Leslie A.

1932   *The Acoma Indians.* US Government Printing Office, Washington, DC.

1962   *The Pueblo of Sia, New Mexico*. US Government Printing Office, Washington, DC.

Whitman, William

1940   The San Ildefonso of New Mexico. In *Acculturation in Seven American Indian Tribes*, edited by R. Linton, pp. 390–460. D. Appleton–Century, New York.

Whitman, William, and Marjorie W. Whitman

1969   *The Pueblo Indians of San Ildefonso: A Changing Culture*. AMS Press, New York.

4

The Archaeology of Dogs at the Precontact Site of Nunalleq, Western Alaska

EDOUARD MASSON-MACLEAN, ELLEN MCMANUS-FRY,
AND KATE BRITTON

With contributions from Carly Ameen, Véronique Forbes, Loïc Harrault,
Claire Houmard, Ana Jorge, Rick Knecht, Paul Ledger, Krista McGrath,
Angela Perri, Anne-Kathrine Runge, Kristina Skillin, and Camilla Speller

For centuries dogs have played a prominent role in the lifeways of many Arctic and subarctic peoples (Morey and Aaris-Sørensen 2002). Dogs were likely an "integral part of [human] adaptation to the Arctic," illustrated by their prominent use in traditional Inuit culture, and possibly among earlier Thule and Paleo-Eskimo groups too, for transportation, hunting, protection and as a potential source of food and fur (Arnold 1979:265; Park 1987:185). In recent years there has been an increased interest in dogs in the archaeological record, particularly focused on the timing, nature and process of dog domestication (e.g., Larson et al. 2012). However, research has also gone *beyond domestication*, examining the management of dogs, their social and cultural significance, and dog-human relationships (e.g., Snyder and Moore 2006). Given their vital role across the circumpolar North, however, surprisingly little research has focused on dogs in this region.

Recent excavations at the precontact site of Nunalleq in the Yukon-Kuskokwim Delta (Y-K Delta), western Alaska, have uncovered a significant proportion of dog bones. Conditions at the site have also resulted in preservation of dog fur and even dog lice in deposits at the site, along with a vast organic and inorganic material culture assemblage. Here, we explore the archaeology of dogs at Nunalleq through multi-stranded cross-disciplinary study. Centered on the osteological analysis of dog remains themselves, we also incorporate advanced archaeological science methodologies and the study of material culture and other bodies of evidence into our analysis, along with the ethnohistoric record. Following the presentation and discussion of the zooarchaeological assemblage of Nunalleq, we draw on the work of diverse specialists working at the site in order to explore three main themes: 1) the utilitarian role of dogs, 2) dogs in foodways, and 3) dogs in social and symbolic space at the site. Our aim is to provide insight into this vital aspect of precontact animal-human relationships in the Y-K Delta and the varied roles, and significance, of the only Indigenous Arctic domesticate.

The Nunalleq Site

Nunalleq (GDN-248) lies on the shores of Kuskokwim Bay in the Y-K Delta, Alaska, approximately five km south of the Yup'ik village of Quinhagak (Figure 4.1).

An area of coastal wet tundra, the Y-K Delta region also includes interior boreal forests, wetlands, and areas of higher ground, including hills and mountains. The resource-rich but seasonal landscape features some of the largest aggregations of waterbirds and runs of anadromous fish in the world. The riparian environment and migrating salmon attract bears and caribou; wolves and foxes are found across the tundra. The coastlines and estuaries provide feeding grounds for small cetaceans and pinnipeds (Alaska Department of Fish and Game 2006).

The region is occupied today by the Central Alaskan Yupiit, who are likely descendants of the Thule—a culture common across the North American Arctic between approximately 1000 and 1400 CE (Raghavan et al. 2014). While the Yupiit are ethnographically well documented, relatively little is known about life in the Y-K Delta precontact, largely due to a previous lack of archaeological research in the region. However, excavations at Nunalleq have recently formed the most extensive exploration of late precontact archaeology in the region to date. With its rich and diverse cultural and ecological assemblage, the site represents a unique research opportunity into precontact lifeways in the Y-K Delta and, in particular, animal-human relationships.

Figure 4.1. Areas of excavation at Nunalleq, with inset map showing the location of the site.

Archaeology at Nunalleq

Since 2009 the Nunalleq site has been the focus of excavations by the University of Aberdeen and the Native corporation Qanirtuuq Incorporated (Fienup-Riordan et al. 2015; Hillerdal 2017; Hillerdal et al. in press) revealing the remains of a semi-subterranean sod and timber dwelling complex. Yup'ik for "old village," Nunalleq was occupied primarily between the late sixteenth and the late sev-

Edouard Masson-MacLean, Ellen McManus-Fry, and Kate Britton

enteenth century during the Little Ice Age, a period between the fifteenth and nineteenth centuries marked by generally colder conditions than today (Ledger et al. 2016; Ledger et al. 2018). The site likely corresponds to the precontact coastal village of Agaligmiut, known from local oral history to have been attacked and set ablaze during a period of regional warfare known as the Bow and Arrow Wars (Fienup-Riordan and Rearden 2016; Funk 2010).

Discontinuous permafrost and waterlogged soils have led to the excellent preservation of organic materials at the site, comprising tens of thousands of artifacts and an extensive assemblage of biological remains including animal bone, fur, baleen, feathers, and human hair. Wooden masks, carved animal bone, hunting implements, anthropomorphic figures, and animalistic artforms carved with images of game animals and other spiritually allied beings attest to the key role of animals in the precontact Yup'ik world.

Following rescue excavations in Area C (2009–2010), severely threatened by coastal erosion, research-led excavations at Nunalleq were undertaken in Areas A and B between 2012 and 2015 (Figure 4.1). At least three phases of occupation (Phases II, III, and IV) were identified, including evidence of architectural remodeling between the most recent Phases II and III (1620–1675 AD) in Area A (Ledger et al. 2018). The numerous projectile points associated with the latest house floor deposits from Phase II (1640/1660–1675 AD) evidence an attack— corresponding with local ethnohistorical accounts of the fall of Agaligmiut— and the thick layers of burned sod and charred timbers attest to the intense fire that led to the subsequent collapse of the structure. The data explored here originate from both the rescue excavations in Area C and the research excavations in Areas A and B, with the bulk of the faunal material coming from the better-documented Phases II and III in Area A.

The Faunal Assemblage

Identification, Composition and Analysis

To date, 10,429 faunal bone fragments have been identified from Nunalleq, the analysis of which was undertaken by two of the authors (Masson-MacLean 2018; Masson-MacLean et al. 2019; McManus-Fry 2015). Based on the number of identified specimens (NISP), marine mammals, fish (notably salmonids), caribou, and dog remains form the majority of the faunal assemblage (Table 4.1).

Salmon and marine mammals were the predominant food source at Nunalleq, based on NISP and meat weights calculated for the mammalian species

Table 4.1. Taxonomic identifications (NISP) and meat weights (kg)

Taxon	2009–2010	2012–2015	Total NISP	% NISP	Estimated Meat Weight (kg)	%
Seals	428	2,341	2,769	26.6%	8,060	28.9%
Fish	22	2,586	2,608	25.0%	-	-
Caribou	272	1,593	1,865	17.9%	4,030	14.5%
Domestic dog	**229**	**1,567**	**1,796**	**17.2%**	**1,770**	**6.4%**
Birds	25	646	671	6.4%	217.7	0.8%
Other land mammals	38	249	287	2.8%	430.15	1.5%
Mollusks	7	132	139	1.3%	-	-
Walrus	17	72	89	0.9%	4,500	16.1%
Fox	13	67	80	0.8%	44	0.2%
Beluga	9	48	57	0.5%	8,775	31.5%
Cetacean other	17	39	56	0.5%	-	-
Wolf	1	11	12	0.1%	43.5	0.2%
Total	1,078	9,351	10429	100%	2,7870.35	100%

(Table 4.1; Masson-MacLean 2018), with caribou also making a non-negligible contribution. This is in agreement with human paleodietary isotope data from the site, where stable carbon ($\delta^{13}C$) and nitrogen ($\delta^{15}N$) isotope ratios of values from human hair suggest a mixed diet but rich in salmon and incorporating higher trophic level marine foods (Britton et al. 2013; Britton et al. 2018). Based on meat weight contributions alone, dogs could have provided approximately 6% of the total non-fish meat weight if they were all consumed. However, as the following sections explain, dogs filled a number of different roles beyond consumption at Nunalleq.

Dog Remains

The Nunalleq fauna includes one of the largest Thule-era dog assemblages from Alaska and as such is a valuable research opportunity. A high proportion of dog remains is not the case for all contemporaneous Alaskan or Thule-era sites and likely reflects differences in the uses (and therefore usefulness) of dogs at

Edouard Masson-MacLean, Ellen McManus-Fry, and Kate Britton

different locales. Variations in local resource availability, modes of transportation, and in hunting methods will have impacted how many dogs were kept at any one time, thereby influencing their representation in the zooarchaeological record.

Skeletal Representation

Based on the 1,796 dog remains identified (NISP), a minimum (MNI, Minimum Number of Individuals) of 78 dogs was calculated. The identification of possible wolf (cf. *Canis lupus*) was based on the much larger size of some *Canis* sp. elements and comparison to modern wolf reference specimens. All dog body parts and elements were represented, although the assemblage was dominated by head and limb bones (Masson-MacLean 2018). The bias in skeletal representation may be related to density-mediated attrition or to the discard of certain elements in an unexcavated part of the village or elsewhere (Friesen and Betts 2002). The abundance of certain elements may also be a function of their use. For example, the abundant head elements recovered were mostly mandibles, which might, in part, be explained by the desire to acquire dog canines. The use of carnivore canines, including domestic dogs, as raw material for making bone-splitting tools and jewelry, such as pendants and amulets, has been attested in other precontact context in Arctic Alaska and around the world (Grouard, Perdikaris and Debue 2013; Jonuks and Rannamäe 2017; Kitching 1963; Lantis 1980:10; Mannermaa et al. 2019), and there was clear evidence of worked dog canines at Nunalleq.

A New Breed? Morphological and Genetic Evidence

The dogs at Nunalleq are similar to dogs found at Thule sites across the Arctic and would have been different from pre-Thule Alaskan dogs in terms of their size and craniofacial morphology (Ameen 2018). Geometric morphometrics revealed no significant variation in the size or shape of the dogs at Nunalleq, suggesting a relatively uniform dog phenotype. Analysis of their crania show a large, elongated brain case, shallowly sloped snout, and wide zygomatic arches, and their mandibles exhibit a sharp ascending ramus and a curved toothrow (Ameen 2018). The Nunalleq dogs, and Thule-era dogs in general, exhibit a phenotype that is morphologically similar to both historic Greenland and Canadian Inuit sled dogs, as well as the modern Greenland Dog breed.

Based on DNA analysis of whole mitochondrial genomes, Nunalleq dogs fall within the diversity of all Thule-era dogs. Diversity of their mitochondrial DNA lineages suggests that the Nunalleq dogs are derived from a novel population introduced to Alaska by Thule peoples (Ameen 2018).

The Utilitarian Role of Dogs at Nunalleq

Domestic dogs can have a range of functions and roles within human societies. From their use as traction animals to protectors of human settlements, from assisting in the hunting of other animals to their direct exploitation for meat, their uses are wide ranging, multifaceted, and not mutually exclusive. In the Y-K Delta, ethnographic and historical accounts allow us to gain an initial understanding of the role of dogs among precontact populations in the region. At Nunalleq, archaeological evidence not only attests to the multiple uses of dogs but also documents practices associated with the management of dogs and their lived experiences.

A Dog's Life

The use of domestic dogs as draught animals is synonymous with perceptions of traditional life in the Arctic. Although such perceptions may not always be accurate reflections of the past, and other uses of dogs (e.g., for hunting) may have been more important, the use of dogs in traction and load carrying was commonplace until the introduction of snowmobiles in many regions (Wolfe et al. 1984:178).

Consistent with evidence from elsewhere in Alaska (Ford 1959:151–153; Stanford 1976:215), a number of components related to dog sleds were identified in the Nunalleq collections, including sled shoes and a grass harness (Rick Knecht, personal communication, 2016). Previous studies of archaeological dog remains in Arctic regions have suggested that the presence of certain vertebral pathologies could be associated with the carrying of heavy packs or the pulling of sleds (Arnold 1979; Morey and Aaris-Sørensen 2002), although no such injuries or skeletal stress markers were identified at Nunalleq. Even so, the presence of material culture associated with traction suggests that the inhabitants of Nunalleq did use their dogs as draught animals to pull sleds and likely also to carry loads of equipment or food on hunting expeditions. It should be noted, however, that other important sledding apparatus, such as trace buckles, are notably absent from the Nunalleq assemblage, which may indicate that traction was not the foremost use for dogs at the site.

Beyond traction, domestic dogs in the region have also traditionally had widespread use in the hunting of other animals, and this may have been the case

Edouard Masson-MacLean, Ellen McManus-Fry, and Kate Britton

at Nunalleq. During the Fifth Thule Expedition (1921–1924), Knud Rasmussen described the use of dogs in breathing-hole hunting among the Central Inuit, where (preferably) hungry dogs are taken out over the ice to lead Inuit hunters to concealed seal-breathing holes by scent alone (Rasmussen 1931). Once holes had been identified, hunters would wait for seals to surface for air and the animal would be harpooned. Historically, dogs would also have been important in hunting terrestrial fauna, such as caribou and musk oxen and even polar bears (Cummins 2013). Therefore, perhaps one of the most important functions of dogs at Nunalleq is likely to have been for use in the hunting of other (wild) animals. Although the direct evidence of hunting at the site is irrefutable, including fishing, sealing, and game-hunting harpoons, hafted arrows, bows and throwing boards, the use of dogs in hunting at Nunalleq is difficult to elucidate. Some, albeit indirect, evidence for these practices may lie in the chemical analyses of human and dog tissues from the site. Stable isotope data from strands of human hair from Nunalleq suggests at least some individuals had strongly seasonal diets and, in some cases, may be indicative of seasonal mobility as part of specialized hunting parties (Britton et al. 2018). Similar short-term dietary variability was displayed in some of the dog fur and claws from the site, analyzed using the same methodologies (McManus-Fry et al. 2018), which may suggest canine companionship or participation during hunting expeditions.

Other than traction and hunting, further practical uses may have included settlement protection and the use of primary and secondary products from the dogs themselves, including their meat. The presence of dogs in the houses and passageways of Nunalleq, evidenced by their fur and lice, coprolites, and even complete preserved bodies. Such evidence is certainly indicative of the close physical association of dogs and humans in the domestic space and may suggest the role of dogs in the securing of that space from intrusion from human or animal threats.

As beasts of burden, and likely participants in potentially dangerous hunting activities, it is probable that the dogs of Nunalleq led hard lives. Ethnographic and historical accounts suggest dogs were often poorly fed (Park 1987). This may have been incidental, in order to preserve food, but at other times withholding food may have been more deliberate. The Netsilik, for example, incentivized dogs' participation in hunting activities by hunger (Balikci 1970). Pulling sleds could be a dangerous activity, with the risk of dogs falling and being run over (Park 1987), in addition to possible long-term physical damage from pulling or carrying heavy loads. Wolves and bears represented significant physical threats, during hunts or otherwise, and in-fighting between dogs could be particularly vicious and near constant (Park 1987). Physical admonishments from their handlers, including beatings and whippings, also seem to have been a common practice by historic Inuit and Eskimo groups according to ethnographic accounts, and pathologies observed on archaeological dog bones seem to indicate that similar treatment of dogs occurred during the precontact period too (Park 1987, 1999; Hill 2018).

Skeletal Pathologies and Trauma

The pathologies observed on dog remains evidence some of the experiences and the management of the dogs at Nunalleq. In traditional Yup'ik culture, dogs that were disobedient, fought, took food, or chewed their harnesses were physically punished or may have been muzzled by skin strips tied around their mouths (Fienup-Riordan 2007). In archaeological studies of dog remains from Arctic contexts, injuries have been identified on bones and interpreted as evidence of discipline or punishment (Losey et al. 2014; Park 1987, 1999). These injuries are generally associated with beatings to the head and face, which can result in fractures to the cranium and facial bones (e.g., Crockford 1997).

At Nunalleq a number of dog bones exhibit pathologies consistent with such physical injuries (Figure 4.2; McManus-Fry 2015:210–211). One maxilla exhibited a fracture of the inferior eye socket, consistent with a blow to the face. An intact cranium had a perforating injury to the right frontal bone, through the frontal sinus and perforating the palatal bone. This could be related to a strong impact from a sharp implement that traveled through the whole skull and would certainly have been fatal, similar to injuries identified by Robert W. Park (1987) on dogs from the Thule site of Porden Point. Cutmarks across the occipital condyles indicate that this dog was decapitated and the skull removed from the upper cervical vertebrae (Figure 4.2). Another complete adult dog skull exhibited a well-healed blunt-force trauma injury to the right frontal bone in the form of a curved indentation. The healed results of a probable similar trauma were also identified on a juvenile skull (McManus-Fry 2015:211). A healed rib fracture was also identified, possibly related to an impact to the side of the body. As well as pathologies consistent with the management of dogs by force, perforations on dog crania likely evidence fighting between dogs at Nunalleq (McManus-Fry 2015:211), as observed at other sites (e.g., Park 1987).

The healed nature of some wounds suggests that the dogs of Nunalleq may have received care and treatment after an injury, or at least that dogs were suf-

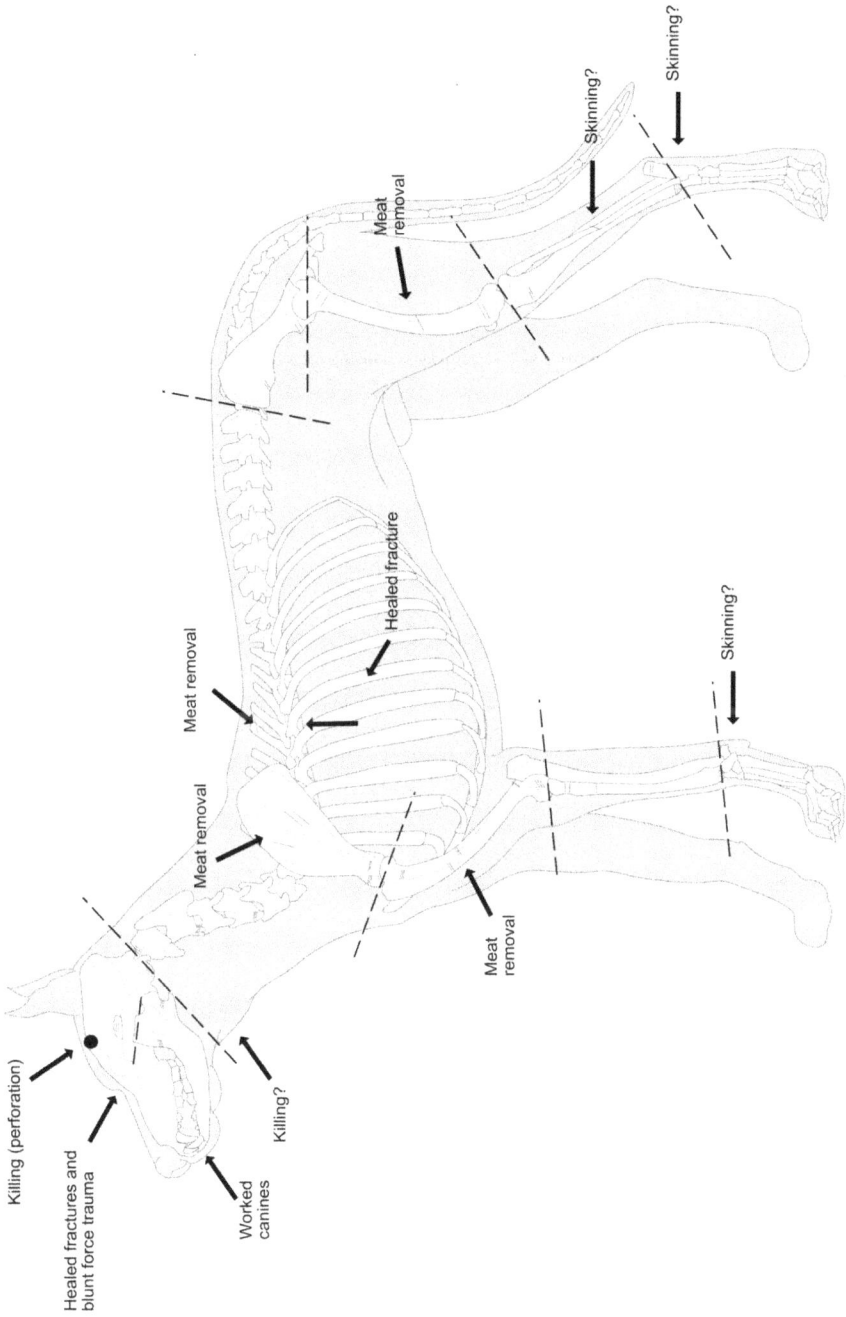

Figure 4.2. Summary of the main modifications and pathologies on domestic dog remains at Nunalleq.

ficiently important and valuable to still be fed and maintained despite a possibly impaired ability to work. Healed wounds include those from human-inflicted injuries described above, and others, such as a fractured and healed (albeit misaligned) right fibula and other skeletal components with evidence of bone thickening and new bone formation consistent with infections (McManus-Fry 2015:212). The care of dogs is also indicated by ethnographic accounts of Inuit hunters making other efforts to protect and strengthen dogs. For example, to protect dogs' feet from cold and cuts on snow and ice, blubber was spread over the pads of paws. Additional efforts could also be made to help ensure the dogs were strong and healthy for hunting and pulling sleds. For example, seal tooth amulets were sometimes tied to dog's necks to ensure hard bites when fighting prey, and caribou sinew hung around the necks of puppies to promote health and strength (Cummins 2013).

Dogs in Primary and Secondary Products

Based on ethnographic and historical evidence from across the Arctic, the dogs of Nunalleq likely had utility beyond their physical actions and living bodies. This is confirmed by both artifactual and ecofactual evidence from the site, including their likely use for skins and furs, tool-making, and other material culture. Their use as meat in human foodways is also likely.

One use for domestic dogs for which there is ample ethnographic evidence among Indigenous Alaskan and Canadian peoples is the use of dog fur and skin for clothing. Dog fur was used in clothing for infants and was also particularly favored for parka ruffs (Issenman 2011; Lantis 1980), as its long guard hairs and uneven texture prevented the build-up of frost around the hood (Issenman 2011:39). Dog skins were also valued for their resistance to shedding and other damage when moist. The use of dog fur in fishing lures (VanStone 1989:13) and as mask decoration (Issenman 2011) is also documented. While preserved skins, some with fur still attached, have been found at Nunalleq, none of these have yet to be confirmed to be canine in origin. Cutmarks, found on more than 20% of the dog bones found at Nunalleq, may, however, be consistent with the removal of feet and skinning—particularly cutmarks observed on tibia and metapodial bones.

At Nunalleq, hair and fur are common finds on house floors. In addition to the isotopic and genetic analyses of the more easily recognizable human hair, a recent pilot study was also conducted on animal fur from the site, including the speciation of samples using light microscopy (Skillin 2016). As part of this

study, fibers that had previously been identified in the matrix of a large proportion of clay lamps from the site (Figure 4.3) were examined and determined to
be dog in all cases.

Given that only one (pheno)type of dog has been found at the site, it is unlikely that wool dogs (a small breed kept for their woolly fur and shorn like
sheep) were raised at Nunalleq specifically for this or other purposes. Instead,
dog fur used in the lamps was probably removed or shed directly from the same
dogs used in other activities at the site. Two types of canid fur, likely guard hairs
and underfur, were identified in the lamps, which may be consistent with the
different seasons these hairs are shed in dogs and the season of lamp production
(Skillin 2016).

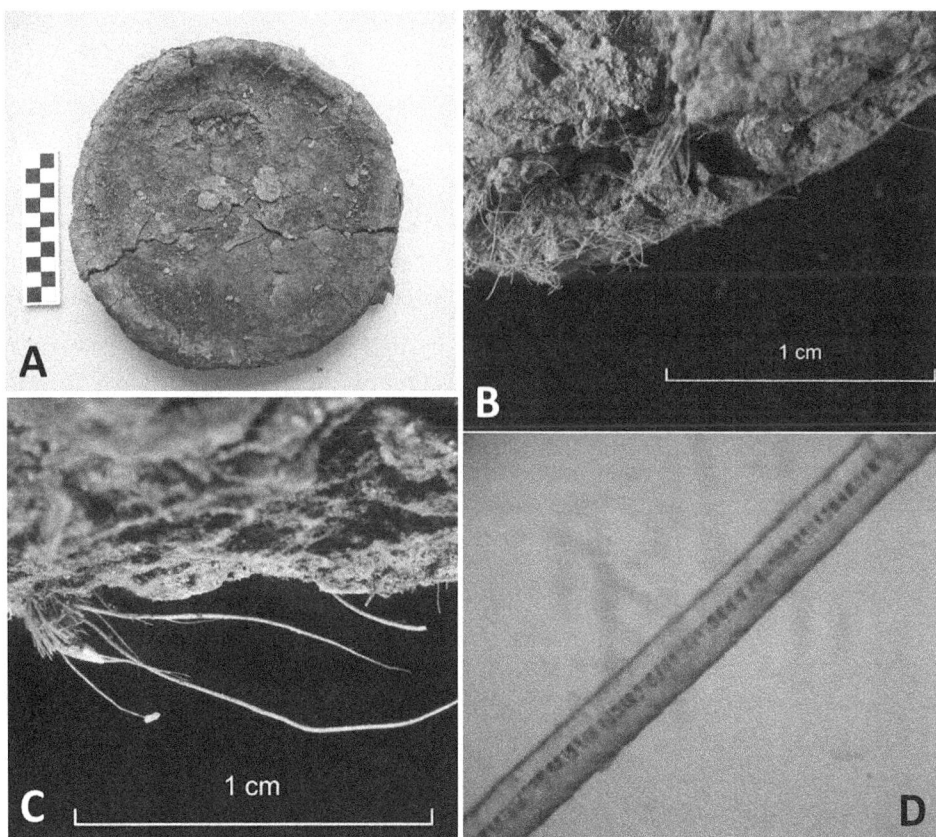

Figure 4.3. An example of a clay lamp from Nunalleq (A), with two types of fur (B), visible during macroscopic
analysis of sherds (C). Analysis via light microscopy (400× magnification) allowed the identification of both dog
underfur and guard hairs (D). Photographs by Ana Jorge (A–C) and Kristina Skillin (D).

While archaeological and ethnographic literature from Alaska and Canada mentions the use of hair or fur as temper for pottery, the Nunalleq study is the first that dog fur has been positively identified in Arctic ceramics. The choice of dog fur for lamps may have been one of practicality (given the abundance of shed dog fur found on house floors at the site) or may reflect a cultural preference. The fact that dog fur was used for lamps but not in the hundreds of pots also found at Nunalleq seems to support a cultural preference. In the same pilot study, fur from other species such as hare and seal were associated with the manufacture of other objects and clothing (Skillin 2016), suggesting the ubiquity of dog fur in lamps results from its preferential selection rather than a lack of other options. These findings are significant as it marks use of a secondary product (fur) that could be "harvested" during the life of Alaska's only Indigenous domesticate. The choice of dog for lamps (bringing light and warmth into the home) may be consistent with contemporary cultural perception of dogs as animals able to transcend wild and domestic spheres.

In addition to the use of dog skin and fur, two further utilitarian uses of canid raw materials were identified at Nunalleq. During the preliminary examination of bone technology at the site, two worked dog canines were identified as being modified to make carving implements, similar to other worked faunal teeth at the site (e.g., fox, bear, mustelid, and beluga). A further final and certainly terminal utilitarian use for dogs at Nunalleq was the (at least occasional) consumption of their meat. Documented historically and ethnographically, dog meat eating, particularly in times of scarcity, was common among circumpolar Indigenous communities (Laugrand and Oosten 2002; Park 1987). At Nunalleq the possible consumption of dog meat and the intricate dietary relationships between humans and the North American Arctic's omnivorous and only domesticate were examined using multiple approaches.

Dogs in Foodways at Nunalleq and Beyond

The consideration of dogs in the foodways of Nunalleq includes two distinct concerns: the need to provision for an omnivorous domesticate whose niche so closely overlaps with its human keepers and also the possibility that dog meat itself could have formed part of the human diet.

Provisioning for the North American Arctic's Indigenous Omnivorous Domesticate

Due to their similar dietary requirements to humans, provisioning for dogs would have represented an additional demand on the subsistence hunting and fishing activities at Nunalleq. Dogs, like humans, would have been dependent on the geographical and seasonal spread of the resources around them as well as the ability of their human keepers to manage their feeding in the face of seasonal variation in prey availability. As with other aspects of the human-canine relationship, historical and ethnographic records provide an insight into the types of foods that dogs in western Alaska may have consumed in the past.

Subsistence-caught fish (either fresh or dried) is a documented staple food for sled dogs in the region (Andersen 1992; Michael 1967:116; Ray 1966:44). Salmon in particular are used today, especially species less desirable for human consumption such as chum salmon, which is known colloquially as "dog salmon" or "dog food" throughout southern Alaska and the Aleutian Islands (Lynn Church, Quinhagak, personal communication, 2015). Elsewhere in Alaska, historical and ethnographic accounts commonly describe the feeding of fish and roe to dogs, especially fermented or frozen fish and roe (e.g., on Nunivak Island; VanStone 1989:31). The feeding of other foods less favored by humans, such as shrimp and birds, has also been described elsewhere (Nelson 1969), as has the feeding of non-favored parts of hunted animals, including caribou lungs and kidneys, to dogs, such as on Nunivak Island (VanStone 1989:30). With seals, non-favored parts would include the organs such as the spleen and lungs, and with walrus, the majority of the carcass, aside from certain organs (the heart, liver, kidneys, brain), ribs, and flippers, which were reserved for human consumption, would have been fed to dogs (Spencer 1959). The remains of marine mammals, washed up after the breakup of sea ice in the spring, may also have formed an important supplement to dogs' diet, and the splitting of carcasses and feeding of dog teams on the beach was a practice common in Quinhagak until the late 1970s (John Smith, Quinhagak, personal communication, 2018).

Richard K. Nelson (1969) notes seasonal differences in dog diet in northern Alaska, including blubber in winter and seal meat in summer. In the region to the north of the Y-K Delta, a seasonally varying diet was also observed; dogs were fed seal, salmon roe, and salmon intestines in the summer and dried salmon heads and spines with flesh adhering in the winter (Jenness 1970:19, 60). The quantity and type of food and frequency of feedings is likely to have varied seasonally as well, reflecting not only the abundance and seasonality of resources but also the energy requirements of the dogs. For example, dogs near Bethel in the Y-K Delta were fed every day in winter but only every other day in summer (Weinland 1884, as cited by Lantis 1980:18).

Biomolecular Evidence for Dog Diet at Nunalleq

Alongside an extensive human dietary study at Nunalleq, the stable isotope analysis of domestic dog remains was also undertaken to reconstruct dogs' diet and how it differed from human diet (Britton et al. 2018; McManus-Fry et al. 2018). Mixing models used to identify probable dietary combinations from carbon and isotope data revealed that the dogs of Nunalleq, like the human inhabitants, were probably eating a range of foods, including marine mammals and terrestrial resources such as caribou, but with a significant amount of protein derived from fish such as salmonids (McManus-Fry et al. 2018).

The feeding of subsistence-caught fish to dogs in the precontact Y-K Delta is consistent with historic and ethnographic evidence. Of fish remains at the site, a large number were identified as salmonids, most likely Pacific salmon or trout (*Oncorhynchus* sp.). While vertebrae were the most common elements found (typical of North Pacific rim sites), salmonid vertebrae are notoriously difficult to identify to species. Various studies have employed different methods to differentiate species, including aDNA, radiography, and osteometrics (Huber et al. 2011; Moss et al. 2014; Orchard and Szpak 2011; Speller et al. 2005). A test sample of vertebrae from Nunalleq (n = 27) were identified using ancient mitochondrial DNA analysis (research by Camilla Speller, Krista McGrath, University of York). This study confirmed the predominance of salmon and identified several *Oncorhynchus* species including chum (n = 11), sockeye (n = 6), Chinook (n = 5), coho (n = 3), and pink (n = 2). Given the small sample size, it is unlikely that this is representative of salmon exploitation at the site, but it does demonstrate that all species of *Oncorhynchus* were exploited (Masson-MacLean 2018). The prevalence of chum is surprising, given that it tends not to be a species favored for human consumption, but may be consistent with the importance of this salmon species in provisioning for dogs at the site.

Coprolite Evidence for Dog Diet and Health at Nunalleq

In addition to the osteological and biomolecular evidence for diet at Nunalleq, another potential source of dietary information for both humans and canids has presented itself in abundance across house floors in the form of coprolites. A pilot study assessing the coprolites is ongoing, including analysis of their provenance and chemical, macro-, and microscopic content. Analysis of fecal stanols via gas chromatography–mass spectrometry (undertaken by Loïc Harrault) showed high contents of coprostanol and epicoprostanol compared to 24-ethylcoprostanol, 24-ethylepicoprostanol, and other phytostanols (see Table 4.2). Further statistical multivariate analysis (Harrault et al. 2019) allowed the positive identification of a number of canid coprolites (Loïc Harrault, personal communication, 2017; see Figure 4.4). Visual assessment of dog coprolites indicates fish bone is present in a number of samples, and biomolecular analysis to identify coprolite content to species is ongoing by Anne-Kathrine Runge.

Paul Ledger and Angela Perri's examination of coprolites using light microscopy revealed a surprising range of pollen and coprophilous fungi, along with the eggs of *Nanophyetus* and *Diphyllobothrium* spp. (Ledger 2018:421; P. Ledger and A. Perri, personal communication, 2017). The *Diphyllobothrium* worm and the *Rickettsia* bacteria, for which the parasite *Nanophyetus salmincola* serves as a vector, can cause severe and potentially fatal conditions in dogs. Such para-

Table 4.2. Distribution (%) and concentration of 5β -stanols

	Distribution *5β-stanols (%)*		*Concentration* *5β-Stanols (µg/g DW)*	
Sample ID	S-15438	S-15375	S-15438	S-15375
Coprostanol	51.8%	47.6%	239.1	25.6
Epicoprostanol	40.6%	22.4%	187.3	12.0
Brassicastanol	0.0%	0.0%	0.0	0.0
Lichestanol	1.3%	13.6%	5.9	7.3
Epibrassicastanol	0.0%	0.0%	0.0	0.0
5β-Campestanol	0.8%	6.7%	3.8	3.6
5β-Epicampestanol	0.6%	0.0%	2.7	0.0
5β-Stigmastanol	0.7%	0.0%	3.1	0.0
5β-Epistigmastanol	0.0%	0.0%	0.0	0.0
5β-Ethylcoprostanol	3.4%	9.7%	15.5	5.2
5β-Ethylepicoprostanol	0.8%	0.0%	3.8	0.0
Total	100.0%	100.0%	461.2	53.7

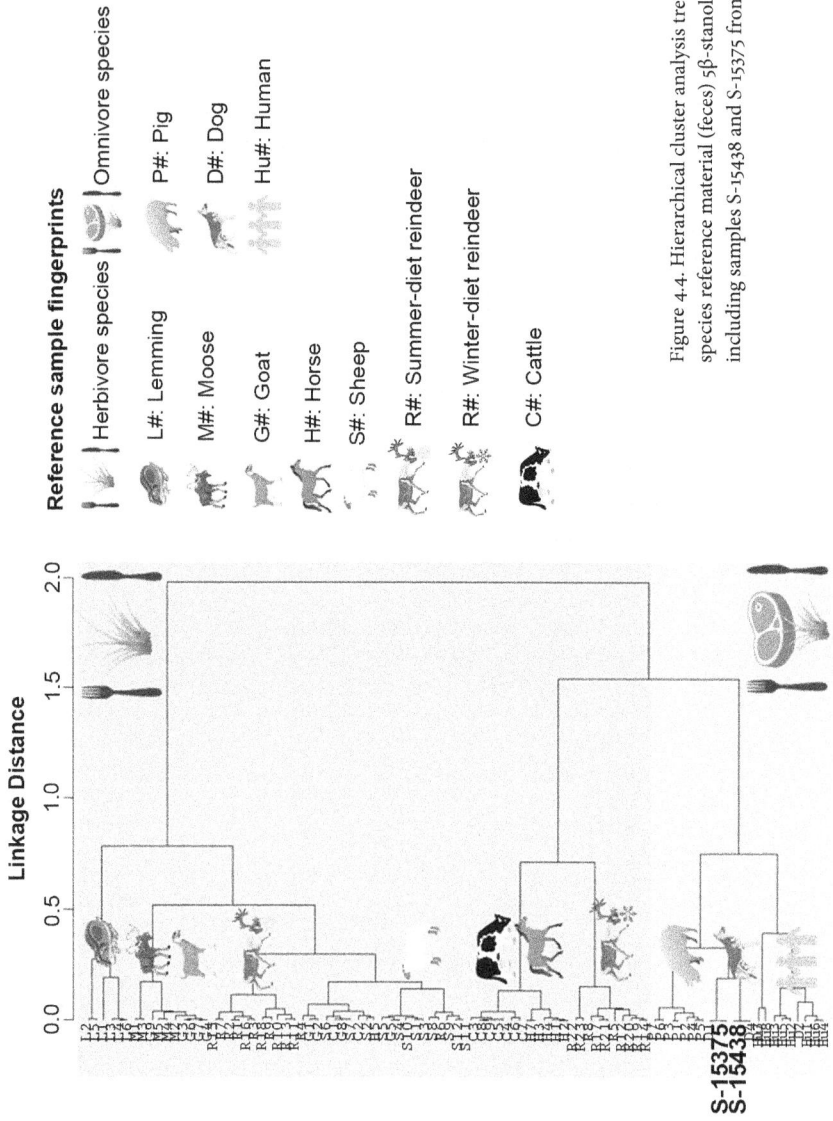

Reference sample fingerprints

Herbivore species | Omnivore species

L#: Lemming   P#: Pig

M#: Moose   D#: Dog

G#: Goat   Hu#: Human

H#: Horse

S#: Sheep

R#: Summer-diet reindeer

R#: Winter-diet reindeer

C#: Cattle

Figure 4.4. Hierarchical cluster analysis tree model showing the distinction between species reference material (feces) 5β-stanol fingerprints and soil sample fingerprints, including samples S-15438 and S-15375 from Nunalleq.

sites and resultant salmon poisoning disease (in the case of *N. salmincola*) are common along the northwest coast of North America (Bathurst 2005) and are associated with the consumption of uncooked fish. This confirms that subsistence-caught salmon likely had a key role in the diet of the dogs of Nunalleq and also indicates that the health status of at least some of the dogs may not have been favorable.

Evidence for Dogs in the Human Diet at Nunalleq

The zooarchaeological analysis of dog remains, including age determination and the analysis of butchery patterns, was undertaken in order to explore the possible consumption of dogs at Nunalleq. Human dietary isotope data, particularly in comparison with dog isotope data, have also provided a useful additional line of evidence for the frequency of dog meat consumption at Nunalleq.

Age at death was estimated based on epiphyseal fusion and tooth eruption (Crockford 2009; Silver 1969:265; Sumner-Smith 1966:306–308) during the faunal analysis (Masson-MacLean 2018; McManus-Fry 2015). There are great limitations to determining the age of dog remains (Hillson 2005:241–242; Sumner-Smith 1966), mainly as a result of early bone fusion rates (most elements are fused before 18 months old) and early eruption of permanent teeth (by 7 months old). Nevertheless, combined epiphyseal fusion and tooth eruption data indicates that young dogs (at least half of which were less than 8–18 months old, and 20–40% of which were less than 7 months old) dominate the Nunalleq assemblage (Masson-MacLean 2018; McManus-Fry 2015). This might be related to their consumption, and indeed there is ethnographic evidence that Alaskan groups raised dogs for meat and consumed juveniles in particular (Spencer 1959:221). The abundance of juveniles may also be related to dog population management through the killing of young individuals (Lantis 1980:13), as dogs require maintenance and large amounts of food (Morey and Aaris-Sørensen 2002:45).

Evidence of the disarticulation and butchery of dog carcasses was also observed at Nunalleq (Masson-MacLean 2018; McManus-Fry 2015). Cutmarks were found on most dog elements, and their location on the bones highlights specific butchery practices (Figure 4.2) such as the systematic separation of the head from the body (71.2% of atlases have cutmarks), the disarticulation of limbs from the carcass (cutmarks on long bone epiphyses, distal scapula, and acetabulum), and the division of the carcass into smaller portions (cutmarks on distal femur and proximal tibia). There was also evidence for the removal of meat on meat-bearing bones such as the scapula, humerus, and femur (transversal cutmarks on shaft), as well as the removal of the feet and the skin (cutmarks on astragalus, calcaneus, and metapodials). The frequencies of cutmarks on just over a fifth of all dog remains does not necessarily suggest that dogs were commonly consumed or formed any significant proportion of the diet. Nevertheless, it is apparent that, in certain circumstances, dogs were being butchered at Nunalleq.

Discussion: Dogs in the Human Diet at Nunalleq and Beyond

There is ample archaeological, historical, and ethnographic evidence for the consumption of domestic dogs from across the North American Arctic. For example, at Porden Point, Devon Island, Robert Park (1999) found that dogs that had probably been used for traction or load carrying were ultimately processed for consumption. Examination of animal bones from more recent (sixteenth- and seventeenth-century) deposits on Kodiak Island included the identification of many dog bones that bore the marks of butchery in the forms of knife cuts (Clark 1974). As at Nunalleq, many of the dog remains were juvenile, and canid gnawing marks suggest that butchered bones were also accessed by dogs (Clark 1974). Robert F. Spencer's (1959) account of life in northern Alaska during the mid-twentieth century states that some inland groups raised dogs for their meat, that they were preferentially killed and eaten "in the puppy stage" (Spencer 1959:223–374), and that the skins were used for clothing. Park (1999) also makes similar observations in northern Alaska but notes that consuming dog meat was generally reserved for times of resource stress. Similarly, Spencer (1959) states that coastal groups in northern Alaska ate dog less often than their inland counterparts, not due to some taboo or prohibition but more due to the economic value of the living dog among coastal groups.

At Nunalleq, a series of stable isotope studies on human hair have pointed to a mixed diet, including marine mammals and some caribou but rich in salmonids (Britton et al. 2013; Britton et al. 2018). This diet was very similar to that of the dogs themselves (McManus-Fry et al. 2018), evidencing the mutual dependence of dogs and people in the foodways of Nunalleq—with dogs aiding subsistence activities through transportation or directly through hunting, and with their owners, in turn, providing at least some of these resources to the dogs. However, cutmarks on dog bones confirm this dietary relationship extended to the consumption of dog meat and that there was no taboo against this at Nunalleq. Age profiles may suggest a favoring of younger animals for this purpose, as described ethnographically in northern Alaska (Spencer 1959), but may also be a reflection of the culling of young, probably male dogs to manage the population, a practice found in many dog-owning cultures (Morey 1986:120).

When viewed together, zooarchaeological and biomolecular data provide a clearer picture of the dietary role of dog meat at Nunalleq. The butchery marks on dog bones are not frequent enough to indicate that dogs formed a large proportion of the human diet and are not consistent with the keeping of dogs solely as a food source. Furthermore, stable isotope data from human hair at the site are not sufficiently enriched in nitrogen-15 relative to the dogs themselves, again implying that dog meat was not consumed regularly or in any great quantity. It is instead more likely that dogs contributed to a strategy of resilience, providing a source of food in periods of scarcity. In this sense, the fate of dogs at Nunalleq was determined by a delicate balance between their usefulness for haulage, hunting, and other living purposes and the nutritional demands they put on the community. When their contribution decreased as a result of age, injury, lack of discipline, or external factors such as changes to prey abundance, they may have been exploited for other resources (their meat, skins, and furs). In this sense, the relationship between humans and dogs would have been a critical aspect of the exploitation of faunal resources at Nunalleq. Their nutritional demands, the similarity between human and dog diet, and mutual dependency in the obtaining of foodstuffs implies that the provisioning of dogs was an important consideration in human subsistence activities. In this way, the role of dogs in foodways at Nunalleq emphasizes the unique position of dogs in the precontact Y-K Delta.

"The Animal Members of Society"

The belief that animals have agency and the conception of them as "other-than-human persons" (Hallowell 1960) is central to the traditional Yup'ik perception of the natural world (Hill 2011). Typically, as with much of the discussion between hunter-gatherers and animals in academic literature, the focus is often placed on the conceptualization of the prey animal and on the complex respect relationship of the hunter's intention (to hunt) and the prey's permission (to allow the hunt; Nelson 1984 [1899]). In historical and ethnographic literature of the region, less has been written about the ontological relationship between humans and their dogs, perhaps due to the misconception that the relationship between domestic animals is more straightforward and relatable to Western scholars conducting research; this is unlikely to have been the case, however. Indeed, for many Arctic communities, dogs may have held a unique sociocultural and even spiritual role. In their discussion of the Canadian Arctic, Frédéric Laugrand and Jarich Oosten (2002:91) describe dogs as "the animal members of society" and highlight the role of dogs (and in particular the killing or maiming of dogs) in Inuit healing rituals.

In traditional Yup'ik culture, dogs are generally respected and are considered wise, particularly for their ability to remember paths they have traveled and guide their owners to safety (Fienup-Riordan 2007). Dogs feature in a number of Yup'ik stories and rituals in which they are sometimes represented as kin. Fienup-Riordan (2007:329) describes a ceremony called Aaniryaraq, celebrated in some coastal and Kuskokwim communities, in which two men, referred to as mothers, lead a group of boys, referred to as their dogs, around the village receiving bowls of akutaq ("Eskimo ice cream" traditionally made with seal fat and berries) from women. The Dog Husband story is a traditional Yup'ik folk tale of how Nunivak Island was populated by a woman from the mainland who married a dog and traveled to the island, where she had several pups, who, through her teaching, came to have human minds (Fienup-Riordan 1983:236–238). In this sense, we can understand that dogs may be perceived as intermediate between the domestic sphere and the external, wild sphere, both practically and symbolically.

Representation of Dogs in Material Culture at Nunalleq

Based on the rich ethnographic record and oral history for the region, animals have traditionally had a central utilitarian and symbolic role in the Yup'ik physical and spiritual world (Fienup-Riordan 2000). The Yup'ik universe was composed of three layered worlds: underwater, land, and sky, with humans living in the terrestrial world. Animals that could transcend these boundaries had a high symbolic value and were often depicted on utilitarian objects or represented in art forms such as carvings (Fienup-Riordan 1990).

In the material culture from Nunalleq, a number of animals are represented (Table 4.3), some of which, such as seals and marine birds, can travel between worlds. Seal remains were also abundant in the faunal record, suggesting they played an important economic as well as symbolic role precontact. This contrasts starkly with marine birds, which are commonly represented in the material culture or art from Nunalleq but whose remains were infrequent at the site, suggesting their symbolic value largely exceeded their utilitarian role. On the other hand, animals that are restricted to the terrestrial world, such as caribou, are not often represented despite the abundance of their faunal remains and their high economic value. For example, not only do caribou provide food, but

Table 4.3. Taxonomic identifications (NISP) in artforms

Taxon	NISP (artforms)	%	NISP (faunal bone)	%
Marine bird	52	26.3%	586	5.7%
Land bird	6	3.0%	85	0.8%
Total birds	58	29.3%	671	6.5%
Seal	67	33.8%	2,769	26.9%
Walrus	8	4.0%	89	0.9%
Cetacean	15	7.6%	113	1.1%
Total marine mammals	90	45.5%	2,971	28.9%
Fish	25	12.6%	2,608	25.3%
Caribou	6	3.0%	1,865	18.1%
Domestic dog	**0**	**0.0%**	**1,796**	**17.5%**
Wolf	2	1.0%	12	0.1%
Other land mammals	1	0.5%	367	3.6%
Total land mammals	9	4.5%	4,040	39.26%
Zoomorphic	16	8.1%	-	-
Total	198	100%	10,290	100%

they were also a valuable source of raw material, including hide for clothing and antler for making hunting implements, tools, and objects (Betts 2016).

While the utilitarian role of dogs at Nunalleq is evident in the archaeology across the site, the iconographic absence of dogs in material culture from the site is notable. This may indeed be consistent with a (possible) spiritual role of dogs or, at the very least, with the notion that they were considered different from other animals.

Dogs in Social Space at Nunalleq

The physical presence of dogs at Nunalleq is evidenced by bones from across the site, both dog bones themselves and also the bones of other animals, particularly caribou, which show ample evidence of dog gnawing (Masson-MacLean 2018; McManus-Fry 2015). Dog gnawing can also be seen on a number of artifact types, particularly discarded wooden labrets that, presumably after months serving as facial piercings, may have had a certain appealing umami flavor. Coprolites found in outside spaces and within the walkways and various structures at Nunalleq also attest to the presence of dogs in social spaces shared with humans.

Study of the invertebrate remains from deposits across the site, including house floors, illuminates activity zones, living conditions, and even the broader environment (see Forbes et al. 2015). In addition to human lice, dog-biting lice have been identified at the site. Not only do these lice provide additional useful information about the health status and parasite load of the dogs of Nunalleq, but—when found in house floor deposits—can provide a proxy for the presence of dogs in the various spaces of the site. Concentrations of dog-biting lice and dog fur, in the site's northwest Structure 5 in particular (Figure 4.5), highlights that this space may have served as a dog sleeping space. While the sheltering of dogs inside structures may have been essential in the coldest conditions for the protection of the dogs themselves, it may also indicate that dogs provided

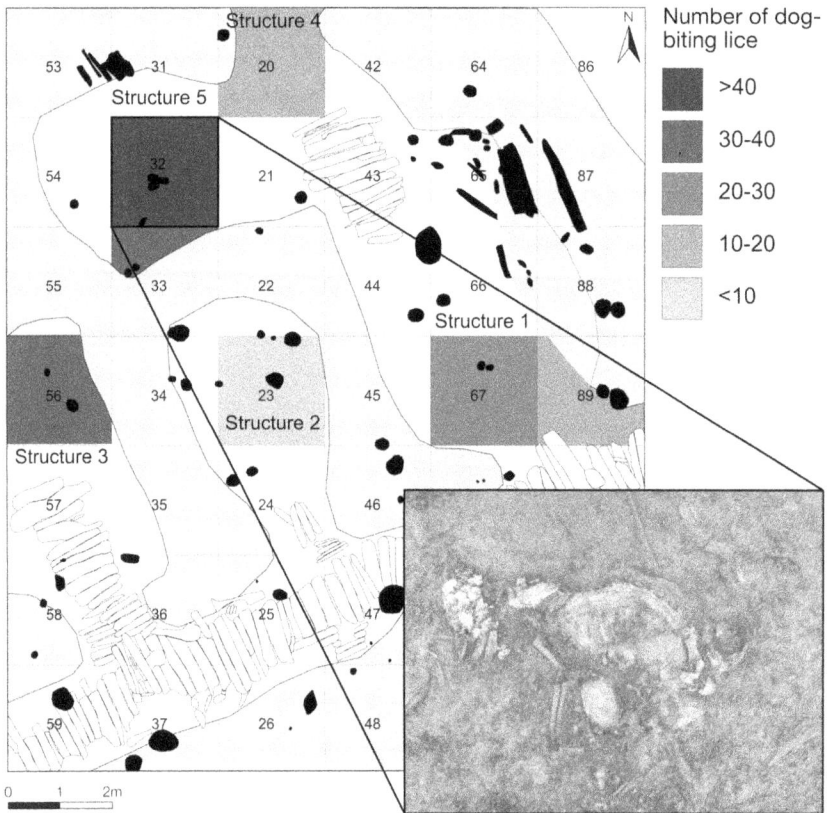

Figure 4.5. Partial plan of Area A of the Nunalleq site, detailing concentrations of dog-biting lice identified in different house floor deposits, with inset of a complete dog found preserved at the site.

protection for those housed at Nunalleq or hint that some animals were kept more like pets.

The burned, complete remains of several dogs were also found in Structure 5 (Figure 4.5, inset). Associated with the final phase of the site and the attack that resulted in its destruction, the complete skeleton of one young dog was likely tied up within the house (evidenced by cordage associated with it) and was probably crushed by falling wooden supports as the house burned. Another complete dog carcass was found in Structure 1, to the western edge of the site, a very young puppy enclosed in a woven grass basket. This carcass, buried with apparent care, again may attest to the special relationship between dogs and humans at Nunalleq, the possible keeping of dogs as pets rather than just as working animals. Both the juvenile dog shown in Figure 4.5 and the very young, likely neonate, dog buried in the basket may also attest to the cultural value and differential treatment of young dogs compared to older animals. The care and attention given here to puppies, their presence in the house and the putative burial, mirrors ethnographic observations that highlight the great care Canadian Inuit took to bring up puppies in order for them to become useful members of society (Laugrand and Oosten 2014:158), thus contrasting with the harsher treatment some adult dogs received (Park 1987).

Concluding Remarks

Nunalleq represents an unparalleled opportunity to investigate the archaeology of dogs beyond their domestication in this understudied region. Evidence of their utilitarian roles, management, and lived experiences is ubiquitous at the site. Artifacts such as sled runners attest to their use as sled dogs, while their abundant skeletal remains demonstrate their diet, their treatment at the hands of their owners, and even their occasional consumption. The identification of dog fur used as temper in the matrix of clay lamps and of burin-like tools manufactured from dog canines are the first such examples recorded at an archaeological site in Alaska. The rich record at Nunalleq, including fur, dog coprolites, and even dog-biting lice found in house floor deposits, also provides evidence for the areas of the site used by dogs as well as their health status and parasite load. Material culture enables further insights into the function of dogs and animal-human relationships at the site. Iconographic forms, particularly of game species, are abundant on the numerous artifact types found, but dogs are conspicuous in their absence from such objects.

This highlights the role of dogs as socioculturally and even spiritually separate from both wild animals and humans. While differential treatment of puppies and adult dogs highlights that *a dog's purpose* might shift during its life, the nuanced record from Nunalleq confirms that, as well as being working animals, dogs pervaded domestic life at the site. Sleeping in side-rooms and manifest as furs and skins, worked bone technology, and even as part of the fabric of lamps, dogs inhabited a unique physical, social, and cultural space in the precontact Yup'ik world.

Acknowledgments

This research was funded by an AHRC (AH/K006029/1) grant awarded to Rick Knecht, Kate Britton, and Charlotta Hillerdal (Aberdeen); an AHRC-LabEx award (AH/N504543/1) to Kate Britton, Rick Knecht, Keith Dobney (Liverpool), and Isabelle Sidéra (Nanterre); a PhD studentship to Ellen McManus-Fry from NERC (2210 GG005 RGA1521); and the MPI-EVA. The on-site collection of samples was carried out by staff and students from the University of Aberdeen, volunteer excavators, and the residents of Quinhagak. We had logistical and planning support for fieldwork by Qanirtuuq Incorporated, Quinhagak, Alaska, and the people of Quinhagak, who we also thank for sampling permissions. Special thanks to Warren Jones and Qanirtuuq Incorporated (especially Michael Smith and Lynn Church) and to all Nunalleq project team members, in Aberdeen and at other institutions, particularly all the contributors who have allowed us to discuss their research on the dogs of Nunalleq in this chapter, which has greatly enriched it. This includes Camilla Speller and Krista McGrath (University of York) for contributions to the section "Biomolecular Evidence for Dog Diet at Nunalleq"; Loïc Harrault (University of Aberdeen and Durham University), Paul Ledger (University of Aberdeen and Memorial University), Angela Perri (Durham University) and Anne-Kathrine Runge (University of York) for research discussed in the section "Coprolite Evidence for Dog Diet and Health at Nunalleq"; Rick Knecht (University of Aberdeen) and Claire Houmard (UMR 7055, Préhistoire et Technologie, National Museum of Denmark) for their work on the technoculture at Nunalleq, as discussed in the sections "Representation of Dogs in Material Culture at Nunalleq" and "Dogs in Primary and Secondary Products"; Ana Jorge and Kristina Skillin (University of Aberdeen) for their research on fur contained in the clay lamps discussed in the section "Dogs in Primary and Secondary Products"; Carly Ameen (University of Liverpool and University of Exeter) for her research on dog morphology and genetic history in the section "A New Breed? Morphological and Genetic Evidence"; and Véronique Forbes (University of Aberdeen and Memorial University) for her research on parasites at the site, as explored in "Dogs in Social Space at Nunalleq."

References Cited

Alaska Department of Fish and Game
2006   *Our Wealth Maintained: A Strategy for Conserving Alaska's Diverse Wildlife and Fish Resources.* Alaska Department of Fish and Game, Juneau.

Ameen, Carly
2018   A New Look at an Old Friend: A Geometric Morphometric Approach to Examining Morphological Diversity and Human-Canid Relationships in New World Prehistory. PhD thesis, University of Liverpool, Liverpool.

Andersen, David B.
1992   The Use of Dog Teams and the Use of Subsistence-Caught Fish for Feeding Sled Dogs in the Yukon River Drainage. Technical Paper, Vol. 121, Alaska Department of Fish and Game, Juneau.

Arnold, Charles D.
1979   Possible Evidence of Domestic Dog in a Paleoeskimo Context. *Arctic* 32(3):263–265.

Balikci, Asen
1970   *The Netsilik Eskimo.* Natural History Press, Garden City, New York.

Barone, Robert
1976   *Anatomie comparée des mammifères domestiques,* Tome 1, Fascicule 2. Vigot frères, Paris.

Bathurst, Rhonda R.
2005   Archaeological Evidence of Intestinal Parasites from Coastal Shell Middens. *Journal of Archaeological Science* 32(1):115–123.

Betts, Matthew
2016   Zooarchaeology and the Reconstruction of Ancient Human-Animal Relationships in the Arctic. In *The Oxford Handbook of the Prehistoric Arctic,* edited by Max T. Friesen, and Owen K. Mason, pp. 81–108. Oxford University Press, New York.

Britton, Kate, Richard A. Knecht, Olaf Nehlich, Charlotta Hillerdal, Richard S. Davis, and Michael P. Richards
2013   Maritime Adaptations and Dietary Variation in Prehistoric Western Alaska: Stable Isotope Analysis of Permafrost-Preserved Human Hair. *American Journal of Physical Anthropology* 151(3):448–461.

Britton, Kate, Ellen McManus-Fry, Olaf Nehlich, Michael P. Richards, Paul M. Ledger, and Richard A. Knecht
2018   Stable Carbon, Nitrogen and Sulphur Isotope Analysis of Permafrost Preserved Human Hair from Rescue Excavations (2009, 2010) at the Precontact Site of Nunalleq, Alaska. *Journal of Archaeological Science: Reports* 17:950–963.

Clark, Donald Woodforde
1974   *Contributions to the Later Prehistory of Kodiak Island, Alaska.* National Museums of Canada, Ottawa.

Crockford, Susan J.

1997   *Osteometry of Makah and Coast Salish Dogs.* Archaeology Press, Simon Fraser University, Burnaby, British Columbia.

2009   *A Practical Guide to in situ Dog Remains for the Field Archaeologist.* Pacific Identifications, Victoria, British Columbia.

Cummins, Bryan David

2013   *Our Debt to the Dog: How the Domestic Dog Helped Shape Human Societies.* Carolina Academic Press, Durham, North Carolina.

Fienup-Riordan, Ann

1983   *The Nelson Island Eskimo: Social Structure and Ritual Distribution.* Alaska Pacific University Press, Anchorage.

1990   *Eskimo Essays: Yup'ik Lives and How We See Them.* Rutgers University Press, New Jersey.

2000   *Hunting Tradition in a Changing World: Yup'ik Lives in Alaska Today.* Rutgers University Press, New Brunswick, New Jersey.

2007   *Yuungnaqpiallerput (The Way We Genuinely Live): Masterworks of Yup'ik Science and Survival.* University of Washington Press, Seattle.

Fienup-Riordan, Ann, and Alice Rearden

2016   *Anguyiim Nalliini/Time of Warring: The History of Bow-and-Arrow Warfare in Southwest Alaska.* Bilingual ed. University of Alaska Press, Fairbanks.

Fienup-Riordan, Ann, Alice Rearden, and Melia Knecht

2015   Irr'inarqellriit/Amazing Things: Quinhagak Elders Reflect on Their Past. *Alaska Journal of Anthropology* 13(2):37–71.

Forbes, Véronique, Kate Britton, and Rick Knecht

2015   Preliminary Archaeoentomological Analyses of Permafrost-Preserved Cultural Layers from the Pre-contact Yup'ik Eskimo Site of Nunalleq, Alaska: Implications, Potential and Methodological Considerations. *Environmental Archaeology* 20(2):158–167.

Ford, James A.

1959   *Eskimo Prehistory in the Vicinity of Point Barrow, Alaska.* Anthropological Papers of the American Museum of Natural History 47(1). American Museum of Natural History, New York.

Friesen, T. Max, and Matthew W Betts

2002   Archaeofaunas and Architecture: Zooarchaeological Variability in an Inuit Semi-subterranean House, Arctic Canada. In *Integrating Zooarchaeology: Proceedings of the 9th Conference of the International Council of Archaeozoology, Durham*, edited by M. Maltby, pp. 65–76. Oxbow, Oxford.

Funk, Caroline

2010   The Bow and Arrow War Days on the Yukon-Kuskokwim Delta of Alaska. *Ethnohistory* 57(4):523–569.

Grouard, Sandrine, Sophia Perdikaris, and Karyne Debue

2013   Dog Burials Associated with Human Burials in the West Indies during the Early Pre-Columbian Ceramic Age (500 BC–600 AD). *Anthropozoologica* 48(2):447–465.

Hallowell, Alfred Irving

1960   Ojibwa Ontology, Behaviour, and World View. In *Culture in History: Essays in Honor of Paul Radin*, edited by S. Diamond, pp. 17–49. Columbia University Press, New York.

Harrault, Loïc, Karen Milek, Emilie Jardé, Laurent Jeanneau, Morgane Derrien, and David Anderson

2019   Faecal Biomarkers Can Distinguish Specific Mammalian Species in Modern and Past Environments. *PLoS ONE* 14(2):e0211119.

Hill, Erica

2011   Animals as Agents: Hunting Ritual and Relational Ontologies in Prehistoric Alaska and Chukotka. *Cambridge Archaeological Journal* 21(3):407–426.

2018   The Archaeology OF Human-Dog Relations in Northwest Alaska. In *Dogs in the North: Stories of Cooperation and Co-domestication*, edited by R. Losey, R. Wishart, and J. Loovers, pp. 87–104. Routledge, New York.

Hillerdal, Charlotta

2017   Integrating the Past in the Present: Archaeology as Part of Living Yup'ik Heritage. In *Archaeologies of "Us" and "Them": Debating History, Heritage and Indigeneity*, edited by C. Hillerdal, A. Karlström, and C.-G. Ojala, pp. 64–79. London: Routledge.

Hillerdal, Charlotta, Richard Knecht, and Warren Jones

2019   Nunalleq: Archaeology, Climate Change and Community Engagement in a Yup'ik Village. (In Press) *Arctic Anthropology*, 56(2).

Hillson, Simon

2005   *Teeth*. 2nd ed. Cambridge University Press, Cambridge.

Huber, Harriet R., Jeffery C. Jorgensen, Virginia L. Butler, Greg Baker, and Rebecca Stevens

2011   Can Salmonids (*Oncorhynchus spp.*) Be Identified to Species Using Vertebral Morphometrics? *Journal of Archaeological Science* 38(1):136–146.

Issenman, Betty Kobayashi

2011   *Sinews of survival: The Living Legacy of Inuit Clothing*. University of British Columbia Press, Vancouver.

Jenness, Aylette

1970   *Dwellers of the Tundra: Life in an Alaska Eskimo Village*. Crowell-Collier Press, New York.

Jonuks, Tõnno, and Eve Rannamäe

2017   Animals and Worldviews: A Diachronic Approach to Tooth and Bone Pendants from the Mesolithic to the Medieval Period in Estonia. In *The Bioarchaeology of Ritual and Religion*, edited by A. Livarda, R. Madgwick and S. Riera Mora, pp. 162–178. Oxbow Books, Oxford.

Kitching, James W.

1963   *Bone, Tooth & Horn Tools of Palaeolithic Man: An Account of the Osteodontokeratic Discoveries in Pin Hole Cave, Derbyshire*. Manchester University Press, Manchester.

Lantis, Margaret

1980   Changes in the Alaskan Eskimo Relation of Man to Dog and Their Effect on Two Human Diseases. *Arctic Anthropology* 17(1):1–25.

Larson, Greger, Elinor K. Karlsson, Angela Perri, Matthew T. Webster, Simon Y. Ho, Yoris Peters, Peter W. Stahl, Philip J. Piper, Frode Lingaas, Merete Fredholm, Kenine E. Comstock, Jaime F. Modiano, Claude Schelling, Alexander I. Agoulnik, Peter A. Leegwater, Keith Dobney, Jean-Denis Vigne, Carles Vilà, Leif Andersson, and Kerstin Lindblad-Toh

2012   Rethinking Dog Domestication by Integrating Genetics, Archaeology, and Biogeography. *Proceedings of the National Academy of Sciences of the United States of America* 109(28):8878–8883.

Laugrand, Frédéric, and Jarich Oosten

2002   Canicide and Healing: The Position of the Dog in the Inuit Cultures of the Canadian Arctic. *Anthropos* 97(1):89–105.

2014   *Hunters, Predators and Prey: Inuit Perceptions of Animals.* Berghahn Books, Oxford.

Lazăr, Cătălin, Monica Mărgărit, and Adrian Bălăşescu

2016   Dogs, Jaws, and Other Stories: Two symbolic Objects Made of Dog Mandibles from Southeastern Europe. *Journal of Field Archaeology* 41(1):101–117.

Ledger, Paul M.

2018   Are Circumpolar Hunter-Gatherers Visible in the Palaeoenvironmental Record? Pollen-Analytical Evidence from Nunalleq, Southwestern Alaska. *Holocene* 28(3):415–426.

Ledger, Paul M., Véronique Forbes, Edouard Masson-MacLean, and Richard A. Knecht

2016   Dating and Digging Stratified Archaeology in Circumpolar North America: A View from Nunalleq, Southwestern Alaska. *Arctic* 69(4):378–390.

Ledger, Paul M., Véronique Forbes, Edouard Masson-MacLean, Charlotta Hillerdal, W. Derek Hamilton, Ellen McManus-Fry, Ana Jorge, Kate Britton, and Richard A. Knecht

2018   Three Generations under One Roof? Bayesian Modeling of Radiocarbon Data from Nunalleq, Yukon-Kuskokwim Delta, Alaska. *American Antiquity*:1–20.

Losey, Robert J., E. Jessup, Tatiana Nomokonova, and Mikhail Sablin

2014   Craniomandibular Trauma and Tooth Loss in Northern Dogs and Wolves: Implications for the Archaeological Study of Dog Husbandry and Domestication. *PLoS ONE* 9(6):e99746.

Mannermaa, Kristiina, Dimitri Gerasimov, Evgeny Girya, and Mikhail V. Sablin

2019   Wild Boar (*Sus scrofa*) Teeth from a Female Burial in Yuzhniy Oleniy Ostrov, Northwestern Russia (c. 6200 cal BC)—Local Rarities or Transported Goods? *Environmental Archaeology* 24(1):79–90.

Masson-MacLean, Edouard

2018   Animals, Subsistence and Society in Yup'ik Prehistory. PhD thesis, University of Aberdeen.

Masson-MacLean, Edouard, Claire Houmard, Rick Knecht, Isabelle Sidéra, Keith Dobney, and Kate Britton,

2019   Pre-contact Adaptations to the Little Ice Age in Southwest Alaska: New Evidence from the Nunalleq Site. *Quaternary International,* in press.

McManus-Fry, Ellen

2015   Pre-contact Ecology, Subsistence and Diet on the Yukon-Kuskokwim Delta. PhD thesis, Department of Archaeology, University of Aberdeen.

McManus-Fry, Ellen, Richard A. Knecht, Keith Dobney, Michael P. Richards, and Kate Britton

2018   Dog-Human Dietary Relationships in Yup'ik Western Alaska: The Stable Isotope and Zooarchaeological Evidence from Pre-contact Nunalleq. *Journal of Archaeological Science: Reports* 17:964–972.

Michael, Henry N.

1967   *Lieutenant Zagoskin's Travels in Russian America, 1842–1844: The First Ethnographic and Geographic Investigations of the Yukon and Kuskokwim Valleys of Alaska.* University of Toronto Press, Toronto.

Morey, Darcy F.

1986   Studies on Amerindian Dogs: Taxonomic Analysis of Canid Crania from the Northern Plains. *Journal of Archaeologial Science* 13:119–145.

Morey, Darcy F., and Kim Aaris-Sørensen

2002   Paleoeskimo Dogs of the Eastern Arctic. *Arctic* 55(1):44–56.

Moss, Madonna L., Kathleen G. Judd, and Brian M. Kemp

2014   Can Salmonids (*Oncorhynchus* spp.) be Identified to Species Using Vertebral Morphometrics? A Test Using Ancient DNA from Coffman Cove, Alaska. *Journal of Archaeological Science* 41:879–889.

Nelson, Edward William

1984 [1899] *The Eskimo about Bering Strait*. In *18th Annual Report of the Bureau of American Ethnology for the Years 1896–97*. Introduction by W. Fitzhugh. Improved reprint. Smithsonian Institution Press, Washington, DC.

Nelson, Richard K.

1969   *Hunters of the Northern Ice*. University of Chicago Press, Chicago.

Orchard, Trevor J., and Paul Szpak

2011   Identification of Salmon Species from Archaeological Remains on the Northwest Coast. In *The Archaeology of North Pacific Fisheries*, edited by Madonna L. Moss, and Aubrey Cannon, pp. 17–29. University of Alaska Press, Fairbanks.

Park, Robert W.

1987   Dog Remains from Devon Island, N.W.T.: Archaeological and Osteological Evidence for Domestic Dog Use in the Thule Culture. *Arctic* 40(3):184–190.

1999   Seal Use and Storage in the Thule Culture of Arctic North America. *Revista de Arqueología Americana* 16:77–97.

Raghavan, Maanasa, Michael DeGiorgio, Anders Albrechtsen, Ida Moltke, Pontus Skoglund, Thorfinn S. Korneliussen, Bjarne Grønnow, Martin Appelt, Hans Christian Gulløv, T. Max Friesen, William Fitzhugh, Helena Malmström, Simon Rasmussen, Jesper Olsen, Linea Melchior, Benjamin T. Fuller, Simon M. Fahrni, Thomas Stafford, Vaughan Grimes, M. A. Priscilla Renouf, Jerome Cybulski, Niels Lynnerup, Marta Mirazon Lahr, Kate Britton, Rick Knecht, Jette Arneborg, Mait Metspalu, Omar E. Cornejo, Anna-Sapfo Malaspinas, Yong Wang, Morten Rasmussen, Vibha Raghavan, Thomas V. O. Hansen, Elza Khusnutdinova, Tracey Pierre, Kirill Dneprovsky, Claus Andreasen, Hans Lange, M. Geoffrey Hayes, Joan Coltrain, Victor A. Spitsyn, Anders Götherström, Ludovic Orlando, Toomas Kivisild, Richard Villems, Michael H. Crawford, Finn C. Nielsen, Jørgen Dissing, Jan Heinemeier, Morten Meldgaard, Carlos Bustamante, Dennis H. O'Rourke, Mattias Jakobsson, M. Thomas P. Gilbert, Rasmus Nielsen, and Eske Willerslev

2014   The Genetic Prehistory of the New World Arctic. *Science* 345(6200): 1255832.

Rasmussen, Knud

1931   The Netsilik Eskimos: Social Life and Spiritual Culture. *Report of the Fifth Thule Expedition* 8(1):1–542.

Ray, Dorothy Jean

1966   H. M. W. Edmonds' Report on the Eskimos of St. Michael and Vicinity. *Anthropological Papers of the University of Alaska* 13(2):1–144.

Silver, I. A.

1969   The Ageing of Domestic Animals. In *Science in Archaeology: A Survey of Progress and Research*, edited by Don R. Brothwell, E. S. Higgs, and Grahame Clark, pp. 283–302. Thames and Hudson, London.

Skillin, Kristina

2016   Splitting Hairs: Testing the Feasibility of Light Microcopy Use on the Identification of Archaeological Cold-Preserved Fur and Hair. MSc Thesis, University of Aberdeen.

Snyder, Lynn M., and Elizabeth A. Moore (editors)

2006 *Dogs and People in Social, Working Economic or Symbolic Interaction*. Oxbow, Oxford.

Speller, Camilla F., Dongya Y. Yang, and Brian Hayden

2005 Ancient DNA Investigation of Prehistoric Salmon Resource Utilization at Keatley Creek, British Columbia, Canada. *Journal of Archaeological Science* 32(9):1378–1389.

Spencer, Robert F.

1959 *The North Alaskan Eskimo: A Study in Ecology and Society*. Smithsonian Institution Press, Washington, DC.

Standford, Dennis

1976 The Walakpa Site Alaska: Its Place in the Birnirk and Thule Cultures. Smithsonian Contributions to Anthropology, Vol. 20. Smithsonian Institution Press, Washington, DC.

Sumner-Smith, Geoff

1966 Observations on Epiphyseal Fusion of the Canine Appendicular Skeleton. *Journal of Small Animal Practice* 7(4):303–311.

VanStone, James W.

1989 *Nunivak Island Eskimo (Yuit) Technology and Material Culture*. Field Museum of Natural History, Chicago.

Wolfe, Robert J., Joseph J. Gross, Steven J. Langdon, John M. Wright, George K. Sherrod, Linda J. Ellanna, Valerie Sumida, and Peter J. Usher

1984 *Subsistence-Based Economies in Coastal Communities of Southwest Alaska*. Technical Paper. Alaska Department of Fish and Game, Juneau.

5

Using Dental Microwear to Understand the Dietary Behavior of Domestic Dogs in Precontact North America

AMANDA BURTT AND LARISA R. G. DESANTIS

The history of dog keeping has come to the forefront of archaeological research in recent years, due in part to advancing technologies for analyzing dog remains in museum collections. Research presented here uses curated dog skeletons to investigate food sharing between people and domestic dogs (*Canis familiaris*) in late precontact North America. Dental microwear texture analysis (DMTA) methodology is applied to analyze tooth surfaces of canids housed at archaeological repositories in Indiana and Wyoming. Archaeologists typically assume domestic dogs were scavengers and that past peoples made little effort to feed them. Domestic dogs have even been described as garbage disposals (Lupo and Janetski 1994:215). Seeing dogs in the past solely as scavengers and not provisioned by human caregivers is problematic and risks undervaluing the interconnectedness of humans and dogs. This research breaks down this singular category of scavenger into two more descriptive categories that can be used to better qualify human-canine food sharing. Using gray wolf (*Canis lupus*) and coyote (*Canis latrans*) dietary behavioral ecologies and DMTA values for comparison, two categories of domestic dog dietary behavior are hypothesized: provisioned consumers and non-provisioned scavengers. These categories are significant because they explain a dog's access to food resources. Categories are determined based on DMTA attributes that suggest either a dog being fed or hunting or scavenging successfully (provisioned consumer) or for signs of potential food stress as inferred via increased carcass utilization (non-provisioned scavenger). These explanatory terms refine the idea of domestic dog scavenging behavior, providing a clearer representation of whether dogs were successfully accessing food resources or were processing bones for the majority of their subsistence. Heavily processing bones would mean that dogs were either provisioned with bones or food resources were inadequate, leaving dogs to exhaust bone refuse.

Bone consumption leaves unique microwear evidence on the surfaces of teeth. DMTA has been used to understand the dietary behavior of carnivores to assess degrees of tough and/or hard food consumption indicative of flesh and bone, respectively (DeSantis 2016). The diets of extant carnivores have been used to better understand dietary behaviors of their extinct relatives (DeSantis et al. 2015, 2019). Research presented here utilizes modern domestic dog relatives, gray wolves and coyotes (with identical tooth arrangements and known feeding behaviors) as a baseline to better understand the diets of domestic dogs living among Indigenous North Americans in the Midwest and on the Northwest Plains.

Research Questions

Domestic dogs in precontact North America filled multiple roles alongside humans (Schwartz 1997) but are most often assumed to be self-sufficient scavengers of food resources (Burleigh and Brothwell 1978:358). While it is safe to assume dogs cohabitating with humans were scavenging food refuse to some degree, this chapter asks, can dental microwear show when domestic dogs are potentially denied access to food resources? In order to answer this question, this research quantifies dental microwear features to determine when domestic dogs are heavily processing bones. If dogs were effectively hunting or consuming fairly fresh kills, their dental microwear will be similar to a dog being intentionally fed. Thus, these two scenarios cannot be differentiated, and both are defined here as *potentially* provisioned consumers. On the other hand, dogs that are heavily processing bone are not effectively acquiring prime food resources or are not allowed access to them (at least for a given point in time during which they are scavenging) and are here defined as non-provisioned scavengers. A non-provisioned scavenger may also be a dog provisioned with bones.

Suggestions have been made that intentionally fed dogs are managed more precisely than dogs that solely scavenge (White et al. 2001; Eriksson and Zagorska 2003). Enacting control requires keeping dogs from seeking out opportunistic feeding opportunities (scavenging), such as tethering or corralling dogs (Ames et al. 2015:279). Identifying attempts to control the diets of dogs has important implications for understanding past human-canine connections, including human perceptions of animal behavior and taboos regarding foods appropriate for dogs.

Dogs who successfully consumed (i.e., provisioned) implies that resources were adequate; unsuccessful (i.e., non-provisioned) scavenging means dogs were exhausting discarded foodstuff (including bones) as a food resource. Archaeological dog remains used in this study provide dental microwear attributes that can be interpreted using the dental microwear attributes of wolves and coyotes. This research indicates that a geographically varied sample of Late Precontact North American domestic dogs are accessing adequate food resources more than being restricted from feeding opportunities, providing evidence that the majority of dogs from archaeological contexts used for this study are provisioned consumers, and fewer are considered non-provisioned scavengers.

Evidence for Understanding the Diets of Late Precontact Dogs

There are several lines of evidence that can and have been used to better understand the lives of dogs in the past (Crockford 2000; Snyder and Moore 2006). They all contribute to understanding ways that dogs were maintained in Native North America and around the world. Taken together, research into the diets of domestic dogs have shown that dogs and humans share foods to varying degrees, and dogs are sometimes not allowed access to food resources for numerous reasons. Several of these lines of evidence are explored here.

Ethnohistoric Accounts of Dog Provisioning

Ethnohistoric documents have helped clarify diverse dog feeding strategies practiced by Native North Americans in the past. With limited documentation of Indigenous peoples describing practices related to feeding and maintaining dogs and vastly differing ways Europeans perceived these practices when encountering and observing people and their dogs, both the ethnographic and historic records are limited in their ability to inform research questions explored here. However, several rich sources enlighten our understanding of human provisioning strategies and provide Indigenous perspectives of dog-keeping practices in the past. Arguably the most informative narrative by an Indigenous person regarding the care of dogs comes from Buffalo Bird Woman (Maaxiiriwia), a Hidatsa elder who shared her traditional knowledge about certain animals and plants with Gilbert Wilson in the early twentieth century.

Wilson then published these accounts in his 1924 work, *The Horse and the Dog in Hidatsa Culture*. The Hidatsa historically occupied sedentary villages in the modern state of North Dakota. Precontact Hidatsa people practiced subsistence strategies that were closely tied to seasons, including horticulture and hunting and gathering (DeMallie and Sturtevant 2001:332).

Specifically, Buffalo Bird Woman gave the following (abbreviated) account of dog feeding practices to Wilson (1924:201) while she was living on the Fort Berthold Reservation in North Dakota:

> As dogs became adult we fed them meat and also cooked corn for them, boiling it into a kind of mush. Anything that turned sour in the lodge, like boiled corn, we gave to the dogs. Any food that was spoiled or for some reason was rejected by the family, was set aside for them. If, on the hunt, an animal was killed that was lean and poor in flesh, it was given to the dogs. . . . In times of scarcity the people cared for their dogs as best they could. They ate the bones that were crushed and broken in cooking and then thrown away. The dogs could chew and gnaw at them and get some food in this way.

Buffalo Bird Woman's account can help guide interpretations of bone consumption by dogs. Within her community, dogs processing large amounts of bone refuse were not necessarily neglected but do indicate a lack of abundant food sources for humans as well as dogs.

Europeans that encountered Native groups had varying understandings and observations of feeding programs employed by Indigenous dog owners. Regarding the Blackfoot, John C. Ewers (1955:307) observed, "The necessity for feeding dogs (which were meat eaters like their masters) must have placed practical limits upon the number of dogs owned in pre-horse days." Dimitri Shimkin, an anthropologist working on the Wind River Reservation, noted this about the Shoshone tribe, "Dogs were highly regarded. They were valuable as watch dogs against the enemy or wolves. In that case they would walk back and forth excitedly and growl. Each family had a couple of dogs. They were fed like people" (Shimkin 1939). Conversely, denying dogs access to food resources has also been noted in various ethnohistoric sources including Claude Lévi-Strauss's *The Way of the Masks,* where a hunting chant regarding dogs not having access to certain animal carcasses is described, "No women shall eat your flesh; no dog shall insult you" (Lévi-Strauss 1988:22). Writings by Jesuit missionaries of Northeastern Canadian tribes in the seventeenth century also noted dogs were not allowed to consume certain prey carcasses, "They hold that fish are possessed of reason, as also the Deer and Moose; and that is why they do not throw to the Dogs either the bones of the latter when they are hunting, or the refuse of the former when fishing; If they did, and the others should get wind of it, they would hide themselves, and not let themselves be taken" (Kenton 1925:25). All of these accounts show assorted aspects of dog feeding practiced by Indigenous peoples.

Osteology

Traditional zooarchaeological methods involving osteological analysis of dog remains from archaeological sites have been used to investigate dog maintenance and diets. For example, Robert J. Losey and colleagues (2014) investigated the tooth conditions and associated skeletal material from 144 historic domestic dogs and 400 gray wolves from the artic regions of North America and Russia. Their study compared the two above-mentioned groups of canids to assess the frequencies of cranial trauma and tooth pathologies. They found that domestic dogs had more occurrences of fractured and missing teeth than wolves in the wild. According to Losey and colleagues, high instances of tooth loss from breakage or subsequent infections suggest that domestic dogs were likely scavenging off bones, or "self-provisioning" as a means of obtaining nutrition during times of food stress (Losey et al. 2014:1). Results from this study are useful for understanding the archaeological signatures of dog provisioning. The authors also posited, as others have, that tooth injury or loss may also occur as the result of injury during prey acquisition or defensive interactions associated with resource competition (DeSantis et al. 2012, 2015; Losey et al. 2014). Tooth breakage is an important component of understanding canid feeding and provisioning patterns, though osteological studies may not always provide the most comprehensive understanding of provisioning strategies in all contexts.

Stable Isotope Analysis

Stable isotope analysis of bone collagen and/or tooth enamel have been used to investigate the diets of canids (DeSantis et al. 2019; Tankersley and Koster 2009). This method requires the destruction of bone or tooth samples to extract tissues for testing. Stable carbon isotope signatures indicate types of plants consumed by an animal, or transferred from prey to predator, in the case of carnivores (Schwarcz and Schoeninger 1991). Specifically, plants that utilize different photosynthetic pathways (and the prey that eat those plants and/or the predator that eat those prey) can be distinguished via stable carbon isotopes (e.g., C4 versus

C3 plants; Cerling et al. 1997 ; DeSantis et al. 2019; Guiry 2012). Nitrogen isotopes signify animal proteins consumed and can place an animal on a trophic spectrum (e.g., evidence for animals consuming other animals or being more omnivorous; Schwarcz and Schoeninger 1991). Nitrogen values can also be used to distinguish between herbivores and carnivores and between marine-based and terrestrial-based diets (Schoeninger et al. 1983; Sponheimer et al. 2003). Studies investigating canid isotopic signatures are not usually focused on understanding dog provisioning by past peoples. Typically, dog remains from archaeological sites are investigated as analogs for their human caregivers, an analytical framework called the canine surrogacy approach (Cannon et al. 1999; Edwards et al. 2017; Guiry and Grimes 2013; Noe-Nygaard 1988; White et al. 2001). This approach uses the isotopic signatures of dog bones as surrogates for human bone when human skeletal material is unavailable or unsuitable for testing. These studies have been invaluable in questions regarding major subsistence patterns, such as the adoption of agriculture (Edwards et al. 2016). The canine surrogacy approach suggests dog diets and their chemical signatures can be used to evaluate the diets of humans living in contemporary communities because dogs theoretically consumed what their humans did or scavenged on human refuse and human feces (Guiry 2012:352; Schulting and Richards 2002). The canine surrogacy approach also assumes that humans and dogs have identical metabolic processes (Guiry 2012).

Previous isotopic analysis of domestic dog skeletal remains suggest dogs were generally fed or scavenged food resources that humans consumed, confirming food sharing between people and dogs. Most studies have shown dietary similarities; however, discrepancies typically involve nitrogen isotopes that may reflect trophic differences between people and dogs or may be due to biochemical differences between humans and canines (Guiry 2012). Bone chemistry can aid in deciphering between types of plants consumed and quantifying meat consumption; however, these analyses are less able to speak to food scarcity in dogs.

Coprolite Evidence

Fewer studies have examined ancient dog coprolites, or fossilized feces, to better understand the diets of domestic dogs (Maldre 2006; Fortier 2015). These studies require the coprolite to be broken down or CT scanned to assess for preserved bones and hard plant matter. Materials are then identified and can be used to recreate the last meals of an animal. In this way, coprolites provide evidence for both foods consumed and environmental reconstruction. Coprolite analysis has also been used to reconstruct the dietary behavior of wild animals, including extinct canids, and has demonstrated an ability to identify the consumption of hard materials, such as bone, that survive the consumption process (Wang et al. 2018). Unlike isotopic analysis, coprolites can reveal the ratio of bone consumed by carnivores, as dental microwear can. These lines of evidence are fruitful for understanding the diets of dogs but dependent on rare finds of preserved dog feces.

Dental Microwear Texture Analysis

The above-mentioned methods are useful for understanding the general makeup of a dog's diet, but they are often unable to quantify a dog's access to adequate food resources. As such, we approached this problem with dental microwear texture analysis. This method is the most current technique for analyzing microwear and has proven informative for understanding the dietary behavior of both extinct and extant canids (e.g., DeSantis et al. 2015, 2019; Tanis et al. 2018; Ungar et al. 2012). Microwear, "the fine structure of worn surfaces," has been used to investigate the diets of a variety of animals, including humans (Hillson 2005:220). Originally, dental microwear studies used a scanning electron microscope to record and analyze tooth surfaces. This process requires the specimen (tooth) be coated with a conducting metal (gold, palladium, or carbon), placed in a pressurized chamber, and scanned with a fine electron beam (Hillson 2005). This scan produces a two-dimensional image that is then quantified by a researcher, who records the tooth surface features. However, these subjective quantifications have been shown to have high observer and recorder bias (DeSantis et al. 2013). The consumption of hard and soft tissue and other organic consumables leave distinct textural features on the surfaces of teeth, making DMTA's three-dimensional application of microwear analysis an appropriate tool for understanding the diets of mammals (DeSantis 2016; Ungar et al. 2008).

Unlike isotopic analyses that are used to infer diet during a broad span of time, microwear is constantly being rewritten and captures only the last few months of dietary behavior before death, what is often referred to as the Last Supper effect (Grine 1986). Access to different foods is often seasonal, meaning microwear values are affected by season (Hogue et al. 2008). DMTA data can indicate if a carnivore was heavily utilizing carcasses, a sign of food stress. Microwear can also be used to understand a specific moment in time, making it the ideal method to investigate a dog's access to adequate food resources during certain seasons, hunting events, and other relevant time periods. DMTA values of domestic dogs associated with human groups in the past illuminate the specific lived experience of individual dogs or communities of dogs and their ability to effectively acquire resources other than bone refuse. This research adds another avenue to the diverse ways anthropologists investigate the diets of past domestic dogs, contributing to the understanding of how humans chose to support canine community members.

DMTA Methodology and Analysis

DMTA scans the wear facet of a tooth (or tooth cast) with a confocal light microscope to generate three-dimensional surface data, as opposed to the traditional two-dimensional images produced by scanning electron microscopes (Scott et al. 2006). DMTA creates point clouds of three-dimensional data that can be analyzed with specialized software that measures multiple characteristics of the tooth surface, including the degree to which features share a similar orientation (anisotropy), changes in surface roughness (complexity), and the relationship between shape and texture of the tooth surface (textural fill volume) (Scott et al. 2006). DMTA employs scale-sensitive fractal analysis instead of a human counter, allowing for a less biased interpretation of tooth surface features and making the analysis repeatable and comparative for future/alternative studies.

DMTA begins with acquiring a mold of the tooth surface to produce a subsequent cast to be used for study. This process has been standardized and is non-destructive, as the original tooth surface has only a molding agent applied (Donohue et al. 2013; Scott et al. 2006). The established procedure for molding and casting teeth is as follows: 1) tooth facets are cleaned with acetone soaked cotton swabs prior to application of regular body polyvinylsiloxane dental impression material (President's Jet, Coltene-Whaledent Corp.); 2) replicas are cast using high-resolution epoxy that is optimized for imaging (Epotek 301, Epoxy Technologies Corp.); 3) these casts are then scanned using a Sensofar Plu Neox optical profiler (Solarius Development, Inc., Sunnyvale, California) using a 100× objective (four total surfaces per tooth; see methods noted in Jones and DeSantis 2017), and data processed using Toothfrax and SFrax software to quantify attribute values of the tooth surface.

DMTA variables used to understand the diets of canids are produced from the median values of four adjoining scans (per Jones and DeSantis 2017) taken from the same facet of the second mandibular molar of each specimen. Complexity, quantified by a process called area-scale fractal complexity ($Asfc$), is a measure of the molar surface at different scales of observation. Higher complexity values correlate with a diet consisting of hard foods (Scott et al. 2006). For carnivores, hard foods are hard tissues such as bone (e.g., DeSantis and Haupt 2014; DeSantis and Patterson 2017, DeSantis et al. 2012, 2015, 2017; Donohue et al. 2013; Schubert et al. 2010; Stydner et al. 2018). Less complex surfaces typically have fewer pits and less rough surface textures (see Figure 5.1 for a schematic of the complexity variable).

Anisotropy, called exact proportion Length-scale anisotropy of relief (*epLsar*), is the measure of striation orientation and is high when striation features are

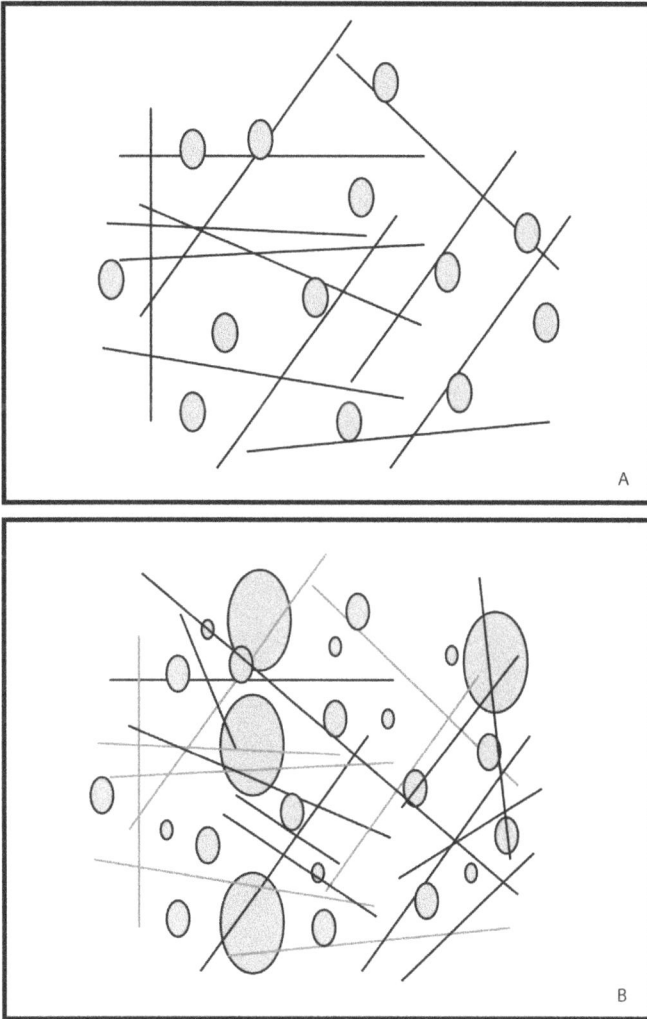

Figure 5.1. A schematic of the complexity (*Asfc*) variable, indicating (*A*) low complexity and (*B*) high complexity.

more parallel, i.e. oriented in the same direction (DeSantis 2016). See Figure 5.2 for a schematic of the anisotropy variable. Values are derived from the length and depth of grooves taken at 5-degree intervals. Low *epLsar* values represent a more heterogeneous surface (Scott at al. 2006:341). Parallel striations on the surfaces of teeth are indicative of tough food consumption; in herbivores this instead indicates the consumption of tough vegetation like tough tree leaves or grass blades. In carnivores, high anisotropy values can indicate flesh consumption (DeSantis 2016; Schubert et al. 2010).

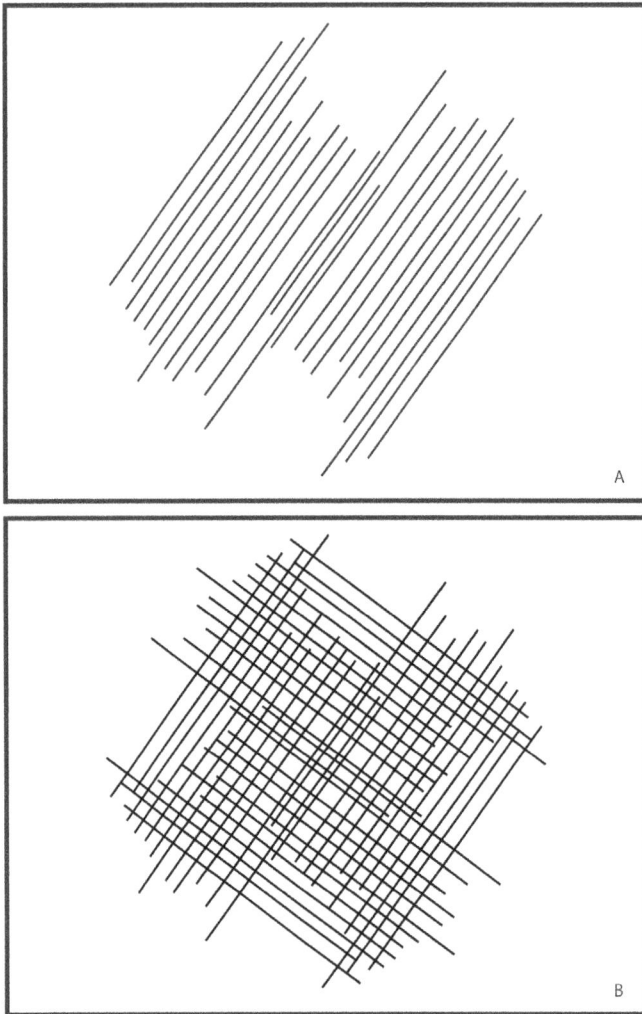

Figure 5.2. A schematic of the anisotropy (*epLsar*) variable, indicating (*A*) high anisotropy, and (*B*) low anisotropy.

Amanda Burtt and Larisa R. G. DeSantis

Complexity and anisotropy are often paired when distinguishing between frugivores, grazers, and browsers, and between obligate carnivores and more omnivorous or scavenging carnivores (DeSantis 2016). Carnivore scavenging behavior is most important for research presented here, with high complexity indicative of a hard (bone) food consumer (DeSantis 2016). Low complexity and high anisotropy values are instead indicative of a tough (flesh) food consumer (DeSantis 2016).

Textural fill volume (*Tfv*) is a measure of the volume of tooth surface features filled with squared cuboids of two different sizes, 10 μm and 2 μm in diameter. This variable is derived from two attributes of the tooth surface, the shape and the texture (Scott et al. 2006). High *Tfv* values are correlated with sizable features that are deep, potentially pits. Heavily pitted tooth surfaces correlate with hard (bone) food consumption; thus, *Asfc* and *Tfv* are often positively correlated (DeSantis et al., 2013).

Mandibular Second Molars

Canids have a generalized dentition; their incisors are small and sharp, with prominent canines and molars that become more complex on the tooth row from anterior to posterior. Canids have four premolars and three molars on their mandibles, though the third molar is significantly reduced and can often be completely absent. Domestic dogs, wolves, and coyotes have the same dental formula and process foods in similar ways. When canids, and mammals more broadly, process foodstuff there are two general phases of mastication. In Phase I, the mouth is tearing and shearing and securing food items, and in Phase II acquired food is crushed and processed for ingestion (Ungar 2010). During Phase II, molars break down matter between the occlusal surfaces of the top and bottom tooth rows, leaving microwear signatures that correlate with food particles being crushed by the force of the bite. The mandibular second molar is used for microwear analysis of canids since the position of this tooth in the dental arcade makes it responsible for the crushing and grinding of hard and tough food matter during Phase II mastication, each leaving a unique dental microwear signature (Ungar et al. 2010). If dogs are consuming large amounts of bone, this is the area in the mouth that will show such behaviors.

The second mandibular molar's anterolingual surface of the hypoconid cusp (Figure 5.3) is the established standard to collect microwear features on canids, an important factor for the ability to compare domestic dogs to previously published microwear data (DeSantis et.al. 2015; Schmitt 2011; Ungar et al. 2010).

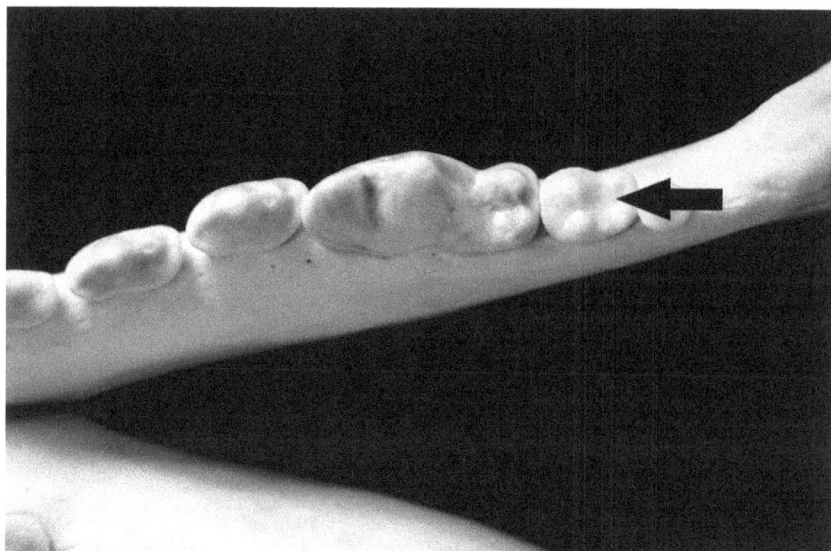

Figure 5.3. Anterolingual surface of the hypoconid on the second mandibular molar.

Dental molds are used to generate casts and must be collected from enamel, not dentin. As molar surfaces experience wear, the enamel will gradually be worn down and sometimes completely wear off, exposing the dentin below (Haupt et al. 2013). Once dentin is exposed over the entire hypoconid region of the second mandibular molar with no remaining enamel, the tooth is no longer suitable for this type of microwear analysis. Archaeological dog remains used for this analysis had preserved enamel on the lower second molar. While several archaeological sites assessed for this study had multiple dogs associated with them, only dogs that had the necessary tooth present were included in this analysis. When mandibular skeletal material associated with teeth used for this study were still intact, measurements were taken following discipline standards (Von den Driesch 1976). Samples used for this study are the only mandibular second molars identified as canid, with the following criteria: preserved microwear, available for research, and housed at one of two archaeological repositories inventoried for this study in Indiana and Wyoming. Determining canids as domestic dogs was based on size and morphology of associated skeletal material. This determination was not always straightforward, especially among the much larger canids recovered from archaeological sites in Wyoming as opposed to smaller canids from Indiana, a challenge addressed later in this chapter.

Comparing Domestic Dogs to Gray Wolves and Coyotes

Modern carnivores, including gray wolves and coyotes, have proven valuable for understanding the dietary behavior of extinct carnivores, especially scavenging behavior. Such studies include investigation of the La Brea Tar Pits, located in Rancho La Brea in the modern state of California, which trapped numerous carnivores and their prey millennia ago during the Pleistocene Epoch. Animals recovered from these pits have been investigated for signs of scavenging behavior before their extinction at the end of the Late Pleistocene. These include animals such as saber-toothed cats and short-faced bears. DMTA has been used to evaluate the dietary behavior of these now-extinct carnivores to see if they were experiencing food stress leading up to their extinction (DeSantis et al. 2012; DeSantis et al. 2015, 2019). These studies are used as a reference and framework for applying similar theoretical understandings for reconstructing the dietary behavior of closely related species. For this research, gray wolves and coyotes are used as behavioral analogs for understanding the normal range of dietary behavior another member of the genus *Canis* may exhibit.

To better understand possible dietary behavior of domestic dogs living with humans, their unmodified wild ancestors, gray wolves, and less related coyotes are employed to establish baseline data. Genetically, gray wolves differ from coyotes by about 4% of mitochondrial DNA sequence, and wolves differ from domestic dogs by about 0.2% (Wayne 1993). This makes wolves and coyotes the domestic dogs' two closest ancestors from a total of 35 species of extant canids (Ungar et al. 2010). By comparing the microwear of domestic dogs, whose dietary behavior is in question, with that of wild canids whose dietary behavior is known, analysis presented here interprets the textures of foods consumed, hard (bone) versus tough (flesh), to better understand a dog's access to adequate food resources. Interpretations are based on: 1) wolves' preference for flesh; and, 2) coyotes' tendency to consume more bone as opportunistic canids preying on small mammals with smaller skeletal structures and as scavengers of ungulate carcasses, often killed by wolves (Paquet 1992).

The dietary behaviors of wolves can differ slightly based on their geographic location, but broadly speaking they prefer large ungulates (e.g., deer, elk). Wolves are able to prey on such large animals due to their physical and social characteristics, including being large-bodied carnivores, having the ability to consume sizable amounts of meat, and traveling and hunting in packs (Mech 1970). Wolves prefer flesh and internal organs and will consume these portions first, typically leaving long bones, vertebrae, the mandible and cranium at the kill site (Mech 1970:186). Wolves will scavenge from carcasses for nutrition if no other resource is available and prefer fresh over frozen carrion (Haynes 1982). Wolves will return to carcasses and process them more completely, consuming bone refuse when preferred food is scarce (Haynes 1982; Mech 1970; Stahler et al. 2006). It is the wolves' preference for flesh that make their dietary behavioral ecology an analog for domestic dogs having access to fresher kills. Dogs that have microwear signatures closely correlated to those of wolves are thus deemed a potentially provisioned consumer.

Coyotes tend to consume carrion and hunt smaller animals, like rabbits; therefore, they come in contact with skeletal material more frequently than wolves, since wolves prefer larger prey, with larger skeletons that aren't consumed entirely (Reid 2006). Coyotes are also known to scavenge more than wolves, are more flexible in their dietary behavior, and tend to be solitary or form small groups (Ewer 1998). In contrast, wolves form social groups and are able to cooperate to take down larger (and fresh) prey (Mech 1970). Coyotes that have DMTA values that do not overlap with wolves are here assigned as analogs for domestic dogs that are non-provisioned scavengers.

Dental microwear data have been used to reconstruct the dietary behaviors of both extant and extinct members of the taxonomic family Canidae (DeSantis et al. 2015, 2019; Ungar et al. 2010). These studies serve as established protocol for determining a canid's access to flesh versus bone. Values generated in previous studies for wolves and coyotes serve as baseline data for comparing domestic dogs. Visualizing these data are helpful for understanding the different yet overlapping dietary behavior of wolves and coyotes. Previous research has shown that plotting complexity and anisotropy in a bivariate plot exemplifies carnivore dietary behavior with regard to hard versus tough foods, or flesh versus bone food consumption (Figure 5.4). High complexity values (x-axis) are associated with bone consumption and high anisotropy values (y-axis) are associated with flesh consumption. Using data points generated by a modern group of wolves (n = 15) (DeSantis et al. 2015, 2019) and a modern group of coyotes (n = 12) (Ungar et al. 2010) there are two designated areas of possible domestic dog behavior based on wolf and coyote behavior: potentially provisioned consumers and non-provisioned scavengers. In this model, dogs are either being fed or have access to adequate food resources or dogs have less access, leaving them to scavenge from bone refuse. As wolves rarely chew on bone, *Asfc* values less than 6.2 suggest adequate food resources. Despite the

Amanda Burtt and Larisa R. G. DeSantis

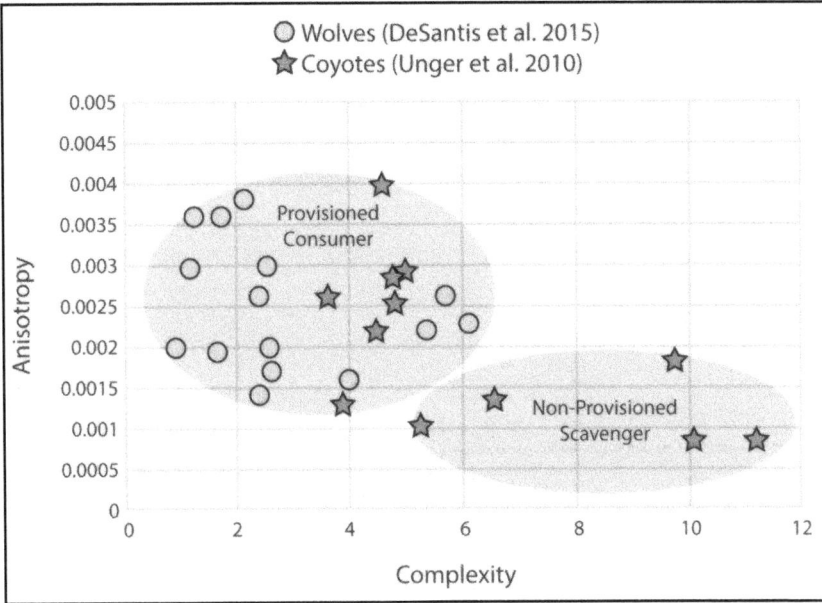

Figure 5.4. Bivariate of complexity and anisotropy plotted for wolf and coyote. Comparative data from DeSantis et al. 2015 and Ungar et al. 2010.

recent publication of additional coyote and gray wolf specimens (DeSantis et al. 2019), out of 126 extant gray wolf and coyote specimens analyzed, only coyotes have *Asfc* values above 6.2.

Dogs from Archaeological Sites in Indiana and Wyoming

Collections curated at Indiana University's Glenn A. Black Laboratory of Archaeology contributed nine individual dogs to this study from seven different archaeological sites across the modern state of Indiana: Albee (12Su1), (n = 1); Angel (12Vg1), (n = 1); Bowen (12Ma610), (n = 1); Haag Site (12D19), (n = 3); Oliver (12Ma1), (n = 1); Stephan-Steinkamp (12Po33), (n = 1); and 12Po437, (n = 1). Dogs from these sites were living with people in agricultural towns and villages from Late Woodland, Mississippian, and Fort Ancient temporal contexts. When plotting complexity and anisotropy, as is customary when analyzing DMTA data, six dogs appear to be accessing adequate food resources, while three dogs appear to be consuming hard food items, likely bones. Of these three, two dogs are from the Haag site and one is from Albee Mounds (Figure 5.5). The dietary behavior of the other six dogs from Indiana archaeological sites show varied provisioning

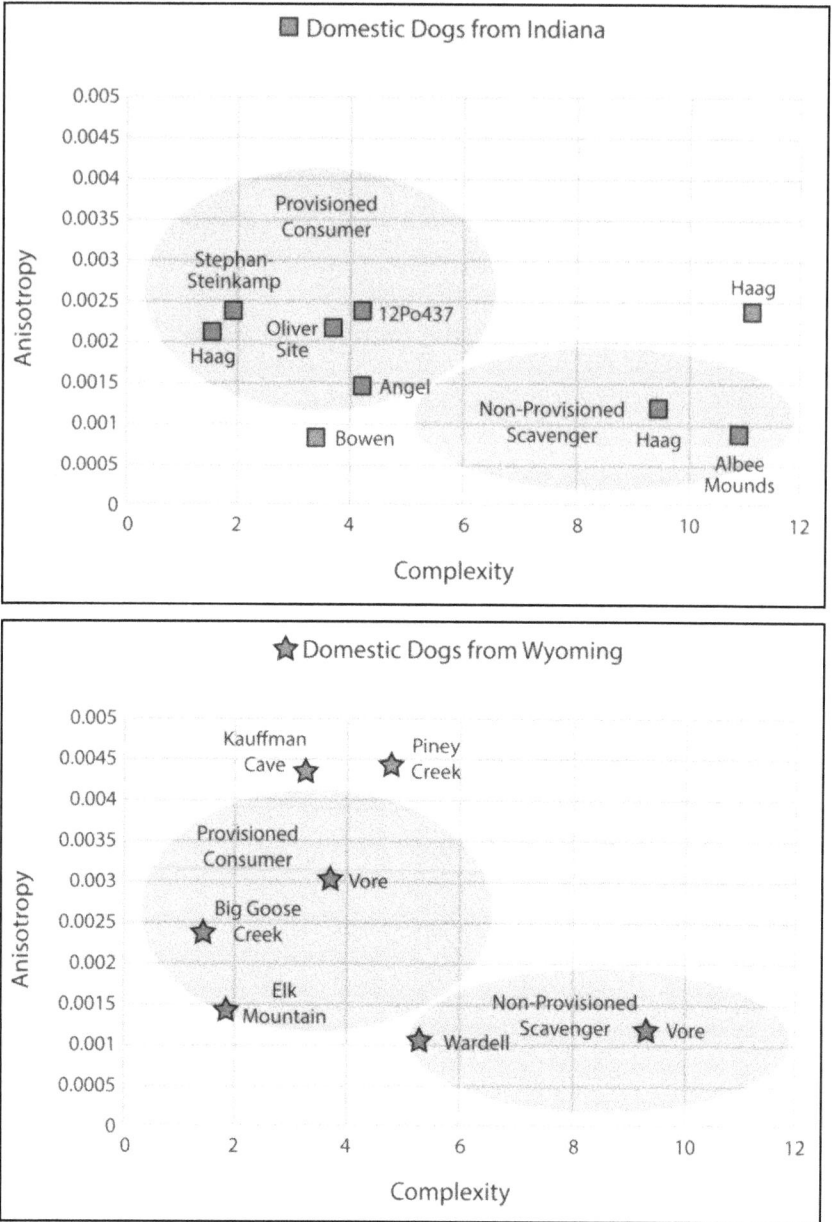

Figure 5.5. Bivariate of complexity and anisotropy plotted for domestic dogs from Indiana and Wyoming.

practices, though visually their diets appear more homogenous, with clustering in the lower left quadrant, than those from Wyoming. Signs of homogenous dog diets imply a more organized feeding program within these town sites or that dogs had consistent access to foods with similar textures (although it is possible that the foods themselves could have been quite different), leaving similar dental microwear signatures on their teeth.

Collections curated at the University of Wyoming Archaeological Repository contributed seven individual dogs to this study from six different archaeological sites across the modern state of Wyoming: Big Goose Creek (48SH313), (n = 1); Elk Mountain (48CR301), (n = 1); Kauffmann Cave (48SH301), (n = 1); Piney Creek (48JO312), (n = 1); Vore (48CK302), (n = 2); and Wardell (48SU301), (n = 1). These sites represent buffalo jumps and corrals, ephemeral camping areas, and a rock shelter and are associated with mobile hunters and gatherers on the Northwest Plains and foothills of the Rocky Mountains. All except one (from Kauffman Cave) of the canids used for this study were also previously examined for their likeness to wolves (Walker and Frison 1982) and were found to be distinctly different. Sizes of several of these canids may indicate that they are of recent wolf genetic admixture, as other researchers noted, "the Wyoming canids, while related to both wolves and prehistoric dogs, appear to be closer in appearance to dogs, a result of the domestication processes acting upon them" (Walker and Frison 1982:154). The canid from Kauffman Cave was tentatively identified as possible wolf (Grey 1962); this animal's DMTA values are consistent with this identification, as they are similar to those observed in wolves.

When charting complexity and anisotropy values, five of seven dogs from Wyoming do not appear to be scavenging off bone refuse and can be considered provisioned consumers (Figure 5.5). However, two dogs, one from Vore and another from the Wardell site, are instead categorized as non-provisioned scavengers based on the wolf and coyote behavioral analogs. Additionally, the seven dogs appear to have subsisted off foods with different texture properties. Some dogs have DMTA attribute values indicative of tough flesh consumption (high anisotropy values) while others indicate brittle bone consumption (high complexity values), suggesting that this sample of dogs had varying degrees of access to food resources. Different access to high value food resources could be reflective of individual roles or relationships dogs had with humans or within communities.

Testing for Regional Differences

Archaeological dogs from Indiana and Wyoming represent geographically and culturally distinct regions of North America, and these dogs lived with people practicing different subsistence strategies. Statistical analysis was used to compare

Table 5.1. Raw DMTA data values for all archaeological dogs

State	Site Name	Site Number	Catalog ID	Asfc Median	epLsar Median	Tfv Median
Indiana	Angel	12Vg1	X11B 3305	4.211	0.0014	12686
Indiana	Albee Mounds	12Su1	WRAZL A67	10.741	0.0008	12903
Indiana	Bowen	12Ma61	WRAZL ff28	3.353	0.0009	12400
Indiana	Haag	12D19	6983–7071f19	10.948	0.0024	16421
Indiana	Haag	12D19	6983–7071f21	9.317	0.0012	12841
Indiana	Haag	12D19	6983–7076f50	1.574	0.0022	11041
Indiana	Oliver	12Ma1	WRAZL A66	3.629	0.0022	11726
Indiana	n/a	12Po437	3831	4.162	0.0024	13087
Indiana	Stephan-Steinkamp	12Po33	6475–1791	1.892	0.0023	11931
Wyoming	Big Goose Creek	48SH313	10629	1.411	0.0023	7780
Wyoming	Elk Mountain	48CR301	C3799	1.803	0.0013	15479
Wyoming	Kauffmann Cave	48SH301	2	3.250	0.0044	12129
Wyoming	Piney Creek	48JO311	Uncatalogued	4.739	0.0044	13305
Wyoming	Wardell	48SU301	22105	5.351	0.0010	13602
Wyoming	Vore	48CK302	VNB34	9.336	0.0011	13504
Wyoming	Vore	48CK302	VNB38	3.672	0.0030	13517

these two samples of domestic dogs to test for regionally specific provisioning strategies. Table 5.1 displays raw DMTA data values for all dogs included in this study, and Table 5.2 presents descriptive statistics of these data. To determine if these variables were normally distributed, Shapiro-Wilk tests were performed and found that these DMTA variables are not all normally distributed.

Non-normally distributed variables compounded by a small sample size required that nonparametric statistical analysis be performed. Mann-Whitney and Kruskal-Wallis tests were run to compare the two regional groups, as well as to compare each group to wolves and coyotes, respectively. Domestic dogs were compared to each other and then each to both wolves and coyotes (raw data for wolves is from DeSantis et al. 2015; raw data for coyotes is from Ungar et al. 2010).

Table 5.3 presents the results from Kruskal-Wallis tests, with a significance value of $p < 0.05$. Results from the Mann-Whitney tests were similar, with nei-

Table 5.2. Descriptive statistics for DMTA values

Domestic Dogs	Statistic	n	Asfc	epLsar	Tfv
Indiana	Mean	9	5.536	0.0017	12782
	Median		4.162	0.0022	12686
	Standard Deviation		3.737	0.0007	1516
	Minimum		1.574	0.0008	11041
	Maximum		10.948	0.0024	16421
	Total Range		9.374	0.0015	5380
	Skewness (Fisher)		0.680	-0.445	1.898
	p for normality (Shapiro-Wilk)		0.044	0.029	0.022
Wyoming	Mean	7	4.223	0.0025	12759
	Median		3.672	0.0023	13504
	Standard Deviation		2.667	0.0015	2406
	Minimum		1.411	0.0010	7780
	Maximum		9.336	0.0044	15479
	Total Range		7.924	0.0034	7699
	Skewness (Fisher)		1.201	0.432	-1.709
	p for normality (Shapiro-Wilk)		0.376	0.162	0.042

Table 5.3. Results from two-sample Kolmogorov-Smirnov test

Asfc	Wolf	Coyote	Wyoming
Indiana	0.070	0.249	0.591
Wyoming	0.282	0.101	1
Wolf	1	**0.001**	0.282

epLsar	Wolf	Coyote	Wyoming
Indiana	0.069	0.603	0.256
Wyoming	0.671	0.470	1
Wolf	1	0.164	0.671

Tfv	Wolf	Coyote	Wyoming
Indiana	0.997	0.492	0.637
Wyoming	0.606	0.891	1
Wolf	1	0437	0.606

ther nonparametric statistical test finding significant differences between these regions across the three measured DMTA variables. These findings suggest that dental microwear signatures of dogs living in regionally and culturally different contexts cannot be distinguished from each other. When compared to wolves and coyotes (Kruskal-Wallis tests), dogs from Indiana and Wyoming (analyzed independently and collectively) are indistinguishable from each other and from both wolves and coyotes. Yet coyotes have significantly higher *Asfc* values than wolves (as was reported by DeSantis and coauthors [2015] and consistent with observed dietary behavior).

Intra- and Intersite-Level Investigations

Domestic dogs living with residents of Late Woodland, Mississippian, and Fort Ancient towns and villages likely had access to different food resources than contemporaneous dogs living with more mobile peoples on the Northwest Plains and Rocky Mountains, yet data from these two regions indicate that dog diets can be variable regardless of their geographic location (i.e., the diets seen in one location are not necessarily more variable than those in the other location). DMTA variables are then most useful for drawing contextual inferences that help enrich site biographies. The Leonard Haag site from Indiana and Elk Mountain and Vore sites from Wyoming are considered as case studies for using dental microwear texture analysis to better understand specific lived experiences of domestic dogs by integrating dental microwear data with interpretations of these sites.

The Leonard Haag site (12D19) in the Central Ohio Valley was occupied continuously by two separate groups of Indigenous peoples spanning different time eras. The first was a Late Woodland occupation from 500 CE to 1000 CE, when people participated in foraging and hunting subsistence practices. The second and final group was the Fort Ancient population, which occupied the site from 1000 to 1300 CE and were primarily agriculturists, subsisting on maize (Reidhead 1977). All three dogs representing the Haag site were recovered from the Fort Ancient component. Two Haag dogs have similar microwear signatures with high complexity values and intermediate anisotropy values (Figure 5.5). These dogs were likely heavily processing discarded bone and can be confidently called non-provisioned scavengers. In contrast, the third dog recovered from the Haag site has the lowest complexity value with average anisotropy, meaning this dog was subsisting on much softer food items than its canine counterparts, either being fed or successfully acquiring other food sources.

The striking difference in the dietary behaviors between these individuals could have several implications. The bone-consuming canines may represent a time of food scarceness and the other a time of abundance, or their treatment may represent different roles held within the community. Dogs could have been seen as individuals with distinct feeding strategies tailored to specific dogs. Three dogs with high complexity values (two from Haag and one from Albee Mounds) also have higher texture fill volume, further indicating heavy bone consumption. While the other Haag dog has the lowest complexity value observed from Indiana dogs, this dog also has lower textural fill volume values than the other two dogs from this site, evidence this dog was provisioned or consumed softer food resources. All three dogs from the Haag site have been interpreted as contemporaneous (Reidhead 1977), yet they were fed or had access to food in dramatically different ways. These data highlight dissimilar ways dogs were treated within this community or could represent dog owners' food security, with times of abundance and times of scarcity.

Vore Buffalo Jump (48CK302), perhaps the most well-known buffalo jump site located in the modern United States, is located in northeastern Wyoming and was used from 1500 to 1800 CE by Indigenous groups of the Black Hills and surrounding areas. This jump was used intensively and now contains the remains of potentially 20,000 bison (Reher and Frison 1980). Both dogs recovered from the Vore site and used for this analysis were found in different unit blocks at approximately the same horizontal floor. One of the two dogs recovered from the Vore site has the highest complexity value from the total Wyoming dog sample, indicating high degrees of bone consumption. Additionally, high textural fill volume values provide further evidence that this dog was not successfully acquiring fresh flesh and was a non-provisioned scavenger. This dog's complexity values plot with the coyotes that were likely scavenging, with only three coyotes having slightly higher complexity values.

Interpreting this dog's scavenging behavior offers several intellectually productive avenues. This dog may not have been owned by the humans who drove buffalo off the cliff but may instead have been unowned and attracted to the carcasses, perhaps feeding off them when killed. Alternatively, the dog could have been taken to the hunt having only had access to bone scraps and was killed during the hunting event, either intentionally or not. Dogs have been known to accompany people to buffalo hunting events; Crow people talk about dogs being involved in driving bison (Crow 1978). It is reasonable to imagine dogs could get hurt or killed and their remains comingled with butchered remains of buffalo. Perhaps a scavenging dog is a sign of an unsuccessful hunting expedition during the animal's recent past, leaving the dog to scavenge off old kills. What is known is that this particular dog's bone consumption behavior, inferred via dental microwear, is well outside the dietary behavior of the domestic dog's closest relative, the gray wolf. Features on the tooth surface represent the dog's last several meals (and potentially several days, weeks, or months). This dog, at some point in its recent past, was not effectively acquiring softer or fresher flesh and can be deemed a non-provisioned scavenger.

Elk Mountain (48CR301) is an open-air site in the southeastern part of Wyoming, used as an ephemeral campsite beginning in the Late Archaic period and continuing through to the contact period (Eckles 2018). The domestic dog recovered from the Elk Mountain site has the second-lowest complexity value (indicating little bone consumption) of Wyoming dogs used for this study. This dog also exhibits a low anisotropy value. Dental microwear values indicate that this dog was neither scavenging off bone refuse nor consuming tough flesh but instead was consuming non-tough, non-hard foods—perhaps cooked fare prepared by humans. This dog is interpreted as either successfully acquiring food resources or being intentionally fed, thus a provisioned consumer.

Conclusion

Domestication theories incorporate scavenging behavior of canids and their attraction to human habitation sites as crucial contact points for human-canine interactions (Driscoll 2009; Morey 2010; Stahl 2016). Research presented here further contextualizes these points, providing evidence for provisioned and non-provisioned dietary behavior among domestic dogs during the late precontact period in North America. It is helpful to think of wolf and coyote comparative DMTA variables as a continuum on which domestic dogs can be placed. Wolves and coyotes access different food resources with some overlap. Areas they do not overlap are especially helpful when thinking of a domestic dog's consumption of tough versus hard textured foods, specifically when investigating food stress or bone consumption. Microwear textures can determine the degree to which carnivores consume flesh or bone (DeSantis 2016). Evidence presented here demonstrates that late precontact North American domestic dogs essentially fall within natural dietary behavioral parameters established by wolves and coyotes, with the majority of domestic dogs being provisioned food resources or successfully acquiring fresher kills and fewer dogs scavenging off carcasses and/or chewing on bones (even provisioned bones). Results show that individual dogs' lived experiences can be explored through their dental microwear texture analysis and site context.

Archaeological research into the human-canine connection continues to employ innovative technologies to examine curated dog remains. Skeletal remains of dogs are our most exact tool for understanding human-canine interactions in the past. Although dog remains are recovered from archaeological sites in various stages of completeness and preservation, each piece can provide details of a dog's lived experience in the care of humans. Teeth are especially helpful as they are more likely to survive in the archaeological record. This survivability has been praised by other researchers: "Excellent preservation, under a wide variety of conditions, is one of the most useful features of dental tissues" (Hillson 2005:206).

The archaeology of dog keeping enriches our understanding of the complex relationships humans have sustained and cultivated with another species across various geographical and temporal landscapes. Finding new ways to investigate this topic contributes to broader anthropological knowledge about relationships among humans and the natural world. Without an adequate analysis of canine provisioning strategies, we undervalue the interconnectedness of humans and dogs, ultimately leading to a limited conceptualization of dog keeping in the past. Human efforts to feed dogs and thus gain more control over them have many implications. Intentionally provisioning dogs could be tied to the value of dogs to people or communities, dog individuality, available resources within communities, or past human understandings of carnivore behavior. In this study, dental microwear texture analysis is used to enrich site biographies and to explore nuanced feeding and alternate scenarios of past domestic dog provisioning strategies employed by Indigenous North Americans.

Acknowledgments

The authors thank the University of Wyoming Archaeological Repository and Indiana University's Glenn A. Black Laboratory of Archaeology for access to

dog skeletons, Laura Scheiber and David Polly for access to laboratory resources at Indiana University, as well as Della C. Cook, Stacie M. King, April
Sievert, coeditor Brandi Bethke, and all of the volume contributors. We would
also like to thank our own provisioned canids, Lila Burtt and Candy DeSantis,
for inspiration and companionship.

References Cited

Ames, Kenneth M., Michael P. Richards, Camilla F. Speller, Dongya Y. Yang, R. Lee.
Lyman, and Virginia L. Butler
2015   Stable Isotope and Ancient DNA Analysis of Dog Remains from Cathlapotle
        (45CL1), a Contact-Era Site on the Lower Columbia River. *Journal of Archaeologi-
        cal Science* 57:268–282.

Burleigh, Richard, and Don Brothwell
1978   Studies on Amerindian dogs, 1: Carbon Isotopes in Relation to Maize in the Diet
        of Domestic Dogs from Early Peru and Ecuador. *Journal of Archaeological Science*
        5(4):355–362.

Cannon, Aubrey, Henry P. Schwarcz, and Martin Knyf
1999   Marine-Based Subsistence Trends and the Stable Isotope Analysis of Dog Bones
        from Namu, British Columbia. *Journal of Archaeological Science* 26(4):399–407.

Cerling, Thure E., John M. Harris, Bruce J. MacFadden, Meave G. Leakey, Jay Quade,
Vera Eisenmann, and James R. Ehleringer
1997   Global Vegetation Change through the Miocene/Pliocene Boundary. *Nature*
        389:153–158.

Crockford, Susan J. (editor)
2000   *Dogs through Time: An Archaeological Perspective.* BAR International Series, Vol.
        889. Archaeopress, Oxford.

Crow, Joe Medicine
1978   Notes on Crow Indian Buffalo Jump Traditions. *Plains Anthropologist* 23(82):249–253.

DeMallie, Raymond J., and William C. Sturtevant (editors)
2001   *Handbook of North American Indians,* Vol. 13, *Plains, Pt. 1.* Smithsonian Institution,
        Washington, DC.

DeSantis, Larisa R. G.
2016   Dental Microwear Textures: Reconstructing Diets of Fossil Mammals. *Surface To-
        pography: Metrology and Properties* 4(2):023002.

DeSantis, Larisa R. G., Jonathan M. Crites, Robert S. Feranec, Kena Fox-Dobbs, Aisling
B. Farrell, John M. Harris, Gary T. Takeuchi, and Thure E. Cerling
2019   Causes and Consequences of Pleistocene Megafaunal Extinctions as Revealed from
        Rancho La Brea Mammals. *Current Biology* 29:2488–2495.

DeSantis, Larisa R. G., and Ryan J. Haupt
2014   Cougars' Key to Survival through the Late Pleistocene Extinction: Insights from
        Dental Microwear Texture Analysis. *Biology Letters* 10(4):20140203.

DeSantis, Larisa R. G., and Bruce D. Patterson
2017   Dietary Behaviour of Man-Eating Lions as Revealed by Dental Microwear Textures.
        Scientific Reports 7(1):904.

DeSantis, Larisa R. G., Blaine W. Schubert, Elizabeth Schmitt-Linville, Peter S. Ungar, Shelly L. Donohue, and Ryan J. Haupt.

2015 Dental Microwear Textures of Carnivores from the La Brea Tar Pits, California, and Potential Extinction Implications. *Contributions in Science, Los Angeles County Museum of Natural History* 42(2015):37–52.

DeSantis, Larisa R. G., Blaine W. Schubert, Jessica R. Scott, and Peter S. Ungar

2012 Implications of Diet for the Extinction of Saber-Toothed Cats and American Lions. *PLoS ONE* 7(12):e52453.

DeSantis, Larisa R. G., Jessica R. Scott, Blaine W. Schubert, Shelly L. Donohue, Brian M. McCray, Courtney A. Van Stolk, Amanda A. Winburn, Michael A. Greshko, and Mackie C. O'Hara

2013 Direct Comparisons of 2D and 3D Dental Microwear Proxies in Extant Herbivorous and Carnivorous Mammals. *PLoS ONE* 8(8):e71428.

Donohue, Shelly L., Larisa R. G. DeSantis, Blaine W. Schubert, and Peter S. Ungar

2013 Was the Giant Short-Faced Bear a Hyper-Scavenger? A New Approach to the Dietary Study of Ursids Using Dental Microwear Textures. *PLoS ONE* 8(10):e77531.

Driscoll, Carlos A., David W. Macdonald, and Stephen J. O'Brien

2009 From Wild Animals to Domestic Pets, an Evolutionary View of Domestication. *Proceedings of the National Academy of Sciences* 106(Supplement 1):9971–9978.

Eckles, David G.

2018 Faunal Remains from the Garrett Allen (Elk Mountain) Site (48CR301). Unpublished manuscript, University of Wyoming Archaeological Repository, Laramie.

Edwards, Kim, Dale Allen Walde, and M. Anne Katzenberg

2016 Searching for Evidence of Maize Consumption at Cluny: Stable Carbon and Nitrogen Isotope Analysis of Dog and Bison Bone Collagen. *Canadian Journal of Archaeology* 40(2):319–331.

Edwards IV, Richard W., Robert J. Jeske, and Joan B. Coltrain

2017 Preliminary Evidence for the Efficacy of the Canine Surrogacy Approach in the Great Lakes. *Journal of Archaeological Science: Reports* 13:516–525.

Eriksson, Gunilla, and Ilga Zagorska

2003 Do Dogs Eat like Humans? Marine Stable Isotope Signals in Dog Teeth from Inland Zvejnieki. In *Mesolithic on the Move: Papers Presented at the sixth International Conference on the Mesolithic in Europe, Stockholm 2000*, edited by L. Larsson, pp. 160–168. Oxbow, Oxford.

Ewer, Rosalie Francis

1998 *The Carnivores*. Cornell University Press, Ithaca, New York.

Ewers, John C.

1955 *The Horse in Blackfoot Indian Culture, with Comparative Material from Other Western Tribes*. US Government Printing Office, Washington, DC.

Fortier, Andrew C.

2015 Preliminary Analyses of Prehistoric Dog Feces (Coprolites) from the Janey B. Goode Site, St. Clair County, Illinois. *Illinois Antiquity* 50(3):16–18.

Grey, D.

1962 The Bentzen-Kaufmann Cave Site 48 SH 301. *Plains Anthropologist* 7(18):237–245.

Grine, Frederick E.

1986 Dental Evidence for Dietary Differences in Australopithecus and Paranthropus: A

Quantitative Analysis of Permanent Molar Microwear. *Journal of Human Evolution* 15(8):783–822.

Guiry, Eric J.

2012　Dogs as Analogs in Stable Isotope-Based Human Paleodietary Reconstructions: A Review and Considerations for Future Use. *Journal of Archaeological Method and Theory* 19(3):351–376.

Guiry, Eric J., and Vaughan Grimes

2013　Domestic Dog (*Canis familiaris*) Diets among Coastal Late Archaic Groups of Northeastern North America: A Case Study for the Canine Surrogacy Approach. *Journal of Anthropological Archaeology* 32(4):732–745.

Haupt, Ryan J., Larisa R. G. DeSantis, Jeremy L. Green, and Peter S. Ungar

2013　Dental Microwear Texture as a Proxy for Diet in Xenarthrans. *Journal of Mammalogy* 94(4):856–866.

Haynes, Gary

1982　Utilization and Skeletal Disturbances of North American Prey Carcasses. *Arctic* 35(2):266–281.

Hillson, Simon

2005　*Teeth*. Cambridge University Press, Cambridge.

Hogue, S. Homes, and Melsheimer, Rebecca

2008　Integrating Dental Microwear and Isotopic Analyses to Understand Dietary Change in East-Central Mississippi. *Journal of Archaeological Science* 35(2):228–238.

Jones, Davis Brent, and Larisa R. G. DeSantis

2017　Dietary Ecology of Ungulates from the La Brea Tar Pits in Southern California: A Multi-proxy Approach. *Palaeogeography, Palaeoclimatology, Palaeoecology* 466:110–127.

Kenton, Edna

1925　The Jesuit Relations and Allied Documents. Albert and Charles Boni, New York.

Lévi-Strauss, Claude

1988　*The Way of the Masks*. University of British Columbia Press, Vancouver.

Losey, Robert J., Erin Jessup, Tatiana Nomokonova, and Mikhail Sablin

2014　Craniomandibular Trauma and Tooth Loss in Northern Dogs and Wolves: Implications for the Archaeological Study of Dog Husbandry and Domestication. *PLoS ONE* 9(6):e99746.

Lupo, K. D., and J. C. Janetski

1994　Evidence of the Domesticated Dogs and some Related Canids in the Eastern Great Basin. *Journal of California and Great Basin Anthropology* 16(2):199–220.

Maldre, Liina

2006　What Did the Bronze Age Dogs Eat? Coprolithic Analyses. In *Dogs and People in Social, Working, Economic or Symbolic Interaction*, edited by Lynn M. Snyder and Elizabeth A. Moore, pp. 44–48. Proceedings of the 9th ICAZ Conference, Durham, 2002. Oxbow, Oxford.

Mech, L. David

1970　*The Wolf: The Ecology and Behavior of an Endangered Species*. Natural History Press, New York.

Morey, Darcy F.

1986　Studies on Amerindian Dogs: Taxonomic Analysis of Canid Crania from the Northern Plains. *Journal of Archaeological Science* 13(2):119–145.

2010   *Dogs: Domestication and the Development of a Social Bond.* Cambridge University Press, Cambridge.

Morey, Darcy F., and M. D. Wiant

1992   Early Holocene Domestic Dog Burials from the North American Midwest. *Current Anthropology* 33(2):224–229.

Noe-Nygaard, Nanna

1988   δ13C-values of Dog Bones Reveal the Nature of Changes in Man's Food Resources at the Mesolithic-Neolithic Transition, Denmark. *Chemical Geology: Isotope Geoscience* 73(1):87–96.

Paquet, Paul C.

1992   Prey Use Strategies of Sympatric Wolves and Coyotes in Riding Mountain National Park, Manitoba. *Journal of Mammalogy* 73:337–343.

Reher, Charles, and George Frison

1980   *The Vore Site, 48CK302: A Stratified Buffalo Jump in the Wyoming Black Hills.* Plains Anthropologist Memoir 16. Plains Anthropological Society, Norman, Oklahoma.

Reid, Fiona

2006   *Peterson Field Guide to Mammals of North America.* Houghton Mifflin Harcourt, Boston.

Reidhead, Van A.

1977   Optimization and Food Procurement at the Prehistoric Leonard Haag Site, Southeastern Indiana: A Linear Programming Approach. PhD dissertation, Indiana University.

Schmitt, Elizabeth T.

2011   Analysis of Bone Crushing Behavior of the Dire Wolf (*Canis dirus*) Using Dental Microwear Texture Analysis. *Electronic Theses and Dissertations,* paper 1269. http://dc.etsu/etd/1269.

Schoeninger, Margaret J., Michael J. DeNiro, and Henrik Tauber

1983   Stable Nitrogen Isotope Ratios of Bone Collagen Reflect Marine and Terrestrial Components of Prehistoric Human Diet. *Science* 220(4604):1381–1383.

Schubert, Blaine W., Peter S. Ungar, and Larisa R. G. DeSantis

2010   Carnassial Microwear and Dietary Behavior in Large Carnivorans. *Journal of Zoology* 280(3):257–263.

Schulting, Rick. J., and Michael P. Richards

2002   Dogs, Ducks, Deer AND Diet: New Stable Isotope Evidence on Early Mesolithic Dogs from the Vale of Pickering, North-East England. *Journal of Archaeological Science* 29(4):327–333.

Schwarcz, Henry P., and Margaret J. Schoeninger

1991   Stable Isotope Analyses in Human Nutritional Ecology. *American Journal of Physical Anthropology* 34(S13):283–321.

Schwartz, Marion

1997   *A History of Dogs in the Early Americas.* Yale University Press, New Haven.

Scott, Robert S., Peter S. Ungar, Torbjorn S. Bergstrom, Christopher A. Brown, Benjamin E. Childs, Mark F. Teaford, and Alan Walker

2006   Dental Microwear Texture Analysis: Technical Considerations. *Journal of Human Evolution* 51(4):339–349.

Shimkin, Dimitri

1939   Field Notes. American Heritage Center, University of Wyoming, Laramie.

Snyder, Lynn M., and Elizabeth A. Moore (editors)

2006 *Dogs and People in Social, Working, Economic or Symbolic Interaction.* Proceedings of the 9th ICAZ Conference, Durham 2002. Oxbow Books, Oxford.

Sponheimer, Matt, Todd Robinson, Linda Ayliffe, Beverly Roeder, Jordan Hammer, Ben Passey, Adam West, Thure Cerling, Denise Dearing, and J. Ehleringer

2003 Nitrogen Isotopes in Mammalian Herbivores: Hair δ15N Values from a Controlled Feeding Study. *International Journal of Osteoarchaeology* 13(1–2):80–87.

Stahl, Peter W.

2016 Old Dogs and New Tricks: Recent Developments in Our Understanding of the Human–Dog Relationship, *Reviews in Anthropology* 45(1):51–68.

Stahler, Daniel R., Douglas W. Smith, and Debra S. Guernsey

2006 Foraging and Feeding Ecology of the Gray Wolf (*Canis lupus*): Lessons from Yellowstone National Park, Wyoming, USA. *Journal of Nutrition* 136(7):1923S–1926S.

Tanis, Brian P., Larisa R. G. DeSantis, and Rebecca C. Terry

2018 Dental Microwear Textures across Cheek Teeth in Canids: Implications for Dietary Studies of Extant and Extinct Canids. *Palaeogeography, Palaeoclimatology, Palaeoecology* 508:129–138.

Tankersley, Kenneth B., and Jeremy M. Koster

2009 Sources of Stable Isotope Variation in Archaeological Dog Remains. *North American Archaeologist* 30(4):361–375.

Ungar, Peter S.

2010 *Mammal Teeth: Origin, Evolution, and Diversity.* Johns Hopkins University Press, Baltimore.

Ungar, Peter S., Kristin L. Krueger, Robert J. Blumenschine, Jackson Njau, and Robert S. Scott

2012 Dental Microwear Texture Analysis of hominins recovered by the Olduvai Landscape Paleoanthropology Project, 1995–2007. *Journal of Human Evolution* 63(2):429–437.

Ungar, Peter S., Jessica R. Scott, Blaine W. Schubert, and Deano D. Stynder

2010 Carnivoran Dental Microwear Textures: Comparability of Carnassial Facets and Functional Differentiation of Postcanine Teeth. *Mammalia* 74(2):219–224.

Ungar, Peter S., Robert S. Scott, Jessica R. Scott, and Mark Teaford

2008 Dental Microwear Analysis: Historical Perspectives and New Approaches. *Technique and Application in Dental Anthropology* 53:389.

Von den Driesch, Angela

1976 *A Guide to the Measurement of Animal Bones from Archaeological Sites: As Developed by the Institut für Palaeoanatomie, Domestikationsforschung und Geschichte der Tiermedizin of the University of Munich,* Vol. 1. Peabody Museum Press, Cambridge, Massachusetts.

Walker, Danny N., and George C. Frison

1982 Studies on Amerindian Dogs, 3: Prehistoric Wolf/Dog Hybrids from the Northwestern Plains. *Journal of Archaeological Science* 9(2):125–172.

Wang, Xiaoming, Stuart C. White, Mairin Balisi, Jacob Biewer, Julia Sankey, Dennis Garber, and Z. Jack Tseng

2018 First Bone-Cracking Dog Coprolites Provide New Insight into Bone Consumption in Borophagus and Their Unique Ecological Niche. *eLife*, 1–28. DOI: 10.7554/eLife.34773.

Wayne, Robert K.

1993   Molecular Evolution of the Dog Family. *Trends in Genetics* 9(6):218–224.

Wilson, Gilbert Livingston

1924   *The Horse and the Dog in Hidatsa Culture*. Anthropological Papers of the American Museum of Natural History, vol. 15, pt. 2. American Museum of Natural History, New York.

White, Christine D., Mary E. D. Pohl, Henry P. Schwarcz, and Fred J. Longstaffe

2001   Isotopic Evidence for Maya Patterns of Deer and Dog Use at Preclassic Colha. *Journal of Archaeological Science* 28(1):89–107.

6

Scavenger and Sentry

The Roles of Dogs at Çatalhöyük, Turkey,
in the Context of the Near Eastern Neolithic

NERISSA RUSSELL

Dog domestication predates agriculture. There are a number of claims for Upper Paleolithic dogs in various Old World locations (Germonpré et al. 2009; Germonpré et al. 2015; Janssens et al. 2018; Musil 2000; Ovodov et al. 2011; Pionnier-Capitan et al. 2011; Sablin and Khlopachev 2002; Vigne 2005/2006), although these remain somewhat controversial (Boudadi-Maligne and Escarguel 2014; Drake et al. 2015; Morey 2014; Perri 2016a). The earliest generally, although not universally, accepted dogs are found in the Epipaleolithic Natufian culture of the Levant at circa 12,500 cal BCE (Davis and Valla 1978; Tchernov and Valla 1997; cf. Quintero and Köhler-Rollefsen 1997), in the context of a foraging culture that was sedentary in some places. Dogs are more widespread in the Near East in the earliest Neolithic, when many settlements practiced plant cultivation but not herding, even crossing the sea to Cyprus. Dogs remained the only animal domesticate until later in the Neolithic, when livestock herding began. Dogs made the transition along with humans from mobile to settled, broad-based foraging, and they apparently became more valuable as humans started farming.

Dogs have played myriad roles in human societies, including companion, hunting aid, guard, pack animal, scavenger, and food source. There are differing ideas about the function or functions of the first dogs, that is, what would motivate humans to share their lives with tame wolves, even if the process of dog domestication is now usually seen as coevolutionary. Popular suggestions include their use in hunting, given that humans and wolves pursue much of the same prey (e.g., Clutton-Brock 1995; Eaton 1969; Mason 1966 [1895]; Musil 2000); their inclination to scavenge and thereby clean up human garbage (e.g., Dekel et al. 2017; Montagu 1942; Zeder 2012); their companionship as pets (e.g., Janssens et al. 2018; Sauer 1969; Serpell 1996); their use as guards for humans and their possessions (e.g., Jouventin et al. 2016; Ronen 2004); or, if domestication is placed later, their use in herding through the modification of wolf hunting behavior to control ungulates (Zeuner 1963). Regardless of the original reason or reasons for dog domestication, settling down and devoting labor to cultivation would change the lives of both humans and dogs, particularly as this was accompanied, roughly speaking, with a shift to a more broad-spectrum subsistence, meaning hunting focused on smaller animals. Livestock herding not only provided new potential roles for dogs as herding aids but also changed their relation to humans. No longer the sole domesticate, their position became more anomalous: not wild but also not raised for food.

My focus here is not on the earliest dogs but on their roles in Near Eastern Neolithic societies as the dogs adapted to these changing circumstances. Since hunting and herding are the main activities through which they could contribute to human subsistence, I will explore evidence that these practices influenced how many dogs were kept. In particular, was there a shift from use of dogs in hunting to use in herding as livestock were added to plant agriculture? I will also consider other potential roles, as food or companions. I will examine these issues through the case study of Çatalhöyük in Turkey, along with a broader look at the Near Eastern Neolithic.

Çatalhöyük and the Near Eastern Neolithic

My geographical coverage encompasses the Levant, Upper Mesopotamia (the middle and upper valleys of the Euphrates, Tigris, and their tributaries), and the Zagros, together comprising the Fertile Crescent; Anatolia (the southeast portion of Anatolia forms part of Upper Mesopotamia, while I divide the remainder into Central and Western Anatolia); and Cyprus. These are key regions in the development of early agriculture. Cyprus is particularly illuminating with respect to human-animal relations because virtually all mammals found on the island in the Holocene were brought there by humans (Vigne et al. 2011). For simplicity's sake, I will use loosely the primarily Levantine

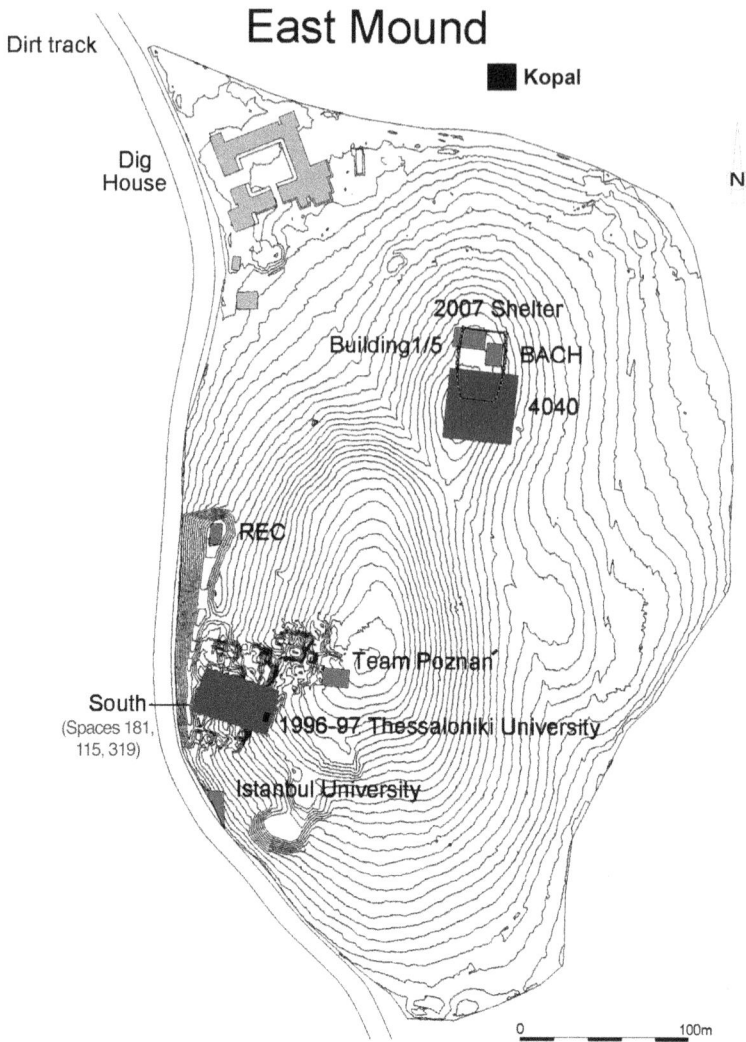

Figure 6.1. Excavation areas on Çatalhöyük East Mound.

chronological system for the Neolithic of this whole area: Pre-Pottery Neolithic A (PPNA) for the earlier aceramic Neolithic, when plant cultivation
probably started; PPNB for the subsequent period when livestock herding
began and when population in the region increased and farming settlements
spread rapidly; and Pottery Neolithic (PN), marking the adoption of ceramic
vessels, subsuming a variety of named cultures. These transitions do not hap-
pen simultaneously across the region discussed, but the PPNA covers roughly

the early tenth–mid-ninth millennia cal BCE, the PPNB roughly mid-ninth–mid-seventh millennia cal BCE (including what is sometimes separated as the PPNC), and the PN starts between circa 7000 and 6500 cal BCE and runs to about 5000 cal BCE.

Çatalhöyük is a large tell site on the Konya Plain in Central Anatolia, excavated by James Mellaart (1967) in the 1960s and more recently by Ian Hodder (2006, 2014). This discussion is based on the analysis of materials from the Hodder excavations through 2008 (Figure 6.1). The Neolithic East Mound was occupied from circa 7100 to 6000 cal BCE, with pottery in use through most of the sequence. The tell is built up from numerous layers of closely packed mudbrick houses, entered through the roofs. There are no streets, but some open spaces existed among the buildings, created when a house went out of use and was not immediately rebuilt. These open areas accumulated middens as neighboring houses dumped their refuse into them, and they were also used for outdoor activities. Many changes in architecture, material culture, and other aspects of life occur circa 6500 cal BCE (Hodder 2013; Hodder and Doherty 2014); this is the division between what I call the earlier and later levels.

Domestic sheep and goats dominate the animal remains throughout the occupation, increasing in the later levels (Figure 6.2). In the earlier levels, sheep and goats (caprines) and dogs are the only domesticates; a few domestic cattle are also present in the later levels (Russell et al. 2013). The main wild taxa are aurochs (wild cattle), wild boar, equids, and deer (mainly red deer).

Dogs at Çatalhöyük

Dogs form about 1% of the identified macromammalian fauna at Çatalhöyük. They were occasionally but not usually eaten throughout the sequence. Three dog specimens, all from midden deposits, show butchering traces: a radius with articulated ulna from the South G site-edge dumps of the earliest occupation, a tibia from a later-period midden with scraping to remove the periosteum and blows for marrow fracture, and a calcaneus with a dismemberment cut/chop mark from some of the latest Neolithic deposits. Other isolated and broken bones may also be the remains of meals, but many dog specimens are intact and often partially articulated. They differ in this way from the domestic livestock animals and also most of the wild animals, which were eaten, used for their fur, or both. This occasional consumption is somewhat similar to the treatment

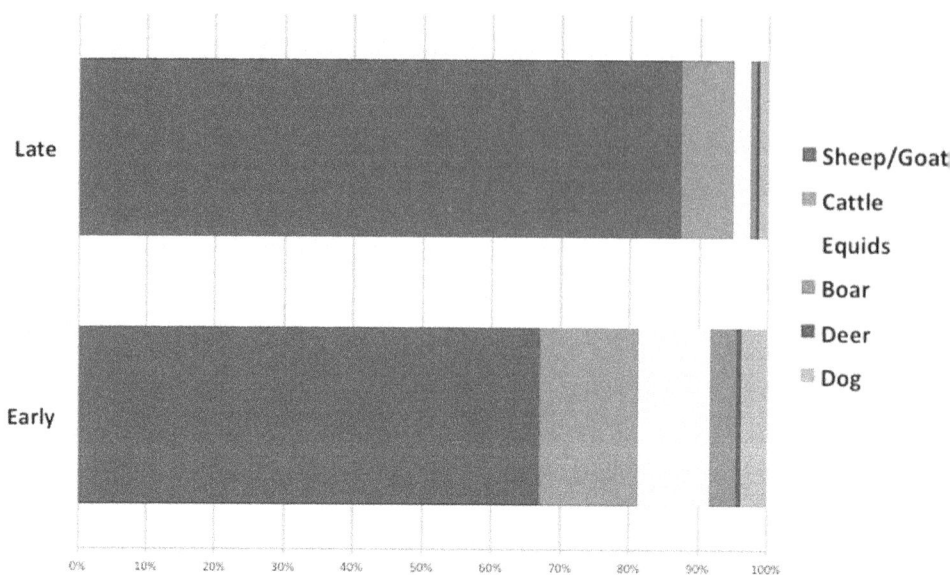

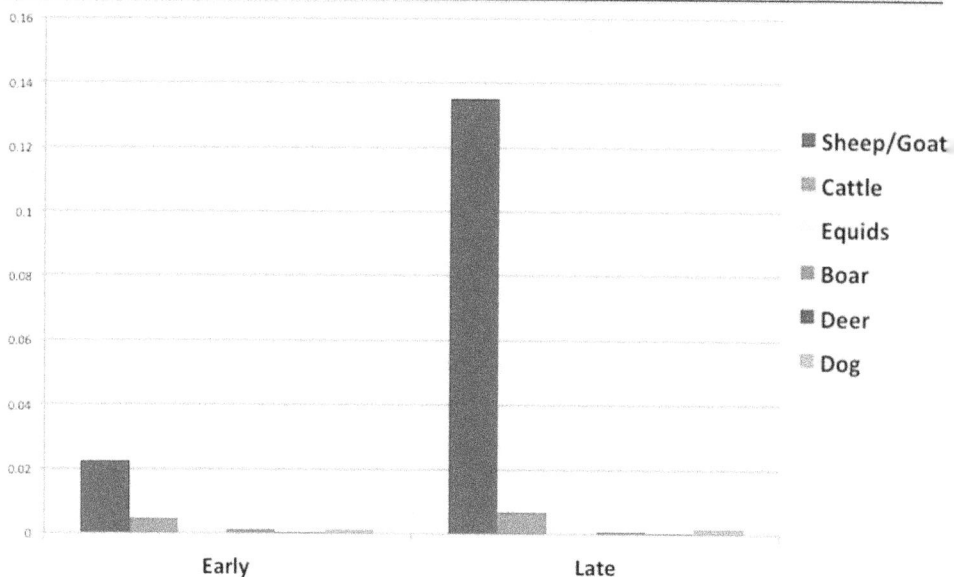

Figure 6.2. *Top:* Relative frequency of dogs and major taxa in the earlier and later levels at Neolithic Çatalhöyük by diagnostic zone (Watson 1979). *Bottom:* Density in midden deposits (diagnostic zones per liter) of dogs and major taxa in the earlier and later levels at Neolithic Çatalhöyük.

of deer and boar, which I argue were subject to partial taboos, meaning some categories of people could not eat them (Russell 2018). However, dogs do not show the same kind of patchy distribution within the site, nor the selection of particular body parts seen in the deer and boar remains. So rather than being eaten by some subgroups, with their remains dangerous to others, dogs and their remains were welcome in the settlement but usually classified as inedible. This makes it likely that eating dogs was an emotionally charged act—perhaps of desperation, or only in particular circumstances.

Although dogs were rarely eaten, there is little evidence to suggest that they were kept as pets at Çatalhöyük. There are no real dog burials at the site, and certainly they are not buried with humans or like humans (below house floors). The lack of gnawed bone in indoor occupation deposits indicates that dogs were not allowed in houses while people lived in them (Russell and Twiss 2017). The dogs do not seem to have been mistreated, in contrast to the high incidence of blunt trauma to the head I have observed in Neolithic southeast Europe (Russell 1993). The only pathology observed in the Çatalhöyük dog specimens is an individual that suffered a penetrating wound to the lower back, breaking some vertebrae and becoming infected. While the dog survived long enough for some healing to occur, this may have been the cause of death. This injury could have resulted from human abuse or from a hunting injury or an accident. Although dogs were generally not abused, canine infant mortality was quite high, especially in the earlier periods (Russell et al. 2013), suggesting that dogs may not have received much care. We might imagine an attitude to dogs resembling what David Blouin (2013) calls the dominionistic form of human-dog relations in contemporary North America (other forms are humanistic and protectionistic): dominionistic owners take a utilitarian approach to their dogs, valuing them for their services but not treating them as persons, and usually keeping them outside the house.

While it is difficult to determine whether dogs were used in hunting or herding, if these were the primary motivations for keeping dogs, one would expect the number of dogs to vary with the proportion of wild or domestic animals, respectively. In the later levels at Çatalhöyük, domestic caprines increase, and some of the cattle are domestic, so that the overall proportion of domestic animals increased and wild ones decreased. Dogs decrease slightly proportionately in the later levels, which on its face suggests that they might have been used primarily in hunting, and certainly not in herding. However, the difficulty with proportions is that it is hard to tell whether sheep are increasing or other animals decreasing. To address this, I examined the density (diagnostic zones per volume excavated) of bones in midden deposits through the occupation (Figure 6.2). Middens catch the remains of most on-site activities, hence they are the best indicator of animal consumption. This analysis shows that caprines increase sharply in the later levels, while cattle remain about the same as earlier (but now including some domestic cattle), and dogs occur at the same density throughout the occupation. Thus the number of dogs seems not to correlate with the proportion of either wild or domestic taxa at Çatalhöyük. This argues against their primary function being either hunting or herding, though they could have participated in these activities.

I propose that people kept dogs at Çatalhöyük largely as guards and garbage processors. A comparison of caprine body part distribution in the digested (dog feces) and undigested material from several midden areas suggests that dogs spent most of their time in these open areas (Russell and Twiss 2017). Residents of nearby houses may have owned the dogs, or these people would at least have been familiar to them. The dogs would surely have acted as guards to the extent of alerting local residents to the arrival of others, which would have been especially useful for people living in houses with roof entrances and no windows. Most of the deposits in the South G middens, then on the edge of the settlement, are heavily worked over by dogs—more so than most on-site middens. So in addition to the dogs living on-site in midden areas, there may also have been a population of pariah dogs on the periphery that did not belong to particular people or families.

While dogs were not buried like humans, a few complete or quasi-complete dog skeletons were placed in houses at closure or in the fill preparatory to constructing the next house, hence foundation deposits. Since house closure involved scouring and stripping the house before (often) placing items in it prior to filling (Russell et al. 2014), these should be considered intentional placements and not simply disposal. In particular, a puppy was placed on top of a platform in Building 3, beneath which humans were buried. Perhaps it was left to guard them in the afterlife. An apparently complete dog, later disturbed by a human burial, was a foundation deposit for Building 6. Another complete dog, however, was put in a midden area outside houses. This last might be an instance of simple disposal, although since dogs lived in these areas in life, it might also have been meant to continue to guard the surrounding houses.

Partial dogs were similarly placed: two dog skulls with articulating mandibles formed part of foundation deposits. A dog scapula was placed along with a cattle scapula (a frequent closing deposit item) near a hearth in the closing layer of Building 51. A large portion of a semi-articulated dog was placed, wrapped around a cattle skull, in an oven in Building 58 prior to filling. The dog seems to have lain exposed elsewhere for a short time, where it was largely defleshed and lost a few pieces. This is the dog with the injured back. If this was a hunting wound, we could interpret this as special treatment for a fallen hunting companion (e.g., Bulmer 1976; Ojoade 1990). However, it was not interred in a regular burial as a human would have been.

Dogs tend to "wolf down" hunks of meat when they feed, thus ingesting bones; they also swallow fragments from bones they gnaw when at leisure. Many of these swallowed bone fragments survive, although altered by digestive acids, and emerge in the feces. Digested bone specimens, especially those in the 1–3 cm range, thus serve as a marker for the presence of dog feces in archaeological deposits (Horwitz 1990; Solomon and David 1990; see Russell and Twiss 2017 for a more extended discussion). Digested bone, most of it almost surely from dog feces, is quite common at Çatalhöyük, forming 7.5% of the mammalian bones from the East Mound assemblage, 9% of those <4 cm (Russell and Twiss 2017). As noted, matches between the proportions of body parts in the digested and un-digested animal bone assemblages of middens suggest that dogs scavenged from the garbage dumped there, and the quantities of digested bone indicate that they consumed large amounts of garbage. Their diet likely also included a substantial quantity of human feces, as has been documented for modern village dogs (But-ler 1998; Butler and du Toit 2002; Sharp 1976). The presence of human feces has been detected through chemical signatures in contexts that also have high levels of bones digested by dogs (many of them larger than humans normally swallow), indicating that dogs had access to human waste (Shillito et al. 2011). If the bile acids that identify human feces survive canine digestion, these could actually be deposits of the feces of dogs that have eaten human excrement.

While scavenging on material including carrion and feces often marks dogs as unclean, the hygienic effect is also appreciated (Bulmer 1976; Hamilton 1972; Montagu 1942; Sharp 1976; Willerslev 2007). Recent work shows that dogs have evolved a greater capacity to digest starch than wolves, and their diet is more omnivorous, making them more effective scavengers around human settle-ments (Arendt et al. 2014; Axelsson et al. 2013). Scavenging dogs reduce large amounts of smelly waste to a smaller amount of (admittedly also smelly) dog excrement. Asian privy pigs, which consumed human and agricultural waste and removed many human pathogens in digestion, provided manure for grow-ing crops that was safer than the direct use of human feces (Nemeth 1998). Dogs probably similarly reduce the prevalence of pathogens in human settlements (Hamilton 1972; Sharp 1976). In particular, they clean up by eating the feces of children too young to use toilet areas (Ojoade 1990; Sharp 1976).

In sum, dogs at Çatalhöyük probably played multiple roles, but there is little indication that their primary function was either hunting or herding or that they were regarded as pets. There is strong evidence that they consumed a large amount of waste, probably including human excrement. In a large, densely inhabited settlement, this service was likely appreciated, if with some ambivalence, and it likely improved human health. Recent studies show that infant mortality and infectious disease were high at Çatalhöyük but intestinal parasites relatively low (Larsen et al. 2019; Ledger et al. 2019), which may be a result of canine processing of human waste. Since dogs lived among the houses, they would inevitably have warned their neighbors of unfamiliar people approaching and may have actively protected houses. Scavenger and sentry appear to have been the major canine roles.

Dogs in the Neolithic Near East

Dogs' roles varied still more across the Neolithic Near East. While somewhat outside the geographical and temporal scope examined here, dogs served as a significant food item, in a diet largely consisting of fish, at seasonal settlements in fifth–fourth millennium cal BCE Neolithic Oman (Maini and Curci 2014). Jean-Denis Vigne and Jean Guilaine (2004) suggest that dogs were introduced early to Cyprus and became feral. At PPNB Shillourokambos, they argue that dogs did not live in the village but were hunted and eaten, given the lack of dog burials or figurines, the absence of gnawed and digested bone, and the presence of roasted dog heads. They note that dog remains and gnawed bones are scarce or absent at contemporary sites on Cyprus (and later aceramic sites contemporary with the Pottery Neolithic on the mainland) and propose that the feral dogs were gradually hunted out. The few Neolithic sites from Cyprus for which I was able to find adequate data (Table 6.1) support a diminishing presence of dogs through time, with a relatively high representation in the PPNA that is reduced in the PPNB.

Cyprus and Oman appear to be particular cases in Neolithic human-canine relations, but the numbers and even presence of dogs at other Neolithic sites are notably variable (Table 6.1). However, if we ignore the small sample from the PPNC (where one of three sites has dogs), dogs appear to be kept more widely through time: dogs occur in 50% of PPNA assemblages (n = 10), 75% of PPNB assemblages (n = 36), and 81% of PN assemblages (n = 32). Dogs are geographically limited in the PPNA. The only occurrence outside the Levant and Cyprus is a single specimen (a humerus) described as dog/wolf from Körtik

Tepe (Arbuckle and Özkaya 2006). This humerus is quite large and could be a wolf. By the PPNB, dogs appear in all regions included here, although they remain rare in the Zagros. In the Pottery Neolithic, dogs occur at most sites in all regions, although some still lack them. While dogs spread through time, their numbers vary. Although there is considerable variability in the proportion of dogs, especially in the PPNB and PN, the average percentage of dogs is 0.6% for the PPNA, dropping to 0.4% in the PPNB, then rising to 0.7% in the PN. If these overall trends are meaningful, more people found it useful to keep fewer dogs as livestock was adopted in the PPNB, while later larger numbers of dogs were again desired.

A previous analysis of faunal patterning across Near Eastern and European Neolithic sites (Bartosiewicz 1990) found a positive correlation between proportions of dogs and of wild taxa, suggesting that dogs were important for hunting. Following up on this for the Near East, with the benefit of data published in the interim, I seek to provide broader context for the patterns observed through the Çatalhöyük sequence, where the lack of correlation of dog frequencies with changes in wild/domestic ratios argues against their major participation in either hunting or herding. As a first approximation, I have tracked down as many faunal reports as I could find for the Neolithic periods of the regions under consideration (Fertile Crescent, Cyprus, Anatolia). I recorded the numbers of wild macromammals (hare-sized and larger), domestic ungulates, domestic caprines (perhaps especially amenable to the use of herding dogs), and dogs (Table 6.1).

Any such comparative exercise faces a number of not fully soluble issues of data comparability. I use NISP (number of identified specimens) as the most consistent quantification technique across assemblages, although this meant excluding a few publications that did not report raw numbers. I have not tried to address inter-analyst differences in identification or the effects of varying archaeological recovery. The latter, especially, may have real consequences for the amount of dogs and caprines, but I hope that gross patterns will still emerge. I have excluded assemblages with fewer than 200 NISP of macromammals as the small sample size is likely to affect proportions (Bartosiewicz 1990). I also exclude reports that span more than one of the periods (PPNA, PPNB, PN) without separating the data, as well as those that do not include all the relevant taxonomic categories (e.g., that lump dogs into "carnivore" or "other" categories), but I do include those that identify only to the level of *Canis* sp. (potentially dog, wolf, and in some places jackal). The beginning of the Pottery Neolithic and the

Table 6.1. Dogs and other fauna at Near Eastern Neolithic sites

Region	Site	Period	Wild	Domestic Ungulates	Domestic Caprine	Canis sp.	Dog	Dog/ Canis sp.	Source
Upper Mesopotamia	Körtik Tepe	PPNA	212	0	0	1	-	1	Arbuckle and Özkaya 2006
Upper Mesopotamia	Mureybet	PPNA	10,480	0	0	0	0	0	Gourichon and Helmer 2008
Upper Mesopotamia	Qermez Dere	PPNA	4,187	0	0	0	0	0	Dobney et al. 1999
Levant	Gilgal I	PPNA	369	0	0	-	7	7	Horwitz et al. 2010
Levant	Hatoula	PPNA	354	0	0	-	0	0	Davis et al. 1994
Levant	Jericho	PPNA	551	0	0	8	-	8	Clutton-Brock 1979
Levant	Netiv Hagdud	PPNA	385	0	0	-	3	3	Tchernov 1994
Levant	Wadi Faynan 16	PPNA	522	0	0	0	0	0	Carruthers and Dennis 2007
Cyprus	Klimonas	PPNA	1,276	0	0	-	22	22	Vigne et al. 2012
Central Anatolia	Pınarbaşı	PPNA	270	0	0	0	0	0	Baird et al. 2018
Zagros	Asiab	PPNB	1,023	81	81	-	0	0	Bökönyi 1977
Zagros	Chogha Bonut	PPNB	222	282	282	0	0	0	Redding 2003
Zagros	Ganj Dareh	PPNB	2,963	4,689	4,689	-	0	0	Hesse 1984
Zagros	Jarmo	PPNB	335	1,071	1,038	10	-	10	Stampfli 1983
Zagros	Tepe Guran	PPNB	37	201	201	0	0	0	Flannery 2014

continued

Region	Site	Period							Reference
Upper Mesopotamia	Cafer Höyük	PPNB	420	3,197	1,739	-	15	15	Helmer 2008
Upper Mesopotamia	Mezraa-Teleilat	PPNB	70	2,406	1,590	-	6	6	Ilgezdi 2008
Upper Mesopotamia	Mureybet	PPNB	376	90	10	3	-	3	Gourichon and Helmer 2008
Upper Mesopotamia	Tell Halula	PPNB	1,604	4,048	2,687	-	230	230	Saña Seguí 1999
Upper Mesopotamia	Tell Sabi Abyad II	PPNB	32	1,278	1,199	-	1	1	van Wijngaarden-Bakker and Maliepaard 2000
Levant	Abu Ghosh	PPNB	9,086	8	8	7	-	7	Horwitz 2003
Levant	Ain Ghazal	PPNB	4,546	13,163	12,139	15	16	31	Köhler-Rollefson et al. 1993; von den Driesch and Wodtke 1997
Levant	Ain Jammam	PPNB	197	852	763	5	-	5	Makarewicz 2009
Levant	Ayn Abū Nukhayla	PPNB	687	1,602	1,048	-	8	8	Dean 2014
Levant	Bāja	PPNB	485	4,783	4,776	-	3	3	von den Driesch et al. 2004
Levant	Basta	PPNB	5,769	14,570	14,570	-	9	9	Becker 1998
Levant	Dhuweila	PPNB	2,681	5	5	3	-	3	Martin 1999a
Levant	Jericho	PPNB	401	388	388	7	-	7	Clutton-Brock 1979
Levant	Motza	PPNB	4,767	96	96	-	0	0	Sapir-Hen et al. 2009
Levant	Qumran Cave 24	PPNB	360	64	64	7	-	7	Alhaique and Gopher 2005
Levant	Tell Aswad	PPNB	1,783	3,330	2,425	3	-	3	Helmer and Gourichon 2017
Levant	Tell Tif'dan	PPNB	126	4,065	3,407	-	3	3	Twiss 2007

Table 6.1.—continued

Region	Site	Period	Wild	Domestic Ungulates	Domestic Caprine	Canis sp.	Dog	Dog/Canis sp.	Source
Levant	Wadi Abu Tulayha	PPNB	1,543	30	27	0	0	0	Hongo et al. 2014
Levant	Wadi Fidan A	PPNB	74	681	681	2	-	2	Richardson 1997
Levant	Wadi Fidan C	PPNB	186	281	281	0	0	0	Richardson 1997
Levant	Wadi Jilat 13	PPNB	1,756	694	694	20	-	20	Martin 1999b
Levant	Wadi Jilat 7	PPNB	1,131	0	0	3	-	3	Martin 1999b
Levant	Wadi Shu'eib	PPNB	109	229	202	1	-	1	Makarewicz 2016
Levant	Wadi Tbeik	PPNB	1,038	0	0	0	0	0	Tchernov and Bar-Yosef 1982
Levant	Yiftahel	PPNB	3,066	1,026	335	5	7	12	Alhaique and Horwitz 2012; Sapir-Hen et al. 2016
Cyprus	Ais Yiorkis	PPNB	11,892	9,723	3,542	-	7	7	Simmons et al. 2018
Cyprus	Kalavasos-Tenta	PPNB	2,002	1,713	789	0	0	0	Croft 2005
Cyprus	Shillourokambos	PPNB	1,420	2,116	991	-	11	11	Vigne et al. 2011
Central Anatolia	Aşıklı Höyük	PPNB	2,978	16,596	16,596	-	2	2	Buitenhuis 1997
Central Anatolia	Boncuklu	PPNB	539	20	20	12	-	12	Baird et al. 2018
Western Anatolia	Ulucak	PPNB	85	2,239	1,741	-	1	1	Çakırlar 2012
Levant	Ain Ghazal	PPNC	1,302	6,217	5,847	3	8	11	Köhler-Rollefson et al. 1993; von den Driesch and Wodtke 1997
Levant	Sha'ar Hagolan	PPNC	89	390	211	0	0	0	Marom 2012

Region	Site	Period							Reference
Levant	Wadi Shuʿeib	PPNC	74	643	485	5	-	5	Makarewicz 2016
Zagros	Jarmo	PN	371	3,053	2,812	26	-	26	Stampfli 1983
Zagros	Qaleh Rustam	PN	2,108	2,056	2,056	2	-	2	Daujat and Mashkour 2017
Zagros	Sarab	PN	1,096	5,978	5,847	128	-	128	Bökönyi 1977
Zagros	Tepe Guran	PN	543	779	779	-	0	0	Flannery 2014
Zagros	Tepe Tulaʾi	PN	46	483	483	-	2	2	Wheeler Pires-Ferreira 1975–1977
Upper Mesopotamia	Çavi Tarlası	PN	75	3,306	1,227	-	14	14	Schäffer and Boessneck 1988
Upper Mesopotamia	Domuztepe	PN	91	5,887	3,080	-	16	16	Kansa et al. 2009
Upper Mesopotamia	Girikihacıyan	PN	41	1,953	1,277	-	26	26	McArdle 1990
Upper Mesopotamia	Mezraa-Teleilat	PN	141	2,072	1,534	-	3	3	Ilgezdi 2008
Upper Mesopotamia	Shams ed-Din Tannira	PN	749	590	485	-	6	6	Uerpmann 1982
Upper Mesopotamia	Tall Aswad	PN	352	459	459	4	-	4	Helmer 1985
Upper Mesopotamia	Tell Amarna	PN	16	421	224	0	0	0	Saña Seguí 2004
Upper Mesopotamia	Tell Boueid II	PN	531	329	283	0	0	0	Saña Seguí 2002
Upper Mesopotamia	Tell Halula	PN	378	4,125	3,116	-	20	20	Saña Seguí 1999
Upper Mesopotamia	Tell Kurdu	PN	765	5,046	2,234	9	-	9	Loyet and Nardulli 2004
Upper Mesopotamia	Tell Sabi Abyad	PN	367	6,483	4,891	-	23	23	Cavallo 2000
Levant	Abu Ghosh	PN	320	26	26	1	-	1	Horwitz 2003

continued

Table 6.1.—continued

Region	Site	Period	Wild	Domestic Ungulates	Domestic Caprine	Canis sp.	Dog	Dog/Canis sp.	Source
Levant	Ain Ghazal	PN	1,155	5,442	5,087	4	25	29	Köhler-Rollefson et al. 1993; von den Driesch and Wodtke 1997
Levant	Azraq 31	PN	815	281	281	22	-	22	Martin 1999b
Levant	Beisamun	PN	150	569	235	-	22	22	Khalaily et al. 2015
Levant	Dhuweila	PN	8,122	39	39	15	-	15	Martin 1999a
Levant	Sha'ar Hagolan	PN	269	1,586	1,011	-	79	79	Marom 2012
Levant	Tell Aswad	PN	191	358	210	0	0	0	Helmer and Gourichon 2017
Levant	Tell Te'o	PN	12	327	124	0	0	0	Horwitz 2001
Central Anatolia	Çatalhöyük	PN	20,784	46,444	46,444	99	571	670	Russell et al. 2013
Central Anatolia	Mersin-Yumuktepe	PN	2	207	158	1	-	1	Buitenhuis and Caneva 1998
Central Anatolia	Pınarbaşı	PN	920	1,304	1,304	22	-	22	Carruthers 2005
Western Anatolia	Bademağacı	PN	297	6,227	2,927	-	70	70	De Cupere et al. 2008
Western Anatolia	Höyücek	PN	90	387	153	-	2	2	De Cupere and Duru 2003
Western Anatolia	Ilıpınar	PN	91	372	301	-	2	2	Buitenhuis 2008
Western Anatolia	Uğurlu Höyük	PN	106	1,322	1,043	0	0	0	Atıcı et al. 2017
Western Anatolia	Ulucak	PN	221	4,413	2,801	-	11	11	Çakırlar 2012

transition from PN to Chalcolithic occur at different times across the regions. I have arbitrarily cut off the PN at 5000 cal BCE.

Domestication poses a particularly tricky set of problems. While zooarchaeologists might disagree about whether particular animal remains derive from domestic or wild animals, I have taken the analysts' assessments at face value, unless the assemblage has been more recently reassessed. Moreover, many assemblages contain a mix of wild and domestic individuals within a taxon, most of which cannot be separated (or it may be uncertain whether the populations were herded). In these cases I have followed as closely as possible the weight of the evidence presented. For example, if the report suggests sheep were probably but not certainly herded, I count them as domestic. In many cases I have had to approximate by, for example, counting all *Ovis* as domestic and all *Sus* as wild even though it is apparent or likely that a few of the sheep are wild and a few pigs domestic. Similarly, if it appears that the *Canis* sp. category is probably mainly dog, I have treated that as equivalent to *C. familiaris*. In sum, the price of broad coverage is a certain amount of fuzziness in the data.

If dogs were used primarily in hunting, we would expect the proportion of dogs to increase with the proportion of wild fauna. The results of this study indicate that there is no consistent relationship between the proportions of dogs and wild fauna (Figure 6.3). For the PPNA, when there are no domestic ungulates, we see a range of dog representation. As noted, half the PPNA sites have no dogs, while those that have them range from 0.5% to 1.9%. Dogs were obviously not uniformly essential to hunting, as half the sites made do without them despite obtaining all their animal food from hunting. In the PPNB, when most sites have domestic ungulates, there is a slightly positive relationship between dogs and wild fauna overall. Broken down by region, Upper Mesopotamia has the strongest positive relationship, although the particularly high proportion of dogs at Halula (3.9%) is not associated with a particularly high proportion of wild fauna (27.3%). There is little relationship between these variables in the Levant and a somewhat negative one in the Zagros. The other areas have fewer than five PPNB assemblages (only the Levant has more than five) and do not show clear patterning. The three PPNC assemblages have low proportions of wild fauna and variable but not very high proportions of dog. The PN assemblages show an overall slightly negative association between dogs and wild fauna, while the regions with five or more assemblages each vary from mildly to strongly negative relationships. Again, the two assemblages with notably high proportions of dogs (Sha'ar Hagolan

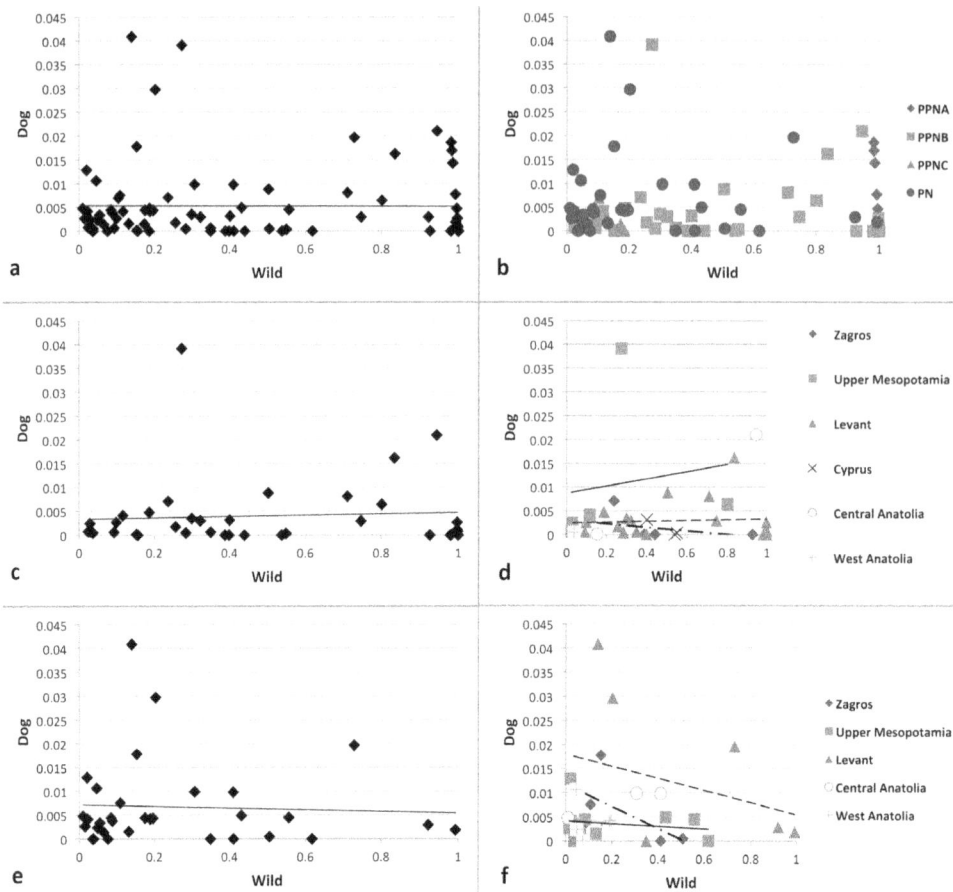

Figure 6.3. Proportion of dogs in relation to proportions of wild macromammals at Near Eastern Neolithic sites: (*a*) all sites in study, (*b*) all sites by period, (*c*) PPNB sites, (*d*) PPNB sites by region, (*e*) PN sites, (*f*) PN sites by region. Trendlines in region diagrams: Zagros, dash-dot; Upper Mesopotamia, solid; Levant, dashed.

4.1%, Beisamun 3.0%) do not have very high amounts of wild fauna. Overall, there is little support for a consistent primary hunting function for dogs in the Near Eastern Neolithic, although they may have played this role at some sites. Finer geographical distinctions and local environmental factors would surely illuminate these differences.

The proportions of wild fauna and domestic ungulates in assemblages obviously have an inverse relationship. However, since wild fauna consists of more than ungulates, the proportion of domestic ungulates is not simply the flip side of the proportion of wild fauna, and it seemed worth examining the relationship

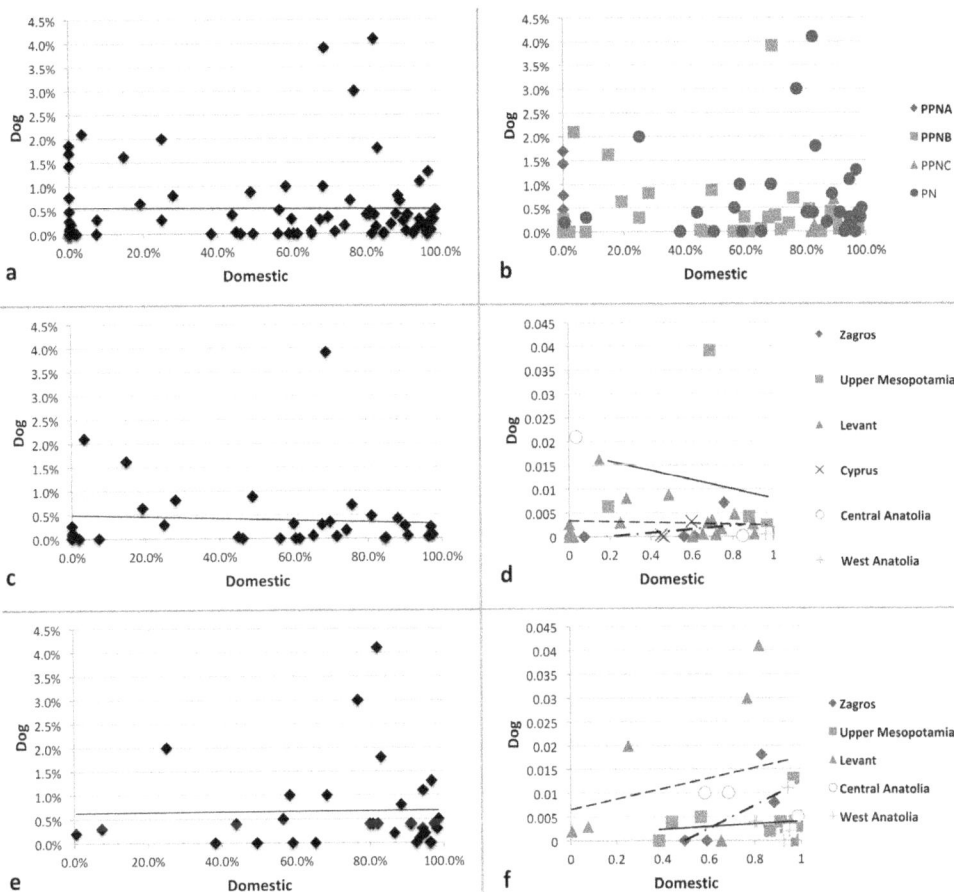

Figure 6.4. Proportion of dogs in relation to proportions of domestic ungulates at Near Eastern Neolithic sites: (*a*) all sites in study, (*b*) all sites by period, (*c*) PPNB sites, (*d*) PPNB sites by region, (*e*) PN sites, (*f*) PN sites by region. Trendlines in region diagrams: Zagros, dash-dot; Upper Mesopotamia, solid; Levant, dashed.

of the proportion of dogs to the proportion of domestic ungulates. If dogs were used primarily for herding, we would expect a positive relationship. However, presumably because the numbers of non-ungulate macromammals in these assemblages are fairly low, the relationships are in fact essentially the inverse of those with the proportion of wild fauna (Figure 6.4): there is an overall lack of relationship, and a generally slightly negative relationship in the PPNB with regional variation mirroring that seen with the wild fauna. While there is overall little relationship in the PN, the regions with larger numbers of assemblages show variably positive relationships. Thus there is little support for the wide-

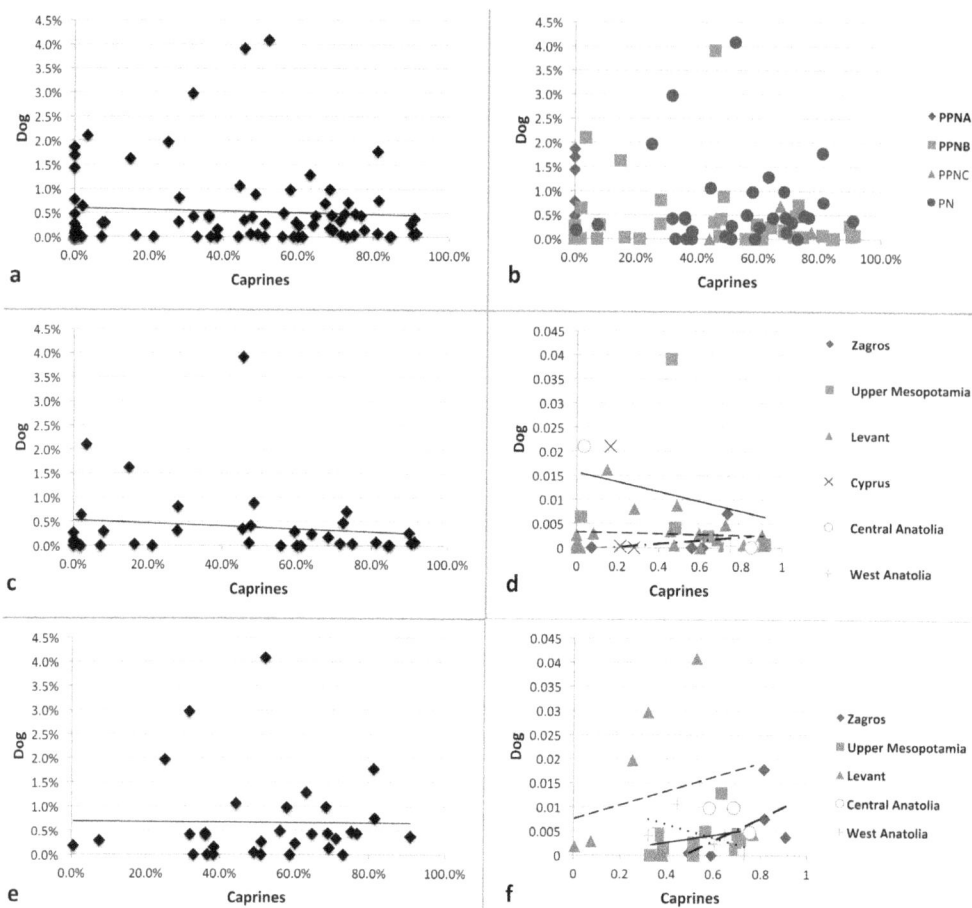

Figure 6.5. Proportion of dogs in relation to proportions of domestic caprines (sheep and goats) at Near Eastern Neolithic sites: (*a*) all sites in study, (*b*) all sites by period, (*c*) PPNB sites, (*d*) PPNB sites by region, (*e*) PN sites, (*f*) PN sites by region. Trendlines in region diagrams: Zagros, dash-dot; Upper Mesopotamia, solid; Levant, dashed; West Anatolia, dotted.

spread primary use of dogs in herding once domestic ungulates appear but some support for this use in the PN in some places. Given the large amount of variability within regions, this may be a more localized practice.

For the most part, caprines dominate the domestic ungulates in these assemblages, so examining the relationship of dogs with caprines alone does not make a lot of difference (Figure 6.5). The negative relationships in the PPNB are slightly accentuated, while in the PN the main difference is that in Western Anatolia, the one region where caprines form a smaller part of the domestic ungulates, the relationship changes from mildly positive with all domestic ungulates to decidedly negative with caprines. These patterns call into question my assumption that dogs are more useful in controlling or protecting small stock, or at least Near Eastern Neolithic dogs and their owners had not developed the skills that would make them useful.

Conclusion

I have juxtaposed a coarse regional analysis of the role of dogs in the Near Eastern Neolithic with a much more contextualized consideration of dogs at Çatalhöyük. Together, they suggest that dogs performed multiple functions at different times and places even as early as the Neolithic, and very likely within single settlements as well. I find little support for their primary use in either hunting or herding (after livestock domestication) at Çatalhöyük or in the Near Eastern Neolithic generally, although these roles may have been important at certain sites. Proportions of dogs do not vary with proportions of either wild or domestic fauna. Interestingly, there is even less evidence in favor of using dogs to herd or protect caprines specifically. At Çatalhöyük, I argue that treatment of dogs and signs of their activities indicate a rather utilitarian human attitude toward dogs and that their primary roles were probably to alert residents to the approach of strangers and to process garbage, perhaps especially human waste. In contrast to PPNB Cyprus (where all dogs may have been feral), dogs were clearly living on-site, in the midden areas among the houses as well as on the site edge.

The regional comparison shows that dogs became more widespread through the Neolithic, so clearly they had some appeal to farmers. Initially found only in the Levant and Cyprus, they expand geographically and occur at a higher percentage of sites within each region during the course of the Neolithic. My focus here is on the Neolithic, but extending comparison to the Epipaleolithic (and finding and excavating more Epipaleolithic sites outside the Levant) would help clarify whether this is a spread from an initial local domestication or a more complex process.

More focused work could illuminate the reasons for the considerable variability in the numbers and even presence of dogs at Near Eastern Neolithic settlements. Local environmental factors likely play some role: Perri (2016b) suggests vegetation has a major effect on dogs' utility in hunting. It would also be very interesting to see more fine-grained analyses exploring dogs' particular roles at other sites, examining the treatment of dog remains and other evidence of their activities (such as gnawed and digested bones) contextually to shed light on human-dog relations. Such studies at Çatalhöyük and Shillourokambos (Vigne and Guilaine 2004) illustrate that variability in numeric representation at least partially derives from differing roles of dogs and differing human attitudes toward them.

References Cited

Alhaique, Francesca, and Avi Gopher
2005 Animal Resource Exploitation at Qumran Cave 24 (Dead Sea, Israel) from the Pre-Pottery Neolithic to the Chalcolithic. In *Archaeozoology of the Near East VI: Proceedings of the Sixth International Symposium on the Archaeozoology of Southwestern Asia and Adjacent Areas*, edited by Hijlke Buitenhuis, Alice M. Choyke, Louise Martin, László Bartosiewicz, and Marjan Mashkour, pp. 139–149. ARC-Publicaties, Vol. 123. ARC, Groningen.

Alhaique, Francesca, and Liora R. K. Horwitz
2012 The Fauna. In *The Pre-Pottery Neolithic B Village of Yiftahel: The 1980s and 1990s Excavations*, edited by Yosef Garfinkel, Doron Dag, Hamoudi Khalaily, Ofer Marder, Ianir Milevski, and Avraham Ronen, pp. 259–278. Bibliotheca Neolithica Asiae Meridionalis et Occidentalis, Vol. 32. Ex Oriente, Berlin.

Arbuckle, Benjamin S., and Vecihi Özkaya
2006 Animal Exploitation at Körtik Tepe: An Early Neolithic Site in Southeastern Turkey. *Paléorient* 32:113–136.

Arendt, Maja-Louise, Tove Fall, Kerstin Lindblad-Toh, and Erik Axelsson
2014 Amylase Activity Is Associated with AMY2B Copy Numbers in Dog: Implications for Dog Domestication, Diet and Diabetes. *Animal Genetics* 45:716–722.

Atıcı, A. Levent, Suzanne E. Pilaar Birch, and Burçin Erdoğu
2017 Spread of Domestic Animals across Neolithic Western Anatolia: New Zooarchaeological Evidence from Uğurlu Höyük, the Island of Gökçeada, Turkey. *PLoS ONE* 12(10):e0186519.

Axelsson, Erik, Abhirami Ratnakumar, Maja-Louise Arendt, Khurram Maqbool, Matthew T. Webster, Michele Perloski, Olof Liberg, Jon M. Arnemo, Ake Hedhammar, and Kerstin Lindblad-Toh
2013 The Genomic Signature of Dog Domestication Reveals Adaptation to a Starch-Rich Diet. *Nature* 495(7441):360–364.

Baird, Douglas, Andrew S. Fairbairn, Emma Jenkins, Louise Martin, Caroline Middleton, Jessica A. Pearson, Eleni Asouti, Yvonne H. Edwards, Ceren Kabukcu, Gökhan Mustafaoğlu, Nerissa Russell, Ofer Bar-Yosef, Geraldine Jacobsen, Xiaohong Wu, Ambroise G. Baker, and Sarah Elliott
2018 Agricultural Origins on the Anatolian Plateau. *Proceedings of the National Academy of Sciences* 115:E3077–E3086.

Bartosiewicz, László
1990 Species Interferences and the Interpretation of Neolithic Animal Exploitation. *Acta Archaeologica Academiae Scientiarum Hungaricae* 42:287–292.

Becker, Cornelia
1998 The Role of Hunting in Pre-Pottery Neolithic Pastoralism and Its Ecological Implications: The Basta Example (Jordan). *Anthropozoologica* 27:67–78.

Blouin, David D.

2013   Are Dogs Children, Companions, or Just Animals? Understanding Variations in People's Orientations toward Animals. *Anthrozoös* 26:279–294.

Bököyi, Sándor

1977   *Animal Remains from Four Sites in the Kermanshah Valley, Iran: Asiab, Sarab, Dehsavar and Siahbid: The Faunal Evolution, Environmental Changes and Development of Animal Husbandry, VIII–III Millennia B.C.* BAR International Series, Vol. 34. British Archaeological Reports, Oxford.

Boudadi-Maligne, Myriam, and Gilles Escarguel

2014   A Biometric Re-evaluation of Recent Claims for Early Upper Palaeolithic Wolf Domestication in Eurasia. *Journal of Archaeological Science* 45:80–89.

Buitenhuis, Hijlke

1997   Aşıklı Höyük: A "Protodomestication" Site. *Anthropozoologica* 25/26:655–662.

Buitenhuis, Hijlke

2008   Ilıpınar: The Faunal Remains from the Late Neolithic and Early Chalcolithic Levels. In *Archaeozoology of the Near East VIII*, edited by Emmanuelle Vila, Lionel Gourichon, Alice M. Choyke, and Hijlke Buitenhuis, pp. 299–322. Travaux de la Maison de l'Orient et de la Méditerranée, Vol. 49. Maison de l'Orient et de la Méditerranée, Lyon.

Buitenhuis, Hijlke, and Isabella Caneva

1998   Early Animal Breeding in South-Eastern Anatolia: Mersin-Yumuktepe. In *Man and the Animal World: Studies in Archaeozoology, Archaeology, Anthropology and Palaeolinguistics in Memoriam Sandor Bökönyi*, edited by Peter P. Anreiter, László Bartosiewicz, Erzsébet Jerem, and Wolfgang Meid, pp. 121–130. Archaeolingua Alapítvány, Budapest.

Bulmer, Ralph

1976   Selectivity in Hunting and in Disposal of Animal Bone by the Kalam of the New Guinea Highlands. In *Problems in Economic and Social Archaeology*, edited by Gale de G. Sieveking, Ian H. Longworth, and Kenneth E. Wilson, pp. 169–186. Duckworth, London.

Butler, James R. A.

1998   The Ecology of Domestic Dogs *Canis familiaris* in the Communal Lands of Zimbabwe. PhD dissertation, Department of Biological Sciences, University of Zimbabwe, Harare.

Butler, James R. A., and Johan T. du Toit

2002   Diet of Free-Ranging Domestic Dogs (*Canis familiaris*) in Rural Zimbabwe: Implications for Wild Scavengers on the Periphery of Wildlife Reserves. *Animal Conservation* 5:29–37.

Çakırlar, Canan

2012   The Evolution of Animal Husbandry in Neolithic Central-West Anatolia: The Zooarchaeological Record from Ulucak Höyük (c. 7040–5660 cal BC, Izmir, Turkey). *Anatolian Studies* 62:1–33.

Carruthers, Denise

2005   Hunting and Herding in Central Anatolian Prehistory: The Sites at Pınarbaşı. In *Archaeozoology of the Near East VI: Proceedings of the Sixth International Symposium on the Archaeozoology of Southwestern Asia and Adjacent Areas*, edited by Hijlke Buitenhuis, Alice M. Choyke, Louise Martin, László Bartosiewicz, and Marjan Mashkour, pp. 85–95. ARC-Publicaties, Vol. 123. ARC, Groningen.

Carruthers, Denise, and Samantha Dennis

2007 The Mammalian Faunal Remains. In *The Early Prehistory of Wadi Faynan, Southern Jordan: Archaeological Survey of Wadis Faynan, Ghuwayr and al-Bustan and Evaluation of the Pre-Pottery Neolithic A Site of WF16*, edited by William D. Finlayson and Steven J. Mithen, pp. 372–386. Oxbow, Oxford.

Cavallo, Chiara

2000 *Animals in the Steppe: A Zooarchaeological Analysis of Later Neolithic Tell Sabi Abyad, Syria*. BAR International Series, Vol. 891. Archaeopress, Oxford.

Clutton-Brock, Juliet

1979 The Mammalian Remains from the Jericho Tell. *Proceedings of the Prehistoric Society* 45:135–157.

Clutton-Brock, Juliet

1995 Origins of the Dog: Domestication and Early History. In *The Domestic Dog: Its Evolution, Behavior, and Interactions with People*, edited by James A. Serpell, pp. 7–20. Cambridge University Press, Cambridge.

Croft, Paul

2005 Mammalian Fauna. In *Vasilikos Valley Project 7: Excavations at Kalavasos-Tenta*, edited by Ian A. Todd, pp. 342–367. Studies in Mediterranean Archaeology, Vol. 71. Paul Åström, Sävedalen.

Daujat, Julie, and Marjan Mashkour

2017 Faunal Remains from the Middle Neolithic Site of Qaleh Rostam. In *Archaeozoology of the Near East 9*, edited by Marjan Mashkour and Mark Beech, pp. 41–58. Oxbow, Oxford.

Davis, Simon J. M., Omri Lernau, and Joelle Pichon

1994 The Animal Remains: New Light on the Origin of Animal Husbandry. In *Le Gisement de Hatoula en Judée Occidentale, Israël*, edited by Monique Lechevallier and Avraham Ronen, pp. 83–100. Mémoires et Travaux du Centre de Recherche Français de Jérusalem, Vol. 8. Association Paléorient, Paris.

Davis, Simon J. M., and François R. Valla

1978 Evidence for Domestication of the Dog 12,000 Years Ago in the Natufian of Israel. *Nature* 276(5688):608–610.

De Cupere, Beatrice, and Refik Duru

2003 Faunal Remains from Neolithic Höyücek (SW-Turkey) and the Presence of Early Domestic Cattle in Anatolia. *Paléorient* 29:107–120.

De Cupere, Beatrice, Refik Duru, and Gülsün Umurtak

2008 Animal Husbandry at the Early Neolithic to Early Bronze Age Site of Bademağacı (Antalya Province, SW Turkey): Evidence from the Faunal Remains. In *Archaeozoology of the Near East VIII*, edited by Emmanuelle Vila, Lionel Gourichon, Alice M. Choyke, and Hijlke Buitenhuis, pp. 367–405. Travaux de la Maison de l'Orient et de la Méditerranée, Vol. 49. Maison de l'Orient et de la Méditerranée, Lyon.

Dean, Rebecca M.

2014 Hunting and Herding at Ayn Abū Nukhayla: The Vertebrate Faunal Assemblage. In *The Sands of Time: The Desert Neolithic Settlement at Ayn Abū Nukhayla*, edited by Donald O. Henry and Joseph E. Beaver, pp. 69–90. Ex Oriente, Berlin.

Dekel, Yaron, Yossy Machluf, Rachel Brand, Oshrat Noked Partouche, Izhar Ben-Shlomo, and Dani Bercovich

2017   Mammal Domestication and the Symbiotic Spectrum. *Proceedings of the National Academy of Sciences* 114(27):E5280.

Dobney, Keith M., Mark Beech, and S. Deborah Jaques

1999   Hunting the Broad Spectrum Revolution: The Characterisation of Early Neolithic Animal Exploitation at Qermez Dere, Northern Mesopotamia. In *Zooarchaeology of the Pleistocene/Holocene Boundary*, edited by Jonathan C. Driver, pp. 47–57. BAR International Series, Vol. 800. Archaeopress, Oxford.

Drake, Abby G., Michael Coquerelle, and Guillaume Colombeau

2015   3D Morphometric Analysis of Fossil Canid Skulls Contradicts the Suggested Domestication of Dogs during the Late Paleolithic. *Scientific Reports* 5:8299.

Driesch, Angela von den, Isabel Cartajena, and Henriette Manhart

2004   The Late PPNB Site of Ba'ja, Jordan: The Faunal Remains (1997 Season). In *Central Settlements in Neolithic Jordan*, edited by Hans-Dieter Bienert, Hans Georg K. Gebel, and Reinder Neef, pp. 271–288. Studies in Early Near Eastern Production, Subsistence, and Environment, Vol. 5. Ex Oriente, Berlin.

Driesch, Angela von den, and Ursula Wodtke

1997   The Fauna of 'Ain Ghazal, a Major PPN and Early PN Settlement in Central Jordan. In *The Prehistory of Jordan II: Perspectives from 1997*, edited by Hans Georg Gebel, Zeidan A. Kafafi, and Gary O. Rollefson, pp. 511–556. Studies in Early Near Eastern Production, Subsistence, and Environment, Vol. 4. Ex Oriente, Berlin.

Eaton, Randall L.

1969   Cooperative Hunting by Cheetahs and Jackals and a Theory of Domestication of the Dog. *Mammalia* 33:87–92.

Flannery, Kent V.

2014   Hunting and Early Animal Domestication at Tepe Guran. In *Excavations at Tepe Guran: The Neolithic Period*, edited by Peder Mortensen, pp 89–105. Peeters, Leuven.

Germonpré, Mietje, Martina Lázničková-Galetová, Robert J. Losey, Jannikke Räikkönen, and Mikhail V. Sablin

2015   Large Canids at the Gravettian Předmostí Site, the Czech Republic: The Mandible. *Quaternary International* 359–360:261–279.

Germonpré, Mietje, Mikhail V. Sablin, Rhiannon E. Stevens, Robert E. M. Hedges, Michael Hofreiter, Mathias Stiller, and Viviane R. Després

2009   Fossil Dogs and Wolves from Palaeolithic Sites in Belgium, the Ukraine and Russia: Osteometry, Ancient DNA and Stable Isotopes. *Journal of Archaeological Science* 36:473–490.

Gourichon, Lionel, and Daniel Helmer

2008   Étude Archéozoologique de Mureybet. In *Le Site Néolithique de Tell Mureybet (Syrie du Nord)*, edited by Juan José Ibáñez Estevez, pp. 115–228. BAR International Series, Vol. 1843. Archaeopress, Oxford.

Hamilton, Annette

1972   Aboriginal Man's Best Friend? *Mankind* 8:287–295.

Helmer, Daniel

1985   Étude de la Faune de Tell Assouad (Djezireh–Syrie): Sondage J. Cauvin. *Cahiers de l'Euphrate* 4:275–285.

2008 Révision de la Faune de Cafer Höyük (Malatya, Turquie): Apports des Méthodes de l'Analyse des Mélanges et de l'Analyse de Kernel à la Mise en Évidence de la Domestication. In *Archaeozoology of the Near East VIII*, edited by Emmanuelle Vila, Lionel Gourichon, Alice M. Choyke, and Hijlke Buitenhuis, pp. 169–195. Travaux de la Maison de l'Orient et de la Méditerranée, Vol. 49. Maison de l'Orient et de la Méditerranée, Lyon.

Helmer, Daniel, and Lionel Gourichon

2017 The Fauna of Tell Aswad (Damascus, Syria), Early Neolithic Levels. Comparison with Northern and Southern Levant Sites. In *Archaeozoology of the Near East 9*, edited by Marjan Mashkour and Mark Beech, pp. 23–40. Oxbow, Oxford.

Hesse, Brian C.

1984 These Are Our Goats: The Origins of Herding in West Central Iran. In *Animals and Archaeology: 3. Early Herders and their Flocks*, edited by Juliet Clutton-Brock and Caroline Grigson, pp. 243–264. BAR International Series, Vol. 202. British Archaeological Reports, Oxford.

Hodder, Ian

2006 *The Leopard's Tale: Revealing the Mysteries of* Çatalhöyük. Thames & Hudson, London.

2013 Becoming Entangled in Things. In *Substantive Technologies at* Çatalhöyük: *Reports from the 2000–2008 Seasons*, edited by Ian Hodder, pp. 1–25. Monumenta Archaeologica, Vol. 31. Cotsen Institute of Archaeology, University of California, Los Angeles.

Hodder, Ian (editor)

2014 *Çatalhöyük Excavations: The 2000–2008 Seasons*. Cotsen Institute of Archaeology, University of California, Los Angeles.

Hodder, Ian, and Chris Doherty

2014 Temporal Trends: The Shapes and Narratives of Cultural Change at Çatalhöyük. In *Integrating Çatalhöyük: Themes from the 2000–2008 Seasons*, edited by Ian Hodder, pp. 169–183. Monumenta Archaeologica, Vol. 32. Cotsen Institute of Archaeology, University of California, Los Angeles.

Hongo, Hitomi, Lubna Omar, Hiroo Nasu, Petra Krönneck, and Sumio Fujii

2014 Faunal Remains from Wadi Abu Tulayha: A PPNB Outpost in the Steppe-Desert of Southern Jordan. In *Archaeozoology of the Near East X*, edited by Beatrice de Cupere, Veerle Linseele, and Sheila Hamilton-Dyer, pp. 1–25. Ancient Near Eastern Studies Supplement, Vol. 44. Peeters, Leuven.

Horwitz, Liora R. K.

1990 The Origin of Partially Digested Bones Recovered from Archaeological Contexts in Israel. *Paléorient* 16:97–106.

2001 The Mammalian Fauna. In *Tel Te'o: A Neolithic, Chalcolithic, and Early Bronze Age Site in the Hula Valley*, edited by Emmanuel Eisenberg, Avi Gopher, and Raphael Greenberg, pp. 171–194. IAA Reports, Vol. 13. Israel Antiquities Authority, Jerusalem.

2003 The Neolithic Fauna. In *The Neolithic Site of Abu Ghosh: The 1995 Excavations*, edited by Hamoudi Khalaily and Ofer Marder, pp. 87–101. Israel Antiquities Authority, Jerusalem.

Horwitz, Liora R. K., Tal L. Simmons, Omri Lernau, and Eitan Tchernov

2010 Fauna from the Sites of Gilgal I, II and III. In *Gilgal: Early Neolithic Occupations in the Lower Jordan Valley: The Excavations of Tamar Noy*, edited by Ofer Bar-

Yosef, A. Nigel Goring-Morris, Avi Gopher, and Tamar Yizraeli-Noy, pp. 263–295. Oxbow, Oxford.

Ilgezdi, Gülçin

2008 The Domestication Process in Southeastern Turkey: The Evidence of Mezraa-Teleilat. PhD dissertation, Gewissenschaftlichen Fakultät, Eberhard-Karls-Universität, Tübingen.

Janssens, Luc A. A., Liane Giemsch, Ralf W. Schmitz, Martin Street, and Stefan Van Dongen

2018 A New Look at an Old Dog: Bonn-Oberkassel Reconsidered. *Journal of Archaeological Science* 92:126–138.

Jouventin, Pierre, Yves Christen, and F. Stephen Dobson

2016 Altruism in Wolves Explains the Coevolution of Dogs and Humans. *Ideas in Ecology and Evolution* 9:4–11.

Kansa, Sarah W., Amanda Kennedy, Stuart Campbell, and Elizabeth Carter

2009 Resource Exploitation at Late Neolithic Domuztepe: Faunal and Botanical Evidence. *Current Anthropology* 50:897–914.

Khalaily, Hamoudi, Tali Kuperman, Nimrod Marom, Ianir Milevski, and Dmitry Yegorov

2015 Beisamun: An Early Pottery Neolithic Site in the Hula Basin. *'Atiqot* 82:1–61.

Köhler-Rollefson, Ilse, Leslie A. Quintero, and Gary O. Rollefson

1993 A Brief Note on the Fauna from Neolithic 'Ain Ghazal. *Paléorient* 19(2):95–97.

Larsen, Clark S., Christopher J. Knüsel, Scott D. Haddow, Marin A. Pilloud, Marco Milella, Joshua W. Sadvari, Jessica A. Pearson, Christopher B. Ruff, Evan M. Garofalo, Emmy Bocaege, Barbara J. Betz, Irene Dori, and Bonnie A. Glencross

2019 Bioarchaeology of Neolithic Çatalhöyük Reveals Fundamental Transitions in Health, Mobility, and Lifestyle in Early Farmers. *Proceedings of the National Academy of Sciences* 116:12615–12623.

Ledger, Marissa L., Evilena Anastasiou, Lisa-Marie Shillito, Helen Mackay, Ian D. Bull, Scott D. Haddow, Christopher J. Knüsel, and Piers D. Mitchell

2019 Parasite Infection at the Early Farming Community of Çatalhöyük. *Antiquity* 93(369):573–587.

Loyet, Michelle, and Frank Nardulli

2004 Tell Kurdu Faunal Analysis. *Anatolica* 30:64–68.

Maini, Elena, and Antonio Curci

2014 New Evidence for Dog Butchering from Prehistoric Coastal Sites in the Sultanate of Oman. In *Archaeozoology of the Near East X*, edited by Beatrice de Cupere, Veerle Linseele, and Sheila Hamilton-Dyer, pp. 403–415. Ancient Near Eastern Studies Supplement, Vol. 44. Peeters, Leuven.

Makarewicz, Cheryl A.

2009 Complex Caprine Harvesting Practices and Diversified Hunting Strategies: Integrated Animal Exploitation Systems at Late Pre-Pottery Neolithic B 'Ain Jamman. In *Zooarchaeology and the Reconstruction of Cultural Systems: Case Studies from the Old World*, edited by Benjamin S. Arbuckle, Cheryl A. Makarewicz, and A. Levent Atıcı, pp. 79–101. L'Homme et l'Animal, Société de Recherche Interdisciplinaire, Paris.

2016 Caprine Husbandry and Initial Pig Management East of the Jordan Valley: Animal Exploitation at Neolithic Wadi Shu'eib, Jordan. *Paléorient* 42:151–168.

Marom, Nimrod

2012   Animals and Society in the Neolithic Settlement at Sha'ar Hagolan. PhD dissertation, Department of Archaeology, University of Haifa.

Martin, Louise

1999a   The Animal Bones. In *The Harra and the Hamad: Excavations and Explorations in Eastern Jordan*, Vol. 1, edited by Alison V. G. Betts, pp. 159–184. Sheffield Archaeological Monographs, Vol. 9. Sheffield Academic Press, Sheffield.

1999b   Mammal Remains from the Eastern Jordanian Neolithic, and the Nature of Caprine Herding in the Steppe. *Paléorient* 25:85–102.

Mason, Otis T.

1966 [1895]   *The Origin of Invention: A Study of Industry Among Primitive Peoples*. MIT Press, Cambridge.

McArdle, John

1990   Halafian Fauna at Girikihaciyan. In *Girikihaciyan: A Halafian Site in Southeastern Turkey*, edited by Patty Jo Watson and Steven A. LeBlanc, pp. 109–120. Institute of Archaeology, University of California, Los Angeles.

Mellaart, James

1967   *Çatal Hüyük: A Neolithic Town in Anatolia*. Thames & Hudson, London.

Montagu, M. F. Ashley

1942   On the Origin of the Domestication of the Dog. *Science* 96(2483):111–112.

Morey, Darcy F.

2014   In Search of Paleolithic Dogs: A Quest with Mixed Results. *Journal of Archaeological Science* 52:300–307.

Musil, Rudolf

2000   Evidence for the Domestication of Wolves in Central European Magdalenian Sites. In *Dogs through Time: An Archaeological Perspective*, edited by Susan J. Crockford, pp. 21–28. BAR International Series, Vol. 889. Archaeopress, Oxford.

Nemeth, David J.

1998   Privy-Pigs in Prehistory? A Korean Analog for Neolithic Chinese Subsistence Practices. In *Ancestors for the Pigs: Pigs in Prehistory*, edited by Sarah M. Nelson, pp. 11–25. MASCA Research Papers in Science and Archaeology, Vol. 15. University of Pennsylvania, University Museum, Philadelphia.

Ojoade, J. Olowo

1990   Nigerian Cultural Attitudes to the Dog. In *Signifying Animals: Human Meaning in the Natural World*, edited by Roy Willis, pp. 215–221. Unwin Hyman, London.

Ovodov, Nikolai D., Susan J. Crockford, Yaroslav V. Kuzmin, Thomas F. G. Higham, Gregory W. L. Hodgins, and Johannes van der Plicht

2011   A 33,000-Year-Old Incipient Dog from the Altai Mountains of Siberia: Evidence of the Earliest Domestication Disrupted by the Last Glacial Maximum. *PLoS ONE* 6(7):e22821.

Perri, Angela R.

2016a   A Wolf in Dog's Clothing: Initial Dog Domestication and Pleistocene Wolf Variation. *Journal of Archaeological Science* 68:1–4.

2016b   Hunting Dogs as Environmental Adaptations in Jōmon Japan. *Antiquity* 90(353): 1166–1180.

Pionnier-Capitan, Maud, Céline Bemilli, Pierre Bodu, Guy Celerier, Jean-Georges Ferrié, Philippe Fosse, Michel Garcia, and Jean-Denis Vigne

2011   New Evidence for Upper Palaeolithic Small Domestic Dogs in South Western Europe. *Journal of Archaeological Science* 38(9):2123–2140.

Quintero, Leslie A., and Ilse Köhler-Rollefson

1997   The 'Ain Ghazal Dog: A Case for the Neolithic Origin of *Canis familiaris* in the Near East. In *The Prehistory of Jordan II: Perspectives from 1997*, edited by Hans Georg K. Gebel, Zeidan A. Kafafi, and Gary O. Rollefson, pp. 567–574. Studies in Early Near Eastern Production, Subsistence, and Environment, Vol. 4. Ex Oriente, Berlin.

Redding, Richard W.

2003   First Report on Faunal Remains. In *Excavations at the Prehistoric Mound of Chogha Bonut, Khuzestan, Iran: Seasons 1976/77, 1977/78, and 1996*, edited by Abbas Alizadeh, pp. 137–147. Oriental Institute Publications, Vol. 120. Oriental Institute of the University of Chicago, Chicago.

Richardson, Jane

1997   An Analysis of the Faunal Assemblages from Two Pre-Pottery Neolithic Sites in the Wadi Fidan. In *The Prehistory of Jordan II: Perspectives from 1997*, edited by Hans Georg K. Gebel, Zeidan A. Kafafi, and Gary O. Rollefson, pp. 497–510. Ex Oriente, Berlin.

Ronen, Avraham

2004   Why Was the Dog Domesticated? In *The Last Hunter-Gatherers in the Near East*, edited by Christophe Delage, pp. 153–160. BAR International Series, Vol. 1320. Archaeopress, Oxford.

Russell, Nerissa

1993   Hunting, Herding and Feasting: Human Use of Animals in Neolithic Southeast Europe. PhD dissertation, Department of Anthropology, University of California, Berkeley.

2018   Neolithic Taboos in Anatolia and Southeast Europe. In *Social Dimensions of Food in the Prehistoric Balkans*, edited by Maria Ivanova, Bogdan Athanassov, Vanya Petrova, Desislava Takorova, and Philipp W. Stockhammer, pp. 14–30. Oxbow, Oxford.

Russell, Nerissa, and Katheryn C. Twiss

2017   Digesting the Data: Dogs as Taphonomic Agents at Neolithic Çatalhöyük, Turkey. In *Archaeozoology of the Near East 9*, edited by Marjan Mashkour and Mark Beech, pp. 59–73. Oxbow, Oxford.

Russell, Nerissa, Katheryn C. Twiss, David C. Orton, and G. Arzu Demirergi

2013   More on the Çatalhöyük Mammal Remains. In *Humans and Landscapes of Çatalhöyük: Reports from the 2000–2008 Seasons*, edited by Ian Hodder, pp. 213–258. Monumenta Archaeologica, Vol. 30. Cotsen Institute of Archaeology, University of California, Los Angeles.

Russell, Nerissa, Katherine I. Wright, Tristan Carter, Sheena Ketchum, Philippa Ryan, E. Nurcan Yalman, Roddy Regan, Mirjana Stevanović, and Marina Milić

2014   Bringing Down the House: House Closing Deposits at Çatalhöyük. In *Integrating Çatalhöyük: Themes from the 2000–2008 Seasons*, edited by Ian Hodder, pp. 109–121. Monumenta Archaeologica, Vol. 32. Cotsen Institute of Archaeology, University of California, Los Angeles.

Sablin, Mikhail V., and Gennady A. Khlopachev

2002   The Earliest Ice Age Dogs: Evidence from Eliseevichi I. *Current Anthropology* 43:795–799.

Saña Seguí, María

1999   *Arqueología de la Domesticación Animal: La Gestión de los Recursos Animales en Tell Halula (Valle del Éufrates-Siria) del 8.800 al 7.000 BP.* Treballs d'Arqueologia del Pròxim Orient, Vol. 1. Universitat Autònoma de Barcelona, Departament d'Antropologia Social i Prehistòria, Barcelona.

2002   The Faunal Remains. In *Tell Boueid II: A Late Neolithic Village on the Middle Khabur (Syria)*, edited by Antione Suleiman and Olivier P. Nieuwenhuyse, pp. 125–140. Subartu, Vol. 11. Brepols, Turnhout.

2004   Analysis of the Faunal Remains of the Halaf Period from Tell Amarna (Syria). In *Tell Amarna (Syrie) I: La Période de Halaf*, edited by Önhan Tunca and Miquel Molist, pp. 245–260. Peeters, Leuven.

Sapir-Hen, Lidar, Guy Bar-Oz, Hamoudi Khalaily, and Tamar Dayan

2009   Gazelle Exploitation in the Early Neolithic Site of Motza, Israel: The Last of the Gazelle Hunters in the Southern Levant. *Journal of Archaeological Science* 36:1538–1546.

Sapir-Hen, Lidar, Tamar Dayan, Hamoudi Khalaily, and Natalie D. Munro

2016   Human Hunting and Nascent Animal Management at Middle Pre-Pottery Neolithic Yiftah'el, Israel. *PLoS ONE* 11(7):e0156964.

Sauer, Carl O.

1969   *Agricultural Origins and Dispersals: The Domestication of Animals and Foodstuffs.* 2nd ed. MIT Press, Cambridge.

Schäffer, Johann, and Joachim Boessneck

1988   Bericht über die Tierreste aus der halafzeitlichen Siedlung Çavi Tarlası (Nibisin/Osttürkei). *Istanbuler Mitteilungen des Deutschen Archäologischen Instituts* 38:37–64.

Serpell, James A.

1996   *In the Company of Animals: A Study of Human-Animal Relationships.* 2nd ed. Cambridge University Press, Cambridge.

Sharp, Henry S.

1976   Man: Wolf: Woman: Dog. *Arctic Anthropology* 13:25–34.

Shillito, Lisa-Marie, Ian D. Bull, Wendy Matthews, Matthew J. Almond, James M. Williams, and Richard P. Evershed

2011   Biomolecular and Micromorphological Analysis of Suspected Faecal Deposits at Neolithic Çatalhöyük, Turkey. *Journal of Archaeological Science* 38:1869–1877.

Simmons, Alan H., Katelyn Di Benedetto, and Levi Keach

2018   Neolithic Kritou Marottou-Ais Giorkis, Cyprus—Living in the Uplands. *Bulletin of the American Schools of Oriental Research* 379:171–195.

Solomon, Su, and Bruno David

1990   Middle Range Theory and Actualistic Studies: Bones and Dingoes in Australian Archaeology. In *Problem Solving in Taphonomy: Archaeological and Palaeontological Studies from Europe, Africa and Oceania*, edited by Su Solomon, Iain Davidson, and Di Watson, pp. 233–255. Tempus, Vol. 2. University of Queensland Anthropology Museum, St. Lucia.

Stampfli, Hans R.

1983 The Fauna of Jarmo with Notes on Animal Bones from Matarrah, the 'Amuq and Karim Shahir. In *Prehistoric Archeology along the Zagros Flanks*, edited by Linda S. Braidwood, Robert J. Braidwood, Bruce Howe, Charles A. Reed, and Patty Jo Watson, pp. 431–483. Oriental Institute Publications, Vol. 105. Oriental Institute of the University of Chicago, Chicago.

Tchernov, Eitan

1994 *An Early Neolithic Village in the Jordan Valley. Part II: The Fauna of Netiv Hagdud.* American School of Prehistoric Research Bulletin, Vol. 44. Peabody Museum, Harvard University, Cambridge.

Tchernov, Eitan, and Ofer Bar-Yosef

1982 Animal Exploitation in the Pre-Pottery Neolithic B Period at Wadi Tbeik, Southern Sinai. *Paléorient* 8:17–37.

Tchernov, Eitan, and François R. Valla

1997 Two New Dogs, and Other Natufian dogs, from the Southern Levant. *Journal of Archaeological Science* 24:65–95.

Twiss, Katheryn C.

2007 The Zooarchaeology of Tel Tif'dan (Wadi Fidan 001), Southern Jordan. *Paléorient* 33:127–146.

Uerpmann, Hans-Peter

1982 Faunal Remains from Shams ed-din Tannira, a Halafian Site in Northern Syria. *Berytus* 30:3–52.

van Wijngaarden-Bakker, Louise H., and Rik Maliepaard

2000 The Animal Remains. In *Tell Sabi Abyad II: The Pre-Pottery Neolithic B Settlement: Report on the Excavations of the National Museum of Antiquities, Leiden in the Balikh Valley, Syria*, edited by Marc Verhoeven and Peter M. M. G. Akkermans, pp. 147–171. Nederlands Historisch-Archaeologisch Instituut, Leiden.

Vigne, Jean-Denis

2005/2006 L'Humérus de Chien Magdalénien de Erralla (Gipuzkoa, Espagne) et la Domestication Tardiglaciaire du Loup en Europe. *Munibe* 57:279–287.

Vigne, Jean-Denis, François Briois, Antoine Zazzo, George H. Willcox, Thomas Cucchi, Stéphanie Thiébault, Isabelle Carrère, Yodrik Franel, Régis Touquet, Chloé Martin, Christophe Moreau, Clothilde Comby, and Jean Guilaine

2012 First Wave of Cultivators Spread to Cyprus at least 10,600 Y Ago. *Proceedings of the National Academy of Sciences* 109:8445–8449.

Vigne, Jean-Denis, Isabelle Carrère, François Briois, and Jean Guilaine

2011 The Early Process of Mammal Domestication in the Near East: New Evidence from the Pre-Neolithic and Pre-Pottery Neolithic in Cyprus. *Current Anthropology* 52(S4):S255-S271.

Vigne, Jean-Denis, and Jean Guilaine

2004 Les Premiers Animaux de Compagnie, 8500 Ans avant Notre Ère? . . . ou Comment J'ai Mangé Mon Chat, Mon Chien et Mon Renard. *Anthropozoologica* 39:249–273.

Watson, John P. N.

1979 The Estimation of the Relative Frequencies of Mammalian Species: Khirokitia 1972. *Journal of Archaeological Science* 6:127–137.

Wheeler Pires-Ferreira, Jane C.

1975–1977   Tepe Tula'i: Faunal Remains from an Early Campsite in Khuzistan, Iran. *Paléorient* 3:275–280.

Willerslev, Rane

2007   *Soul Hunters: Hunting, Animism, and Personhood among the Siberian Yukaghirs.* University of California Press, Berkeley.

Zeder, Melinda A.

2012   Pathways to Animal Domestication. In *Biodiversity in Agriculture: Domestication, Evolution, and Sustainability*, edited by Paul Gepts, Thomas R. Famula, Robert L. Bettinger, Stephen B. Brush, Ardeshir B. Damania, Patrick E. McGuire, and Calvin O. Qualset, pp. 227–259. Cambridge University Press, Cambridge.

Zeuner, Frederick E.

1963   *A History of Domesticated Animals.* Harper and Row, New York.

7

Dog Days to Horse Days

The Introduction of the Horse and Its Impact on Human-Dog Relationships among the Blackfoot

BRANDI BETHKE

The Blackfoot refer to the period before European contact as "the time when dogs were used either as pack animals or for drawing travois" (Ewers 1955:44–48). During these dog days, humans walked the plains of North America, hunting on foot, using dogs to transport not only their kill but also their possessions. With the introduction of horses, it was possible for the people to travel further and transport more, which in turn expanded their spatial-temporal reality, changed social structures, and altered value concepts as the horse became an important new symbol of wealth and power. The close association between dogs and horses is universal on the northern plains (Hämäläinen 2003:846). Within plains research, this relationship has most often been characterized as framing the horse as a "new and improved" dog.

More recent scholarship focusing on the horse in the plains is now moving away from a paradigm of viewing the horse as merely an intensifier of existing cultural traits and toward a framework that acknowledges that the horse had a significant, lasting impact on Native peoples. Nevertheless, this interpretation of the horse as essentially an "upgraded" dog has persisted. Although prior experience with domesticated dogs did facilitate the incorporation of horses into the daily lives of Plains people, this chapter explores the fundamental differences between these two animals in order to better characterize both the continuity and change that occurred within Blackfoot culture following the introduction of the horse, including how this transition impacted the role and value of dogs. As this work demonstrates, it is important not only to recognize these animals as active agents in this exchange but also to frame these relationships within a Blackfoot ontology.

The Blackfoot People

The Blackfoot Confederacy, or Nitsitapii, is made up of Algonquian-speaking peoples who have occupied northern Montana, southern Alberta, and western Saskatchewan on a permanent basis for centuries, although their ancestors and archaeological predecessors inhabited this region for millennia (Brink 2008; Duke 1991; Kehoe 1960:440; Peck 2011:10, 445; Peck and Hudecek-Cuffe 2003:77, 90; Reeves 1983; Tovias 2011:1; Vickers and Peck 2009; Zedeño et al. 2014). Prior to their forced settlement on reservations and reserves by the US and Canadian governments in the late nineteenth century, the Blackfoot were a seasonally nomadic people who focused their annual economic cycle on hunting bison (Zedeño et al. 2014). There is ample evidence that bison were at the center of their worldviews during this time, serving as an organizing principle of social, ceremonial, and religious life (Ewers 1958; Grinnell 1962; Schaeffer 1934; Schultz 1962). Today, the Blackfoot people reside in three reserves in Alberta and one reservation in Montana. These contemporary land divisions roughly correspond to three Blackfoot divisions known at the time of European contact: Siksika (Blackfoot), Kainai (Blood), and Piikani (Piegan) (Dempsey 2001; Tovias 2011). The Piikani are further categorized into northern and southern divisions (Piikani Nation and the Blackfeet Tribe of Montana); however, this is an arbitrary split imposed by the International Boundary between the United States and Canada. Historically, these bands were rather loosely integrated politically but had close social, ceremonial, and kinship ties.

Blackfoot Dogs

Dogs existed even before humans. When Old Man Napi came to create the world, he brought his pet (a dog or a wolf) with him from the sky (Raczka 2017), and the culture hero, slayer Kutoyis (Blood-Clot) is said to have had a dog called Sis-sume (John Murray, personal communication, 2014). When asked how the Blackfoot first obtained dogs, one Blackfoot elder responded that they "have always had them" (John Murray, personal communication, 2014). Blackfoot dogs, like the majority of those belonging to northern Plains groups, were generally described as large, robust, and "wolf-like," although more medium-sized varieties are also known from the archaeological record (Ewers 1958:10; Grinnell 1961:92; Schultz 1962:194–195; Roe 1955:14). There is some evidence that selective breeding was practiced to obtain these desired traits, as Wissler (1910:91) explained:

> the dogs were large and stronger than now, some of them standing about seventy-five cm. in height; that many dogs were able to drag tipi poles and that the strongest ones hauled skin tipi covers. . . . It appears that formerly, before horses became numerous, some selective breeding was practiced to provide large, strong dogs for travois use.

Similar accounts describe the crossing of wolves and dogs to create "wolf-dog" hybrids (SC-252 Morgan Diary 1862). Writing in the 1870s, Lieutenant James Bradley (1900:278) described Blackfoot dogs as "very similar in appearance to the large gray wolf."

Blackfoot Horses

It is currently understood from historical accounts that horses made their way to the northwestern plains via the ancient Rocky Mountain trade network connecting the Rio Grande valley to the central Rockies (Ewers 1955:5–19; Haines 1938a, 1938b; Hämäläinen 2003:845). This trade network carried horses, along with the knowledge of how to use and train them, to the Shoshone and Kootenai people by 1700, to the Blackfoot and the Crow by the 1720s, and elsewhere to the north and east by the 1750s. The Cayuse or "Indian pony" descends from Barb horses introduced from North Africa into Spain after the Muslim Conquest in the eighth century (Denhardt 1947:20–22; Ewers 1955:33; Hungry Wolf 2006:92). The adult male Cayuse averaged a little under 14 hands in height, weighed approximately 700 pounds, and had a large head in proportion to its body. They were said to possess good eyes, a large, round barrel chest, heavy shoulders and hips, small, fine, strong limbs, small feet, and a wide range of solid and mixed hide colors (Ewers 1955:33).

The most widely cited narrative of the Blackfoot's first encounter with a horse comes from Saukamappee, an elderly Cree man living among the Blackfoot during this period. In 1787 Saukamappee related the story of how the Blackfoot first obtained the horse to the English fur trader David Thompson. In this account, Saukamappee claimed that, sometime between 1723 and 1728, he joined several Blackfoot bands that planned to slip into "Snake Indian" territory to hunt bison and deer and, they hoped, "to see a horse of which we had heard so much" (Tyrrell 1916:334). Locating the mounted Shoshones was difficult for the pedestrian Blackfoot, but finally, "as the leaves were falling," they encountered a horse that "was killed by an arrow shot into his belly" (Tyrrell 1916:334). The group gathered around the dead animal, trying to make sense of him:

> we all admired him, he put us in mind of a Stag that had lost his horns; and we did not know what name to give him. But as he was a slave to Man, like the dog, which carried our things, he was named the Big Dog. (Tyrrell 1916:334)

While Saukamappee's report is the earliest recorded account of a Blackfoot encounter with horses, several other traditional stories of where and from whom the Blackfoot obtained their first horses also exist from this period (Ewers 1955:18; Glover 1962:246–247; Hungry Wolf 2006:1445; Nabokov 1992:42–44; Schultz 1962:321; Wissler 1910:19). Therefore, it is likely that these first horses were acquired from multiple exchanges. In addition to historical narratives describing how they first obtained horses, the Blackfoot also have oral traditions explaining the origin of horses as gifts from Old Man Napi, Thunder, the Water Spirit, and the Morning Star (Ewers 1955:291–297; Jackson 2000:10; John Murray, personal communication, 2014; Allan Pard, personal communication, 2014; Paul Raczka, personal communication, 2014).

Of the three Blackfoot groups, the Piikani were likely the first to acquire the horse because they typically ranged south of the Kainai and Siksika. The Piikani, in turn, must have shared their horses with their Kainai and Siksika relatives soon thereafter (Binnema 2001:93). The eighteenth century witnessed the widespread adaptation of horses to their primary uses among the Blackfoot—as burden bearers and transport animals in moving camp and as aids in hunting and warfare (Ewers 1955:334). By the time Hudson Bay Company trader Anthony Henday first encountered the Blackfoot in 1754, he reported that they had completely adopted an equestrian lifestyle (Burpee 1908:289, 299, 337).

The Human-Dog-Horse Relationship within a Blackfoot Ontology

Within Plains research horses have most commonly been understood as a product of updated technology. Wissler, for example, explains "to such a culture the horse would most surely be a new and superior dog; he would like any greatly improved appliance enrich and intensify development in certain established directions" (Wissler 1914:18–19). However, this characterization of dogs and horses may not be the most appropriate interpretive framework for understanding this transition within a Blackfoot worldview. In contrast to Western belief systems that often see animals "in utilitarian terms, as objects to manipulate, use and consume" (Hill 2011:408), Indigenous cultures tend to conceive of animals as social beings whose daily interactions are based on reciprocal relationships (Hill 2013; Losey et al. 2011; Nadasdy 2007). These interactions with animals are not just spiritual but one element in a complex social life linking humans to other elements of their landscape, such as plants, significant places, spiritual beings, and other humans. Recognizing this worldview constitutes a shift from viewing animals as *objects* toward an understanding of animals as *subjects* (Hill 2013:118), which has implications for how we conceive of animals and their capacities for enacting change within societies in the past (e.g., Descola 2013; Fijn 2011; Ingold 2000, 2006; Kirksey and Helmreich 2010; Kohn 2013; McCormack 2018; Nadasdy 2007).

One of the most basic frames of reference for the Blackfoot people is the concept of medicine power (Denman 1968:27; McFee 1972:44). Within a Blackfoot worldview, animals and other nonhuman persons are able to aid humans through the transfer of their power by such mediums as visions or dreams, pipe bundles, or medicine bundles (Barsh and Marlor 2003:587; Bastien 2004; Denman 1968:30–32; Ewers 1958:163; Grinnell 1962:262; Harrod 2000:45–46; Lokensgard 2010:84; John Murray, personal communication, 2014; Raczka 2011; Wissler 1912:276–277). Animals are understood as active agents in these exchanges, similar to what Hill (2011:407–408) describes as "animals as other-than-human persons . . . capable of acting with forethought and of affecting human health and well-being." These relationships replicate human-to-human interactions that frame community organization and are built around the basic principles of generosity, reciprocity, and civic obligations. As one elder explains, "in those days they had their dogs and horses to speak to them. And they know what to say" (M-37:11). As such, these relationships are not passive but instead require consistent negotiations as animals are consulted with for a variety of reasons, from the applied (such as subsistence power) to the more abstract (such as healing medicines or advice in certain situations). In return for their assistance, animals are venerated based on what they provided to humans in the form of both economic benefits as well as spiritual knowledge and power (Pepion 1999:131). Therefore, it may be more appropriate to understand the introduction of the horse and its effects within a framework of changing relationships between humans and animals—specifically what dogs and horses were able to provide to the relationship as well as what humans were required to reciprocate for these benefits—as opposed to viewing these animals as only technological objects.

Dogs within a Blackfoot Worldview

Similar to many cultures worldwide, within the Blackfoot world dogs occupied an "ambiguous ontological position" (Hill 2018:96) as a liminal animal, straddling the human and nonhuman worlds and occupying often contradictory roles (McCormack 2018:139). Dogs came from the sky and are one of three manifestations of the same sky spirit (dog, wolf, and coyote; Carol Murray, personal communication, 2014). Blackfoot dogs, therefore, were conceptually and sometimes literally (wolf-dog hybrids) both wild and domestic. They served their masters but also had their own agency beyond the needs of their humans (John Murray, personal communication, 2014). As a result, dogs had a complex social standing within Blackfoot society that had implications for how they were used, valued, and understood.

Within this system, dogs functioned in several different capacities both before and after the introduction of the horse. Dogs, like many other animals of Blackfoot country, were understood to possess I'ta'kiwa ("has-a-spirit") and were consulted in this way (Bastien 2004:13; Ewers 1958:163; Grinnell 1962:260). In addition to its economic use as a pack animal, the dog was respected and valued within Blackfoot culture for its ability to provide companionship, loyalty, and protection (Bastien 2004:13). As Morris explains to Pepion (1999:131), "They used dogs for transportation. They knew the power and spirit of that dog. The spirit of the dog was highly recognized. They were used as protectors; as warners; name it, I could go on how powerful that dog is. They knew all these things. It began with the dogs that relate to everything."

There are several stories that attest to dogs as protectors from both physical and spiritual harm (Uhlenbeck 1912; Wissler and Duvall 1908). For example, Uhlenbeck (1912:199–200) recounts a story told to him about a man who was saved by his dog when he was out hunting alone in the summer and was secretly approached by members of another tribe. The dog, who had just had puppies, went out at night to get a drink and was shot with an arrow by the hostile party. She quickly ran back to her camp, alerted the man of the approaching enemies, and led the man and her pups to safety just as the enemy came to their lodge to attack. As Uhlenbeck (1912:200) explains, "his dog saved (that man's) life. (Since that time) he loved (the dog)." In another story recounted to Wissler and Duvall (1908:71–72), dogs again are responsible for saving the lives of humans by creating springs after water in the streams and lakes was taken away by the Sun and the Moon. After making the springs the dogs turned to their leader, an old white medicine-dog, who prayed to the Sun and Moon on their behalf. On the eighth day they sent rain. "Even to this day," Wissler and Duvall (1908:72) write, "all the people have great respect for their dogs because of this." Dogs are also thought to possess the power to alert people to the presence of "ghostly beings who did not make it to Omahksspa'tsikoi, the Sand Hills (the place where the dead live)" (Bastien 2004:13).

Because of these qualities, some dogs were viewed as valued members of the Blackfoot community and were known to have been used as trade items in several types of transactions, such as in marriage contracts or in exchange for goods or other rites (Tom Crawford, personal communication, 2014; Ewers 1968:11; Uhlenbeck 1912:81). Not all dogs were equal within this system, however. Training, intelligence, behavior, and physical qualities all influenced the perceived value of an individual dog (Ewers 1955:312). Apart from their economic value, some dogs were also known to be highly regarded by their owners on a more personal level. While most Blackfoot dogs in the past were considered working animals by today's standards, there were individual dogs who were highly regarded and given individual names (Tom Crawford, personal communication, 2014). Some dogs were even given their own tipis by their owners (McClintock 1999:180). The Blackfoot, like other Plains peoples, were known to keep many different species as companion animals, such as wolves, foxes, badgers, and even tamed bears (Hungry Wolf 2006; Schultz 1907:309, 371–372; Uhlenbeck 1912:128). Therefore, although accounts are sparse, it is likely that in addition to their duties around camp, some dogs were regarded as personal animals and valued by their owners for the companionship they provided.

The role of dogs within Blackfoot spiritual life prior to the contact period is not well known by anthropologists. As Ewers (1955:316) reports, "if the Blackfoot Indians looked upon dogs as sacred animals in the days when dogs were their only domesticated animals, their descendants appear to have no traditions regarding that attitude. I have found no trace in Blackfoot culture of a dog cult organized for the express purpose of appealing to dog spirits for aid in doctoring or influencing the actions of dogs." However, the origin and use of dog medicine is recorded by Clark Wissler (1912:54) and Wissler and D. C. Duvall (1908:109).

Dog parts were included in bundles, dog songs were sung during transfer ceremonies, and dogs were exchanged for some sacred rites and objects both before and after the introduction of the horse (Ewers 1955:289; McClintock 1999:87–88; Wissler 1912:177, 184, 83). Describing one part of the Beaver Bundle opening ceremony, Wissler (1912:184) recounts, "the next song was known as the dog song. He picked up a dog's tail, and after shaking it handed it to a man. While the man danced everyone barked and howled in imitation of a dog. The dancer ended with a howl." The Blackfoot also have a dog society, known by several names, including the Brave Dog Society, Crazy Dog Society, Mad Dog Society, and All-Crazy Dogs Society, which was considered one of the policing groups that kept order and enforced discipline in the camps and during the hunt (Grinnell 1962:104–112, 220–224; Tovias 2011:2; Wissler and Duvall 1908:107–109). Members in this society were regarded as having great power because they were composed of past chiefs who had "earned a reputation for bravery and strictness" (Crowshoe and Manneschmidt 2002:16).

While it was clear that some dogs were highly regarded within Blackfoot society, a number of negative connotations relating to dogs also existed, including the association of dogs as dangerous or unclean. In some instances, medicine pipe owners were advised to keep away from dogs. Wissler and Duvall (1908:90) explain one of the origins of this fear:

> When the Thunder left the woman and elder child behind, he said that if dogs ever attempt to bite them, they would disappear. One day a dog rushed into the lodge and snapped at the boy, after which nothing was seen of him or his mother, and to this day the owner of a medicine-pipe is afraid of dogs.

For this reason, dogs were not allowed within the tipi during a transfer ceremony (Wissler 1912:133, 139, 172, 449, 457, 574). Similar apprehensions toward dogs were felt by bundle owners (Wissler 1912:260). At the same time, there were taboos against bundle and pipe owners hurting a dog. As Ewers (1955:278) explains, medicine pipe owners "must not strike a dog or horse, nor cut a horse's tail." Wissler (1912:173–174) recounts a similar warning to Beaver Bundle owners: "he must not strike a dog, nor kill any kind of bird or animal."

Nevertheless, the Blackfoot did manage their dogs with physical repercussions. When a dog was being trained or misbehaving, its behavior was corrected physically as well as with calls and commands (Callahan 1997; Roe 1955:31–32). Additionally, while dogs were not used for food by the Blackfoot except at times of extreme starvation (Ewers 1955:167; 1958:87; John Murray, personal communication, 2014; McClintock 1999:179; Paul Raczka, personal communication, 2014; Schultz 1907:57–59, 350–352; 1962:77; Wissler 1910:20), there are accounts of the ritual killing of dogs for particular ceremonies and religious rites, for example:

> Another ritual privilege included the shooting of dogs at the Sun Dance. After the dances, the Bear Pigeons would roam through the camp shooting and killing dogs that were either not a recognized breed or that were not marked by their owners. In the dog days, they would even kill a dog pulling a travois. Dogs with gray mounts, shaggy coats, or bobbed tails were spared: these dogs resembled bears; the color made no difference. If a dog owner wished to protect his animal he would take it to the Bear Pigeons and pay a member to paint the face of the dog with "real paint," a reddish ochre. A plume headpiece would be attached as further identification. If a dog approached Pigeons while they were stealing food, it would be shot—unless it was marked (or of a privileged breed), in which case it would be fed. If a dog should escape wounded, and run into a tipi, an Old Man Comrade would be required to come and count war coups or stealing coups before the dog could be removed and killed. (PR2009.0336/0001:198)

However, it is unclear if this specific practice extended back to precontact times. There is also evidence to suggest that dogs were sometimes killed at the graves of their owners prior to the introduction of the horse, although the practice is not recorded after European contact (Ewers 1955:317–318).

Differences between Dogs and Horses

Unlike the dog, the horse's place within Blackfoot society is not ambiguous, and horses are in all accounts highly regarded for their utilitarian, spiritual, and intrinsic value. In contrast to dogs, there are almost no negative connotations associated with horses, which to the Blackfoot were, as Schultz (1962:77) explains, "sacred animals of almost human attributes . . . that they loved almost as much as they did their children." A survey of available literature as well as consultation with tribal members suggests that while dogs are in all accounts described as "friends," horses are typically described as "family." This linguistic difference is important for understanding not only the significant roles that these animals played within the lives of their humans but also how these relationships differed.

As indicated by the traditional names for the horse, "big dog" or "elk-dog," there was a clear association in the mind of the Blackfoot people between the two animals (Baldwin 1994:70; Ewers 1955:16; Umfreville 1790:202). This association was based not on physical appearance but instead on the initial relationship that the horse had with the Blackfoot people as a domesticated animal used for traction—"he was a slave to Man, like the dog, which carried our things" (Tyrrell 1916:334). Immediately following the horse's introduction, therefore, the horse shared a similar relationship to that of the dog as a domesticated burden-bearer, which in turn allowed for its rapid incorporation into Blackfoot life. However, this human-horse relationship quickly evolved in response to the skills and capabilities horses possess that dogs do not, the most significant of these advantages being the horse's superior traction and transport power that offered mobility benefits and stimulated the development of equestrian hunting. This new relationship between humans and horses rapidly transformed almost all aspects of Blackfoot culture, including the way they used and understood their dogs.

To better understand these unique relationships between the Blackfoot people and their pack animals, one must examine key differences between dogs and horses that led to differential advantages of the human-horse relationship, as well as new obligations in terms of care and maintenance. These dissimilarities and their implications have been discussed at length by Wissler (1914), Wilson (1924), Haines (1938a, 1938b), Ewers (1955), Roe (1955), Dickason (1980), Hämäläinen (2003), Landals (2004), and Bethke (2017). The following sections summarize and expand on these discussions through the inclusion of new information acquired from original ethnographic interviews with Piikani tribal members, primary source documents and recordings from repositories in the United States and Canada, and archaeological data.

Transport and Mobility

The rapid rate of adoption of the horse by the Blackfoot and other Plains groups has been universally explained by the differential advantages that the horse provided, as compared to the dog, in terms of traction, transport, and mobility.

Prior to obtaining horses, the Blackfoot were dependent on the use of dogs as pack animals (Ewers 1958:91; Grinnell 1962:187; Wissler and Duvall 1908:92). On average, it is estimated that Blackfoot dogs pulling the travois were able to carry a load of anywhere from 50 to 100 pounds, depending on their body size (Ewers 1955:306, 1958:10; Grinnell 1961:92, 1962:187; Hanson 1986:96; Roe 1955:14). The horse, Ewers (1955:308, 1958:94) estimates, was eight times more efficient than a dog in terms of traction power. The adaptation of the travois to the horse further facilitated ease of transport. Ewers (1955:18) recounts in the Blackfoot oral tradition of Sits-in-the-Night how the horse's first use was as a beast of burden:

> After a time a woman said, "Let's put a travois on one of these big dogs just like we do on our small dogs." They made a large travois and attached it to one of the horses. The horse did not jump or kick as it was led around camp. It seemed gentle. Later a woman mounted the horse and rode it with travois attached. According to this tradition the Blackfoot did not employ horses for riding, to hunt buffalo, or to war until after they were adapted to transport use with the travois.

Using the travois, a horse could drag a load four to five times heavier than it could carry on its back (Carlson 1998:39; Roe 1955:16). An increase in carrying power provided the mechanism and opportunity to accumulate material wealth, resulting in the adoption of larger tipis as well as the ability to transport larger quantities of storable food and a variety of possessions (Bastien 2004; Carlson 1998; Denman 1968; Ewers 1955:307–308; Grinnell 1962; Landals 2004:224; Raczka 2011:4; Wissler 1914:11).

Beyond simply providing more power, horses also proved to be better at transport in other ways. Ewers (1958:10–11) suggests that dogs were not as well-trained as we typically envision and thus could cause additional difficulties and delays with their poor behavior. Packhorses, which were well-trained and naturally predisposed to follow the herd, did not suffer from these behavioral issues, making the business of moving camp an easier task.

The horse increased not only the weight that could be transported but also the speed and distance that could be traveled. The intersection of increased traction power and transport resulted in the horse's most crucial advantage over the dog: its ability to carry human riders. This created something never before experienced in the lives of the Blackfoot people—a mode of transportation beyond their own feet, which bestowed on the horse a special role within Blackfoot society that set it apart from all other animals, including the dog (Dietz 2003:189). With the horse, a single person or small groups could now leave on individual missions without having to uproot the entire camp. This became especially important for hunting, raiding, warfare, and trade and also made it possible to travel to other camps to visit relatives or friends more frequently, encouraging trade and creating more time for social and ceremonial activities (Bastien 2004:15).

Hunting and Subsistence

As a result of these advantages, horses became an integral component of the Blackfoot bison hunting complex (Bethke 2019). Dogs were never an important factor in the bison hunt (Ed LeMieux, personal communication, 2014; Schaeffer 1978). Although dogs were used to transport meat following the butchery of a kill, they were typically muzzled and kept out of the vicinity of a communal hunt (Henry 1809:294; Roe 1955:365; Uhlenbeck 1912:40; Wissler 1910:37–38). While limited numbers of canid remains are commonly found at precontact bison kill sites in the region, these most likely result from later processing activities as opposed to casualties of the actual hunt—either dogs that were brought in to use as pack animals or wolves attracted to the kill site that were accidentally or purposefully killed for raw materials (Peck 2011). Canid bone beads found in processing areas away from the main kill site at the late precontact Kutoyis Site, for example, evidence this activity (Bethke et al. 2018:883), and similar canid bone beads are commonly found at Old Women's Phase campsites in various stages of manufacture throughout the region (Peck and Vickers 2006:72).

Following their adoption into the bison hunting complex, horses came to occupy a position of considerable prominence not only in economic exchanges as a valuable new indication of wealth but also in Blackfoot religious beliefs and rituals as a source of powerful new animal medicines that could be used to obtain bison as well as other benefits (Bethke 2019). This association with bison—the single most significant economic and spiritual resource for people inhabiting the northwestern plains for more than a millennium—caused the horse, and by extension horse medicine (*ponokâmita saám*), to become one of the most sacred and powerful animals within the Blackfoot world (Ewers 1955:258–260, 317; Carol Murray, personal communication, 2014; John Murray, personal communication, 2014; Allan Pard, personal communication, 2014). The fact that traditional accounts of the origin of horses credit the first horses to Old Man Napi, sky spirits, or underwater spirits further highlights their significance since they follow the Blackfoot pattern of attributing the origin of their most sacred possessions to one or more of these spirit sources (Ewers 1955:297).

This association between bison hunting and horses gave horses a key logistical and spiritual advantage over dogs, who were never linked to bison in this way since they did not possess hunting power. Within this new system, the concept of domestic animal transitioned from a loyal helper to an essential hunting partner, which in turn elevated the economic and spiritual value of the horse and simultaneously reduced the practical and religious value of the dog.

Care and Maintenance

Although the horse brought with it considerable power, the Blackfoot people also had to devote significantly more time and energy to maintain these relationships because horses required more in terms of not only practical care but also religious obligations than dogs did. With the horse came an array of new knowledge about horsemanship, breeding, and care. While previous experience with dogs did provide the Blackfoot with a framework for caring and training domesticated animals (Sheldon Carlson, personal communication, 2014; Allan Pard, personal communication, 2014), the horse required new training methods and the implementation of husbandry practices (Ewers 1955:300; Landals 2004:246). Horse care encompassed day-to-day duties as well as long-term herd management strategies. Maintaining horse herds demanded considerably more time, energy, and expertise than maintaining packs of dogs (Osborn 1983:583).

A key difference between dogs and horses is their feeding requirements. Dogs are omnivores and scavengers. Blackfoot dogs were typically provisioned with essentially the same diet as their human companions; thus time spent thinking about feeding them was relatively minimal (Ewers 1955:51, 307; Wissler 1910:24). Horses, on the other hand, are herbivores and as such require large amounts of accessible vegetation for grazing. Before the introduction of the horse, the Blackfoot planned their nomadic existence around the seasonal movements of bison. This shift from an omnivorous to herbivorous pack animal required a significant increase in attention paid to eating habits (Hämäläinen 2003; Hanson 1986:97; Landals 2004; Oliver 1962:14). As a result, good horse pasturage became as vital as finding good hunting territory in the selection of camp locations (Carson 1998:38; Landals 2004). It also necessitated more frequent camp movements as horses exhausted the surrounding landscape quicker than dogs or humans (Krech 1999:138; Zedeño et al. 2014:28).

Another major difference between dogs and horses is their hydration requirements. Dogs require relatively little water compared to horses. As a result, water for humans and dogs could be easily transported. The water requirements for horses, especially a large herd, are much greater. While Ewers (1955:146) reports accounts of water being transported during camp movements following the arrival of the horse, he notes that this practice was not common and could not sustain a large herd for more than one or two days of movement. Therefore, the equestrian Blackfoot had to be constantly aware of available fresh water for their horses (Ewers 1955:307; Landals 2004), which in turn caused a shift in Blackfoot settlement patterns and use of the landscape (Bethke 2017).

Finally, a major distinction between dogs and horses has to do with their behavioral characteristics. Dogs are pack animals and as such exhibit loyalty and duty to the pack, of which they consider their humans to be a part (Landals 2004:244). Horses, on the other hand, are herd animals and therefore do not possess the same sense of allegiance, instead being easily led by the will of the group leader. This difference in the behavior of the two animals makes it almost impossible to steal even a single dog but very easy to steal a large horse herd all at once (Ewers 1955:301; Landals 2004:244). Furthermore, horses were the target of these thefts more frequently because they were highly valued in ways that dogs were not. Therefore, while there are many historic and ethnographic accounts of horse raiding, there is no evidence of dog theft among the Blackfoot or other groups in the region (Ewers 1955:312).

In addition to being stolen, horses, unlike dogs, will stray under certain conditions and feel no need to return (Ewers 1955:301; Landals 2004:248). In order to protect their horses, the Blackfoot had to develop new methods of securing their domestic stock, including tying their most prized horses near their tipis, corralling them inside the camp, hobbling them, using natural topography to conceal and separate herds, and employing dogs as guards (Ewers 1955:38–42, 301, 312; Jackson 2000:11; Landals 2004:248–249; Schultz 1962:182, 259).

If lost or stolen, a horse was much more difficult to replace than a dog. Dogs have a faster breeding and maturation cycle than horses that requires relatively little in terms of human intervention or specialized knowledge. Although a family would be able to quickly and easily replenish its dog population, horse breeding programs among the Blackfoot were infrequent before the reservation period, and most horses were obtained from trading (which was costly) or raiding (which was risky) (Denman 1968:102). As a result, access to horses was more limited than access to dogs. Furthermore, dogs are much easier to train and thus could be made useful more quickly and efficiently than horses, which require expert knowledge, equipment, a longer time period, and more risk to break and train. Therefore, while any family could have as many dogs as needed to transport their goods with no dependence upon specialized knowledge or medicine power in order to obtain them, horses were often acquired at a higher cost.

The Dog in Equestrian Blackfoot Culture

These differences in husbandry concerns coupled with growing instrumental and intrinsic value of horses altered the relationship between the Blackfoot people, their animals, and their landscape. While dogs continued to be viewed by the Blackfoot as close companions and partners after the adoption of the horse, their relationship had to be redefined within this equestrian Blackfoot culture, where they were no longer the only domesticated animal. The value of dogs decreased as horses "relegated them to a place of secondary importance as burden bearers" (Ewers 1955:312). Similar accounts were given by tribal members. As one individual puts it, "dogs didn't mean as much after the horse" (Tom Crawford, personal communication, 2014). This new station manifested itself in several different ways, impacting both the dog's utilitarian value as well as its spiritual importance. For example, before the horse, dogs were given the duty of transporting medicine pipes and bundles when moving camp. Following the introduction of the horse, dogs were no longer allowed to carry these sacred objects, and a special horse was painted and designated by each owner for their transport (Crowshoe and Manneschmidt 2002:82; Wissler 1912:175).

While the horse may have impacted the relationship between the Blackfoot and their dogs, it did not completely replace it (Carol Murray, personal communication, 2014; Allan Pard, personal communication, 2014; Paul Raczka, personal communication, 2014). Indeed, dogs remained an important part of equestrian Blackfoot society, existing alongside humans and horses in several capacities (Ewers 1955:309; Allan Pard, personal communication, 2014). Although the use of dogs for transport following the introduction of the horse is sometimes viewed as an indication of poverty, historic and ethnographic accounts attest to the fact that dogs continued to be used, even among those families who had an abundance of horses, since they remained useful for auxiliary transport and light camp work (Ewers 1943:609–610, 1955:136, 309; Roe

1955:20). Carrying relatively light loads, dogs could keep up with the horses in the moving of camp (Ewers 1955:136; Henderson 1994, 2005). Furthermore, dogs provided an insurance mechanism since they could better withstand winter conditions, starvation, disease, and theft (Ewers 1955:141; Landals 2004:247).

In addition to their continued use as pack animals, dogs could serve their masters in ways that horses could not, such as the important role of camp guard (Ewers 1955:207–208; Carol Murray, personal communication, 2014; Allan Pard, personal communication, 2014; Schultz 2002:99). Dogs were related to horses directly in this way, as they were relied on extensively to guard horses within the camp, although the Blackfoot people were aware that they often were ineffective in this position (Ewers 1955:207–208).

In the reservation period, dogs also earned a new job as herders of horses, cattle, and sheep (Carol Murray, personal communication, 2014). These dogs differed physically from their predecessors as Euro-American encroachment, forced assimilation efforts, and the effects of newly introduced dog diseases eventually led to the decline of native dog populations (McCormack 2018:119). By the turn of the nineteenth century, dogs owned by the Blackfoot began to become increasingly diverse as smaller dog breeds used for herding by Euro-American populations were introduced (Tom Crawford, personal communication, 2014; Allan Pard, personal communication, 2014).

In addition to these services, dogs continued to be a component of Blackfoot religion, including playing an important role in bundle ceremonies and society life (Glenbow 2013:55; Carol Murray, personal communication, 2014; Pepion 1999; Paul Raczka, personal communication, 2014). As one tribal member explains,

> You know, all horses are medicine, the dogs are medicine, everything, all the animals are connected in the spiritual way. And the dog was the most sacred, because it is the first one that we had, they moved their camps with them. Then the horse came, and the horse surpassed the dog in significance. But still they used the dog, the dog was still important. (Tom Crawford, personal communication, 2014)

Today dogs have in many ways continued to be important characters within modern Blackfoot society, functioning as a source of both traditional power and value while at the same time developing into working partners within farming and ranching communities as well as filling the role of household pet (Carol Murray, personal communication, 2014).

Conclusion

Beyond their applied functions, animals provide humans with an important conceptual resource. The way a culture views, treats, and interacts with animals influences and is influenced by the way they experience, understand, and view themselves within the world (Harrod 2000; Hill 2011). The economic relationship humans have with animals, for example, has a great influence on human social organization as well as how animals are conceptualized within these systems. At the same time, however, understanding these relationships from only an economic point of view may ignore other important aspects of human-animal interactions beyond simply their practical utility (Hill 2011; Russell 2012). Recognizing how the many elements of these culturally specific relationships may combine is important for understanding not only what these relationships may tell us about human cultural systems but also how animals may influence or change these systems. Within Blackfoot culture, dogs and horses were understood not as technological objects but as dynamic actors in the community that engage in reciprocal relationships with humans. This understanding allows one to better characterize both the change and continuity of Blackfoot cultural institutions following the introduction of the horse within an Indigenous ontology of human-animal relationships.

Prior to acquiring the horse, the Blackfoot had a substantial commitment to the dog- and bison-centered Plains pedestrian complex. The apparent speed at which the Blackfoot made adjustments to both their daily lives and long-term cultural institutions to accommodate horses was remarkable (Peck 2011:433). They would not have given up this pedestrian system, which had worked to their advantage for thousands of years, unless the benefits of this new animal outweighed the significant adjustments to their way of life. Although horses were adopted for a number of activities (many of which were formerly performed by or continued to be performed in conjunction with dogs), their ability to carry human riders and subsequently be used in the bison hunt represents their most important advantage over the dog.

The rapid rise of the horse to this place of prominence within Blackfoot culture attests to the fact that, for the Blackfoot people, the horse became more than just a "new and superior dog" (Wissler 1914). Instead, the horse was a completely new animal that brought with it its own set of abilities, expectations, and obligations, altered the habits of daily life, served to develop new skills and technical expertise, enriched the material culture, and irrevocably changed the way in which the Blackfoot obtained their most important resource—bison.

As a result, Blackfoot people developed a different relationship with their horses than they previously had with their dogs, creating a new equestrian lifeway centered around horses and the advantages they brought to nomadic life. Despite functioning as pack animals, guards, religious figures, and even companions, dogs were never as integral to Blackfoot culture as the horse (Bastien 2004:13; Denman 1968:63; Ewers 1955:309; Tom Crawford, personal communication, 2014). Yet even as the horse engulfed the reality of the Blackfoot world, they did not completely forsake their trusted canine companions. Instead, the human-dog relationship was renegotiated within this new, horse-centered existence.

Acknowledgments

I would like to thank the Blackfeet Nation and individuals who participated in this project, in particular John and Carol Murray, Allan Pard, Paul Raczka, Sheldon Carlson, Tom Crawford, and Ed LeMieux. Their guidance and input were instrumental to this research. This work also benefited from comments and discussion from María Nieves Zedeño, TJ Ferguson, Mary Stiner, Barnet Pavao-Zuckerman, Alison Landals, Joey Williams, and Sarah Trabert. I would like to also thank my coeditor, Amanda Burtt, and all of the volume contributors. This work was funded by a National Science Foundation Doctoral Dissertation Improvement Grant (1521950).

References Cited

Baldwin, Stuart J.
1994   Blackfoot Neologisms. *International Journal of American Linguistics* 60:69–72.
Bamforth, Douglas B.
1988   *Ecology and Human Organization on the Great Plains*. Plenum Press, New York.
Barsh, Russel Lawrence, and Chantelle Marlor
2003   Driving Bison and Blackfoot Science. *Human Ecology* 31:571–593.
Bastien, Betty
2004   *Blackfoot Ways of Knowing: The Worldview of the Siksikaitsitapi*. University of Calgary Press, Calgary.
Bethke, Brandi
2017   The Archaeology of Pastoralist Landscapes in the Northwestern Plains. *American Antiquity* 82(4):798–816.
2019   Revisiting the Horse in Blackfoot Culture: Evaluating the Development of Nomadic

Pastoralism on the North American Plains. *International Journal of Historical Archaeology*. DOI: 10.1007/s10761-019-00502-1.

Bethke, Brandi, María Nieves Zedeño, Geoffrey Jones, and Matthew Pailes

2018   Complementary Approaches to the Identification of Bison Processing for Storage at the Kutoyis Complex, Montana. *Journal of Archaeological Science: Reports* 17:879–894.

Burpee, Lawrence (editor)

1908   *York Factory to the Blackfeet Country: The Journal of Anthony Hendry, 1754–55*. Proceedings and Transactions of the Royal Society of Canada, 3rd series. Royal Society of Canada, Ottawa.

Bradley, James H.

1900   Affairs at Fort Benton from 1831 to 1869: From Lieut. Bradley's Journal. *Contributions to the Historical Society of Montana* 3:203–205.

Brink, Jack

2008   *Imagining Head-Smashed In: Aboriginal Buffalo Hunting on the Northern Plains*. Athabasca University Press, Edmonton.

Carlson, Paul Howard

1998   *The Plains Indians*. Texas A&M University Press, College Station.

Crowshoe, Reg, and Sybille Manneschmidt

2002   *Akak'stiman: A Blackfeet Framework of Decision-Making and Mediation Process*. University of Calgary Press, Calgary.

Dempsey, Hugh A.

2001   Blackfoot. In *Handbook of North American Indians*, Vol. 13, *Plains*, edited by R. DeMallie, pp. 604–628. Smithsonian Institution Press, Washington, DC.

Denhardt, Robert M.

1947   *The Horse of the Americas*. University of Oklahoma Press, Norman.

Denman, Clayton Charlton

1968   Cultural Change among the Blackfeet Indians of Montana. PhD dissertation, University of California, Berkeley.

Descola, Philippe

2013   *Beyond Nature and Culture*. University of Chicago Press, Chicago.

Dickason, Olive Patricia

1980   A Historical Reconstruction for the Northwestern Plains. *Prairie Forum* 5:19–37.

Dietz, Ute Luise

2003   Horseback Riding: Man's Access to Speed? In *Prehistoric Steppe Adaptation and the Horse*, edited by Colin Renfrew, Marsha Levine, and Katie Boyle, pp. 189–202. McDonald Institute for Archaeological Research, Cambridge.

Duke, Philip

1991   *Points in Time: Structure and Event in a Late Northern Plains Hunting Society*. University Press of Colorado, Niwot.

Ewers, John C.

1955   *The Horse in Blackfeet Indian Culture: With Comparative Material from Other Western Tribes*. Smithsonian Institution Bureau of American Ethnology, Bulletin 159. US Government Printing Office, Washington, DC.

1958   *The Blackfoot: Raiders on the Northwestern Plains*. University of Oklahoma Press, Norman.

Ferris, Neal

2009 *The Archaeology of Native-Lived Colonialism.* University of Arizona Press, Tucson.

Fijn, Natasha

2011 *Living with Herds: Human-Animal Coexistence in Mongolia.* Cambridge University Press, Cambridge.

Fran Fraser's Blackfoot Culture Collection, ca. 1930s–1973.

1969 M-37 (manuscript). Rosie Ayoungman Interviews. Glenbow Museum Archives, Calgary.

Glenbow Blackfoot Gallery Committee

2013 *The Story of the Blackfoot People: Niitsitapiisinni.* Glenbow Museum, Calgary.

Grinnell, George B.

1961 *Pawnee, Blackfoot, and Cheyenne: History and Folklore of the Plains from the Writings of George Bird Grinnell.* Scribner, New York.

1962 *Blackfoot Lodge Tales: The Story of a Prairie People.* University of Nebraska Press, Lincoln.

Haines, Francis

1938a The Northward Spread of Horses among the Plains Indians. *American Anthropologist* 40:429–437.

1938b Where Did the Plains Indians Get Their Horses? *American Anthropologist* 40:112–117.

Hämäläinen, Pekka

2003 The Rise and Fall of Plains Indian Horse Cultures. *Journal of American History* 90:833–862.

Hanson, Jeffery R.

1986 Adjustment and Adaptation on the Northern Plains: The Case of Equestrianism among the Hidatsa. *Plains Anthropologist* 31:93–107.

Harrod, Howard L.

2000 *The Animals Came Dancing: Native American Sacred Ecology and Animal Kinship.* University of Arizona Press, Tucson.

Henderson, Norman

1994 Replicating Dog Travois Travel on the Northern Plains. *Plains Anthropologist* 39:145–159.

2005 *Rediscovering the Prairies: Journeys by Dog, Horse and Canoe.* TouchWood Editions, Victoria, British Columbia.

Henry, Alexander

1809 *Travels and Adventures in Canada and the Indian Territories between the Years 1760 and 1776.* I. Riley, New York.

Hill, Erica

2011 Animals as Agents: Hunting Ritual and Relational Ontologies in Prehistoric Alaska and Chukotka. *Cambridge Archaeological Journal* 21:407–426.

2013 Archaeology and Animal Persons: Toward a Prehistory of Human-Animal Relations. *Environment and Society: Advances in Research* 4:117–136.

2018 The Archaeology of Human-Dog Relations in Northwest Alaska. In *Dogs in the North: Stories of Cooperation and Co-Domestication,* edited by Robert J. Losey, Robert P. Wishart, and Jan Peter Laurens Loovers, pp. 87–104. Routledge, New York.

Hungry Wolf, Adolf

2006 *The Blackfoot Papers,* Vol. 1, *Pikunni History and Culture.* Good Medicine Cultural Foundation, Browning, Montana.

Ingold, Tim

2000   *The Perception of the Environment: Essays on Livelihood, Dwelling and Skill.* Routledge, London.

2006   Rethinking the Animate, Re-Animating Thought. *Ethnos* 71:9–20.

Jackson, John C.

2000   *The Piikani Blackfeet: A Culture under Siege.* Mountain Press, Missoula.

Kehoe, Thomas F.

1960   Stone Tipi Rings in North-Central Montana and the Adjacent Portion of Alberta, Canada: Their Historical, Ethnological, and Archeological Aspects. *Anthropological Papers* 173:421–473.

Kidd, Kenneth E.

1986   *Blackfoot Ethnography.* Archaeological Survey of Alberta Manuscript Series, Vol. 8. Alberta Culture, Historical Resources Division, Edmonton.

Kirksey, S. Eben, and Stefan Helmreich

2010   The Emergence of Multispecies Ethnography. *Cultural Anthropology* 25:545–76.

Kohn, Eduardo

2007   How Dogs Dream: Amazonian Natures and the Politics of Transspecies Engagement. *American Ethnologist* 34:3–24.

Krech, Shepard, III

1999   Chapter 5: Buffalo. In *The Ecological Indian: Myth and History*, pp. 123–150. W. W. Norton, New York.

Landals, Alison

2004   Horse Heaven: Change in Late Precontact to Contact Period Landscape Use in Southern Alberta. In *Archaeology on the Edge: New Perspectives from the Northern Plains*, edited by J. Kelley and Brian Kooyman, pp. 231–262. University of Calgary Press, Calgary.

Leslie Corness Fonds

1970   PR2009.0336/0001 (manuscript). The Pigeons, a Society of the Blackfoot Indians. Paper presented by John C. Hellson at a Conference held in Edmonton, Alberta. Provincial Archives of Alberta, Edmonton.

Lewis Henry Morgan Papers

1862   SC-525 (manuscript). Lewis Henry Morgan Diary. Montana Historical Society Research Center Archives, Helena.

Losey, Robert J., Vladimir I. Bazaliiskii, Sandra Garvie-Lok, Mietje Germonpré, Jennifer A. Leonard, Andrew L. Allen, M. Anne Katzenberg, and Mikhail V. Sablin

2011   Canids as Persons: Early Neolithic Dog and Wolf Burials, Cis-Baikal, Siberia. *Journal of Anthropological Archaeology* 30:174–189.

McClintock, Walter

1999   *The Old North Trail: Life, Legends and Religion of the Blackfeet Indians.* University of Nebraska Press, Lincoln.

McCormack, Patricia

2018   An Ethnohistory of Dogs in the Mackenzie Basin (Western Subarctic). In *Dogs in the North: Stories of Cooperation and Co-Domestication*, edited by Robert J. Losey, Robert P. Wishart, and Jan Peter Laurens Loovers, pp. 105–153. Routledge, New York.

Nadasdy, Paul

2007   The Gift in the Animal: The Ontology of Hunting and Human-Animal Society. *American Ethnologist* 34:25–43.

Oliver, Symmes C.

1962 *Ecology and Cultural Continuity as Contributing Factors in Social Organization of the Plains Indians.* University of California Publications in American Archaeology and Ethnology, Vol. 48. University of California Press, Berkeley.

Osborn, Alan J.

1983 Ecological Aspects of Equestrian Adaptations in Aboriginal North America. *American Anthropologist* 85:563–591.

Peck, Trevor

2011 *Light from Ancient Campfires: Archaeological Evidence for Native Lifeways on the Northern Plains.* Athabasca University Press, Edmonton.

Peck, Trevor, and Caroline R. Hudecek-Cuffe

2003 Archaeology on the Alberta Plains: The Last Two Thousand Years. In *Archaeology in Alberta: A View from the New Millennium*, edited by J. W. Brink and J. F. Dormaar, pp. 72–103. Archaeological Society of Alberta, Medicine Hat.

Peck, Trevor, and Roderick J. Vickers

2006 Buffalo and Dogs: The Prehistoric Lifeways of Aboriginal People on the Alberta Plains, 1004–1005. In *Alberta Formed, Alberta Transformed*, edited by Catherine Anne Cavanaugh, Michael Payne, and Donald Grant Wetherell, pp. 54–85. University of Alberta Press, Edmonton.

Pepion, Donald

1999 Blackfoot Ceremony: A Qualitative Study of Learning. MA Thesis, Montana State University, Bozeman.

Raczka, Paul

2011 Ponokamita Saam—Horse Medicine of the Blackfoot People. In *Horses and Bridles of the American Indians*, edited by Ned Martin, Mike Cowdrey, and Jody Martin, pp. 2–17. Hawk Hill Press, Niscasio, California.

2017 *A Blackfoot History, The Winter Counts: Sikaitapi Itsinniiki, Telling the Old Stories.* Blackfoot Books, Choteau, Montana.

Reeves, Brian O. K.

1983 *Culture Change in the Northern Plains, 1000 B.C.–A.D. 1000.* Occasional Papers of the Archaeological Survey of Alberta, Vol. 20. Alberta Culture Historical Resources Division, Edmonton.

Roe, Frank Gilbert

1955 *The Indian and the Horse.* University of Oklahoma Press, Norman.

Russell, Nerissa

2012 *Social Zooarchaeology: Humans and Animals in Prehistory.* Cambridge University Press, Cambridge.

Schaeffer, Claude E.

1978 The Bison Drive of the Blackfeet Indians. *Plains Anthropologist* 23:243–238.

Scheiber, Laura L., and Judson Byrd Finley

2011 Mobility as Resistance: Colonialism among Nomadic Hunter-Gatherers in the American West. In *Hunter-Gatherer Archaeology as Historical Process*, edited by Kenneth E. Sassaman and Donald H. Holly Jr., pp. 167–183. University of Arizona, Tucson.

Schultz, James Willard

1907 *My Life as an Indian.* Fawcett Publications, Greenwich, Connecticut.

1962 *Blackfeet and Buffalo.* University of Oklahoma Press, Norman.

2002 *Blackfeet Tales from Apikuni's World.* University of Oklahoma Press, Norman.

Silliman, Stephen
2005 Culture Contact or Colonialism? Challenges in the Archaeology of Native North America. *American Antiquity* 70:55–74.

Tovias, Blanca
2011 *Colonialism on the Prairies: Blackfoot Settlement and Cultural Transformation, 1870–1920.* Sussex Academic Press, Brighton and Eastbourne.

Tyrrell, J. B. (editor)
1916 *David Thompson's Narrative of His Explorations in Western America, 1784–1812.* Champlain Society, Toronto.

Uhlenbeck, C. C.
1912 *A New Series of Blackfoot Texts from the Southern Peigans Blackfoot Reservation, Teton County, Montana.* J. Muller, Amsterdam.

Umfreville, Edward
1790 *The Present State of Hudson's Bay: Containing a Full Description of That Settlement, and the Adjacent Country; and Likewise of the Fur Trade, with Hints for Its Improvement, &c. &c.; To Which Are Added, Remarks and Observations Made in the Inland Parts, During a Residence of Near Four Years; A Specimen of Five Indian Languages; and a Journal of a Journey from Montreal to New-York.* Charles Stalker, London.

Vickers, Roderick J., and Trevor R. Peck
2009 Identifying the Prehistoric Blackfoot: Approaches to Nitsitapii (Blackfoot) Culture History. In *Painting the Past with a Broad Brush: Papers in Honor of James Valliere Wright,* edited by David L. Keenlyside and Jean-Luc Pilon, pp. 473–497. Mercury Series Archaeology Paper, Vol. 170. Canadian Museum of Civilization, Gatineau.

Wilson, Gilbert Livingstone
1924 *The Horse and the Dog in Hidatsa Culture.* AMS Press, New York.

Wissler, Clark
1910 *Material Culture of the Blackfeet Indians,* Vol. V. Anthropological Papers of the American Museum of Natural History, New York.
1912 *Ceremonial Bundles of the Blackfoot Indians,* Vol. VII. Anthropological Papers of the American Museum of Natural History, New York.
1914 The Influence of the Horse in the Development of Plains Culture. *American Anthropologist* 16:1–25.

Wissler, Clark, and D. C. Duvall
1908 *Mythology of the Blackfoot Indians,* Vol. II. Anthropological Papers of the American Museum of Natural History, New York.

Zedeño, María Nieves, Jesse A. B. Ballenger, and John R. Murray
2014 Landscape Engineering and Organizational Complexity among Late Prehistoric Bison Hunters of the Northwestern Plains. *Current Anthropology* 55:23–58.

8

Exotic Dogs and Indigenous Humans
in Tropical Northeastern South America

PETER W. STAHL

Domestic dogs (*Canis lupus familiaris*) are currently encountered almost everywhere in South America, and although ubiquitous throughout the tropical lowlands, their appearance in much of Amazonia may have been relatively recent. Where incorporated into Indigenous societies, dogs are generally used in hunting game, and the relative esteem afforded them tends to be directly associated with their role in predation. This stands in marked contrast to other exotic animal domesticates, whose treatment ranges from curiosity to benign neglect and cruelty. Despite their famed proclivity for keeping tamed "pets," Indigenous people domesticated few, if any, endemic animals in the neotropical lowlands. This is particularly noteworthy as it contrasts starkly with the wide variety of endemic plants that were brought under various forms of domestication.

Preserved specimens of precolumbian dogs have been identified in some Andean archaeological contexts, although their earliest appearance in Amazonia is conjectural. They may have been present in northeastern South America, but their status is poorly known. However, the archaeological association of humans and endemic canids, particularly fox species, is widespread and ancient in South America, where anecdotal evidence insinuates the taming of endemic canids in many areas of the continent. This is particularly well documented in the tropical lowlands of northeastern South America, which may have served as a precolumbian center for the distribution of early canids into the Caribbean.

In this chapter, I explore the relationship between exotic dogs and Indigenous humans in northeastern South America. I emphasize that the esteem bestowed on hunting dogs by their owners can differ markedly from their attitude toward other exotic domesticates, including dogs that play no apparent role in predation. I suggest that this attitude may have its basis in a shared ontological perspective, which considers a qualitatively different relationship between Indigenous Amazonians and their endemic faunas from one generally held for exotic domesticates. The aberrant esteem bestowed upon exotic hunting dogs today may be based on an earlier template of endemic canids that were tamed and trained but never domesticated because it was logically incongruent to do so.

Canids in the Tropical Lowlands of Northeastern South America

Although the timing and location of its early appearance is debated, the dog (*Canis lupus familiaris*) is believed to have been introduced by migrant human populations into North America, where it is identified in early Holocene archaeological contexts (Morey 2010; Tito et al. 2011) long after its domestication involving Pleistocene populations of Eurasian gray wolf (Druzhkova et al. 2013; Frantz et al. 2016; Larson et al. 2012; Thalman et al. 2013). The exotic dog first appeared somewhat later in western South America, based upon a few scattered identifications of specimens in Andean archaeological contexts (Stahl 2012:115), and eventually entered the continent's southern cone with agriculturalists at a relatively late date (Schwartz 1997; Prates et al. 2009). Identifying its early presence in the tropical lowlands is hampered by a lack of preserved archaeological data; however, specimens from the margins of Amazonia in northern coastal Venezuela (Linares 1987) and southeastern Brazil (Guedes et al. 2017) provide dates during the mid-first millennium AD.

In his comprehensive review of hunting dogs in the neotropical lowlands, Jeremy Koster (2009) notes the relative absence of domesticated dogs in much of Amazonia. Although dogs were eagerly imported from adjoining highland areas, some Amazonian societies only first acquired them during the twentieth century. He hypothesizes that Amazonians may have declined to accept dogs when presented with the opportunity. Other factors, such as high mortality under harsh tropical conditions, may also have hindered their diffusion into the area (Koster 2009:592–593). The argument is strengthened by Peter Mitchell's (2017) suggestion that endemic infectious disease may have constrained the early expansion of exotic dogs into neotropical environments. The exotic domesticated dog appeared on a continent where only a few endemic animals were domesticated, including Andean camelids (*Lama glama* and *Vicugna pacos*), cuy (*Cavia porcellus*), and Muscovy duck (*Cairina moschata*). The relative paucity of endemic animal domesticates in Amazonia can seem paradoxical, especially in an area celebrated for the enormous array of endemic plants that were brought under various forms of cultivation (Clement 1999) and considering the famous proclivity of Indigenous Amazonians for keeping all sorts of animal "pets."

There is no species of *Canis* among the contemporary endemic canids of South America, which include short-eared dog (*Atelocynus microtis*), crab-eating fox (*Cerdocyon thous*), maned wolf (*Chrysocyon brachyurus*), bush dog (*Speothos venaticus*) and six species of foxes (*Lycalopex*, also *Pseudalopex* and *Dusicyon* in the literature). Where was the source for Amazonian dogs? Are today's domesticates descendants of post-Conquest introductions? Had a Eurasian dog arrived in the area with earlier colonizers? Were altogether different and endemic canids associated with Indigenous societies? Were any or all of these earlier canids hybridized?

Elsewhere, I have suggested the possibility that at least some Indigenous Amazonians may have already had their own autochthonous version of the domesticated dog in the form of tamed endemic canids (Stahl 2013). The earliest European documents describe encounters with canids in the Caribbean islands. These animals were probably introduced by humans from northern South America or potentially from eastern Central America. These early canids could have been tamed endemic canids or dog hybrids introduced via trade networks from northern South America into the Caribbean. The scarce direct archaeological evidence is of little assistance for deciphering the status of precolumbian canids in greater Amazonia, and DNA studies suggest that native dogs were extensively replaced by post-Conquest dogs (Castroviejo-Fisher et al. 2011). However, widespread archaeological associations of fox and humans are recorded from an early date (Stahl 2012), and historic accounts mention that humans were taming foxes and hybridizing foxes and dogs in various areas of the continent (Stahl 2013). Highly esteemed hunting dogs, including tamed foxes and hybrids, were circulated via an old and far-reaching trade network that persisted into recent times and was centered in northeastern South America.

Indigenous Hunters, Traders, and Canids
in Northeastern South America

In the early decades of Spanish exploration and conquest, the official chronicler of the Indies wrote of shy, little, non-barking dogs that were brought to the Caribbean coast for trade from the lands of the Caribes (Oviedo y Valdés 1946 [1526]:Capítulo 26:491). An ancient and extensive trading network among the Indigenous societies of northeastern South America (Figure 8.1) subsequently became known to the Spanish in the eighteenth century and to the Dutch and English in the early nineteenth century (Coppens 1971). Central trade items in

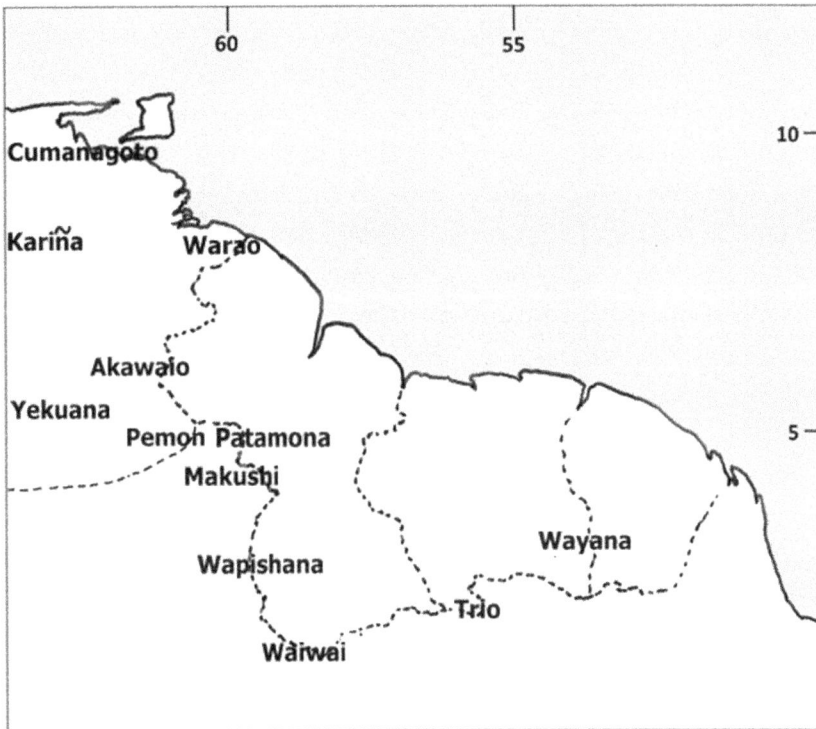

Figure 8.1. Approximate locations of some Indigenous societies in Northeastern South America. Various alternate spellings, names, and incorporated groups are often encountered, including Warao (Guaraúno); Kariña (Matihuana, Mawisha); Akawaio (Guaica, Ingarikó, Kapon, Kapong, Waicá); Yekuana (Dekuana, Maionggong, Makiritare, Pawaná, So'to), Pemon (Arekuna, E'ti, Kamarakoto, Pemong, Taulebang, Taulipang, Taurapang, Taurepan); Patamona (Ingarikó, Kapon, Kapong); Makushi (E'ti, Macuxi, Pemon); Wapishana (Wapixana, Wapichana); Trio (Tirió, Tiriyó); Wayana (Upurui, Roucouyen). For issues involving alternative names, see Butt 1973. All except Wapishana (Arawakan) are speakers of Cariban languages.

this network included esteemed hunting dogs. During the course of his boundary survey for the British government in 1842, German explorer Robert Schomburgk wrote glowingly of dogs obtained from the Waiwai and Taruma that were used as a "kind of merchandise or Article of barter between them and their neighbours" (Rivière 2006:96).

The Waiwai of extreme southern Guyana and northern Brazil are perhaps the most celebrated dog trainers and traders in the area. Through trade with Akawaio, Wapishana, Trio, and others, their prized dogs, cassava graters, and apron belts were exchanged for goods obtained in expanding networks that reached the coast and beyond. Waiwai mastery of dogs may have been originally obtained from the Taruma, a non-Cariban speaking group believed to have lived on the lower Río Negro during the seventeenth century and moved into the upper Essequibo area during the nineteenth century before being absorbed by the Waiwai in the first half of the twentieth century (Brett 1868; Farabee 1918; Fock 1963; Guppy 1958; Howard 2001; Mentore 2005; Rivière 1969; Roth 1924; Thurn 1883; Yde 1965). The Yekuana of western Venezuela are also celebrated for training desired hunting dogs, which were traded to their Akawaio, Pemon, Sanumá, and Yanomami neighbors. Akawaio middlemen transported dogs to the coast in exchange for products with which they returned to the interior (Barandiaran 1962; Butt Colson 1973; Coppens 1971; Sponsel 1981; Taylor 1974). It has also been suggested that the coastal Cumanagoto were supplied with dogs by the Kariña (Civrieux 1980), and that the Wayana of eastern Guiana raised great numbers of dogs, which were one of their principal resources for sale (Hurault 1968).

Any precise identification of the kinds of canids involved in this trade network is complicated by its evolving nature in time and space. In 1842 Schomburgk lost one of his beloved dogs, described as "a cross breed between the Taruma dog and the *Canis cancrivorus*," to a jaguar attack (Rivière 2006:194). Later, in a letter to Charles Darwin (1868:23) he mentioned that coastal Arawaks repeatedly told him how they improved their dogs through crossings with the crab-eating fox. He also described the Waiwai and Taruma dogs as uncommonly large, with short white hair in black patches, broad heads, and long muzzles, like a cross between greyhounds and pointers (Darwin 1868:23; Rivière 2006:96). In the late nineteenth century, Everard Thurn (1883:232) concurred that fox-dog hybrids produced the best hunting dogs. Indeed, the crab-eating fox has long been identified as the indigenous dog of the area (e.g., Latcham 1922:54). Known to the Macushi as *maikang*, Walter Roth (1924:553) notes that "a tamed maikang has an especial value for the Indians in that it makes an excellent cross with their dogs, the cross being especially good hunters. . . . A tamed maikang is one of the most treasured possessions of an Indian, who will feed it on cooked flesh, fish, and fruit, especially ripe plantains." Mammalogists affirmed that the crab-eating fox (*Cerdocyon thous*) is easy to domesticate and that it was mated with domestic dogs to produce usable hybrids (Cabrera and Yepes 1960:130; and see Stahl 2012, 2013). It is interesting to note that both archaeological specimens from coastal Venezuela identified as *Canis* and *Cerdocyon* retain similar preserved evidence for captivity (Linares 1987). The bush dog (*Speothos venaticus*), or *ai*, has also been identified as the precolumbian hunting dog of eastern Venezuela (Civrieux 1980; Darwin 1868:23; and see Stahl 2012, 2013).

It is informative to consider the local Indigenous linguistic referents for dogs. Exotic domesticates recently introduced into South America were often referred to by borrowings or modifications of colonial words, onomatopoeic names, descriptive comparison to endemic animals, or simply as male or female (Nordenskiöld 1922). Indigenous languages in northeastern South America largely borrow colonial words for dogs. Charles Waterton (1891:111) argued strongly against the existence of precolumbian dogs in Guiana, noting that Indigenous Caribs regularly adopted Spanish words for recent introductions, including dogs (e.g., Simpson 1940:295, 1941:8; Wilbert 1972:96). Roth (1924:552), however, recounts Alexander von Humboldt's mention that in the early half of the sixteenth century local dogs of the Orinoco were called *maios* and *auries*, the latter a Maipurean (Arawakan) name used into recent times. Importantly, Carib names are specifically maintained for dogs among Pemon, Makushi, and Waiwai (e.g., Latcham 1922:54; Roth 1924:553; Simpson 1940:295, 1941:8), and interestingly the latter refer to dogs as *xapari* but call the recently introduced cat *kamaraci*, or "little jaguar" (Howard 2001:242).

Indigenous societies in the area often use dogs in predation, through active hunting of game, opportunistic hunting undertaken in association with another activity, or guarding against being hunted by forest predators. The many factors governing if and how dogs are used in these activities tend to be interrelated (Figure 8.2). Dogs, singularly or in large packs, regularly assist in the hunting of larger game by variously tracking, chasing, cornering, driving, or extricating tapirs and especially peccaries (Barandiaran 1962; Farabee 1924; Fock 1963; Guppy 1958; Hurault 1968; Thurn 1883). Dogs are also used to extricate smaller forest game, particularly large rodents, often while humans tend to their gardens

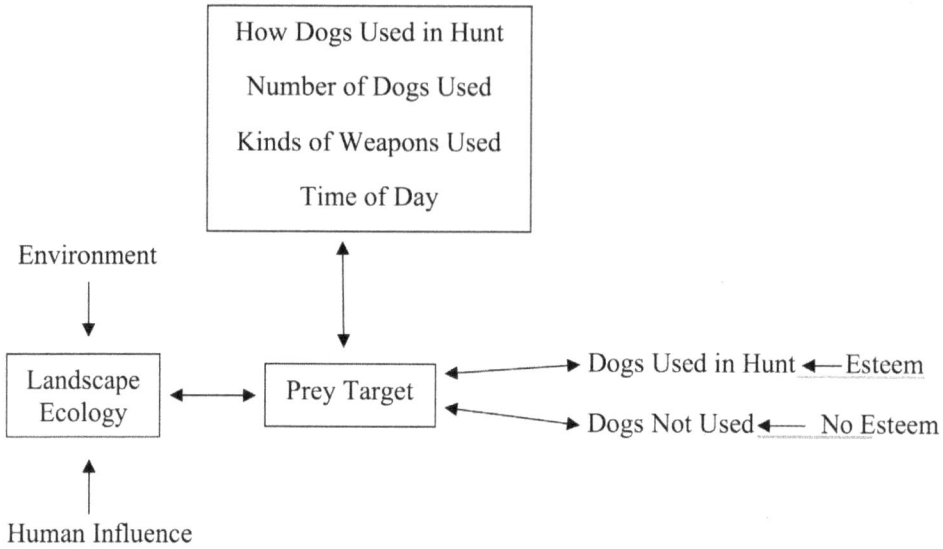

Figure 8.2. Potential factors affecting the relative esteem in which dogs are held by Indigenous Amazonians.

(Koster 2009:537; Roth 1922:121; Wilbert 1972). Early historical accounts identify their role in hunting large endemic Caribbean *hutia* rodents (Stahl 2013). Dogs are also used to warn of and protect against human, animal, and spirit predators (e.g., Guppy 1958:166; Smole 1976:179; Sponsel 1981; Yde 1965:102).

Through their participation in predation, dogs receive varying amounts of esteem from Indigenous humans. Thurn (1883:232) noted that the Taruma trained each dog to hunt a certain kind of game. More recently, Catherine Howard (2001:255) noted that a Waiwai dog's relative worth is based upon both its appearance and expertise in the kinds of game it hunts, rated on a descending scale from tapir to armadillo. So valuable were dogs that Schomburgk claimed "among the Indians of the interior a good hunting dog like a marriageable girl commands a gun" (Rivière 2006:161). Dogs were the most valuable trade item for the Trio, and a good one was worth an ax, sheath knife, scissors, cloth, and beads (Rivière 1969:53). In exchange for a trained adult male hunting dog, the Yekuana would receive a new shotgun from their Pemon trading partners (Coppens 1971:50).

Esteem for good hunting dogs was particularly pronounced in Waiwai society where a dog's hunting skill was closely associated with a man's reputation; a bartered dog could be worth as much as 200 to 500 dollars in trade items (Howard 2001:247–248). Waiwai settlements could contain more dogs than humans. Prized hunting dogs were tethered to raised platforms along the perimeter walls of the house in order to protect them from the ubiquitous ectoparasites on the dwelling floor. Their daily needs were attended to by women, who carried them to the river to be bathed so their feet never touched the ground (Farabee 1918, 1924; Fock 1963; Guppy 1958; Mentore 2005). Nicholas Guppy (1958:165) was moved to declare: "Even more than the English the Wai-Wais deserve to be famous as dog-lovers. Their dogs are, collectively, the world's most pampered. . . . They spend most of their adult days reclining, in the ease of Oriental potentates, on their shelves, or even in their own hammocks." Dogs also figure prominently in the Waiwai origin myth; two dogs appear with the first humans, whose children are exhorted to keep them as pets (Fock 1963:42). At death, a Waiwai's personal belongings are destroyed and a favored dog killed (Fock 1963:164) and occasionally buried to accompany its human companion into the afterlife (Roth 1924:652, 660).

The fate of dogs that play no role in predation is entirely different. Unlike the pampered hunting dogs, Thurn (1883:232) noted that every house swarmed with an "undue number of miserable looking curs." Howard (2001:255) noted that dogs not participating in the hunt are considered valueless. These worthless dogs could be used as decoys in gardens if jaguars attacked, providing the women with a chance to escape (Roth 1924:554). Otherwise these often-squalid animals appeared to be of no use (e.g., Simpson 1940:402), and "ordinary dead dogs are merely thrown away in the forest" (Fock 1963:166). Worthless dogs in many ways assume the same status as other exotic animal domesticates.

Indigenous societies throughout northeastern South America variably acquired exotic animal domesticates. Although pigs, cows, horses, donkeys, mules, cats, and chickens are certainly known, they play no, or extremely insignificant, economic roles in Indigenous society. Throughout South America, these animals are referred to by onomatopoeic names (especially in the case of the chicken), derivations from European languages, modified comparisons to wild endemics, or not at all (Nordenskiöld 1922). For example, Camarakotos call the chicken *kŏroitoko* and the pig *kochino*; other exotic animal domesticates were never introduced and have no names (Simpson 1940, 1941). Some Carib groups might keep exotic domesticates, but they are never eaten, and pigs are obtained as sucklings from criollos for fattening and resale (Henley 1982:42; Thomas 1982:47).

The divide between endemic faunas that can be eaten and exotic domesticated faunas that are almost never eaten is perhaps best illustrated in the case of the chicken, which is found practically everywhere. Chickens, especially white varieties, tend to be kept for their feathers. They can serve as playthings or, much like young endemic birds, perhaps as pets. They can be admired for their novelty, singing, or behavior, and along with their eggs, they can be kept for sale to colonists. However, Indigenous people rarely consume chickens or their eggs, and if they do it is usually only under specific circumstances, such as accidental death (Barandiaran 1962:15; Farabee 1924:201; Guppy 1958:34; Henley 1982:47; Hurault 1968:6; Rivière 1969:41; Roth 1924:556; Smole 1976:185; Thomas 1982:42). Alan Campbell (1995:22) details the interesting encounter of Waiwai with chickens: "When they were first given chickens by the Brazilians they found it difficult to understand that they were supposed to kill them and eat them from time to time. When they got round to it, they decided that the only way to kill them was with a bow and arrow, as if they were game." Clearly, Indigenous attitudes that define the relationships between humans and animals, whether locally available or exotic and "domesticated" or "wild," require a different perspective.

Relational Ontology, Game Animals, Pets, Exotic Domesticates, and Dogs

Indigenous Amazonians are celebrated for surrounding themselves with a striking array of endemic animal others. Often referred to as "pets," these animals can be suckled, cared for like children, kept as amusement, or ignored. Collectively, they are not eaten, bred, or in any way domesticated. Exotic animal domesticates, if present, might be prized for admired traits, acquired from colonists and fattened for resale, allowed to disperse freely around the residence and completely disregarded, or treated harshly. They are usually neither mated nor raised as domesticates, nor are they eaten, or if they are eaten, only under special circumstances. However, Indigenous attitudes toward canids, at least in northeastern South America, can appear to be somewhat ambivalent, depending upon context. Endemic canids trained for hunting were tame, but not domesticated. Exotic dog–endemic canid hybrids could not be bred successfully, only minimally due to chromosomal incompatibility and their resulting sterile offspring (Stahl 2013:523). Exotic dogs that are raised and trained for hunting are highly valued. Those having no role in predation tend to be treated like exotic animal domesticates and at times with extreme cruelty (e.g., Cormier 2003:115; Santos-Granero 2009:182).

It might be easily argued that the differential treatment bestowed a highly trained exotic hunting dog is simply a function of its predatory skill and related value as a trade commodity, especially when compared to a worthless ordinary exotic dog with no special skill. However, if relative esteem were only a function of economic value, then why are exotic chickens or pigs not similarly esteemed as valuable trade items? The relationship between exotic dogs and Indigenous humans is likely more complex and based in a shared Amazonian logic that underscores the relationship between humans and animals. Why can endemic animals be consumable as game yet non-consumable as pets? Why is the concept of animal domestication alien to Indigenous Amazonians? Why can exotic dogs, unlike other introduced animal domesticates, be intentionally bred?

Indigenous Amazonians organize their relations with other occupants of a cohabited universe on the basis of human society. Animals assume a certain social equivalence to humans as they reside in their own villages, speak their own languages, and participate in their own cultural settings. Humans therefore differ from animals only in their outward appearance, as both are imbued with similar interior qualities like rational thought, intentionality, and reflexivity. Humans relate to and connect with sentient animals through established kinship networks (Århem 1996; Descola 1992, 1996, 2001, 2013; Fausto 2007; Viveiros de Castro 1998, 2004). Indigenous Amazonians understand that, as sentient others are organized in similar ways, the only manner in which they differ is in their outward shape (Taylor 1996); their human condition is that of a "transitory corporeal envelope" (Descola 2013:31), an "outward clothing" (Descola 2013:131) in which humans are veiled as animals (Viveiros de Castro 1998:480).

While humans are differentiated from others through visible and tangible expressions of their "physicality" or external form, they are the same as others through their "interiority," or all internal properties such as a soul or mental consciousness (Descola 2013:116). As shared interiority enables animals to conform to social norms and possess ethical precepts, it permits communicative relations between humans and non-humans (Descola 2013:129). Humanity or animality is simply a state or condition (Descola 2013:241; Viveiros de Castro 1998:472). All beings see in the same way, yet what may differ between them is what they see (Viveiros de Castro 1998:477; 2004:471) because any being in possession of a soul (its interiority) has a point of view that creates the object it perceives (Viveiros de Castro 1998:476; 2004:467). Following the logic of their perspectival multinaturalism, humans are fully aware that while perceiving the outward appearance of an animal, the animal simultaneously perceives itself as human (Viveiros de Castro 2004:466).

This shared relational ontology generates a central conflict for Indigenous Amazonians: if an animal is endowed with a similar interiority or soul, how can a hunter simply take its life as quarry and consume it as food (Descola 2013:16)? Through established kinship reckoning, hunter and prey relate as affines, which defines the hunter-prey relationship as one governed by exchange (Århem 1996:191). The connection between Indigenous Amazonian humans and animals involves potentially reversible relationships of exchange, predation, and gift (Descola 2013:311), often involving recycling of souls, negotiation, or reciprocity (Conklin 2001:182; Descola 1992:116; Erickson 2000; Fausto 2007:498). For example, dead humans become peccaries to be hunted (Conklin 2001:xxi), howlers that were once humans become prey (Cormier 2003:142), game is released from invisible villages by spirit masters upon negotiation with shamans (Shepard 2002:119), or humans are prey of spirits (Conklin 2001:182). Rather than mastery over prey, hunting and consuming game is a transaction (Conklin 2001:182).

If hunting and consumption among Indigenous Amazonian humans and endemic game animals is a transaction, then what are pets? Young endemic animals, often orphaned offspring of hunted game, are introduced into residential contexts and adopted into families. Universally, while under the care of adoptive parents, they are neither eaten nor bred. The status of the tamed pet has changed through adoptive filiation, whereby an affine from the outside is progressively consanguinized via familiarization until it is assimilated to society and produced as fully social affinal kin (Cormier 2002; Costa 2016; Descola 2001, 2013; Erickson 2000; Fausto 1999; Norton 2015; Santos-Granero 2016; Taylor 2001). In cases where former pets revisit the vicinity of their adopted home after having been returned to their previous abode, they are never hunted, as "it would be like killing my own children" (Shepard 2002:110). Since the time of Francis Galton (1883) it continues to be comforting to consider animal domestication as a natural consequence of pet keeping. On a fundamental level, in the relational universe of Indigenous Amazonians, pet keeping is not proto-domestication because it cannot be.

With the possible exception of the Muscovy duck, whose early history of domestication is poorly understood (Stahl 2005), Indigenous Amazonians did not domesticate any animals, at least in the way that we commonly think of the term. Philippe Descola (1994, 2013) has considered the ontological implications of animal domestication in Amazonia, underscoring that the dichotomy of wild/domesticated is anything but a universally shared concept (Descola 2013:48). Other ways to connect humans with animals involve potentially irreversible and hierarchical relationships, especially involving production and protection (Descola 2013:311). In the shared relational ontology of Indigenous Amazonians, production is an alien concept because the relations between subjects condition "production," not the other way around (Descola 2013:324). Although pet keeping may involve protecting animals against starvation, predation, and possibly abandonment, pets as consanguinized affines are part of the human kinship network. Philippe Erickson (2000:22) cogently admonishes that far from constituting an initial step in domestication, pet keeping is firmly centered on hunting and predation.

Amazonia is replete with various endemic animals that are "worthy candidates for domestication" (Smole 1976:185; also see Descola 2013:379; Stahl 2014:224); however, animal domestication is not a necessary outcome of simple availability. Domestication necessitates a change in relations that would require compatibility with the overall logic that governs human-animal relations (Descola 2013:377–378). Minimally through their experience with pet keeping, Indigenous Amazonians are not only aware of the basics of animal domestication (Descola 2013:379); they also understand that "most animals are already domesticated" through their relationship with spirit animal masters (Descola 2013:384). However, "between taming of game animals and domestication there is a boundary that the Amerindians of the tropical regions have always refused to cross" (Descola 2013:382). Indigenous Amazonians have enthusiastically accepted introduced technology when presented with the opportunity. However, it is easier to add a new tool to one's inventory than it is to invent a new relationship, which would involve a complete reorientation of existing principles governing human-animal relations (Descola 1994:341). Domestication would require the eradication of an animal's exteriority, and attaining mastery over an animal would require reorienting established relations between humans and spirit masters; "an animal in tropical South America can only be seen as the subject ... of an egalitarian relationship between two persons" (Descola 2013:384).

Exotic animal domesticates introduced into contexts where relations between humans and animals are shaped by animistic logic can be treated with ambivalence. However, they often occupy a niche distinct from endemic animals. The exigency of market economies may draw Indigenous Amazonians into stock rearing when exotic animal domesticates may be resold to colonists from whom they were obtained for fattening, but they are generally not consumed. They may be admired for some feature and kept like pets, yet they are usually not eaten. They may be treated with cruelty or utter neglect and their dead bodies discarded with trash. In some cases they may also be hunted like endemic game, which is made possible by transferring an established relation with game animals to recently introduced animals (Descola 1994:342). Similarly, Campbell (1995:22) observed Waiwai who could only conceive of killing and eating chickens when hunted like game with a bow and arrow. However, exotic animals are seldom bred or treated like domesticates. To the Guajá of northeastern Brazil, dogs, cats, chickens, and pigs are non-Indian pets; they are unlike kin-based forest life as they have no soul (Cormier 2003:96, 115).

How are we then to understand an exotic animal that is not only bred and trained but eagerly obtained through long-distance trade networks, like the highly valued and esteemed hunting dogs of northeastern South America? Descola (2013:385) has suggested that the introduction of European animal domesticates, foremost the dog, was met with few major difficulties. Much like the introduction of a new technical object or tool, it did not necessitate more than some minor adjustments in taxonomies; how the dog was to be regarded was mostly transmitted with the animal itself rather than involving any serious reorientation of human-animal relations. However, in northeastern South America, where the exotic dog may have only been a recent postcolumbian introduction, like a pig or a chicken, the relationship between previously unknown exotic dogs and Indigenous humans would have possibly required only minimal or no ontological adjustments because Indigenous Amazonians were already taming endemic foxes.

Any taming of habitually hunted endemic faunas, whether pets or hunting companions, remains provisional and conditional. However, this protective relationship is not easily transferred by Indigenous Amazonians to a relationship of absolute and irreversible subordination associated with Eurasian animal domesticates. Endemic game animals cannot be transferred into this domesticated relationship because the human-animal relations that govern it are foreign. No endemic faunas were domesticated, but it might be possible to enter into a domesticated relationship providing the latter was not completely alien (Descola 2013:388–389). It may have been possible to readily adopt the exotic dog because endemic foxes were already being tamed, suggesting that their ontological relationship was previously established and understood. However, even though the exotic dog may have filled a preexisting relationship and could thus be accepted and even bred, no other exotic animals were domesticated. Amazonian ontological relationships ensured that it would "remain confined to a niche that (would) impede its transportation to other objects" (Descola 2013:389).

Conclusion

The exotic domesticated dog is conspicuous in lowland neotropical contexts in which other exotic animal domesticates such as chickens, cats, pigs, cows, horses, donkeys, and mules were at best only partially integrated into the Indigenous social fabric and from which endemic animal domesticates appear to have been completely excluded. The exotic dog, like other exotic animal domesticates, may have only been recently introduced into Amazonia. However, unlike the other exotic animals, in northeastern South America it was not only fully integrated but could be intentionally bred and hybridized with endemic canids as a trained and highly valued hunting companion that was eagerly obtained by many Indigenous societies through a vast Indigenous trading network.

The neotropical lowlands of South America were home to the majority of endemic plant domesticates in the Western Hemisphere. However, with the possible exception of the Muscovy duck, no comparable endemic animals were domesticated. Although Indigenous Amazonians are celebrated for the many and varied animals that they avidly keep as pets, they did not enter into domesticatory relationship with endemic animals. Nevertheless, the popular belief of pet keeping as a form of incipient or proto-domestication continues to hold currency. For Indigenous Amazonians this perception is not only incorrect, but its implied corollary that their aptitudes might somehow be on the verge of domesticating animals, though not quite at the requisite stage of development necessary for its implementation, is offensive. Indigenous Amazonians are fully aware of domestication in its entirety, and as Stephen Hugh-Jones (2001:246) has cogently stated, the failure to domesticate endemic animals has less to do with opportunity than with ideas, as "true domestication is probably something more inconceivable than impossible."

Descola (1994, 2013) has suggested that endemic animals could not be domesticated because the domesticatory relationship violates a shared Indigenous Amazonian concept of appropriate relations between humans and animal others. It is as inconceivable to domesticate an endemic game animal as it is to eat a pet. However, it may not have been impossible to accept a domesticatory relationship with an introduced exotic hunting dog, particularly in areas where a history of taming endemic canids for hunting had been long established. Raising domestic dogs and interbreeding them with endemic canids to produce hybrids that developed out of a long-standing relationship of taming endemic faunas, which are also potentially consumable as food, could also account for early reports circulating in the Spanish main of imported dogs that were eaten. Nevertheless, the required hierarchical and irreversible relationship between humans and animal others of domestication was never transferred to endemic animals because it violated established relationships and was therefore inconceivable (Descola 2013:389).

References Cited

Århem, Kaj
1996   The Cosmic Food Web: Human-Nature Relatedness in the Northwest Amazon. In *Nature and Society: Anthropological Perspectives*, edited by Philippe Descola and Gísli Pálsson, pp. 185–204. Routledge, London.
Barandiaran, Daniel de
1962   Actividades Vitales de Subsistencia de los Indios Yekuana o Makiritare. *Antropológica* 11:1–29.
Brett, William H.
1868   *The Indian Tribes of Guiana: Their Condition and Habits*. Bell and Daldy, London.
Butt Colson, Audrey
1973   Inter-tribal Trade in the Guiana Highlands. *Antropológica* 34:1–70.
Cabrera, Angel, and José Yepes
1960   *Mamíferos Sudamericanos*, Vol. 1. 2nd ed. Ediar, Buenos Aires.
Campbell, Alan Tormaid
1995   *Getting to Know Waiwai: An Amazonian Ethnography*. Routledge, London.
Castroviejo-Fisher, Santiago, Pontus Skoglund, Raúl Valadez, Carles Vilà, and Jennifer A. Leonard
2011   Vanishing Native American Dog Lineages. *BMC Evolutionary Biology* 11:73.
Civrieux, Marc de
1980   Los Cumanagoto y sus Vecinos. In *Los Aborigenes de Venezuela*, edited by W. Coppens, pp. 27–240. Instituto Caribe de Antropología y Sociología, Monografía 26. Fundación La Salle de Ciencias Naturales, Caracas.
Clement, Charles R.
1999   1492 and the Loss of Crop Genetic Resources: 1. The Relation between Domestication and Human Population Decline. *Economic Botany* 53:188–202.
Conklin, Beth A.
2001   *Consuming Grief: Compassionate Cannibalism in an Amazonian Society*. University of Texas Press, Austin.

Coppens, Walter

1971 Las relaciones comerciales de las Yekuana del Caura-Paragua. *Antropológica* 30:28–59.

Cormier, Loretta Ann

2002 Monkey as Food, Monkey as Child: Guajá Symbolic Cannibalism. In *Primates Face to Face: Conservation Implications of Human-Non-human Primate Interconnections*, edited by A. Fuentes and L. D. Wolfe, pp. 61–84. Cambridge University Press, Cambridge.

2003 *Kinship with Monkeys: The Guajá Foragers of Eastern Amazonia*. Columbia University Press, New York.

Costa, Luiz

2016 Fabricating Necessity: Feeding and Commensality in Western Amazonia. In *Ownership and Nurture: Studies in Native Amazonian Property Relations*, edited by M. Brightman, C. Fausto, and V. Grotti, pp. 81–109. Berghahn, New York.

Darwin, Charles

1868 *The Variation of Plants and Animals under Domestication*, Vol. 1. John Murray, London.

Descola, Philippe

1992 Societies of Nature and the Nature of Societies. In *Conceptualizing Society*, edited by Adam Kuper, pp. 107–126. Routledge, London.

1994 Pourquoi les Indiens d'Amazonie n'ont-ils pas domestiqué le Pécari? Généalogie des Objets et Anthropologie de l'Objectivation. In *De la Préhistoire aux Missiles Balistiques: l'Intelligence Sociale des Techniques*, edited by Bruno Latour and Pierre Lemonnier, pp. 329–344. La Découverte, Paris.

1996 Constructing Natures: Symbolic Ecology and Social Practice. In *Nature and Society: Anthropological Perspectives*, edited by Philippe Descola and Gísli Pálsson, pp. 82–102. Routledge, London.

2001 The Genres of Gender: Local Models and Global Paradigms in the Comparison of Amazonia and Melanesia. In *Gender in Amazonia and Melanesia*, edited by Thomas A. Gregor and Donald Tuzin, pp. 91–114. University of California Press, Berkeley.

2013 *Beyond Nature and Culture*. University of Chicago Press, Chicago.

Druzhkova, A. S., O. Thalmann, V. A. Trifonov, J. A. Leonard, N. V. Vorobieva, N. D. Ovodov, A. S. Graphodatsky, and R. K. Wayne

2013 Ancient DNA Analysis Affirms the Canid from Altai as a Primitive Dog. *PLoS ONE* 8(3):e57754. doi:10.1371/journal.pone.0057754.

Erickson, Philippe

2000 The Social Significance of Pet-Keeping among Amazonian Indians. In *Companion Animals and Us: Exploring the Relationships between People and Pets*, edited by A. L. Podberscek, E. S. Paul, and J. A. Serpall, pp. 7–26. University of Cambridge Press, Cambridge.

Farabee, William Curtis

1918 *The Central Arawaks*. Anthropological Publications, Vol. 9. University Museum, University of Pennsylvania, Philadelphia.

1924 *The Central Caribs*. Anthropological Publications, Vol. 10. University Museum, University of Pennsylvania, Philadelphia.

Fausto, Carlos

1999 Of Enemies and Pets: Warfare and Shamanism in Amazonia. *American Ethnologist* 26:933–956.

2007   Feasting on People: Eating Animals and Humans in Amazonia. *Current Anthropology* 48:497–530.

Fock, Niels

1963   *Waiwai: Religion and Society of an Amazonian Tribe.* Ethnographic Series, Vol. 8. National Museum, Copenhagen.

Frantz, Laurent A. F., Victoria E. Mullin, Maud Pionnier-Capitan, Ophélie Lebrasseur, Morgane Ollivier, Angela Perri, Anna Linderholm, Valeria Mattiangeli, Matthew D. Teasdale, Evangelos A. Dimopoulos, Anne Tresset, Marilyne Duffraisse, Finbar McCormick, László Bartosiewicz, Erika Gál, Éva A. Nyerges, Mikhail V. Sablin, Stéphanie Bréhard, Marjan Mashkour, Adrian Bălășescu, Benjamin Gillet, Sandrine Hughes, Olivier Chassaing, Christophe Hitte, Jean-Denis Vigne, Keith Dobney, Catherine Hänni, Daniel G. Bradley, and Greger Larson

2016   Genomic and Archaeological Evidence Suggest a Dual Origin of Domestic Dogs. *Science* 352:1228–1231.

Galton, Francis

1883   *Inquiry into Human Faculty and Its Development.* Macmillan, London.

Guedes Milheira, R., D.L. Loponte, C. García Esponda, A. Acosta, and P. Ulguim

2017   The First Record of a Pre-Columbian Domestic Dog (*Canis lupus familiaris*) in Brazil. *International Journal of Osteoarchaeology* 27:488–494.

Guppy, Nicholas

1958   *Wai-Wai: Through the Forests North of the Amazon.* John Murray, London.

Henley, Paul

1982   *The Panare: Tradition and Change on the Amazonian Frontier.* Yale University Press, New Haven.

Howard, Catherine V.

2001   *Wrought Identities: The Waiwai Expeditions in Search of the "Unseen Tribes" of Northern Amazonia.* PhD dissertation. Department of Anthropology, University of Chicago, Chicago.

Hugh-Jones, Stephen

2001   The Gender of Some Amazonian Gifts: An Experiment with an Experiment. In *Gender in Amazonia and Melanesia*, edited by Thomas A. Gregor and Donald Tuzin, pp. 245–270. University of California Press, Berkeley.

Hurault, Jean

1968   *Les Indiens Wayana de la Guyane Française: Structure Sociale et Cotume Familiale.* Orstom, Paris.

Koster, Jeremy

2009   Hunting Dogs in the Lowland Neotropics. *Journal of Anthropological Research* 65:575–610.

Larson, Greger, Elinor K. Karlsson, Angela Perri, Matthew T. Webster, Simon Y. W. Hoe, Joris Peters, Peter W. Stahl, Philip J. Piper, Frode Lingaas, Merete Fredholm, Kenine E. Comstock, Jaime F. Modianom, Claude Schelling, Alexander I. Agoulnik, Peter A. Leegwater, Keith Dobney, Jean-Denis Vigne, Carles Vilà, Leif Anderssond, and Kerstin Lindblad-To

2012   Rethinking Dog Domestication by Integrating Genetics, Archaeology, and Biogeography. *Proceedings of the National Academy of Science* 109:8878–8883.

Latcham, Ricardo E.

1922   *Los Animales Domesticos de la America Precolombina,* Vol. 3. Imprenta Cervantes, Santiago.

Linares, Omar J.

1987   Evidencias de Domesticación en Cánidos Precolombinos del Oriente de Venezuela. *Boletín de la Asociación Venezolana de Arqueología* 4:38–48.

Mentore, George

2005   *Of Passionate Curves and Desirable Cadences: Themes on Waiwai Social Being.* University of Nebraska Press, Lincoln.

Mitchell, Peter

2017   Disease: A Hitherto Unexplored Constraint on the Spread of Dogs (*Canis lupus familiaris*) in Pre-Columbian South America. *Journal of World Prehistory* 30(4):301–349. DOI: 10.1007/s10963-017-9111-x.

Morey, Darcy F.

2010   *Dogs: Domestication and the Development of a Social Bond.* Cambridge University Press, Cambridge.

Nordenskiőld, Erland

1922   *Deductions Suggested by the Geographical Distributions of Some Post-Columbian Words Used by the Indians of South America.* Comparative Ethnographical Studies, Vol. 5. Elanders, Gőteborg.

Norton, Marcy

2015   The Chicken or the *Iegue*: Human-Animal Relationships and the Columbian Exchange. *American Historical Review* 120:28–60.

Oviedo y Valdés, Gonzalo Fernández de

1946 [1526]   *Sumario de la Natural Historia de las Indias.* Bibliotéca de Autores Españoles desde la Formación de Lenguaje hasta Nuestro Dias, Vol. 22. Historiadores Primitivos de Indias 1:471–51. Real Academía Española, Madrid.

Prates, Luciano, Francisco J. Prevosti, and Mónica Berón

2010   First Records of Prehispanic Dogs in Southern South America (Pampa-Patagonia, Argentina). *Current Anthropology* 51:273–280.

Rivière, Peter

1969   *Marriage among the Trio: A Principle of Social Organization.* Clarendon Press, Oxford.

Rivière, Peter (editor)

2006   *The Guiana Travels of Robert Schomburgk, 1835–1844,* Vol. 1, *Explorations on Behalf of the Royal Geographic Society, 1835–1839.* Hakluyt Society Third Series, Vol. 16. Ashgate, Aldershot.

Roth, Walter E.

1922   *Richard Schomburgk's Travels in British Guiana 1840–1844,* Vol. 1. Daily Chronicle Office, Georgetown.

1924   An Introductory Study of the Arts, Crafts, and Customs of the Guiana Indians. *Annual Report of the Bureau of American Ethnology* 38:25–743.

Santos-Granero, Fernando

2009   *Vital Enemies: Slavery, Predation, and the Amerindian Political Economy of Life.* University of Texas, Austin.

2016   Masters, Slaves and Real People: Native Understanding of Ownership and Humanness in Tropical American Capturing Societies. In *Ownership and Nurture: Studies* in *Native Amazonian Property Relations*, edited by M. Brightman, C. Fausto, and V. Grotti, pp. 36–62. Berghahn, New York.

Schwartz, Marion

1997   *A History of Dogs in the Early Americas.* Yale University Press, New Haven.

Shepard, Glenn H.

2002   Primates in Matsigenka Subsistence and Worldview. In *Primates Face to Face: Conservation Implications of Human-Non-human Primate Interconnections*, edited by A. Fuentes and L. D. Wolfe, pp. 101–136. Cambridge University Press, Cambridge.

Simpson, George Gaylord

1940   Los Indios Kamarakotos: Tribu Caribe de la Guyana Venezolana. *Revista de Fomento* 3 (22–25):197–660.

1941   Some Carib Indian Mammal Names. *American Museum Novitates* 1119:1–10.

Smole, William J.

1976   *The Yanoama Indians: a Cultural Geography.* University of Texas Press, Austin.

Sponsel, Leslie E.

1981   *The Hunter and the Hunted in the Amazon: An Integrated Biological and Cultural Approach to the Behavioral Ecology of Predation.* PhD dissertation. Department of Anthropology, Cornell University, Ithaca.

Stahl, Peter W.

2005   An Exploratory Osteological Study of the Muscovy Duck (*Cairina moschata*) (Aves: Anatidae) with Implications for Neotropical Archaeology. *Journal of Archaeological Science* 32(6):915–929.

2012   Interactions between Humans and Endemic Canids in Holocene South America. *Journal of Ethnobiology* 32:108–127.

2013   Early Dogs and Endemic South American Canids of the Spanish Main. *Journal of Anthropological Research.* 69:515–533.

2014   Perspectival Ontology and Animal Non-Domestication in the Amazon Basin. In *Antes de Orellana: Actas del 3er Encuentro Internacional de Arqueología Amazónica*, edited by Stéphen Rostain, pp. 221–231. Instituto Francés de Estudios Andines, Quito.

Taylor, Anne C.

1996   The Soul's Body and Its States: An Amazonian Perspective on the Nature of Being Human. *Journal of the Royal Anthropological Institute* 2:201–215.

2001   Wives, Pets, and Affines: Marriage among the Jivaro. In *Beyond the Visible and the Material*, edited by L. M. Rival and N. L. Whitehead, pp. 47–56. Oxford University Press, Oxford.

Taylor, K. I.

1974   *Sanumá Fauna: Prohibitions and Classifications.* Fundación La Salle de Ciencias Naturales, Caracas.

Thalmann, O., B. Shapiro, P. Cui, V. J. Schuenemann, S. K. Sawyer, D. L. Greenfield, M. B. Germonpré, M. V. Sablin, F. López-Giráldez, X. Domingo-Roura, H. Napierala, H-P. Uerpmann, D. M. Loponte, A. A. Acosta, L. Giemsch, R. W. Schmitz, B. Worthington, J. E. Buikstra, A. Druzhkova, A. S. Graphodatsky, N. D. Ovodov, N. Wahlberg, A. H. Freedman, R. M. Schweizer, K.-P. Koepfli, J. A. Leonard, M. Meyer, J. Krause, S. Pääbo, R. E. Green, and R. K. Wayne

2013   Complete Mitochondrial Genomes of Ancient Canids Suggest a European Origin of Domestic Dogs. *Science* 342:871–874.

Thomas, David John

1982 *Order without Government: The Society of the Pemon Indians of Venezuela.* University of Illinois Press, Urbana.

Thurn, Everard F. Im

1883 *Among the Indians of Guiana.* Kegan Paul, Trench, London.

Tito, Raul Y., Samuel L. Belknap III, Kristin D. Sobolik, Robert C. Ingraham, Lauren M. Cleeland, and Cecil M. Lewis Jr.

2011 DNA from Early Holocene American Dog. *American Journal of Physical Anthropology* 145:653–657.

Viveiros de Castro, Eduardo

1998 Cosmological Deixis and Amazonian Perspectivism. *Journal of the Royal Anthropological Institute* 4:469–488.

2004 Exchanging Perspectives: the Transformation of Objects into Subjects in Amerindian Ontologies. *Common Knowledge* 10:463–484.

Waterton, Charles

1891 *Wanderings in South America.* Thomas Nelson and Sons, London.

Wilbert, Johannes

1972 *Survivors of El Dorado: Four Indian Cultures of South America.* Praeger, New York.

Yde, Jens

1965 *Material Culture of the Waiwái.* Ethnographic Series, Vol. 10. National Museum, Copenhagen.

9

Between Ethnography and Prehistory

The Case of the Australian Dingo

LOUKAS KOUNGOULOS AND MELANIE FILLIOS

Australian Aborigines and dingoes have the oldest surviving canine-human relationship in the world. Dingoes occupy a unique place in the evolution and understanding of this bond and are culturally and historically important on a global scale. Dingoes offer a rare snapshot of dog domestication because they last shared a common ancestor with domestic dogs more than 5,000 years ago and have not undergone more recent artificial selection (Cairns and Wilton 2016). The antiquity of this relationship and, until quite recently, their genetic isolation from modern breeds sets them apart from domestic dogs.

Dingoes are not native to Australia. While the identity of their initial "masters" remains a mystery (Fillios and Taçon 2016), this commensal relationship implies a canine-human bond was well established so that the first dingoes to arrive in Australia were already "domesticated." Recent genetic evidence, coupled with the occurrence of biting lice from Australian marsupials on the Southeast Asian mainland, supports the idea that dingoes likely arrived in waves, accompanying sea-faring peoples who may have brought canines back and forth from locations around Southeast Asia (Cairns et al. 2017; Smith and Litchfield 2009). Despite the dingo's relatively recent arrival to Australia, the genetic isolation reflected in their mitochondrial DNA and the long history of Australian Aborigines' existence without Europeans makes this relationship one of the oldest examples of the human-dog relationship worldwide.

Archaeological and genetic evidence suggests dingoes were introduced to

Australia around 4,000–5,000 years ago, but the details of that introduction remain unclear. Equally enigmatic is the nature of the relationship between people and dingoes. Most of what we know about Aboriginal peoples' relationship with them is based on nineteenth- and twentieth-century European observations of Aborigines interacting with dingoes and recently introduced domestic dogs. Anthropologists returning from twentieth-century fieldwork in arid central Australia initiated debate over the extent to which Aboriginal people utilized dingoes and dogs in their daily lives.

In more recent years the focus of dingo research has changed. Researchers have questioned the taxonomic classification of dingoes (e.g., Crowther et al. 2014; Jackson et al. 2017; Smith et al. 2019) with a more political agenda directed toward their role in ecosystem management and destruction. At the same time, there is a renewed focus on clarifying their geographic and genetic history as a key to their origins (Cairns et al. 2017; Fillios and Taçon 2016). The relationship between dingoes and people has thus been approached from two main avenues: archaeology and written sources. The material evidence, though sparse, speaks to a complex relationship with a significant role in Aboriginal cosmology. Dingoes feature in rock art and are present in ritual burials, both with and without people (Gunn et al. 2010, 2012; Pardoe 1996; Taçon and Pardoe 2002).

In contrast, the ethnographic literature paints a more Eurocentric picture of this relationship, focusing instead on their role as companions, camp dogs, and of course hunting aids. Few have asked whether these scenarios can or should be used to interpret the precontact period (see Meggitt 1965). Additionally, and importantly, there has been a tendency to conflate dingoes with domestic dogs. They are not the same (Crowther et al. 2014; Smith et al. 2019) and do not display the same behavioral traits. Their rapport with Aborigines was also different.

We suggest that while ethnography and historical documents provide valuable sources of information, they must be critically interrogated. Relying upon these sources to infer the nature of the dingo-human relationship in the precontact period is problematic for two reasons. Domestic dogs arrived in Australia with the earliest European settlers and were quickly adopted by Aborigines (Hayden 1975). The early canids recorded in association with Aborigines were therefore often domestic dogs. Twentieth-century observations were also largely based on substantially altered subsistence regimes. Where alternative food sources and proficient European hunting breeds were present, the traditional risk of involving dogs in hunting large game was mitigated. As domestic dogs behave very differently than dingoes, observations of historical canids have limited value in inferring the precontact relationship between humans and dingoes. Assumptions drawn from historical and ethnographic observations assume a static, one-size-fits-all relationship between Aboriginal people and dingoes. In contrast, precontact Aboriginal culture was rich and varied, aptly reflected in the diversity of languages and material culture.

This chapter explores these issues in greater detail within the context of hunting. Given the persistent questions surrounding our understanding of the relationship between Aboriginal peoples and dingoes, an overview of this relationship is well overdue. To address this significant gap in our understanding of the precontact period in Australia, we first delineate the different ways in which dingoes and Aboriginal people interacted. We describe the archaeological evidence and contrast it with the written and ethnographic data. We then turn a critical eye toward the way ethnographic analogy has been used in the interpretation of this relationship. In particular, we question recent interpretations regarding the purported role of dingoes in altering the gendered division of labor, specifically hunting (Balme and O'Connor 2016), and suggest that a non-critical use of ethnographic data regarding women hunting with domestic dogs has resulted in the creation of an archaeological spandrel, an inaccurate projection of precontact dingoes reconstructed from fundamentally different conditions.

Archaeological Evidence

Dingoes were brought to Australia by people, as they would have been incapable of making the large, deep sea water crossing alone. While we do not know whether their initial role was as a traded commodity, a casual passenger, or part of a complex commensal relationship, we can be reasonably certain they were domesticated. Archaeological evidence suggests dingoes were widespread within Australia by circa 3,500 years ago, although recent genetic work argues for even greater antiquity (Cairns et al. 2017). Skeletal evidence exists from a variety of geographic locations, including Western Australia (Madura Cave, Nullarbor, 3,450 years ago; Milham and Thompson 1976), New South Wales (Wombah Midden, 3,230 years ago; McBryde 1982) and Victoria (Fromm's Landing, 3,170 years ago; Mulvaney et al. 1964).

In contrast to many of the early written accounts, the archaeological evidence speaks clearly to the diverse role played by this enigmatic species. Dingoes feature prominently in Aboriginal mythology throughout Australia (e.g., Rose, 1992). Evidence of their spiritual role is highlighted by rock art and ritual burials. Although artistic representations are rare (Pardoe 1996), several images from Arnhem Land (Gunn et al. 2010) and other places across the continent, such as dingo paw stencils, exist from New South Wales and the Northern Territory (Gunn et al. 2010; Taçon et al. 2010). Dingo's Lair in Wollemi National Park, New South Wales, contains several large depictions drawn with charcoal (Figure 9.1; Taçon et al. 2012).

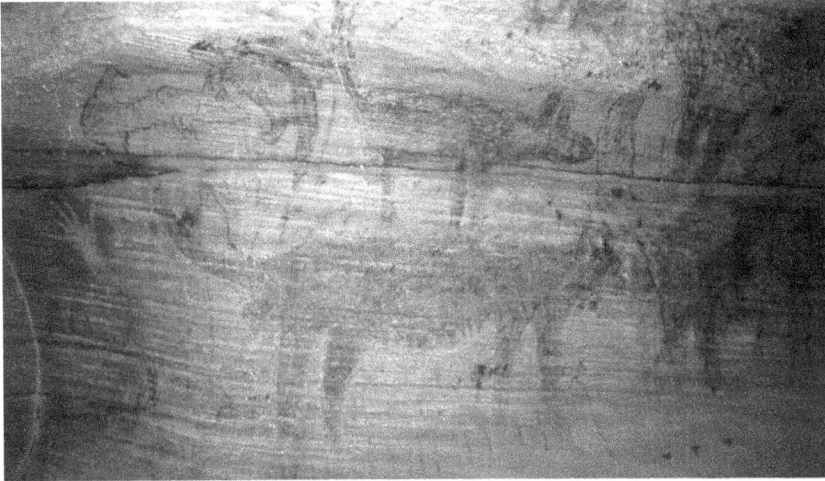

Figure 9.1. Rock drawings of dingoes, Dingo's Lair, Wollemi National Park, New South Wales, Australia. Photo credit: Fillios and Taçon 2016.

Figure 9.2. Rock painting of a dingo and Ancestral figure, Laura region, Queensland, Australia. Photo credit: Fillios and Taçon 2016.

At a few locations, dingoes are depicted in association with humans, such as in Kakadu National Park and north Queensland (Figure 9.2).

Spirituality

Dingoes have played, and continue to play, an active, nuanced role in the belief systems of Aborigines. Indigenous spirituality, often referred to as the Dreaming, describes how the world was created. The two species that feature most prominently in the Dreaming are the snake and dingo (Smith and Litchfield 2009), with the dingo associated with the supernatural more than any other animal (Kolig 1978; Rose 1992). Although Aboriginal people had variable relationships with dingoes, their spiritual importance transcends clan boundaries. Within Indigenous cosmology dingoes typically act as rebel anti-creators, an archetype possibly inspired by their insubordinate, liminal existences fluctuating between the wilderness and human society (Kolig 1978). They were widely considered guardians against the supernatural, spiritual sentinels who alerted people of invisible marauders and helped drive them away (Kolig 1978; Meggitt 1965). Their spiritual importance is further bolstered by intentional dingo burials from Arnhem Land (Gunn et al. 2010, 2012) and several sites across southeastern Australia (Gollan 1980, 1984; Pardoe 1996). Dingoes are the only species on mainland Australia known to be given intentional burial by Aborigines. Culturally, behaviorally, technologically, symbolically, and socially, the dingo holds an unparalleled place in the history of the oldest continuous culture in the world.

Other Cultural Changes?

Despite the renewed attention on the dingo's origin, discussion surrounding the impact dingoes could have had on Aboriginal peoples already in Australia is limited. The idea that cultural changes could have resulted from their introduction is unpopular, yet once the dingo arrived, it made its presence felt in every aspect of Aboriginal society. According to Smith and Litchfield (2009:115), "dingoes became objects of ownership, items for bartering . . . and held deep cultural and spiritual significance." However, the notion that dingoes may have shaped some of the raft of Holocene cultural transformations is rarely discussed. Melanie Fillios and Paul Taçon (2016) suggested that Toalean hunter-gatherer groups could have brought the dingo, while Fillios and colleagues (2010) examined the possibility that dingoes altered Australian ecosystems, thereby impacting available food sources to Indigenous peoples. Most recently, Jane Balme and Susan O'Connor (2016) broached this idea from a gendered division of labor perspective, arguing that dingoes enabled women to become hunters.

Anthropological Perspectives on Human-Dingo Relationships

While dingoes were revered spiritually continent-wide, relationships between dingoes and Aboriginal peoples varied. At European contact, dingoes were recorded as living with some Aborigines and not others. Their variable role is highlighted by ethnographic evidence documenting the taboo placed on eating their meat by some (Meehan et al. 1999) and not by others (Meggit 1965). Evidence shows that some groups regarded them as well-cared-for companions (e.g., Hamilton 1972; Meggit 1965), while others had little to do with them. Fillios and colleagues (2010) proposed that dingoes could have played both a commensal and competitive role with people.

Although early Europeans identified dingoes as having several functions, such as cleaning, warmth, and a mythological or spiritual role, the bulk of discussion on dingoes has focused on hunting. Ethnographically, this focus has translated into a keen interest in how their role in hunting may have applied to precontact Australia, echoing larger, international processualist trends in the anthropological community. Clutton-Brock (1995:15) suggested the relationship between Indigenous Australians and their dogs represents "part of the living heritage of hunter-gatherer culture." Discussions like these first began in earnest with James Downs's (1960) suggestion that anthropologists should look to relationships of traditional peoples and hunting dogs to understand how dogs first came to be domesticated. Meggitt (1965) used historical literature and his own experiences with Western Desert Aborigines to address this issue. He argued that from the limited data it could only be said that dingoes and dogs made infrequent and largely insignificant contributions to family meat intake outside of rainforest areas where suitable game was abundant.

Mervyn Meggitt's rebuttal of the "widespread" acceptance of dingoes being efficient hunting companions generated responses from anthropologists. Isobel White (1972) related her own experiences in Yalata, South Australia, where people with access to guns and vehicles instead relied upon domestic dogs to chase and kill kangaroo. In contrast, Annette Hamilton's (1972) observations in the Everard Ranges, South Australia, were that while dogs were frequently involved in hunting kangaroo, they rarely made worthwhile contributions, and a different kind of smaller dog was used commonly to capture rabbits. Brian

Hayden (1975) described hunting methods in Cundeelee, Western Australia, as commonly involving dogs but not being as reliable as traditional stalking methods or rifle-based approaches. Despite these observations, using dogs was preferable in practice, as it involved less energy expenditure on the hunter's part. Utilizing historical texts, he also argued that, in contrast to Meggitt (1965) and Hamilton (1972), it is likely dingoes played similar roles in the past and that this was not limited to special ecological areas like the rainforest but included scrub and semi-arid environments.

Others pointed out the inherent risks and dangers of taking dingoes and dogs hunting. Descriptions from Richard Gould (1969a, 1969b) and Erich Kolig (1978) indicated that domestic canids would be deliberately excluded from "serious" hunting expeditions using both stalking and rifle-based approaches. Due to their tendency to scare off game, dingoes and dogs were involved in hunting primarily during "family" occasions with parties of women and children, partly because the men did not want their involvement in their own expedition (e.g., Gould 1969a, 1969b; Hamilton 1972). Kolig (1978) related that a dingo brought on one such hunting trip disappeared quickly and was found having almost entirely consumed a wallaby, claiming they were notorious for this sort of behavior.

From these debates, the concept of domestic dingoes as hunting aids was refined somewhat to acknowledge that while the practice of involving dogs was common, it rarely resulted in significant contributions of meat. In recent decades, however, a new perspective focusing on the hunting relationship of women and domestic canids has emerged, beginning with the fieldwork of Betty Meehan and colleagues in Arnhem Land. Meehan's team (1999) described the large numbers of small game (overwhelmingly goanna) captured by women with the aid of dogs. Sibylle Kästner (2012) compiled numerous firsthand Indigenous accounts emphasizing that female hunters were frequently accompanied by dogs.

Such evidence led Balme and O'Connor (2016) to argue that woman-dingo hunting relationships originated following the arrival of dingoes in the mid-Holocene. They argue that with the assistance of dingoes, women were able to contribute larger amounts of meat derived from smaller species to the family's diet. This resulted in the increased proportions of small and medium-sized species observed in many mid- to late Holocene faunal assemblages (Fillios et al. 2010). While Balme and O'Connor's (2016) proposal that dingoes played a key role in altering traditional gender roles by enabling women to hunt with dogs appears to be consistent with archaeological evidence for a shift in prey body size during the time of the dingo's initial introduction, a more comprehensive examination of historical texts finds issues with this idea.

Hunting with Dingoes and Dogs

To contextualize the assistive hunting capacities of dingoes, it should be noted that canids in general do not have any particular biological issues with helping humans hunt Australian fauna (large or small) in Australian landscapes. Ecological studies have established that wild dingoes are frequent and effective predators that control the populations of large macropods and emu (Caughley et al. 1980; Fillios et al. 2010; Pople et al. 2000). However, as related by Balme and O'Connor (2016) and Loukas Koungoulos (2017), the available literature suggests that historical dingoes were more effective at helping humans procure small- or medium-sized game rather than larger ones like kangaroo and emu. This is likely due to their role in increasing encounter rates with smaller prey often hidden to humans (e.g., Koster 2008). European observers from approximately 1780 to 1980 remark that dingoes were used in hunting, but details are frustratingly limited, often not specifying the type of game (e.g., Beveridge 1899; Finlayson 1943; Giles 1889; Grey 1841). George Barrington (1795), Andrew Russell (1840), Gerard Krefft (1865), James Dawson (1881), and Samuel Carter (1911), all describe using dingoes to hunt kangaroo, while Walter Roth (1897) additionally describes hunting of emu with dingoes (Table 9.1). Some of these early observers use the term "dog," but due to their early contexts, they have been generally accepted as referring to dingoes (Balme and O'Connor 2016; Hayden 1975; Koungoulos 2017; Meggitt 1965; White 1972). Others from after 1900 and especially after 1950 that describe hunting large game with "dogs" might be considered more dubious (e.g., Long 1971; Peasley 1983).

In most accounts, game size is limited to small to medium prey. Smaller taxa hunted with dingoes assisting in some capacity include arboreal marsupials such as tree kangaroo (Lumholtz 1889) and possums (Eyre 1841; Nind 1831; Smyth 1878), snakes and lizards (Chewings 1936; Curr 1886; Petrie 1904; Smyth 1878; Thomson 1949), rats (Chewings 1936; Smyth 1878), bandicoots and quolls (Thomson 1949), echidnas (Thomson 1949) and smaller macropods (Dawson 1881; Nind 1831; Thomson 1949). Early reports imply that dingoes were primarily valued in hunting for their keen sense of smell (Eyre 1841; Lumholtz 1889;

Table 9.1. Ethnographic evidence for dingoes and hunting

Mode of Hunting Assistance	Description of Role	Prey Types	Biome	References
Pointing	Keen senses are used to help track or locate prey, and may include capture depending on size.	Bandicoot, echidna, kangaroo lizard, possum, rat, snake, sugar glider, tree kangaroo, wallaby	Tropical savannah, desert, temperate forest, rainforest	Eyre (1841), Lowe (ca. twentieth century), Lumholtz (1889), Nind (1831), Pickering (1992), Smyth (1878) Thomson (1949), Turner and Blyton (1995)
Trapping	Drive fleeing prey into a constrained space or net where it can be extracted by hunter.	Bandicoot, echidna, goanna, kangaroo, possum, quoll, rat, wallaby, wombat	Temperate forest, rainforest	Eyre (1841), Keats (1988), Stokes (1846), Pickering (1992), Thomson (1949)
Ambush	Drive prey toward waiting hunter ambush or beaters.	Emu, euro, kangaroo, wallaby	Temperate forest, tropical savannah	Fountain (1907), Lawrence (1986), Pickering (1992), Russell (1840), Thomson (1949)
Pursuit	Chase prey and kills or otherwise prevents escape until the hunter can arrive.	Euro, kangaroo, wallaby	Temperate forest, tropical savannah	Barrington (1975), Beveridge (1899), Dawson (1880), Pickering (1992), Roth (1897)

Nind 1831; Roth 1897; Smyth 1878; Thomson 1939), which helped to locate and track prey, and for their ability to flush prey from hiding places (e.g., Keats 1988; Nind 1831). Conversely, accounts that describe dingoes being used to chase and run down game (especially large species), are rare for several reasons:

Biology: some early observers noted that dingoes were simply too slow to capture large, fast prey like kangaroo and emu (Barrington 1795; Nind 1831). Exceptions seem to occur where the quarry was hindered by injury (Beveridge 1899) or by difficult terrain (Krefft 1865; Pickering 1992; Roth 1897). Koungoulos (2017) suggested that lowered efficiency in hunting large game was related to prey speed rather than size alone, as wombats and large monitor lizards may qualify as "large" in terms of body weight but due to their lesser locomotive capacities could still be captured using dingoes.

Loukas Koungoulos and Melanie Fillios

Biogeography: Differences in vegetation and physical terrain shape hunting practices. For example, in some areas the obstructing presence of dense vegetation could be used to more efficiently capture macropods by using dingoes to drive them into nets strung between trees (Keats 1988) or into ambushes of armed people (Fountain 1907; Russell 1840). This may explain the larger number of accounts of dingoes being used to help capture large game coming from the more heavily forested eastern coastal areas of Australia. In contrast, in the open spaces of central Australia dingoes could not be used in this way. The tendency of dingoes to put game to flight means they could not be incorporated into the stalking- and concealment-based methods popular in central Australia, but it made them valuable where flushing- and driving-based methods were favored.

Historical context: In the mostly Central Australian traditional communities where anthropologists worked in the twentieth century and from which we derive the most detailed observations of hunting, dingoes had mostly been replaced by domestic dogs (Hamilton 1972). In these open environments where dingoes once may have been used to chase large game, we lack historical evidence to make a reasonable judgment of how this was carried out. In some instances, people observed using dogs deny they ever used dingoes to hunt in the past (Hamilton 1972; Meehan et al 1999). While the use of dingoes in hunting spanned all the major biogeographic and cultural regions of mainland Australia, it was not practiced by every historically documented people. Even neighboring groups had different attitudes to using canids to hunt, resulting in a patchwork of localities in which their assistance was or was not historically utilized.

Pat Lowe's (twentieth-century) experiences observing a camp dingo raised from a wild pup in the Great Sandy Desert indicate the variety of ways dingoes could contribute reliably to the food supply. One female dingo known as the best hunter, Yukayarra, embarked on individual hunts in the early morning, returning with prey that she dropped at the feet of her master. She would bury excess prey for hunters to later recover, as well as regurgitate prey swallowed whole on command. Lowe recounts that dingoes also accompanied people on the hunt. It is important to recognize that the prey in this example were goannas, one of the species most commonly procured with dingoes throughout Australia. Anthropological debate regarding their role in hunting primarily focused on large game like kangaroo, euro, and emu, and it is perhaps for that reason that the overall consensus was that dingoes made few contributions. Lowe's observations indicate at least *four* mechanisms by which dingoes could help contribute meat to the family group, at least from smaller animals like goannas.

While secure evidence of dingoes being used to hunt large game is scant, the same cannot be said of domestic breeds. The colonial literature is replete with accounts of Europeans using their hunting dogs to procure large macropods and emu, as well as a range of smaller animals, though not without danger of injury to the dog (Eyre 1841; Oxley 1820; Sturt 1843, 1849; Tench 1793). Aboriginal people appear to have had mixed success using domestic dogs to hunt large game in the twentieth century. Groups in Victoria (Cahir and Clark 2013; Smith and Litchfield 2009) and Tasmania excelled at the task (Jones 1970). Edward Snell (1988 [1850]) recounted an incident where Aborigines took a hunting dog from his party without permission but soon returned with two kangaroos. Having previously hunted alongside the dogs and Europeans, the Aborigines' own tracking expertise allowed them to make ample use of the dogs' hunting skills alone. The later availability of European guns in the twentieth century is further considered to have altered the way dogs were used in hunting game (Cahir and Clark 2013), but the sparse evidence does not permit a thorough analysis of exactly how guns came into play.

More detailed accounts of the assistive hunting capacities of Indigenous-associated canids tend to come from the twentieth century and in particular from the reports of anthropologists. From these we learn that domestic dogs could also be serious liabilities while hunting large game. They had a tendency to reveal the hunting party's presence, attacking prematurely and losing the prey, or even eating the captured prey before the hunters' arrival (Gould 1969a, 1969b, 1970; Hamilton 1972; Kolig 1978; Meggitt 1965). Consequently, they too were often deliberately left behind by hunters pursuing large species (Basedow 1925; Gould 1969a, 1969b; Meehan et al 1999). Inconsistencies in the effectiveness of using dogs to hunt in Australian environments seem to derive from differences in quality of training (Hamilton 1972) and whether their presence was suited to the predominant method of hunting already used (Hayden 1975).

Here it is probably prudent to group dingo-domestic hybrids closer to domestic dogs, as there are numerous accounts attesting to the effective use of hybrids in hunting kangaroo and emu (Berndt and Berndt 1945; Gould 1969a; Griffith 1845; Horne and Aiston 1924; Lockwood 1962). Disparity is apparent in Gould's observations (1969a) from the Gibson Desert. He notes the "scrawny" dingoes accompanying kangaroo hunters scared the game off and instantly devoured the small lizards they did manage to catch. Conversely, one large dingo-sheepdog hybrid was trained to chase and kill kangaroo and did so successfully. Settlers such as John Lort Stokes (1846) were interested in cross-breeding dingoes with foxhounds to produce a kangaroo-hunting breed, mostly because of the former's keen sense of smell and other senses. Fred Cahir and Ian Clark (2013) note some Victorian groups intentionally bred an efficient kangaroo- and emu-hunting strain by crossing dingoes with kangaroo dogs (a greyhound-mastiff cross). Many modern Australian working breeds have a degree of dingo heritage (Smith 2015).

Domestic Dogs in Australia and Their Integration into Aboriginal Lifestyles

While detailed accounts of Indigenous-associated "dogs" are critical in forming an analogous understanding for precontact human-dingo interactions, we do not know whether many such descriptions refer to dingoes or domestic breeds. This may be because the observer viewed dingoes as dogs and did not use separate terms. Some seem to use the two terms at different times without denoting whether there is actually any distinction between the animals (e.g., Thomson 1940). Others at least use the terms "wild dog" or "native dog" to denote dingoes (e.g., Eyre 1841). It is plausible that some could not tell the difference between a pure dingo and a dingo-domestic hybrid.

The establishment of domestic dogs and hybrids in Aboriginal groups has likely been underestimated in antiquity. Balme and O'Connor (2016) state that some Aboriginal groups living in remote areas such as arid central Australia may not have even seen domestic dogs "until the 1940s." They suggest the accounts mentioned by Hayden (1975) "almost certainly" refer to dingoes because they took place in the "late nineteenth or early twentieth century." Similarly, in an international review of historical hunting dogs, Karen Lupo (2017) stated that European dogs did not reach the Australian interior until the 1950s–1960s. Evidently such sentiments are so that we can feel more secure about using accounts of unspecified historical "dogs" to discuss the utilitarian role of precontact dingoes. But is this appropriate? In their effort to isolate pure dingo specimens for study, Crowther et al. (2014) gave the cutoff date of 1900 to exclude the influence of domestic dogs, based on the reasoning that Australia was sparsely populated before 1900. This seems reasonable for wild dingoes, as it reduces the scope of domestic escapees' contributions to wild dingo gene pools. Historical texts show, however, that the same concept does not hold for Indigenous-associated "camp" dingoes, because Aborigines deliberately sought to acquire domestic dogs from Europeans and did so immediately after contact.

The establishment of European dogs throughout Tasmania (where there are no dingoes) provides a situation potentially similar to that which occurred on the mainland away from European eyes (Jones 1970). Dogs—mostly large, strong hunting breeds such as greyhounds—were acquired from Europeans on the eastern coast and were quickly transported through social networks, such that Aboriginal people on the western side of the island meeting Europeans for the first time already had dogs with them. In the Tasmanian setting, dogs became a great utility in procuring meat for their masters but were also valued for their companionship, altogether attaining a great social value, which led to instances of dogs being presented as gifts (Jones 1970). Although such dramatic popularity of dogs was probably encouraged in Tasmania by the prior lack of dingoes, the available evidence indicates mainland Aboriginal people exhibited a similar enthusiasm for domestic dogs (Meggitt 1965).

Domestic dogs arrived with the first European settlers in the late eighteenth century, and sources suggest that some Indigenous communities rapidly sought to acquire this new, more subservient domestic dog (Hayden 1975). From the beginning of European contact, Aborigines acquired domestic breeds through different forms of exchange, in many cases actively pursuing such transactions. Snell (1988 [1850]) recounts the "theft" of hunting dogs by Aborigines, mirroring one mode of dog "acquisition" in Tasmania suggested by Rhys Jones (1970). Charles Darwin (1839) similarly mentions that Aborigines of the Bathurst area were constantly seeking to "borrow" the greyhounds that European settlers were using to hunt kangaroo locally. Memorably, Charles Sturt (1849) recalls an instance where locals of Mount Harris, New South Wales, were so keen to acquire the dogs of two escaped Irish convicts that the tense situation over their ownership ended with the convicts' deaths. In other instances, Europeans took the initiative. Settlers gave hunting breeds to Aboriginal people as a type of formalized gift to help in placating them (Darwin 1839; Mitchell 1839; Todd 1835), while sealers and whalers likely acted as sources of domestic dogs through trade (Cahir and Clark 2013), as in Tasmania (Ryan 1981).

The interest in European dogs over dingoes was not related strictly to hunting but also to aspects of companionship that dingoes, who usually left the camp upon maturity (Smith and Litchfield 2009) and are well known for their independent and aloof nature, might have lacked. Dawson (1881) states that despite being superior to domestic dogs "in several respects," dingoes in Otways (southern Victoria) communities were nonetheless replaced by them for the latter's more affectionate and agreeable social disposition. Kolig (1978) observed a similar situation in northwestern Australia, noting domestic dogs were easier to acquire, less troublesome, and better suited to living close to humans. Ian Abbott (2008) further suggests Aborigines in Western Australia held higher value in European dogs than dingoes (Moore 1842), perhaps because their clearer bark was valued as a warning of danger (Freycinet 2001). Dawson (1831) and Richard Semon (1899) both observed that the offspring of dingo-domestic unions tended to take the nature of the domestic parent.

For several parts of Australia there is substantial historical evidence suggesting the establishment of domestic dogs at Aboriginal camps between 1800 and 1900, in many cases explicitly referring to hunting roles. Ida Lee (1906) describes that in kangaroo hunts, Aborigines of the Bathurst area in the 1830s used dogs, which were "as a rule" black, or white with red spots, the latter probably indicating domestic heritage; Darwin (1839) remarked that greyhounds were highly active there. Dogs most likely spread quickly through eastern Australia. In the 1820s pioneer Robert Dawson, traveling from Sydney to Port Stephens, noted "almost every" community had domestic dogs, using them to hunt kangaroo and wallaby (Dawson 1831). Tom Petrie (1904) recalls during his father's time (1830s–1870s) in the Moreton Bay region of Queensland, dingoes, never having been very good at hunting kangaroo, had been replaced in this role by "those of the white man," as described by Semon (1899) for the Gladstone area. On the Yorke Peninsula in South Australia Aboriginal people were also "acquiring" kangaroo dogs by this time (Snell 1988 [1850]). In Western Australia, sources compiled by Abbott (2008) indicate that by 1833 settlers were concerned (for their livestock) that others were supplying dogs to Aboriginal people, leading to government regulations against this trade, and stray kangaroo dogs were also adopted by Aborigines. Further north near Broome, the Karajarri, who had close contact with Europeans circa 1900, trained their "dogs" to capture kangaroo, goanna, and feral cat (Skyring and Yu 2008).

The best evidence for the integration of early domestic dogs into subsistence systems comes from Victoria, where Aborigines had close relationships with dingoes (Cahir and Clark 2013). These authors suggest that hunting dogs known to have been present at 1820s sealing camps and military garrisons were quickly acquired by Aboriginal people through trade. Accordingly, M. A. Parker (1916) recalled examining Indigenous-associated canids with clear greyhound and collie ancestry circa 1840 in central Victoria. Similarly, western Victorian groups had acquired kangaroo dogs to cross with their dingoes by the 1840s (Griffith 1845). Robert Brough Smyth (1878) implies that dogs at Aboriginal camps were primary domestic breeds that had replaced camp dingoes and notes that wild dingoes had been nearly exterminated in Victoria by that time. Perhaps most significant is Krefft's (1865) account, commonly regarded as a pre-1900 source for "dingoes" being used to hunt kangaroo. He notes the same Aboriginal people would take and keep Europeans' dogs:

> Women do not hesitate to suckle pups; and it is not to be wondered at, that under such circumstances, the dogs become much attached to the Aborigines: and if only with them for a few nights, they seldom follow their white master again. . . . A well-bred dog left with blackfellows for a few days, is a lost dog for ever. (Krefft 1865:372–373)

Evidence of domestic dogs in arid zone communities is also attested to by pre-1900 reports. The multitude of Aboriginal groups met by early explorers (invariably accompanied by dogs) would have seen their canine companions. It is possible that early meetings between camp dingoes and domestic dogs occurred during the stays of explorers at Aboriginal camps or when their dogs were lost, but no such interactions seem to have been recorded. The two canid relatives seem to have caused each other some consternation in these early days (e.g., Semon 1899; Stormon 1977), and Stokes (1846) recalls that his "pet" dingo fought viciously with domestic dogs. In terms of domestic dogs explicitly associated with arid zone Aborigines, the earliest example comes from the Horn Scientific Expedition of the 1890s to the heart of central Australia, which documented there the presence of "mongrel dogs," elsewhere referring to dingoes by that name (Horn and Spencer 1896). Spencer and Gillen (1889) claim that domestic dogs had "supplanted" dingoes in Aboriginal social contexts and that "all over" Australia scores of "mongrels" of variable appearance are seen at "every native camp." Soon afterwards, George Horne and George Aiston (1924:32) commented the following, regarding dogs used to hunt emu circa 1912, in the region east of Lake Eyre: "No trace of the wild dog can now be seen in them. Greyhound, Irish terrier and fox terrier seem to predominate." Later anthropologists Ronald and Catherine Berndt (1945) remark that circa 1941 Indigenous inhabitants of Ooldea (north of the Nullarbor Plain) would struggle to find a hunting dog that *was not* of domestic heritage. It would seem from these accounts that several arid zone communities had become saturated with domestic dogs by 1900, if not earlier.

While some remote Aboriginal groups evaded direct contact with domestic dogs until the mid-twentieth century, dingoes residing in arid zone communities could not have escaped domestic admixture for long. Even very remote groups could have come into contact with domestic breeds through family who had contact with Europeans. The above accounts are complemented well by recent genetic research by Kylie Cairns and colleagues (2017), which established that a Y-DNA haplogroup (H1) associated with European dog breeds was present even in dingo lineages that were certified by previous genetic tests to be "pure." Cairns and colleagues (2017) suggest that this interbreeding was not modern and took place immediately following the start of colonization (long before dingo purity benchmarks were determined). Proximity to European settlements including livestock and sealing/whaling stations likely played a significant factor in the temporal and spatial pattern of domestic dog dispersals, generally facilitating earlier access to communities living closer to the coast. Victoria, eastern New South Wales, and coastal South Australia appear to have been compromised by the presence of domestic dogs by 1830–1850. In central Australia the process was probably delayed by a few decades, so that hybrid or domestic mongrels were already ubiquitous in some areas by 1890.

Twentieth-Century Ethnography of Women Hunting with Dogs

Evidence of domestic dogs in nineteenth-century Aboriginal communities presents major concerns for efforts to reconstruct precontact subsistence roles from historical interactions between Aboriginal people and "dogs." Excluding accounts that do not explicitly identify the canids as dingoes drastically reduces the sample of reference materials from which to understand their use in historical hunting, let alone speculate on their *precontact* role. It can be confidently said that dingoes were useful in helping find and capture small and medium size game species, while their use in hunting large game was more sporadic in scope, frequency, and efficiency. But is it appropriate to rely on observations of women and domestic dogs in the twentieth century to argue that the arrival of dingoes triggered social reorganization in the mid-Holocene? There are several reasons why this analogy, as employed by Balme and O'Connor (2016), is troublesome.

Most observations of Aborigines hunting with "dogs" in the twentieth century, and some from the nineteenth century, describe domestic dogs or hybrids, not pure dingoes. In the study areas described by Hamilton (1972), Hayden (1975), Meehan and colleagues (1999), and White (1972), people had already abandoned the practice of obtaining wild dingo pups and were accompanied exclusively or overwhelmingly by domestic dogs. Of the large camp dog populations observed, it is apparent that a select few were used to hunt, the rest considered useless in this endeavor. Differences in efficiency between dingoes and domestic breeds in capturing smaller game are probably not great, but there are some apparent differences in their application. The keen noses of dingoes suggest that they were equals of hunting breeds at locating prey species. Accordingly, Stokes (1846) used his "pet" dingo to trap and extract rabbits in similar fashion to domestic dogs described by Horne and Aiston (1924) and Hamilton (1972). Domestic dogs helped capture some small species, including lizards, snakes, feral cats, and rabbits, as did dingoes (Hamilton 1972; Lockwood 1962; Meehan et al. 1999), but it seems domestic dogs did not commonly replace dingoes in the hunt for echidna, possum, bandicoot, and tree kangaroo, perhaps because these were quarries where the scenting ability of dingoes was the primary reason for their involvement.

Twentieth-century accounts, however, are dominated by dogs involved in the capture of *larger* prey like kangaroo, euro, wallaby, and emu (Berndt and Berndt 1945; Campbell 1956; Hamilton 1972; Hayden 1975; Horne and Aiston 1924). It is also important to recognize that European settlement heavily influenced the availability of game species. Efforts in the 1800s using lethal control to prevent dingo depredation of livestock took huge tolls on the apex predator's population, resulting in a well-known explosion of macropod numbers to plague proportions (e.g., Krefft 1865). Combined with landscape alterations such as dams, livestock watering, and pasture management systems that increased access to water and food resources, considerably larger macropod populations would have provided greater incentive to hunt them with capable domestic dogs. Additionally, two of the small species commonly procured by dogs for women were actually introduced exotics that rapidly colonized large swathes of Australia—feral cats (Meehan et al. 1999) and rabbits (Hamilton 1972; Horne and Aiston 1924).

These observations were made from Aboriginal societies whose subsistence regimes had been greatly impacted by various environmental changes. Groups such as the Anbarra and Anangu that hosted Meehan and colleagues (1999) and White (1972), had lived at Christian missions (located great distances from their homelands). Although they had returned to traditional lifestyles as part of the 1970s "outstation movement," they retained connections with Europeans that altered many aspects of life, including subsistence. Aborigines described by Hayden (1975), White (1972), and Meehan and colleagues (1999) were to different degrees reliant upon flour, sugar, and meat from European sources and used modern hunting equipment. Despite preferences for traditional foods, the availability of external food served as critical safety nets for the society, which shaped the role of traditional subsistence practices.

Similarly, we may also consider Abbott's (2008) comments that Aborigines in Western Australia as early as 1892 no longer needed dogs to hunt for them because they relied on settlers' provisions. Indeed Hayden (1975) states that because of this very safety, dogs could be freely involved in hunting, as the risk of failure was no longer linked to a risk of death. Accordingly, hunting with dogs had become for these Aborigines, a type of recreational or traditional leisure activity rather than a practice borne out of necessity to survive. Similar statements might be made about events discussed by Meehan and colleagues (1999) and White (1972), where dogs usually accompanied foraging parties that included men, women, and children. Meehan and colleagues (1999) state that on average five dogs were taken on foraging trips (including for non-game resources like shellfish or yams) usually with women and children, and women tended to own the most dogs. Can it really be considered a special division of labor that these dogs happened to attack and catch small animals when accompanying their mistresses out foraging, as described by Hayden (1975)?

Although extensive review by Kästner (2012) challenges the old idea that Aboriginal women did not partake in hunting whatsoever, it does not seem that any particular relationship between women and dingo- or dog-assisted hunting, nor one with a focus on small prey, is supported by ethnographic literature. Women were the primary hunters of lizards (Meehan et al. 1999) and rabbits (Hamilton 1972) but also accompanied and utilized dogs that were hunting kangaroo (Hamilton 1972; Kaberry 1939; Koch 1993; White 1972). Kästner (2012) related some instances of twentieth-century dogs acquiring game for Aboriginal women. Some sources describe women in a passive role, where the dog did all the "work" (Duncan-Kemp 1964; Kaberry 1939; Koch 1993), while others place them in an active role, where they finished off the kangaroo with clubs after the dogs had run them down (Endicott 1999). In a different sense, Kolig (1978) states that women often hunted with dogs, although this endeavor was rarely successful and always very strenuous. But there are also several references to *men* taking dogs with them hunting (Hamilton 1972; Kaberry 1939; Keats 1988; Krefft 1865; Long 1971; Meehan et al. 1999). Balme and O'Connor's (2016) claim that the accounts of Hayden (1975) and Hamilton (1972) are evidence of dogs being more closely associated with women's foraging trips *rather than* men's is not supported by the content of those publications. The sole hunter actively using a dog Hayden

(1975) described at Cundeelee was male, while both men and women hunted in Hamilton's (1972) Everard Ranges work area. Furthermore, Gould (1969a, 1969b) specifies that dingoes and dogs accompanied women mainly so that they would not trouble the men going hunting.

It is probably telling that few nineteenth-century historical sources specify or imply that women were associated with dingo- or dog-assisted hunting. Here, when women were mentioned as being involved, it was in game drives that involved the whole family group as well as its dogs (e.g., Russell 1840). Hence, impressions of women specifically having close hunting relationships with dogs, and regarding smaller game in particular, derive from twentieth-century foraging contexts. It seems likely that the close bonds of companionship between woman and dog transcend archaeological or historical periods, especially for older women that were widowed or without children. In such cases dingoes probably played an active role in supplementing *personal* (rather than family or community) diet, similar to the practice of supplemental bone nutrient extraction observed historically (Smith 2000).

While the introduction of dingoes likely substantially altered subsistence practices in precontact Australia, the resulting scenarios are unlikely to have resembled those seen in twentieth century Aboriginal communities using domestic dogs. Rather, the ethnographic data suggests that women could benefit passively from their canine companions' bringing them food while out for unrelated tasks, as much as they could actively using dogs to hunt. Moreover, European colonization forever changed the very nature of hunting with dogs by downgrading its importance to nutrition, introducing complementary technologies such as guns and vehicles, altering the types of game available, and changing the ease with which different species could be captured with the assistance of modern domestic breeds. We can use ethnography to envisage the ways in which dingoes supplemented people's diets, resulting in zooarchaeological trends, but we cannot project the social dynamics of these historical societies into the ancient past.

Conclusion

The relationship between Australian Aboriginal peoples and dingoes was nuanced and complex. Dingoes played a key role in spirituality across the continent, yet there is immense variability between groups in belief systems and the ways in which this remarkably enigmatic species was viewed. This variability is echoed in technological and cultural differences continent-wide and is clearly visible in the different names by which dingoes were known: *mimi, warrigal, ngupanu, papa, parrutju, tjantu, wanaparri, yinura,* and *maliki* (Smith and Litchfield 2009). Stranger still, dingoes were never "domesticated" by Aborigines, and yet they were incorporated into the Dreaming and became part of daily life in a variety of ways. The seemingly disparate accounts of early Europeans have been largely neglected in favor of gendered arguments for dingoes' role in changing hunting practices. However, these early accounts are invaluable for their documentation of this variable relationship. The caveat emptor in this relationship, however, is the tendency of modern researchers to conflate dingoes with domestic dogs, an oversight we have shown leads to erroneous assumptions about the *dingo*-human relationship.

Just as with modern domestic dogs, the human-canine relationship in the Australian past was complex. Dingoes were viewed in a variety of ways and were privy to an almost endless variety of human-animal relationships, ranging from companion to competitor to hunting aid. Perhaps, then, the dingo is not enigmatic at all. Rather, perhaps the relationship between dingoes and humans should be seen as dynamic and variable—a rapport that transcends conventional perceptions of the domesticated-domesticator relationship to one of a managed interaction between mutual parties, a rare symbiotic relationship in which neither side is the dominator. The dingo was not domesticated in Australia, and perhaps it is our Eurocentric perception of humans continually dominating canines upon which continued misconceptions of dingoes are founded.

References Cited

Abbott, Ian
2008 Historical Perspectives of the Ecology of Some Conspicuous Vertebrate Species in Southwest Western Australia. *Conservation Science Western Australia* 6(3):1–214.
Balme, Jane, and Susan O'Connor
2016 Dingoes and Aboriginal Social Organization in Holocene Australia. *Journal of Archaeological Science: Reports* 7:775–781. DOI:10.1016/j.jasrep.2015.08.015.
Barrington, George
1795 *A Voyage to Botany Bay with a Description of the Country, Manners, Customs, Religion &c. of the Natives.* C. Lowndes, London.
Basedow, Herbert
1925 *The Australian Aboriginal.* F. W. Preece, Adelaide.
Berndt, Ronald, and Catherine Berndt
1945 *A Preliminary Report of Field Work in the Ooldea Region, Western South-Australia.* Australian Medical, Sydney.
Beveridge, Peter
1889 *The Aborigines of Victoria and Riverina.* M. L. Hutchinson, Melbourne.

Cahir, Fred, and Ian Clark

2013   The Historic Importance of the Dingo in Aboriginal Society in Victoria (Australia): A Reconsideration of the Archival Record. *Anthrozoös* 26:185–198. DOI:10.2752/175303713X13636846944088.

Cairns, Kylie, Sarah Brown, Ben Sacks, and William Ballard

2017   Conservation Implications for Dingoes from the Maternal and Paternal Genome: Multiple Populations, Dog Introgression, and Demography. *Ecology and Evolution* 00:1–21.

Cairns, Kylie, and Alan Wilton

2016   New Insights on the History of Canids in Oceania Based on Mitochrondrial and Nuclear DNA. *Genetica* 144(5):553–565.

Carter, Samuel

1911   *Reminiscences of the Early Days of the Wimmera*. Norman Bros., Melbourne.

Caughley, Graham, Gordon Grigg, Judy Caughley, and G. J. E. Hill.

1980   Does Dingo Predation Control the Densities of Kangaroos and Emus? *Australian Wildlife Research* 7:1–12. DOI:10.1071/WR9800001.

Chewings, Charles

1936   *Back in the Stone Age*. Angus and Robertson, Sydney.

Cleland, John Burton

1966   The Ecology of the Aboriginal in South and Central Australia. In *Aboriginal Man in South and Central Australia*, edited by Bernard Cotton, pp. 111–58. Government Printer, Adelaide.

Clutton-Brock, Juliet

1995   Origns of the Early Dog: Domestication and Early History. In *The Domestic Dog: Its Evolution, Behavior, and Interactions with People*, edited by James Serpell, pp. 7–20. Cambridge University Press, Cambridge.

Crowther, Mathew, Melanie Fillios, Nicholas Colman, and Mike Letnic

2014   An Updated Description of the Australian Dingo (*Canis dingo Meyer*, 1793). *Journal of Zoology* 293:192–203. DOI:10.1111/jzo.12134.

Curr, Edward Micklethwaite

1886   *The Australian Race*, Vol. 2. John Ferres, Government Printer, Melbourne.

Darwin, Charles

1839   *The Voyage of the Beagle*. Internet Wiretap Online Edition. Available online at http://www.gutenberg.org/cache/epub/944/pg944-images.html.

Dawson, James

1881   *Australian Aborigines: The Languages and Customs of Several Tribes of Aborigines in the Western District of Victoria, Australia*. Australian Institute of Aboriginal Studies, Canberra.

Dawson, Robert

1831   *The Present State of Australia*. Smith, Elder, Cornhill, London.

Downs, James

1960   Domestication: An Examination of the Changing Social Relationships between Man and Animals. *Kroeber Anthropological Society Papers* 22:18–67.

Duncan-Kemp, Alice

1964   *Where Strange Paths Go Down*. W.R. Smith and Paterson, Brisbane, Australia.

Endicott, Karen

1999   Gender Relations in Hunter-Gatherer Societies. In *The Cambridge Encyclopedia of*

Hunters and Gatherers, edited by R. B. Lee and R. Daly, pp. 411–418. Cambridge University Press, Cambridge.

Eyre, Edward John

1845 *Journals of Expeditions of Discovery into Central Australia*. T.&W. Boone, London.

Finlayson, Hedley Herbert

1943 *The Red Centre: Man and Beast in the Heart of Australia*. Angus and Robertson, Sydney.

Fillios, Melanie, Chris Gordon, Freya Koch, and Mike Letnic

2010 The Effect of a Top Predator on Kangaroo Abundance in Arid Australia and Its Implications for Archaeological Faunal Assemblages. *Journal of Archaeological Science* 37:986–993.

Fillios, Melanie, and Paul Taçon

2016 Who Let the Dogs In? A Review of the Recent Genetic Evidence for the Introduction of the Dingo to Australia and Implications for the Movement of People. *Journal of Archaeological Science: Reports* 7:782–792.

Fountain, Paul

1907 *Ramblings of an Australian Naturalist, from the Notes and Journals of Thomas Ward*. John Murray, London.

Freycinet, Louis de

2001 *Reflections on New South Wales, 1788–1839*. Hordern House, Sydney.

Giles, Ernest

1889 *Australia Twice Traversed*. Sampson Low, Marston, Searle & Rivington, London.

Gollan, Klim

1980 Prehistoric Dingo. PhD dissertation, Department of Archaeology, Australian National University, Canberra.

1984 The Australian Dingo: In the Shadow of Man. In *Vertebrate Zoogeography and Evolution in Australasia,* edited by Mike Archer and Georgina Clayton, pp. 921–927. Hesperia Press, Carlisle.

Gould, Richard

1969a *Yiwara: Foragers of the Australian Desert*. Scribner, New York.

1969b Subsistence Behaviour among the Western Desert Aborigines of Australia. *Oceania* 39(4):253–274. DOI:10.1002/j.1834–4461.1969.tb01026.x

Grey, George

1841 *Journal of Two Expeditions of Discovery in North-West and Western Australia*. T.&W. Boone, London.

Griffith, Charles James

1845 *Present State and Prospects of Port Phillip*. William Curry, Dublin.

Gunn, Robert, Ray Whear, and Leigh Douglas

2010 A Dingo Burial from the Arnhem Land Plateau. *Australian Archaeology* 71:11–16.

2012 A Second Recent Canine Burial from the Arnhem Land Plateau. *Australian Archaeology* 74:103–105.

Hamilton, Annette

1972 Aboriginal Man's Best Friend? *Mankind* 8:287–295. DOI:10.1111/j.1835-9310.1972.tb00049.x.

Hayden, Brian

1975 Dingoes: Pets or Producers? *Mankind* 10:10–15. DOI:10.1111/j.1835-9310.1975.tb00906.x.

Horn, William, and Baldwin Spencer

1896   Report on the Work of the Horn Expedition to Central Australia. *Mammalia*. Macmillan, London.

Horne, George, and George Aiston

1924   *Savage Life in Central Australia*. Macmillan, London.

Jackson, Stephen, Colin Groves, Peter Fleming, Ken Aplin, Mark Eldridge, Antonio Gonzalez, and Kristofer Helgen

2017   The Wayward Dog: Is the Australian Native Dog or Dingo a Distinct Species? *Zootaxa* 4317:201–224. http://dx.doi.org/10.11646/zootaxa.4317.2.1

Jones, Rhys

1970   Tasmanian Aborigines and dogs. *Mankind* 7:256–271. DOI:10.1111/j.1835-9310.1970.tb00420.x.

Kaberry, Phyllis

1939   *Aboriginal Woman: Sacred and Profane*. Routledge Classic, London.

Kästner, Sibylle

2012   *Hunter-Gatherers and Gatherer-Hunters: How Australian Aboriginal Women Caught Animals*. LIT Verlag, Berlin.

Keats, Norman Charles

1988   *Wollumbin: The Creation and Early Habitation of the Tweed, Brunswick, and Richmond Rivers of N.S.W.* N. C. Keats, Point Clare, New South Wales.

Koch, Grace

1993   *Kaytetye Country: An Aboriginal History of the Barrow Creek Area*. Institute for Aboriginal Development Publications, Alice Springs, Australia.

Kolig, Erich

1978   Aboriginal Dogmatics: Canines in Theory, Myth and Dogma. *Bijdragen tot de Taal-Land-en Volkenkunde* 134:84–115. DOI:10.1163/22134379-9000022597.

Koster, Jeremy

2008   Hunting with Dogs in Nicaragua: An Optimal Foraging Approach. *Current Anthropology* 49(5):935–944.

Koungoulos, Loukas

2017   Canis Dingo and the Australian Fauna Trend: A New Explanatory Model Integrating Ecological Data. *Journal of Archaeological Science: Reports* 14:38–45.

Krefft, Gerard

1865   On the Manners and Customs of the Aborigines of the Lower Murray and Darling. *Transactions of the Philosophical Society of New South Wales*, pp. 357–374.

Lawrence, Roger

1967   Aboriginal Habitat and Economy. Master's thesis, Australian National University, Canberra.

Lee, Ida

1906   *The Coming of the British to Australia 1788 to 1829*. Longmans Green, London, New York and Bombay.

Lockwood, Douglas

1962   *I, the Aboriginal*. Rigby, Adelaide, Australia.

Long, Jeremy

1971   Arid Region Aborigines: The Pintubi. In *Aboriginal Man and Environment in Australia*, edited by Derek John Mulvaney and Jack Golson, pp. 262–270. Australian National University Press, Canberra.

Lumholtz, Carl

1889 *Among Cannibals: Account of Four Years Travels in Australia, and Camp Life with the Aborigines of Queensland*. Charles Scribner's Sons, New York.

Lupo, Karen

2017 When and Where Do Dogs Improve Hunting Productivity? The Empirical Record and Some Implications for Early Upper Paleolithic Prey Acquisition. *Journal of Anthropological Archaeology* 47:139–151.

Lowe, Pat

ca. twentieth century. *Dogs and Their People*. Unpublished paper.

McBryde, Isabel

1982 *Coast and Estuary: Archaeological Investigations on the North Coast of New South Wales at Wombah and Schnapper Point*. Canberra: Australian Institute of Aboriginal Studies.

Meehan, Betty, Rhys Jones, and Annie Vincent

1999 Gulu-kula: Dogs in Anbarra Society, Arnhem Land. *Aboriginal History* 23:83–106.

Meggitt, Mervyn

1965 The Association between Australian Aborigines and Dingoes. In *Man, Culture and Animals*, Vol. 78, edited by Anthony Leeds and Andrew Vayda, pp. 7–26. American Association for the Advancement of Science, Washington, DC.

Milham, Paul, and Peter Thompson

1976 Relative Antiquity of Human Occupation and Extinct Fauna at Madura Cave, Southeastern Western Australia. *Mankind* 10:175–180.

Mitchell, Thomas Livingstone

1839 *Three Expeditions into the Interior of Eastern Australia: With Descriptions of the Recently Explored Region of Australia Felix and of the Present Colony of New South Wales*. T.&W. Boone, London.

Moore, George Fletcher

1842 *A Descriptive Vocabulary of the Language in Common Use amongst the Aborigines of Western Australia . . .* Orr, London.

Mulvaney, John, Graham Lawton, Charles Twidale, Neil Macintosh, Jack Mahoney, and Norman Wakefield

1964 Archaeological Excavation of Rock Shelter No. 6 Fromm's Landing, South Australia. *Proceedings of the Royal Society of Victoria* 77:479–516.

Nind, Scott

1831 Description of the Natives of King George's Sound (Swan River Colony) and Adjoining Country. *Journal of the Royal Geographical Society of London* 1:21–51. Available at https://archive.org/details/jstor-1797657, accessed July 15, 2016.

Oxley, John

1820 *Journals of Two Expeditions into the Interior of New South Wales, Undertaken by Order of the British Government in the Years 1817–18*. John Murray, London.

Pardoe, Colin

1996 Dogs Changed the world. *National Dingo News* Spring:19–29.

Parker, M. A.

2002 Boyish Recollections of Victoria 70 years ago, Mount Alexander Mail, 22, 23, 24 June 1916. Reproduced in *A Successful Failure, a Trilogy: the Aborigines and Early Settlers*, edited by Geoff Morrison, pp. 306–311. Geoff Morrison, Harcourt.

Peasley, William

1983   *The Last of the Nomads.* Fremantle Arts Centre Press, Perth.

Petrie, Tom

1904   *Reminiscences of Early Queensland.* Watson, Ferguson, Brisbane.

Pickering, Michael

1992   Garawa Methods of Game Hunting, Preparation and Cooking. *Records of the South Australian Museum* 26:9–23.

Pople, A. R., G. C. Grigg, S. C. Cairns, L. A. Beard, and P. Alexander

2000   Trends in the Numbers of Red Kangaroos and Emus on Either Side of the South Australian Dingo Fence: Evidence for Predator Regulation. *Wildlife Research* 27:269–276. DOI: 10.1071/WR99030.

Rose, Deborah Bird

1992   *Dingo Makes Us Human: Life and Land in an Australian Aboriginal Culture.* Cambridge: Cambridge University Press.

Roth, Walter Edmund

1897   *Ethnological Studies among North-West-Central Queensland Aborigines.* Queensland Government Printer, Brisbane.

Russell, Andrew

1840   *A Tour through the Australian Colonies in 1839, with Notes and Incidents of a Voyage Round the Globe, Calling at New Zealand and South America.* 2nd ed. David Robertson, Glasgow.

Ryan, Lyndall

1981   *The Aboriginal Tasmanians.* University of Queensland Press, St. Lucia, Australia.

Semon, Richard

1899   *In the Australian Bush and on the Coast of the Coral Sea.* Macmillan, London.

Skyring, Fiona, and Sarah Yu

2008   Strange Strangers: First Contact between Europeans and Karajarri People on the Kimberley Coast of WA. In *Strangers on the Shore: Early Coastal Contacts in Australia,* edited by Peter Veth, Peter Sutton, and Margo Neale, pp. 60–75. National Museum of Australia Press, Canberra.

Smith, Pamela

2000   Dietary Stress or Cultural Practice: Fragmented Bones at the Puntutjarpa and Serpent's Glen Rockshelters. *Australian Archaeology* 51:65–66.

Smith, Bradley

2015   *The Dingo Debate: Origins, Behaviour and Conservation.* CSIRO, Australia.

Smith, Bradley, Kylie Cairns, Justin Adams, Thomas Newsome, Melanie Fillios, Eloise Deaux, William Parr, Mike Letnic, Lily van Eeden, Robert Appleby, Corey Bradshaw, Peter Savolainen, Euan Ritchie, Dale Nimmo, Clare Archer-Lean, Aaron Greenville, Chris Dickman, Lyn Watson, Katherine Moseby, Tim Doherty, Arian Wallach, Damian Morrant, and Mathew Crowther

2019   Taxonomic Status and Nomenclature of the Australian Dingo: The Case for *Canis dingo* Meyer, 1793. *Zootaxa* 4564:173–197. DOI:10.11646/zootaxa.4564.1.6

Smith, Bradley, and Carla Litchfield

2009   A Review of the Relationship between Indigenous Australians, Dingoes (*Canis dingo*) and Domestic Dogs (*Canis familiaris*). *Anthrozoös* 22:111–128. DOI: 10.2752/175303709X434149.

Smyth, Robert Brough

1878   *The Aborigines of Victoria.* J. Ferres, Melbourne.

Snell, Edward

1988 [1850]   *The Life and Adventures of Edward Snell: The Illustrated Diary of an Artist, Engineer and Adventurer in the Australian Colonies 1849 to 1850.* Edited by T. Griffiths. Angus and Robertson and the Library Council of Victoria, North Ryde, Australia.

Spencer, Baldwin, and Francis James Gillen

1889   *The Native Tribes of Central Australia.* University of Adelaide, Adelaide, Australia.

Stokes, John Lort

1846   *Discoveries in the Australia; With an Account of the Coasts and Rivers Explored and Surveyed during the Voyage of H.M.S. Beagle.* T.&W. Boone, London.

Stormon, Edward James

1977   *The Salvado Memoirs.* University of Western Australia Press, Nedlands.

Sturt, Charles

1833   *Two Expeditions into the Interior of Southern Australia*, Vol. 2. Smith, Elder, London.

Taçon, Paul, and Colin Pardoe

2002   Dogs Make Us Human. *Nature Australia* 27(4):52–61.

Taçon, Paul, Michelle Langley, Sally May, Ronald Lamilami, Wayne Brennan, and Daryl Guse

2010   Ancient Bird Stencils in Arnhem Land, Northern Territory, Australia. *Antiquity* 84(324):416–427.

Taçon, Paul, Wayne Brennan, Matthew Kelleher, and David Pross

2012   Differential Australian Cave and Rock Shelter Use during the Pleistocene and Holocene. In *Sacred Darkness: A Global Perspective on the Ritual Use of Caves*, edited by H. Moyes, pp. 135–148. University Press of Colorado, Boulder.

Tench, Watkin

1793   *A Complete Account of the Settlement at Port Jackson.* G. Nicol and J. Sewell, London.

Thomson, Donald

1949   Arnhem Land: Explorations among an Unknown People, Part III, On Foot across Arnhem Land. *Geographical Journal* 114:305–332. DOI:10.2307/178988.

Todd, William

1835   *Journal June–November 1835.* Typescript copy MS. 11335. La Trobe Library, Melbourne.

Turner, John, and Greg Blyton

1995   *The Aborigines of Lake Macquarie: A Brief History.* Lake Macquarie City Council, Australia.

White, Isobel

1972   Hunting Dogs at Yalata. *Mankind* 8:201–205. DOI:10.1111/j.1835-9310.1972.tb00436.x.

10

Powerful Pups

A Case Study for Dog Sacrifice in Archaic Rome from the Area Sacra di Sant'Omobono

VICTORIA MOSES

Roman dogs were diverse, both in terms of their physical appearance and in the functions they served. While iconography and epigraphy tend to focus on their roles as working animals or beloved pets, some ancient texts suggest that dogs also served as sacrificial victims for religious ceremonies and medicinal rites.[1] Romans viewed dogs as powerful beings with the ability to absorb disease, protect against evil, and guide humans through transitions, such as childbirth and death (De Grossi Mazzorin and Minniti 2006). At the same time, they were also associated with the underworld, evil, and impurity (Sassù 2016; Toynbee 1973:122–124). Zooarchaeological evidence adds to this data, revealing that, while the majority of animals sacrificed by the Romans were livestock (sheep, goat, pig and cattle), dogs also featured in sacrificial and medicinal rites associated with civic foundations, childbirth, death, pestilence, and protection (De Grossi Mazzorin and Minniti 2006; Mackinnon 1999; Soren 2003; Wilkens 2006). This chapter presents preliminary research reporting zooarchaeological evidence from one of Rome's earliest temples, the Area Sacra di Sant'Omobono, dating to the early sixth century BCE. This research is part of the Sant'Omobono Project, directed by Monica Ceci, Paolo Brocato, and Nicola Terrenato, that aims to reexamine, record, and compile all the evidence from the site's previous archaeological work and undertake new excavations. The faunal remains from Sant'Omobono indicate that dogs were sacrificed in this prominent early Roman sanctuary (Ioppolo 1972; Tagliacozzo 1989; Moses 2019). There was a consistent choice in fetal, neonatal, and juvenile dogs, indicating that the age of the sacrificial animal was an important criterion for the ritual. Ancient sources often make the distinction that puppies were pure animals that could be used in many medicinal and purification rites.[2] Findings from research presented here reveal that motivations for sacrifices at the temple fall into two main categories: livestock animals that were sacrificed to return a share of subsistence bounty and dogs that were sacrificed for purification and possibly for assistance with childbirth in connection with the deity Mater Matuta. This chapter argues that archaeological evidence for the practice of animal sacrifice in Archaic Rome reveals the foundations for the continuation of this practice during times of social change. Dog sacrifices are well documented in later written sources and in archaeological contexts. Dog sacrifices at Sant'Omobono were a precursor for these later rites.

Dogs in Animal Sacrifice

Faunal remains from animal sacrifice leave material evidence of ancient rituals. Roman life was centered around religion, and one of the major foci and long-standing traditions of Roman religious ritual was animal sacrifice (Beard et al. 1998b:148; Scheid 2007:263). While some rituals required the sacrifice of animals not typically consumed, most sacrificial rituals involved livestock animals, such as sheep, goats, cattle, and pigs (Ekroth 2014:330). These sacrifices were a routine part of religious practices, and some scholars argue that any consumption of meat would have entailed some degree of ritual (Ekroth 2007; Scheid 2012:93).

By later Roman periods, offering animal sacrifices would have involved set practices overseen by religious officials who conducted rites and interpreted signs. The traditional components of these official sacrificial rites (as summarized by Beard et al. 1998b:148) include 1) the procession (*pompa*) of victims to the altar, 2) prayer of the main officiant and offerings of libations at the altar, 3) pouring of wine and grain over the animal's head, 4) killing of the animal by slaves, 5) divination by examining entrails, and 6) burning of selected parts on the altar followed by a banquet during which the rest of the meat is consumed. Descriptions of these acts are known from later sources, and such animal sacrifice scenarios probably stemmed from Archaic period components. One iconographical representation to support the antiquity of these practices is the Hydria Ricci, a vessel from western central Italy dating from the Etruscan period (530–520 BCE), which depicts several of these sacrificial elements in sequence (Cerchiai 1995).

In contrast, dog sacrifices existed outside the realm of typical animal sacrifices of livestock or wild animals since dogs are not commonly considered food outside of ritual or medicinal contexts (Alcock 2006:66), are often named (Toynbee 1973:108–122), and arguably humanized far beyond any other animal. Because of these differences, the sacrifice of dogs functioned differently than the typical meat offering to the gods.

Dogs in ritual contexts are well documented in pre-Roman and Roman Italy.[3] Adult dogs have been interpreted as transitional guides associated with the underworld (De Grossi Mazzorin and Minniti 2006), while younger dogs, like the ones at Sant'Omobono, appear to be preferred more when performing purification rituals or ritual consumption.

The Archaic Period in Rome

By the end of the sixth century BCE, Rome was an urban center (Smith 1996a: 151–152, 2005:108; Terrenato 2010, 2011). The change from a more modest settlement occurred rapidly from the end of the Bronze Age through the Archaic period (Fulminante 2014:66–132). At this transitional time, the city of Rome was one settlement among many (such as the nearby centers of Veii and Gabii) that underwent an "urban explosion" (Becker et al. 2009:629), including a shift from hut compounds to stone complexes and an increase in monumental architecture such as the temple at Sant'Omobono (Fulminante 2014:96; Hopkins 2016).

In Rome the Archaic period also marked the time when the roles and economic obligations of the elite and non-elite were being formalized (Momigliano 2008). These social changes accompanied an increased population density during this period of urbanization and set the foundation and structure for the future of Rome. One of these changing social components was a greater formalization in the religious structure (Beard et al. 1998a:5). Archaeological evidence in burials and other ritual settings shows ritual activity was common in Archaic Rome, and many of these activities, such as the continual use and reuse of the sanctuary space at Sant'Omobono, continued for centuries following their beginnings in the Archaic period (Smith 2007:35–36, 38). By the end of the Archaic period, the Roman religious framework was largely established (Beard et al. 1998a:5). This included the formation of religious groups, building of monumental temples, creation of specific festivals and religious rites, and formalization of how the gods were integrated into daily life, among other aspects of religion.

While the Archaic period is important for understanding Rome's growth, archaeological data from this time period within the city of Rome itself is sparse. This scarcity is largely the result of the volume of anthropogenic deposits above the Archaic period levels due to the continuous occupation of Rome from the Iron Age through modern times (Becker et al. 2009:629). However, recent excavations, such as the one at Sant'Omobono, have offered new and important data for understanding Rome's formative years (Fulminante 2014:66–132). This archaeological evidence is our only direct source into this time period because, except for a few short inscriptions, our earliest surviving Roman texts were written centuries later. For this reason, archaeological evidence from this period gives insights into the transition into the Roman traditions that began at this time (Smith 2007:36).

Introduction to the Area Sacra di Sant'Omobono

One site that represents the new monumentalization of religious structures during the Archaic period is the Area Sacra di Sant'Omobono, an urban sanctuary that served a religious function. It is located in downtown Rome, just east of the Tiber Island (Figure 10.1). This central location was a significant area throughout Rome's occupation as a major access point to the city from the Tiber and as part of the Forum Boarium (Brock 2016:657; Marra et al. 2018:20).

The site of Sant'Omobono has a long history of occupation. Evidence for Bronze Age habitation in the city of Rome is usually absent (Brock and Terrenato 2016:654), but the earliest evidence for occupation at Sant'Omobono dates to the late second millennium BCE based on radiocarbon dating of charred seeds that were associated with ceramic sherds (Brock and Terrenato 2016). Religious structures at Sant'Omobono were continuously built and rebuilt from at least the sixth century BCE to the present day (Brocato et al. 2016; Diffendale et al. 2016; Terrenato et al. 2012). While there were possibly earlier religious activities and structures, the most substantial archaeological evidence from the early use of this site comes from the Archaic period temple, which dates to the early sixth century BCE and was likely dedicated to Fortuna or Mater Matuta, a goddess associated with women and childbirth (Diffendale et al. 2016). The temple's stone podium is one of the earliest known in Italy (Diffendale et al. 2016:11). Architectural terra-cottas that adorned the temple relate to at least

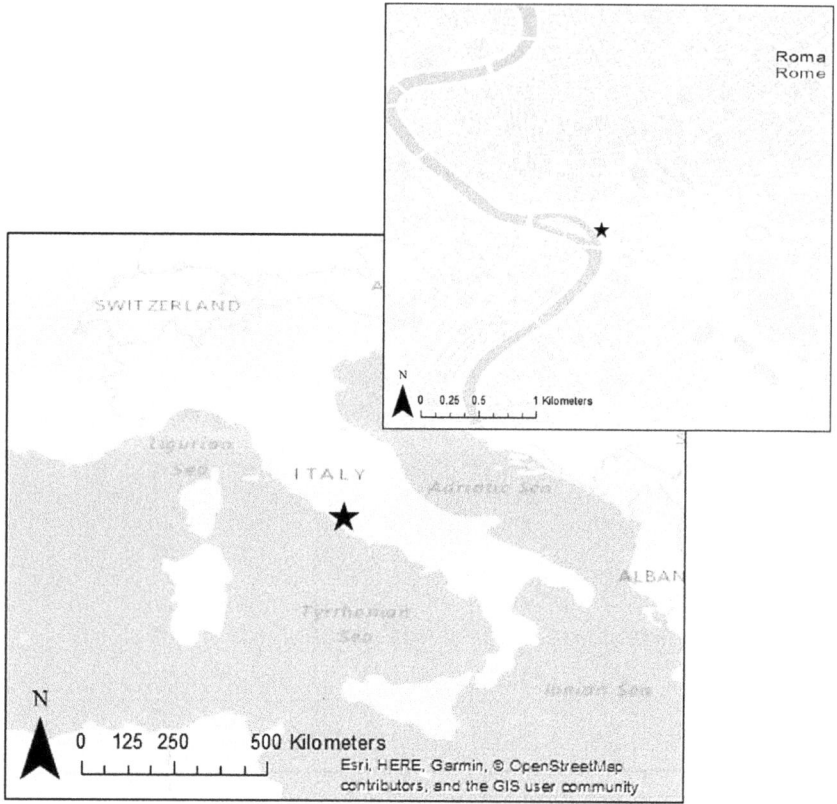

Figure 10.1. Location of the Area Sacra di Sant'Omobono.

two construction phases in the sixth century (Diffendale et al. 2016:13). Outside the temple was an altar (Diffendale et al. 2016:11). The artifacts associated with the temple include a wide range of votive offerings: *impasto* (courseware) items such as miniatures and models of bread, fineware imported from Greece, *bucchero* (Etruscan fineware) vessels including miniatures, bronze rings, and other bronze items, amber, an inscribed lion figure made from ivory, and a variety of other items (Diffendale et al. 2016:19–20). It is also possible that there was another temple, an Archaic period twin temple, that has yet to be uncovered. While the earliest temple was in use during the Archaic period, it was later demolished and replaced by twin Republican temples dedicated to Fortuna and Mater Matuta (Diffendale et al. 2016). The site also includes late Republican *tabernae*, medieval dwellings, and the modern church of Sant'Omobono (Diffendale et al. 2016).

Sant'Omobono was discovered in the 1930s during massive construction and reorganization projects around the city that revealed several statues and an altar (Brocato and Terrenato 2017). Following these findings, Sant'Omobono was designated as a significant archaeological site and has been protected from development since then. From the 1930s through today, the site has seen intermittent archaeological excavations. Before beginning new excavations at the site, the Sant'Omobono Project compiled a comprehensive report on the previous excavations, and these studies are ongoing (Terrenato et al. 2012). Four of the excavations reported animal remains from the Archaic temple levels. Giovanni Ioppolo (1972) reported the fauna from the 1962–1964 excavations of Settore IID and Settore IVE. Antonio Tagliacozzo (1989) reported the fauna from the 1974–1975 excavations of Settore I. Victoria Moses (2019) reported the faunal remains from the 1953 Gjerstad excavations of Settore C and the 2013 Area D10 excavations.

In 2013 and 2014, the Sant'Omobono Project excavated to a depth several meters below the surface, reaching the temple podium 14 m below the floor of the modern church (Diffendale et al. 2016:7). The project used a modern excavation methodology that involved the hand-collection of artifacts and water-screening of matrix containing archaeological material using a 1 cm screen. In addition to material from these more recent excavations, faunal material from the 1953 Gjerstad excavation of the temple was also analyzed for this study to establish a comprehensive overview of the animal sacrifice at Sant'Omobono. While these four areas around the temple were excavated at different times and some of the faunal data was reported in different ways, the remains reported here are all associated with the Archaic period temple. These different reporting methods limit which zooarchaeological data can be quantified. The publication of the complete analysis includes additional details on all the taxa in the faunal assemblage and their interpretation (Moses 2019). One of the notable features of this faunal assemblage is the presence of the remains of several dogs, particularly crania of juvenile dogs, along with other sacrificed domestic animals.

Animal Sacrifice at Sant'Omobono

As one of the earliest temples in the city of Rome, the animal remains from the Archaic period temple at Sant'Omobono represent some of the first religious rituals in the newly urbanized city and reflect the establishment of religious practices that formed the foundation of Roman religion for centuries to follow. At Sant'Omobono, analysis criteria for identifying animal sacrifice were modified from Daniela Klokler (2008) to include the following characteristics: 1) distinctive biases to specific animal parts; 2) presence or absence of unusual butchery patterns, burning, or other modifications; 3) abundance of a specific age, sex, and species; 4) presence of exotic, rare, or expensive taxa; 5) differential preservation; and 6) association with other materials linked to ritual, such as architecture or votive vessels. These characteristics help guide the following interpretation of the assemblage from Sant'Omobono. The strongest indicators that animals were sacrificed and ritually interred at the site are the association between the faunal remains and the temple podium, architectural terra-cottas, and votive offerings paired with the characteristics of the faunal remains such as the abundance of young sheep/goat, age profiles indicating a preference for juvenile dogs, and the selection for dog crania.

The faunal remains largely consist of sheep/goat, followed in prevalence by pig and cattle (Table 10.1). Since the non-mammalian and indeterminate bones were not quantified in detail in previously published faunal reports from the site, only those animals identified to species are included in this discussion.

Table 10.1. NISP for mammal remains from Area Sacra di Sant'Omobono Archaic temple

Taxon	Common Name	Settore IID, IVE	Settore I	Settore C	Area D10	Total NISP
Mammalia						
Bos taurus	Cattle	42	124	4	18	188
Ovis aries	Sheep			2	5	8
Capra hircus	Goat				3	3
Ovis aries/Capra hircus	Sheep/Goat	191	1294	27	140	1652
Sus scrofa domesticus	Pig	232	624	14	101	971
Canis familiaris	Dog	6	38		9	53
Castor fiber	Beaver	1				1
Lepus sp.	Hare				1	1
Equus sp.	Equid				1	1
Cervus elaphus	Red Deer	1			2	3
Determinate Mammal Total		**473**	**2,080**	**47**	**290**	**2,881**

Dogs were consistently present throughout the stratigraphic layers associated with the temple in small percentages (1.8% of the mammal NISP overall). While dog remains represented a much smaller NISP than sheep, goat, cattle, and pig, their consistent presence within sacrificial deposits indicates that from Rome's earliest years dogs were sacrificed, at least occasionally.

Wild animals and non-mammalian remains were rare but included red deer (*Cervus elaphus*), birds such as chicken (*Gallus gallus*), pigeon (*Columba palumbus*), and duck (*Anas domestica*), beaver (*Castor fiber*), hare (*Lepus* sp.), and fish such as seabream (*Sparus aurata*), and a few fragments of reptile and amphibian bones. It is difficult to assess whether all of these remains were intentionally deposited (especially small animals that can be invasive or attracted to human activities, such as reptiles and amphibians), but the secure association with the temple and other artifacts, as well as the other characteristics of the faunal assemblage, indicate that most of the fauna were the remains of animal sacrifice.

Portions of sacrificed animals from Sant'Omobono included all areas of the skeleton, but there was a forequarter bias for sheep/goat. For cattle and pigs, there was no significant overrepresentation or underrepresentation of specific areas of the skeleton. In contrast, almost all dog offerings were cranial (Figure 10.2, Figure 10.3).

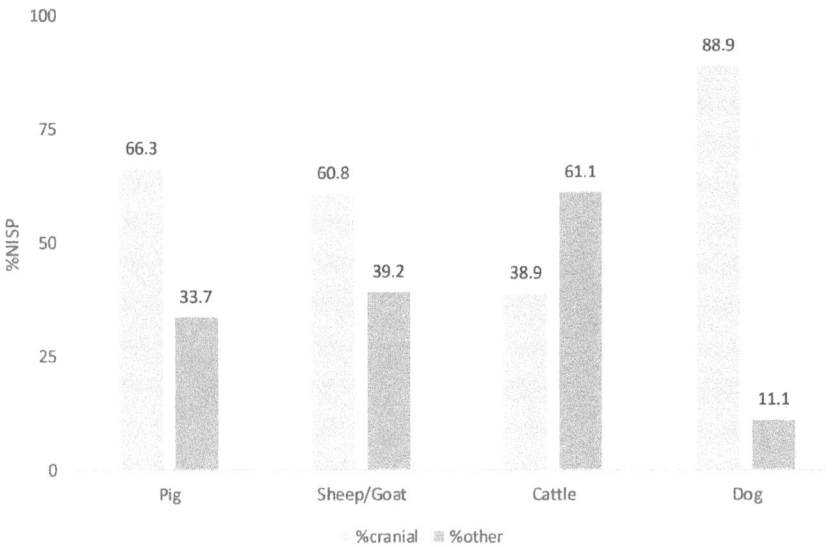

Figure 10.2. Comparison of skeletal element distribution for the faunal data from the 2014 excavations of Area D10, Area Sacra di Sant'Omobono. Archaic temple levels show prevalence of dog crania compared to other animals by %NISP.

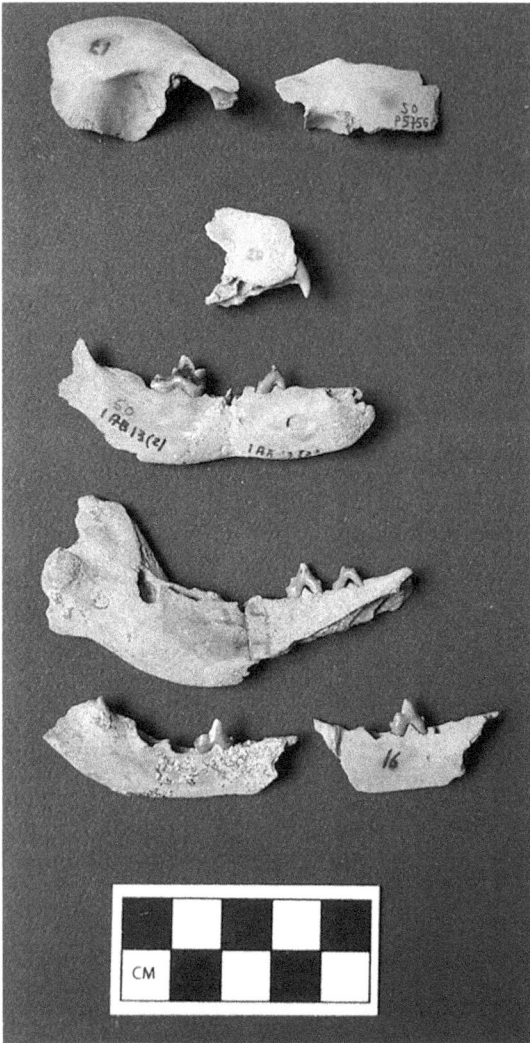

Figure 10.3. Some of the very young dog remains from the Area Sacra di Sant'Omobono. Photo taken by the author at the Museo Nazionale Preistorico Etnografico Luigi Pigorini.

Aging data indicates consistent age-at-death patterns of animals sacrificed at the temple that differ from many other contemporaneous deposits not associated with sanctuaries (see Minniti 2012 for discussion of contemporary domestic deposits). Age is often an important factor in selection for sacrifice, so consistency in age is one indicator of a special deposit. While many of the animals, especially pigs and cattle, were sacrificed as adults, the sheep, goats, and dogs recovered from the site were largely juvenile. The rare taxa did not have enough data to establish age-at-death patterns.

Most of the sheep/goat were under six months old, based on epiphyseal fusion (Figure 10.4). Tooth wear also shows a high proportion of sheep/goats less than six months old (Tagliacozzo 1989:68). This consistency in age and selection for young animals among sheep/goat matches expectations for ritual assemblages in that it displays an atypical age-at-death assemblage from domestic deposits. This indicates that age was an important factor in selecting animals for sacrifice at the site since this pattern does not match other expectations for animal husbandry, such as for raising animals for meat production or secondary products. The ages of the dogs, based on tooth eruption and epiphyseal fusion, are overwhelmingly very young; most canid remains are puppies with ages ranging from zero to two months old. MNI (minimum number of individuals) counts from the temple deposits include 11 fetal or neonatal individuals, 3 juvenile individuals, and 4 adult dogs (Figure 10.5). Aging data, therefore, indicates that at Sant'Omobono, young dogs were preferred for sacrifice over adult dogs. Interestingly, there were no signs of butchery or burning on the dog remains so there is no evidence for how dogs were killed or whether they were consumed.

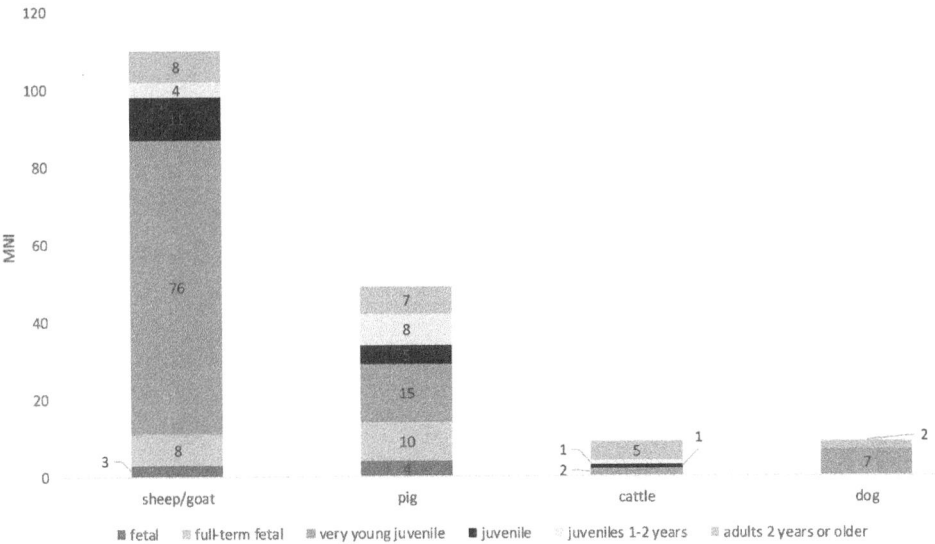

Figure 10.4. Sant'Omobono age data from epiphyseal fusion from the largest temple assemblage at the site. Age structure expressed as minimum number of individuals (MNI). Very young juvenile corresponds to an age of 0–2 months for dogs, 1–6 months for sheep/goats, and 1–3 months for pigs. Juveniles refer to sheep/goats aged 6–12 months and pigs aged 3–12 months. Cattle age ranges were not specified. Data from Settore I (Tagliacozzo 1989).

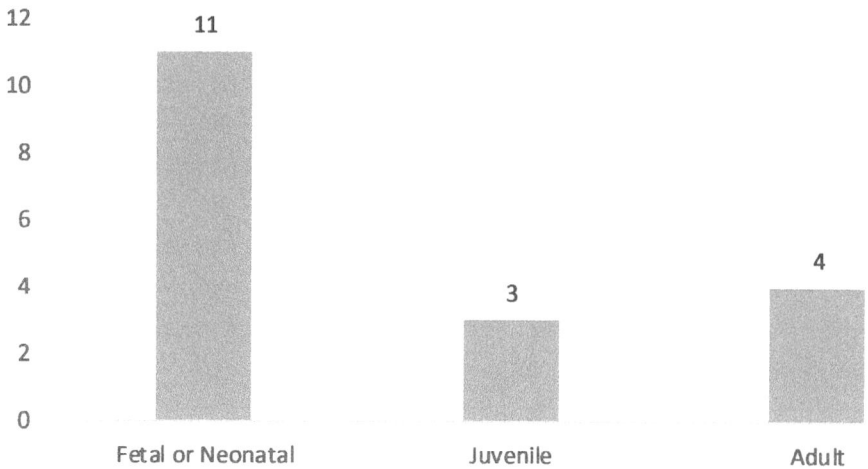

Figure 10.5. Summary of the dog remains from the Archaic temple contexts. These show a high number of very young dogs by minimum number of individuals (MNI).

Identification of Animal Sacrifice at the Area Sacra di Sant'Omobono

While not all criteria set out by Klokler (2008) were observed in the assemblage, there were distinctive biases to certain animal parts, abundance of a specific age and species, and association with other materials linked to ritual, such as architecture or votive vessels. The abundance of very young sheep/goat when compared to other domestic settings or sites, such as at Gabii (Moses in preparation; also see Minniti 2012), and the association of remains with temple architecture and votive items all strongly indicate that the animal remains recovered for this study represent the remains of ritual sacrifice that occurred during the Archaic period. Since there is little consistency in skeletal element or side of body for the sheep/goats, pigs, and cattle, it is possible that some of these remains are from communal consumption as opposed to offerings. Some of the deposits around the temple may represent disposal after different activities. The remains could represent either the portion of the carcass that was left as an offering or the rest of the carcass that was most likely consumed by participants after the sacrifice. Skeletal elements and butchery patterns might not represent how offerings were treated, but the taxa and age-at-death data represent the animals selected for sacrificial slaughter.

Interpreting Dog Sacrifice at Sant'Omobono

While there are earlier examples of dog remains found in ritual contexts around Italy (Wilkens 2006:131), the evidence from Sant'Omobono suggests that even in its formative years dog sacrifice was occurring regularly in Rome. The remains of dogs do not make up a large percentage of the identified species, but they are present throughout the contexts associated with the temple. It is likely that the activities occurring at Sant'Omobono heavily influenced Roman religion because of the temple's origin in the Archaic period and its geographic prominence within the city. Therefore, practices at Sant'Omobono were likely repeated at other sites, or at least at the Republican temples that replaced the Archaic temple at Sant'Omobono.

Their common but lesser presence compared to other domesticates found at the site shows that they were sacrificed often but not at the scale and level of other animals (see Moses 2019 for complete analysis of the assemblage including ritual identification and analysis of all taxa). Cranial remains are the most common offerings of dogs at Sant'Omobono. Offerings from animals that were commonly consumed reflect a portion of edible meat, while the dog remains are comprised primarily of cranial elements that are not typically consumed. This different selection for skeletal element is not unintentional and indicates that animals that were consumed were sacrificed for different purposes than dogs. There is no evidence for dog consumption at Sant'Omobono since there are no signs of burning or butchery. Similarly, despite the selection of young sheep/goat and young dog, the reasoning behind this may not be the same. While caprines were typically consumed, and very young sheep/goat would have been an especially prestigious foodstuff, dogs were not seen as typical food outside ritual consumption (Alcock 2006:66). At Sant'Omobono, adult dogs associated with rituals practices may represent different motivations for dog sacrifice or perhaps the use of an adult dog when a younger dog was unavailable.

The meaning and motivation of the dog sacrifices at Sant'Omobono relies on their special role in Roman society and their symbolic potency. Dog sacrifice was a powerful offering used not only in a few specific named rites described in texts but also in situations in which dog sacrifice would help avoid negative outcomes during transitions such as childbirth or foundation rites or to curtail perceived pollution such as pestilence on crops or personal medical problems (De Grossi Mazzorin and Minniti 2006; Sassù 2016; Smith 1996b; Toynbee 1973:122–124). Observed both in texts and archaeologically, the age of the dog is an important indicator of its status as pure or polluted. While other animal sacrifices are standard offerings to the gods, puppy sacrifices at Sant'Omobono are most likely related to the use of the "pure" status of young dogs as a tool. It is possible that the sacrifice is linked to childbirth, given that dogs are associated with several childbirth deities (Toynbee 1973:123). This connection is likely given the fact that the Archaic period temple at Sant'Omobono is possibly linked to Mater Matuta, a goddess associated with mothers and birth. This link is tenuous, however, since whether the Archaic temple was dedicated to Mater Matuta or Fortuna is debated, with little archaeological evidence proving either (Diffendale et al. 2016, Smith 1996a:160). Additionally, at the contemporaneous sanctuary dedicated to Mater Matuta at Satricum, only 0.1% of the faunal assemblage was canine (Prummel and Bouma 1997). This is a smaller presence of dog compared to the almost 2% from Sant'Omobono. The same sacrificial practice was not in place at Satricum even though they may have been dedicated to the same deity. This inconsistency in the percentage of dog among the sacrificed remains shows that the deity did not necessitate a strictly prescribed sacrifice in this period, or perhaps another deity was represented at Sant'Omobono who called for different sacrifices.

Instead of a connection with childbirth, the canine offering at Sant'Omobono may also have been left in order to cure disease or subvert risks, possibly associated with agriculture, childbirth, death, building and wall foundations, and other risky ventures and transitions. As a major water access point into the city, these sacrifices could also be linked to passage into the city or voyages. While there are many possible interpretations, the selection of young dogs and the association between puppies as pure versus adult dogs as polluted drawn from ancient texts and from archaeological examples suggests that puppy sacrifices at Sant'Omobono were for purification. The presence of primarily juvenile dog remains at Sant'Omobono suggests that young canids were particularly powerful for these rituals.

Who Was Making Offerings at the Sanctuary?

As Rome transitioned from a modest settlement into a major urban site and later the center of an empire, there is a question of who was involved in rituals and who had access to "public" or monumental sanctuaries like the one at Sant'Omobono. While many later religious rituals were strictly codified and limited to a select group of practitioners, the evidence from Sant'Omobono indicates individuals had access to the sanctuary during the Archaic period. These visitors would have made or overseen animal sacrifices.

One line of evidence for a variety of visitors includes the diversity in ritual, both in terms of animal sacrifice (such as the lack of consistency in taxa and skeletal element) and for other offerings. While there was a large proportion of very young sheep and goats sacrificed at the site, other domesticates and wild animals were also offered. There was little consistency in skeletal element distribution of non-canid remains, also indicating little codification and oversight over the rituals taking place at the sanctuary. In addition to the range of animal sacrifice that took place at the site, the votive offerings, or non-animal artifacts associated with the temple, include both elite and non-elite offerings. These range from coarseware to miniature *bucchero* (Etruscan fineware) and other precious objects (Brocato et al. 2016; Diffendale et al. 2016:19–20; Pisani Sartorio et al. 1989; Terrenato et al. 2019). The coarseware and ceramic bread offerings would have entailed minimal resources to acquire and were related to food offerings, either symbolic or literal. The range of other luxury items, including worked ivory, amber, bronze, and fineware, indicate more elite offerings. Some of the offerings are typically related to men and some to women, so it is likely that both had access to the sanctuary and made offerings (Diffendale et al. 2016:20). At Sant'Omobono, the possible connection to Mater Matuta and the association between puppy sacrifice and childbirth reinforces the role of the individual in animal sacrifice during Rome's early years. If these offerings were made by pregnant women or their families to aid in childbirth, the dog sacrifices at Sant'Omobono represent very personal acts specific to the needs of individual women. However, this is impossible to confirm given the evidence.

In addition to the evidence for a variety of men, women, elite, and non-elite visitors making a range of offerings, there is also the suggestion of religious specialists. There were several modified sheep/goat astragali, or knucklebones, that were often used as dice or as divination tools in the ancient world (De Grossi Mazzorin and Minniti 2013; Gilmour 1997; Moses 2019). Here, in context at the temple, these dice were most likely divination tools (Moses 2019). Interestingly, later written sources indicate that "the dog" is the least favorable of these rolls, linking dogs, divination, and evil (David 1962:15). If the dice were divination tools as opposed to personal items, this indicates the sanctuary was also frequented by formal religious specialists who had the knowledge to interpret divination dice. These findings show that a range of people had access to the temple and made offerings based on individualized needs, whether as non-elite visitors, elite visitors, or religious specialists. Many people had access to the sanctuary, so dog sacrifices could have been enacted by any of those individuals.

Conclusion

Dogs played varied and nuanced roles in Roman life as evidenced in literary, artistic, and archaeological evidence (Toynbee 1973:102–124). Their value as loyal companion animals extended beyond their roles as lapdogs and working dogs into religious and ritual worlds. The use of dogs in medicinal and sacrificial rites relates to the Romans' broader belief system, in which dogs are associated with the underworld and the afterlife as well as protection (De Grossi Mazzorin and Minniti 2006, Toynbee 1973:122–124). Within this system, dogs were viewed as the ideal sacrifice in times of need since they can traverse from this world to the underworld and are also attributed with qualities such as loyalty and servitude to their human masters (De Grossi Mazzorin and Minniti 2006). Dogs could interact with evil on a human's behalf, protecting them from danger. The dogs' power also extended to other protective rites beyond childbirth and death, such as crop protection, pestilence avoidance, and foundation rites.

The zooarchaeological remains from the Area Sacra di Sant'Omobono show the perceived power of dogs, specifically juvenile domestic dogs. The preliminary findings of this study illustrate how dog sacrifice diverges from the typical food offerings represented by livestock animals. While the specific motivation for each puppy sacrifice at Sant'Omobono could have been in reaction to several tense situations, such as aiding pregnant women or protecting from disease by absorbing pollution, these possibilities are all linked by the roles of dogs as guardians associated with death and passage between worlds and that puppies were specifically capable of fulfilling these ritual requirements because of their status as pure and unpolluted. The rituals at Sant'Omobono during the Archaic period were influential in the foundation of Roman religion and laid the framework for future rites. These "powerful pups" sacrificed at Sant'Omobono show the potency of dogs in Roman ritual in Rome's formative years.

Acknowledgments

Thank you to the volume editors, Brandi Bethke and Amanda Burtt, for their planning and helpful comments. Joey Williams provided excellent suggestions as well. The Sant'Omobono Project is promoted by the Sovrintendenza ai Beni Culturali di Roma Capitale in collaboration with the Università della Calabria and the University of Michigan. I am very grateful for the support of the directors and my colleagues, including directors Paolo Brocato, Monica Ceci, and Nicola Terrenato, as well as the excavation and lab teams associated with this project. This research was conducted with funding from the Etruscan Foundation Fieldwork Fellowship and the University of Arizona School of Anthropology. Thank you to the American Academy in Rome for support during editing this chapter. Thank you to Laura Motta for her guidance during my fieldwork at Sant'Omobono. Thank you to Francesca Alhaique and Antonio Tagliacozzo at the Museo Nazionale Preistorico Etnografico Luigi Pigorini for support and access to materials.

Notes

1. While it is inadvisable to project modern Western ideals of dogs as pets ("personal animals" might be a better term) onto the past (Mackinnon 2010:293, citing Gilhus 2006:29), zooarchaeological evidence, iconography, and text show the Romans often anthropomorphized and cared for dogs. Zooarchaeological evidence indicates that these animals were sometimes cared for into old age and Roman dog remains show little signs of abuse (Mackinnon 2010:305; Mackinnon and Belanger 2006). We also see an increased range in size and morphology of dog skeletons from the Roman period as opposed to the Neolithic and Iron Age, as Romans bred dogs for specific roles, including small lap-sized breeds (De Grossi Mazzorin and Tagliacozzo 1997, 2000).

2. While far from an exhaustive list and here presented without discussing the merits and challenges of each text, the following are examples of ancient texts that are helpful to understanding how puppies and dogs were used in ritual: Dogs as medicine (often specifically puppies): Pliny, *Natural History*, Book XXIX, 58, 98–101, 111, 114, 117, 133; Book XXX, 21–22, 27–8, 35, 46, 51, 53, 69–70, 72–4, 76, 81–2, 93, 98, 105, 109, 111, 114, 119, 121, 123, 133; Book XXX 42, 64. Consumption of dogs and especially puppies: Hippocrates *Epidemics* 7.62 Sacred Disease; Pliny, *Natural History*, Book XXIX.14 (specifically on purification through puppy blood) and XXIX.57–58; Galen, *On the Powers of Foods*, 3.1 pp. 6.664–665; Plutarch, *Moralia: Roman Questions*, 52. Dogs in agricultural rights such as protection against disease: Festus, *Breviarum*, 358L, 39L; Varro, *On the Latin Language*, Book VI, 16; Columella, *De Re Rustica*, Book X, 342–343; Pliny, *Natural History*, Book XVIII 69; Ovid, *Fasti*, Book IV, 901–942. Puppy sacrifice in Lupercalia as purification of the city: Plutarch, *Moralia: Roman Questions*, 68.

3. For dogs in text, iconography, and archaeology in pre-Roman and Roman Italy, see De Grossi Mazzorin and Minniti 2006, 2010; Mackinnon 2004; Wilkens 2006; and sources within these such as Curci and Tagliacozzo 1995; De Grossi Mazzorin 1990; Prummel 1997; Ricci et al. 2000; Wilkens 1996; Wilkens and Delussu 2002. For broader Roman and Greek evidence of dog in text, iconography, and archaeology, see Bodson 1980, 2000; Brewer et al. 2001; Mackinnon 2014:270–274; Merlen 1971; Sassù 2016; Smith 2006; Toynbee 1973:102–124; Trantalidou 2006. For additional examples of dogs in rituals, both archaeologically and in text, see Alhaique 2018; Soren 2003; Smith 1996b.

References Cited

Alcock, Joan

2006   *Food in the Ancient World.* Greenwood Press, Westport, Connecticut.

Alhaique, Francesca

2018   Four Dogs in a Road (to Say Nothing of the Fox). Paper presented at the 1st Annual Meeting of Dogs, Past and Present, Rome, Italy.

Beard, Mary, John North, and Simon Price

1998a *Religions of Rome,* Vol. 1. Cambridge University Press, Cambridge.

1998b *Religions of Rome,* Vol. 2. Cambridge University Press, Cambridge.

Becker, Jeffrey, Marcello Mogetta, and Nicola Terrenato

2009   A New Plan for an Ancient Italian City: Gabii Revealed. *American Journal of Archaeology* 113(4):629–642.

Bell, Catherine

1992   *Ritual Theory, Ritual Practice.* Oxford University Press, New York.

1997   *Ritual: Perspectives and Dimensions.* Oxford University Press, New York.

Bodson, Liliane

1980   Place et function du chien dans le monde antique. *Ethnozootechnie* 25:13–21.

2000   Motivations for Pet-Keeping in Ancient Greece and Rome: A Preliminary Survey. In *Companion Animals and Us: Exploring the Relationships between People and Pets,* edited by Anthony Podberscek, Elizabeth Paul, and James Serpell, pp. 27–41. Cambridge University Press, Cambridge.

Brewer, Douglas, Terence Clark, and Adrian Phillips

2001   *Dogs in Antiquity, Anubis to Cerberus: The Origins of the Domestic Dog.* Aris & Phillips, Warminster, England.

Brocato, Paolo, Monica Ceci, and Nicola Terrenato

2016   *Ricerche nell'area dei templi di Fortuna e Mater Matuta,* Vol. I. Università della Calabria Press, Calabria.

Brocato, Paolo, and Nicola Terrenato

2017   The Archaic Temple of S. Omobono: New Discoveries and Old Problems. In *The Age of Tarquinius Superbus: Central Italy in the Late 6th Century BC,* Vol. 29, edited by Patricia Lulof and Christopher Smith, pp. 97–106. Babesch/Peeters, Leeuven, Paris, Bristol, Connecticut.

Brock, Andrea

2016   Envisioning Rome's Prehistoric River Harbor: An Interim Report from the Forum Boarium. *Etruscan Studies* 19:1–22.

Brock, Andrea, and Nicola Terrenato

2016   Rome in the Bronze Age: Late Second-Millennium BC Radiocarbon Dates from the Forum Boarium. *Antiquity* 90:654–664.

Brück, Joanna

1999   Ritual and Rationality: Some Problems of Interpretation in European Archaeology. *European Journal of Archaeology* 2(3):313–344.

Cerchiai, Luca

1995   Il Programma Figurative dell'Hydria Ricci. *Antike Kunst* 38(2):81–91.

Columella

1955   *On Agriculture and Trees, III.* Translated by Edward S. Forster. Harvard University Press, Cambridge.

Curci, Antonio, and Antonio Tagliacozzo

1994 Il pozzetto rituale con scheletro dicavallo dall'abitato neolitico di Le Cerquete-Fianello (Maccarese-RM), Alcune considerazioni sulla domesticazione del cavallo e la sua introduzione in Italia. In *Origini XVIII*, pp. 297–350.

David, Florence Nightingale

1962 *Games, Gods, and Gambling*. Hafner, New York.

De Grossi Mazzorin, Jacopo

1990 Ossa di avvoltoio. In *La grande Roma dei Tarquini*, edited by Mauro Cristofani, p. 274. L'Erma di Bretschneider, Rome.

De Grossi Mazzorin, Jacopo, and Claudia Minniti

2006 Dog Sacrifice in the Ancient World: A Ritual Passage? In *Dogs and People in Social, Working, Economic, or Symbolic Interaction*, edited by Lynn M. Snyder and Elizabeth A. Moore, pp. 62–66. Oxbow, Oxford.

De Grossi Mazzorin, Jacopo, and Antonio Tagliacozzo

1997 Dog Remains in Italy from the Neolithic to the Roman Period. *Anthropozoologica* 25(26):429–440.

2000 Morphological and Osteological Changes in the Dog from the Neolithic to the Roman Period in Italy. In *Dogs through Time: An Archaeological Perspective*, edited by Susan Crockford, pp. 141–161. BAR International Series, Vol. 889. Archaeopress, Oxford.

2013 Ancient Use of the Knuckle-Bone for Rituals and Gaming Pieces. *Anthropozoologica* 48(2):371–380.

Diffendale, Daniel, Nicola Terrenato, Paolo Brocato, and Andrea Brock

2016 Sant'Omobono: An Interim Status Quaestionis. *Journal of Roman Archaeology* 29:7–42.

Ekroth, Gunnel

2007 Meat in Ancient Greece: Sacrificial, Sacred, or Secular? *Food and History* 5(1):249–272.

2014 Animal Sacrifice in Antiquity. In *The Oxford Handbook of Animals in Classical Thought and Life*, edited by Gordan Lindsay Campbell, pp. 324–354. Oxford University Press, Oxford.

Festus

1967 *The Breviarium of Festus*. Translated by John Eadie. Bloomsbury, London.

Fogelin, Lars

2007 The Archaeology of Religious Ritual. *Annual Review of Anthropology* 36:55–71.

Fulminante, Francesca

2014 *The Urbanization of Rome and Latium Vetus: From the Bronze Age to the Archaic Era*. Cambridge University Press, New York.

Galen

2002 *On the Properties of Foodstuffs*. Translated by Owen Powell. New York, Cambridge University Press.

Gilhus, Ingvild Sælid

2006 *Animals, Gods and Humans: Changing Attitudes to Animals in Greek, Roman and Early Christian Thought*. Routledge, London.

Gilmour, Garth

1997 The Nature and Function of Astragalus Bones from Archaeological Contexts in the Levant and Eastern Mediterranean. *Oxford Journal of Archaeology* 16(2):167–175.

Hippocrates

1995   *Epidemics,* Vol. 7. Translated by Wesley D. Smith. Harvard University Press, Cambridge.

Hopkins, John

2016   *The Genesis of Roman Architecture.* Yale University Press, New Haven.

Insoll, Timothy

2004   *Archaeology, Ritual, and Religion.* Routledge, London.

Ioppolo, Giovanni

1972   I reperti ossei animali nell'area archeologica di S. Omobono. In *Rendiconti,* Vol. XLIV, *Anno Academica 1971–1972, Atti Della Pontificia Accademia Romana Di Archeologia Serie III,* pp. 3–46. Tipografia Poliglotta Vaticana, Rome.

Klokler, Daniela

2008   Food for Body and Soul: Mortuary Ritual in Shell Mounds (Laguna Brazil). PhD dissertation, University of Arizona, Tucson.

Mackinnon, Michael

1999   Animal Bone Remains. In *A Roman Villa and a Late Roman Infant Cemetery: Excavation at Poggio Gramignano Lugnano in Teverina,* edited by David Soren and Noelle Soren, pp. 533–594. L'Erma di Bretschneider, Rome.

2004   Production and Consumption of Animals in Roman Italy: Integrating the Zooarchaeological and Textual Evidence. *Journal of Roman Archaeology* 54:1–264.

2007   State of the Discipline: Osteological Research in Classical Archaeology. *American Journal of Archaeology* 111(3):473–504.

2010   "Sick as a Dog": Zooarchaeological Evidence for Pet Dog Health and Welfare in the Roman World. *World Archaeology* 42(2):290–309.

2014   Pets. In *The Oxford Handbook of Animals in Classical Thought and Life,* edited by Gordon Lindsay Campbell, pp. 269–280. Oxford University Press, Oxford.

Mackinnon, Michael, and Kyle Belanger

2006   In Sickness and in Health: Care for an Arthritic Maltese Dog from the Roman Cemetery of Yasmina, Carthage, Tunisia. In *Dogs and People in Social, Working, Economic, or Symbolic Interaction,* edited by Lynn Snyder and Elizabeth Moore, pp. 38–43. Oxbow, Oxford.

Marra, Fabrizio, Laura Motta, Andrea Brock, Patrizia Macrì, Fabio Florindo, Laura Sadori, and Nicola Terrenato

2018   Rome in Its Setting: Post-glacial Aggradation History of the Tiber River Alluvial Deposits and Tectonic Origin of the Tiber Island. *PLoS ONE* 13(3).

Merlen, Rene

1971   *De Canibus: Dog and Hound in Antiquity.* J. A. Allen, London.

Minniti, Claudia

2012   *Ambiente, sussistenza e articolazione sociale nell' Italia centrale tra Bronzo medio e Primo Ferro,* Vol. 2394. Archaeopress, Oxford.

Momigliano, Arnaldo

2008   The Rise of the Plebs in the Archaic Age of Rome. In *Social Struggles in Archaic Rome: New Perspectives on the Conflict of the Orders,* edited by Kurt Raaflaub, pp. 168–184. Blackwell, Malden, Massachusetts.

Moses, Victoria

2019   Zooarchaeological Analysis of the Area Sacra di Sant'Omobono. In *Ricerche nell'area dei templi di Fortuna e Mater Matuta,* Vol. II, edited by Nicola Terrenato, Paolo Brocato and Monica Ceci, pp. 137–171. Università della Calabria Press, Calabria.

2020 The Zooarchaeology of Early Rome: Meat Distribution and Consumption in Public and Private Spaces (9th–6th centuries BCE) (working title). Unpublished PhD dissertation, School of Anthropology, University of Arizona, Tucson.

O'Day, Sharyn Jones, Wim Van Neer, and Anton Ervynck

2004 *Behaviour behind Bones: The Zooarchaeology of Ritual, Religion, Status and Identity,* Vol. 1. Oxbow Books, Oxford.

Ovid

1929 *The Fasti of Ovid.* Translated by James Frazier. Macmillan, London.

Pisani Sartorio, Giuseppina, Paola Virgili, and Giovanni Ioppolo

1989 *Il Viver Quotidiano in Roma Arcaica: Materiali dagli scavi del Tempio Arcaico nell'area sacra di S. Omobono.* Edizioni Procom, Rome.

Pliny the Elder

1956 *Natural History.* Translated by William H. S. Jones. Harvard University Press, Cambridge.

Plutarch

1957 *Moralia: Roman Questions,* Vols. I–IV. Translated by Harold Cherniss and William C. Helmbold. Harvard University Press, Cambridge.

Prummel, Wietske, and Jelle Bouma

1997 Animal Offerings at Borgo Le Ferriere (Latium, Italy). *Anthropozoologica* 25, 26: 531–537.

Ricci, Giovanni, Paolo Brocato, and Nicola Terrenato

2000 L'età delle mura, La fase 2, Le prime mura. In *Palatium e Sacra Via. Roma, Bolletino di Archeologia,* edited by Andrea Carandini and Paolo Carafa, pp. 31–33. Bolletino di Archeologia, Rome.

Sassù, Alessio

2016 Through Impurity: A Few Remarks on the Role of the Dog in Purification Rituals of the Greek World. In *Animals in Greek and Roman Religion and Myth,* edited by Patricia A. Johnson, Attilio Mastrocinque, and Sophia Papaioannou, pp. 393–418. Cambridge Scholars, Newcastle upon Tyne.

Scheid, John

2007 Sacrifices for Gods and Ancestors. In *A Companion to Roman Religion,* edited by Jörg Rupke, pp. 263–271. Blackwell, Malden, Massachusetts.

2012 Roman Animal Sacrifice and the System of Being. In *Greek and Roman Animal Sacrifice: Ancient Victims, Modern Observers,* edited by Christopher Faraone and Fred Naiden, pp. 84–96. Cambridge University Press, Cambridge.

Smith, Christopher

1996a *Early Rome and Latium.* Clarendon Press, Oxford.

1996b Dead Dogs and Rattles: Time, Space, and Sacrifice in Iron Age Latium. In *Approaches to the Study of Ritual: Italy and The Ancient Mediterranean,* edited by John Wilkins, 73–89. Accordia Specialist Studies on the Mediterranean, Vol. 2. Accordia Research Center, London.

2005 The Beginning of Urbanization in Rome. In *Mediterranean Urbanization, 800–600 BC,* edited by Robin Osborne and Barry Cunliffe, pp. 91–112. Oxford University Press, Oxford.

2007   The Religion of Archaic Rome. In *A Companion to Roman Religion*, edited by Jörg Rupke, pp. 263–271. Blackwell, Malden, Massachusetts.

Smith, Kate

2006   *Guides, Guards and Gifts to the Gods: Domesticated Dogs in the Art and Archaeology of Iron Age and Roman Britain*. Archaeopress, Oxford.

Soren, David

2003   Can Archaeologists Excavate Evidence of Malaria? *World Archaeology* 35(2):193–209.

Tagliacozzo, Antonio

1989   Analisi dei resti faunistici dell'area sacra di S. Omobono. In *Il Vivero Quotidiano in Roma Arcaica: Materiali dagli scavi del Tempio Arcaico nell'area sacra di S. Omobono*, pp. 65–69. Edizioni Procom, Rome.

Terrenato, Nicola

2010   Early Rome. In *The Oxford Handbook of Roman Studies*, edited by Alessandro Barchiesi and Walter Scheidel. Oxford University Press, Oxford.

2011   The Versatile Clans: Archaic Rome and the Nature of Early City-States in Central Italy. In *State Formation in Italy and Greece Questioning the Neoevolutionist Paradigm*, edited by Nicola Terrenato and Donald Haggis, pp. 231–244. Oxbow, Oxford.

Terrenato, Nicola, Paolo Brocato, Giovanni Caruso, Anna Maria Ramieri, Hilary Becker, Ivan Cangemi, Graziano Mantiloni, and Carlo Regoli

2012   The S. Omobono Sanctuary in Rome: Assessing Eighty Years of Fieldwork and Exploring Perspectives for the Future. *Internet Archaeology* 31.

Terrenato, Nicola, Paolo Brocato, and Monica Ceci

2019   *Ricerche nell'area dei templi di Fortuna e Mater Matuta*, Vol. II. Università della Calabria Press, Calabria.

Toynbee, Jocelyn

1973   *Animals in Roman Life and Art*. Cornell University Press, Ithaca, New York.

Trantalidou, Katerina

2006   Companions from the Oldest Times: Dogs in Ancient Greek Literature, Iconography, and Osteological Testimony. In *Dogs and People in the Social, Working, Economic or Symbolic Interaction*, edited by Lynne Snyder and Elizabeth Moore, pp. 96–120. Oxbow, Oxford.

Varro

1938   *On the Latin Language*. Translated by Roland Kent. Harvard University Press, Cambridge.

Wilkens, Barbara

1996   Un saggio di scavo sull'acropoli di Olbia: la fauna. In *Da Olbìa ad Olbia. 2500 anni di storia di una città mediterranea*, edited by Attilo Mastino and Paola Ruggeri, pp. 353–355. Chiarella, Sassari.

2006   The Sacrifice of Dogs in Ancient Italy. In *Dogs and People in Social, Working, Economic, or Symbolic Interaction*, edited by Lynn Snyder and Elizabeth Moore, pp. 131–136. Oxbow, Oxford.

Wilkens, B., and F. Delussu

2002   I resti faunistici. In *L'agorà di Eraclea Lucana*, edited by Giampiero Pianu, pp. 299–342. Carocci, Rome.

11

Conclusion

Conceptualizing and Investigating
our Relationships with Dogs

ROBERT J. LOSEY

Dogs are the focus of a groundswell of interest for historians, anthropologists, and archaeologists, but also for many biological scientists. My suspicion is that this relates to many scholars' real love for dogs and other canids, but perhaps I am projecting my own adoration of these creatures onto others. Another factor stimulating this burgeoning of dog research is that the social sciences and humanities themselves are changing. Multispecies ethnography, human-animal studies, and posthumanism more broadly all have emerged in the last 15 years or so (DeMello 2012; Kirksey and Helmreich 2010; Mullin 2002; Wolfe 2010), pushing many disciplines to come to terms with the reality that human lives are always enmeshed with other living things. We are far from the only subjects and agents to be considered when studying "human society." Such developing approaches stand in stark contrast to most histories, ethnographies, and archaeologies, which typically relegate animals to the categories of symbols, prey or food, and capital—objects of human concern and production, or mere background noise.

Anthropology in particular has seized these emerging ideas, generating a wealth of literature on human-animal relations, including some papers and books on dogs and domestication (e.g., Anderson et al. 2017; Fijn 2011; Kohn 2007; Loovers 2015; Losey et al. 2018b; Swanson et al. 2018). These works and the scholarship that inspired them have been particularly influential on how I envision our lives with dogs. They strongly color this conclusion and at the same time appear subtly or overtly in many of the chapters in this volume. A second trend in this collection is the utilization of methods that do more than classify archaeological skeletal remains as dog, dingo, wolf, or hybrid. While not often explicitly noted, these methods derive from other historical sciences, particularly human osteoarchaeology and paleontology. These methods are employed by those seeking to know more about past animals, about the courses of their lives, and how these lives interwove with those of other species.

Below I begin by discussing some of the emergent conceptual issues facing the contributors to this volume and that problematize the study of humans and dogs more widely. From there I turn to some of the persistent methodological challenges that exist in the study of archaeological canid remains.

Domestication

The title of this volume is *Dogs: Archaeology beyond Domestication,* and this is an apt description of its contents judging from how domestication is typically portrayed in high-level analytical papers (Losey et al. 2018a). Archaeologists, geneticists, and morphologist commonly advertise domestication in such publications as a highly significant threshold passed long ago by dogs and other domestic animals. To study domestication, one must examine the origins of a domestic animal, and everything after that point is somehow different—mere husbandry or animal keeping. In fact, it is rare to see the word "domestication" used to describe anything other than the earliest genetic or morphological manifestations of this process. Conversely, it is equally clear that conceptually oriented papers define domestication as a process and a relationship, and definitely not as a discrete moment, morphology, or genotype. This contrast in practice versus theory reveals our often-misplaced preference for one part of the history of domestication over others.

Domestication by even a strict definition is a form of evolution wherein humans influence or control the breeding of animals over multiple successive generations. There is no non-arbitrary end or threshold to pass here, and domestication is not a morphotype or a genotype. These latter things are the signs we look to as evidence of a process, not the process itself. Larson and Burger (2013:198) clearly state that "because the evolution of domestic animals is ongoing, the process of domestication has a beginning but not an end." In other words, domestication is not just the advent of animal speciation within a human niche revealed through bodily change. Rather, it is a continuing process of animals closely evolving with humans and with many other things and organisms. We really cannot get beyond domestication with dogs—we are still domesticating them. Dogs can be domestic, not domesticated or finished. Further, like all evolutionary relationships, domestication is a social process. Breeding alone does not ensure the multigenerational nature of domestication. In fact, no species evolves in isolation from other things, somehow outside of its niche, nor does any living thing evolve in relation to just one other species. Domestication is also multidirectional, affecting the experiences and evolution of the other living things, and humans are no exception.

Machines and Human Adaptive Strategies?

I have often struggled to find useful language for describing aspects of our relationships with dogs. Do we use dogs for hunting, pulling sleds, or companionship? Are dogs what enabled people to be mobile or colonize new areas? Are dogs our biotechnologies? My argument here is not that humans and dogs are in symmetrical relationships, both freely engaging in such daily activities with some sort of mutual understanding or shared goals. Rather, portraying domestic animals as just part of our adaptive strategies renders them mindless machines, mere tools that are wielded as we see fit. They cease to be living things without emotions, social lives, forms of communication, and intentions. Such language is also unidirectional, failing to acknowledge the ways in which people serve and enable dog lives. We are in many instances *their* biotechnologies, but taking such a viewpoint requires that we try to consider life from not just a human position.

Dogs have their own agendas, and this is no more evident than when we are trying to accomplish something with them. For example, study of the effectiveness of dogs in pursuing different types of prey shows that dogs can choose their own prey species to pursue, despite all human efforts to dissuade them (Koster 2008). We also clearly do not hunt just with dogs but sometimes also for them. In some situations, dogs must be provisioned by people. We fish, hunt, milk, farm, and cook to feed them, and in turn they hunt, herd, protect, and haul as part of these processes. Episodes of colonization and daily or seasonal migration are also not as we often portray them. People never travel alone—we move as multispecies packages. We are accompanied by pathogens, parasites, and of course also domestic animals and their companion species, such as fleas. Dogs clearly can assist in human movement by carrying packs and pulling sleds and in this sense are used for our mobility. But this wording is misleading, as in these processes they are moving too, along with our obligations to them.

Ontologies and Practices of Non-Domestication

Our histories with animals—how we have practically engaged with them—shape how we understand their places in the world, including their relations to us. How we understand the world also guides how we interact with animals that are new to us. This appears beautifully in two of the chapters in this volume, Peter W. Stahl's contribution on dogs in South America, and Loukas Koungoulos and Melanie Fillios's chapter on dingoes in Australia. Both chapters provide examples of people who chose not to breed dogs but still lived and even worked alongside them. Stahl argues that dogs arrived comparatively recently to people of northeastern South America. The notion of domesticating these animals was inconceivable to some people of this region because to do so violated how they already understood and related to indigenous animals. Natasha Fijn (2018) recently has made a quite similar argument regarding dingoes among Aboriginal groups in Australia. There dingoes were not bred, but people hunted with them and cared for them in various ways. As Koungoulus and Fillios's chapter shows, dingoes were also readily incorporated into Aboriginal cosmologies.

In both cases, one could argue that we are seeing domestication play out in ways beyond the scope of our rather restrictive definitions. We could of course trivialize these practices by referring to them as mere "pet keeping." In this case, we then must ask ourselves why we value the breeding of domestication and its bodily outcomes more than the rest of the relationships between people and these animals. In other words, why is breeding more important or a greater achievement than hunting with dingoes or highly valuing hunting dogs and caring for them? If we truly value pet keeping as much as animal breeding, why do we not see articles regularly published in *Nature* and *Science* on this topic? Perhaps notions of domestication as causing revolutionary change are still at work. We still believe in the Neolithic Revolution, even though we know that it was a very slow revolution in many cases, if it was a revolution at all. Or perhaps we value the bodily outcomes of breeding more than the relationships that constitute this process. The former are seen as somehow more real, more measurable, than past or present lived experiences.

Methodologies

Several papers in this volume exemplify the remarkable ways in which scholars can now apply a suite of analytical tools to archaeological dog remains to tease out details of these animals' lives, and in some cases the use of their body parts after death. Studies of dog diet are perhaps most advanced, and here include the use of stable isotope and dental microwear analyses. Such research moves away from assessing dog diet merely as a means of approximating what humans were eating. Here questions essentially focus on how or even if dogs were being provisioned by humans. Assessing such feeding and provisioning practices is important in understanding numerous aspects of our past relations with dogs.

In many cases, a community's ability to provision its dogs was a major constraint on both the number of dogs that were present and their roles in those communities. Certainly in parts of northern Siberia, sled dogs were only common in the historic period where fishing and marine mammal hunting provided economical sources of dog food (Davydov and Klokov 2018). More broadly, most of the world's dogs today are in fact street animals that survive largely by scavenging on human food refuse (Coppinger and Coppinger 2016). They are in a sense fed by people but often not intentionally or directly. Dogs can of course also hunt effectively for themselves in some locations and seasons. In parts of the North American Arctic, for example, sled dogs were left in the non-sledding season on islands for weeks or months at a time to fend for themselves (Boas 1974; Weyer 1932). Disentangling these various feeding and dietary practices (being fed, scavenging, self-provisioning) is challenging because they potentially produce the same sorts of archaeological signatures. Further, some dogs probably relied on all three feeding practices over the course of their lives as their social positions and bodies were changing.

Isotope studies provide only generalized pictures of dogs' diets over the span of a few months or years (in most cases) but say little about the qualities of those foods. Microwear studies can better pinpoint the qualities or textures of the food eaten, at least for a few weeks prior to death, but say little about longer-term patterns or the overall contribution of different types of food. Neither method can really get at how such foods were obtained. These challenges are difficult or perhaps even impossible to resolve. In an ideal world of unlimited time and financial resources, integrating isotope and microwear studies could be attempted. Additionally, such findings could be analyzed in light of other data such as dental wear and tooth loss patterns, body size estimations, and coprolite studies (to name just a few).

Sex and age are two of the most basic sets of biometric data for the study of any animal. These critical details unfortunately still remain remarkably difficult to assess in canids remains. This problem also plagues the osteoarchaeological analysis of the world's most studied species, modern humans (c.f., Milner and Boldsen 2016). Unfortunately, little effort seems to be happening on the canid osteology front in terms of improving such methods (but see Ruscillo 2006). I nonetheless cannot help but imagine what zooarchaeologists could learn if we could correlate aging data with dental microwear patterns. Were dogs in the past relying more on coarse-textured foods as they aged? Perhaps even better yet would be to examine aging and sexing data in relation to each other, particularly to explore culling and sacrificing practices in the past. Were mostly male dogs culled, and what might we infer about the effects of these practices on population size, genetic structure, and morphology? Aging and sexing methods will of course never be infallible. Regardless, we should aim to upgrade existing methods to allow us to better assign canid specimens to categories with some known degree of probability of being correct, just as is done in human osteology.

Baseline data for various conditions in dogs and other canids are also badly needed. For example, how often do free-ranging wolves, dingoes, street dogs, hunting dogs, or herding dogs experience fractures in different parts of their bodies? We really do not know if there are patterns in trauma experiences that might be useful for identifying past behaviors because reliable comparative data is lacking. Additionally, we also still have few methods or data for differentiating the natural attritional changes in dogs' bodies, such as wear and tear on the joints, from those associated with specific patterns of habitual activity. In other words, are the pathological lesions we observe the result of specific working lives, or rather the skeletal signs of dogs growing to old age?

Throughout the volume, some of the most informative methods used to understand past dogs are also the most basic: archaeological context and ethnographic and historic analogy. It is difficult for me to imagine better evidence for human-dog emotional bonds than dog burials, for example, or stronger indication of dog sacrifice than finding their butchered remains in places of clear spiritual significance. This site-specific information should be the starting point for most archaeological analyses but can be surprisingly hard to track down, especially for old collections. Contextual information is even more useful when paired with detailed osteological and bone chemistry analyses.

Documents provide very compelling and rich datasets for interpretation and can sometimes be usefully paired with archaeological data. Often such materials are used in more of a survey mode to provide broad comparative data that is used to make inferences about the past. Some parts of our past history with dogs, though, seem to have no good modern analogs, such as the initial phase of the domestication process. In other cases, information available about a particular way of being with dogs is potentially misleading about relations in prehistory. For example, we have little information about dog travois practices because these ways of working with dogs dwindled after the adoption of the horse. Detailed accounts based on statements by a handful of individuals shape most of what we know about dog travois use. Understanding of dog sledding suffers a similar bias, but for different reasons. Studies of modern racing dog sleds (e.g., Coppinger and Coppinger 2001) heavily color some interpretations of sledding in the past (Pitulko and Kasparov 2017). Racing with dogs versus working with them on a daily basis for travel and hunting seem to me like very different ways of being together, in very different contexts. Body processes involved in pulling sleds must be similar, but preferences for certain body sizes and behaviors are likely to be quite distinct.

Conclusion

Dogs can be a pleasure to live with and to study, and it is encouraging to see the social sciences focus a bit of their attention on our relations with these animals. Increasing the relevance of our studies of dogs to our academic disciplines will depend on further development, improvement, and integration of our theories and methods. This volume makes good strides in this direction by presenting a series of inspired looks at dogs in many different societies. Hopefully this trend will continue to build momentum into the future.

References Cited

Anderson, David G., Jan Peter Laurens Loovers, Sara Asu Schroer, and Robert P. Wishart
2017   Architectures of Domestication: On Emplacing Human-Animal Relations in the North. *Journal of the Royal Anthropological Institute* 23:398–416.
Boas, Franz
1974   *The Central Eskimo*. Coles, Toronto.
Coppinger, Raymond, and Lorna Coppinger
2001   *Dogs: A Startling New Understanding of Canine Origin, Behavior and Evolution*. Scribner, New York.

2016 *What Is a Dog?* University of Chicago Press, Chicago.

Davydov, Vladimir, and Konstantin Klokov

2018 Dogs, Reindeer and Humans in Siberia: Threefold Synergetic in the Northern Landscape. In *Dogs in the North: Stories of Cooperation and Co-Domestication*, edited by Robert J. Losey, Robert P. Wishart, and Jan Peter Laurens Loovers, pp. 45–60. Routledge, London.

DeMello, Margo

2012 *Animals and Society: An Introduction to Human-Animal Studies.* New York: Columbia University Press.

Fijn, Natasha

2011 *Living with Herds: Human-Animal Coexistence in Mongolia.* Cambridge University Press, Cambridge.

2018 Dog Ears and Tails: Different Relational Ways of Being with Canines in Aboriginal Australia and Mongolia. In *Domestication Gone Wild: Politics and Practices of Multispecies Relations*, edited by Heather Anne Swanson, Marianne Elisabeth Lien, and Gro B. Ween, pp. 72–93. Duke University Press, Durham.

Kirksey, S. Eben, and Stefan Helmreich

2010 The Emergence of Multispecies Ethnography. *Cultural Anthropology* 25(4):545–76.

Kohn, Eduardo

2007 How Dogs Dream: Amazonian Natures and the Politics of Transspecies Engagement. *American Ethnologist* 34(1):3–24.

Koster, Jeremy M.

2008 Hunting with Dogs in Nicaragua: An Optimal Foraging Approach. *Current Anthropology* 49:935–944.

Larson, Greger, and Joachim Burger

2013 A Population Genetics View of Animal Domestication. *Trends in Genetics* 29(4): 197–205.

Loovers, Jan Peter Laurens

2015 Dog-Craft: A History of Gwich'in and Dogs in the Canadian North. *Hunter-Gatherer Research* 1(4):387–419.

Losey, Robert J., Tatiana Nomokonova, Andrei V. Gusev, Olga P. Bachura, Natalia V. Fedorova, Pavel A. Kosintsev, and Mikhail V. Sablin

2018a Dogs Were Domesticated in the Arctic: Culling Practices and Dog Sledding at Ust'-Polui. *Journal of Anthropological Archaeology* 51:113–126.

Losey, Robert J., Robert P. Wishart, and Jan Peter Laurens Loovers (editors)

2018 *Dogs in the North: Stories of Cooperation and Co-Domestication.* Routledge, London.

Milner, George R., and Jesper L. Boldsen

2016 Estimating Age and Sex from the Skeleton: A Paleopathological Perspective. In *A Companion to Paleopathology*, edited by Anne L. Grauer, pp. 268–284. Wiley-Blackwell, Oxford.

Mullin, Molly

2002 Animals and Anthropology. *Society and Animals* 10:387–393.

Pitulko, Vladimir V., and Aleksei Kasparov

2017 Archaeological Dogs from the Early Holocene Zhokhov Site in the Eastern Siberian Arctic. *Journal of Archaeological Science: Reports* 13:491–515.

Ruscillo, Deborah

2006   The Table Test: A Simple Technique for Sexing Canid Humerii. In *Recent Advances in Ageing and Sexing Animal Bones*, edited by Deborah Ruscillo, pp. 62–67. Oxbow, Oxford.

Swanson, Heather Anne, Marianne Elisabeth Lien, and Gro B. Ween (editors)

2018   *Domestication Gone Wild: Politics and Practices of Multispecies Relations.* Duke University Press, Durham.

Weyer, Edward Moffat

1932   *The Eskimos, Their Environment and Folkways.* Yale University Press, New Haven.

Wolfe, Cary

2010   *What Is Posthumanism?* University of Minnesota Press, Minneapolis.

Contributors

Brandi Bethke, Oklahoma Archeological Survey, University of Oklahoma, Norman

Kate Britton, Department of Archaeology, University of Aberdeen, Aberdeen, and Department of Human Evolution, Max Planck Institute for Evolutionary Anthropology, Leipzig

Amanda Burtt, Department of Geography, Royal Holloway University of London

Larisa R. G. DeSantis, Department of Biological Sciences, Vanderbilt University, Nashville

Melanie Fillios, School of Humanities, University of New England, Armidale, New South Wales

Emily Lena Jones, Department of Anthropology, University of New Mexico, Albuquerque

Loukas Koungoulos, Department of Archaeology, University of Sydney, Sydney, New South Wales

Robert J. Losey, Department of Anthropology, University of Alberta, Edmonton

Edouard Masson-MacLean, Department of Archaeology, University of Aberdeen, Aberdeen

Ellen McManus-Fry, Department of Archaeology, University of Aberdeen, Aberdeen

Victoria Monagle, Department of Anthropology, University of New Mexico, Albuquerque

Victoria Moses, School of Anthropology, University of Arizona, Tucson

Angela R. Perri, Department of Archaeology, Durham University, Durham, United Kingdom

Nerissa Russell, Department of Anthropology, Cornell University, Ithaca, New York

Peter W. Stahl, Department of Anthropology, University of Victoria, Victoria, British Columbia

Index

Page numbers in *italics* followed by *t* and *f* indicate tables and figures.

www.ingramcontent.com/pod-product-compliance
Lightning Source LLC
Chambersburg PA
CBHW050808270326
41926CB00026B/4614